THEOLOGY AS A LIFE

OTHER TITLE BY J.H. THORNWELL

In addition to *Theology as a Life* Solid Ground Christian Books has also published a companion volume by Thornwell titled:

Whatsoever Things Are True - These seven Discourses on Truth were written and preached in the Spring of 1851 from the text, "Finally, brethren, whatsoever things are true, think on these things." Philippians 4:8. They were delivered at the Chapel of the College at Columbia, South Carolina, by James Henley Thornwell who was serving as both President and Chaplain.

"Thornwell is a giant and nowhere is his mental and spiritual strength seen better than in his treatment of ethics. His application of Scripture to all of life is illuminating and exemplary. *Discourses on Truth* deserves to be a standard reference." - **Dr. Nick Willborn**

"Thornwell abounds with riches of multifaceted brilliance. Theology, biblical interpretation, philosophy, ethics all take on an attractive hue under the pen of Thornwell. His essays on truth perhaps are more relevant now than when he first wrote them. An age that sees truth as personal, subjective, and existential [therefore relative] needs the clear light of *Thornwell's Discourses*. Christian will learn to think about the glory of having truth, living by truth, and receive new conviction in the task of the propagation of truth." - **Dr. Tom J. Nettles**

Of Thornwell the following two statements should suffice:

J.W. Alexander once wrote the following of one of Thornwell's sermons, *"His sermon was a model of what is rare, viz.: burning hot argument, logic in ignition, and glowing more and more to the end."*

Dr. D. Martyn Lloyd-Jones said of him, *"Thornwell was one of the greatest preachers that America has ever produced."*

Call us at 205-443-0311
Visit us on web at solid-ground-books.com

THEOLOGY AS A LIFE

Theological Discourses
From the Heart of J.H. Thornwell

JAMES H. THORNWELL

SOLID GROUND CHRISTIAN BOOKS
BIRMINGHAM, ALABAMA USA

Solid Ground Christian Books
PO Box 660132
Vestavia Hills AL 35266
205-443-0311
mike.sgcb@gmail.com
www.solid-ground-books.com

THEOLOGY AS A LIFE
Theological Discourses from the Heart of J.H. Thornwell

by James Henley Thornwell (1812-1862)

First Solid Ground edition in February 2012

These discourses are taken from Volume II of *The Collected Works of J.H. Thornwell* most recently published by Solid Ground Christian Books.

Cover design by Borgo Design
Contact them at borgogirl@bellsouth.net

ISBN- 978-159925-2759

CONTENTS

I. Outline of the Covenant of Grace and Testimony to Sublapsarianism. - 17

I. OUTLINE OF THE COVENANT OF GRACE
Recapitulation of the Heads to which Theology was reduced in the previous Lectures.
1. Those essential principles of moral government which are involved in the relations of a rational, responsible creature to its Creator and Ruler.
2. The second head includes the dispensation under which man was placed after his creation, commonly called the Covenant of Works.
3. The third great department of Theology is that which relates to redemption, and that is the topic on which we are to enter now. The scheme of redemption, otherwise called the Covenant of Grace or Redemption. Principles common to it and the Covenant of Works. Its distinct peculiarities. Logical order of the topics involved in the discussion of the Covenant of Grace.

II. SUBLAPSARIANS AND SUPRALAPSARIANS.
1. Moral significance of the distinction between these parties.
2. The question whether the Divine decrees are conditioned.
3. Three opinions as to the order of the Divine decrees.
4. The state of the question between Sublapsarians and Supralapsarians. Reasons in support of Sublapsarianism.
5. The true order of the Decrees. The New School order.

III. TESTIMONIES TO SUBLAPSARIANISM
1. The Helvetic Confession, Chapter X.
2. The Gallic Confession, Section XII
3. The Anglican Confession, Article XVII.
4. The Scotch Confession, Section 8.
5. The Confession of Dort, Article XVI.
6. The Synod of Dort, Canons VI. to XI.

IV. PREDESTINATION AS HELD BY SUBLAPSARIANS
1. The decree respects man *as fallen.* Objections to Supralapsarian view.
2. The decree respecting man as fallen is absolutely sovereign.
3. The decree is to everlasting life, and the means to that end.
4. The decree is eternal.
5. (1) Sublapsarian order of the decrees. (2) Supralapsarian order.
(3) General-atonement-Calvinist' order. Redemption includes the general proposition of salvation.

II. THEOLOGY AS A LIFE IN INDIVIDUALS AND IN THE CHURCH: BEING A REVIEW OF BRECKINRIDGE'S SUBJECTIVE THEOLOGY. - 34

An account of the design of Dr. Breckinridge's work.
1. Remarks upon the first point of the first book—the posture of the world under the condemnation of sin as modified by grace.
2. Upon the second point—the nature and provisions of the Covenant of Grace.
3. The third point—the conditions of the covenant with respect to the sinner. Strictures upon the author's views. Faith maintained as the sole condition.
4. Upon the main subject of the treatise—the exhibition of the work of grace upon the human soul.
5. Upon the doctrine of the book as to the Church. The nature of the Church. Its relation to the State and to secular institutions.
6. Upon Dr. Breckinridge's views as to the future of the kingdom of God.
7. Estimate of the merits of the work.

III. THE NECESSITY AND NATURE OF CHRISTIANITY. -55

Description of the Apostle Paul at Athens. Analysis of his sermon on Mars' Hill. Effects of the sermon.
1. The necessity of Christianity does not spring simply from man's ignorance. Its necessity not that of a mere revelation. Not simply a republication of natural religion. Christianity discriminated from natural religion. Peculiar contents of each system. Necessity of Christianity that of a scheme which contemplates a work to be done as well as truths to be revealed.
2. The necessity of Christianity does not arise from the want of a new principle of government. It does not make sin pardonable upon mere

repentance. Maintains the principle of distributive justice. Provides for the pardon of sin in consistency with that principle.

3. The necessity of Christianity not a necessity created by the demands of governmental policy. The theory of meditation which grounds it upon public policy discussed. Dr. Wardlaw's views considered.

4. The necessity and nature of Christianity as a scheme which reconciles the pardon of the guilty with the perfections of God and the principles of His government. The distinctive provisions of Redemption.

IV. ELECTION AND REPROBATION.   -105

    I. *A precise statement of these doctrines* as held by Presbyterians.
    II. *Scriptural proofs* that Election—
1. Is personal.
2. Contemplates man as a fallen being.
3. Is unto everlasting life or salvation.
4. Is from eternity.
5. Is sovereign. The Arminian view discussed. Elements and proofs of Reprobation.

    III. *A consideration of prominent objections* to Election and Reprobation—
1. That they are inconsistent with the justice of God.
2. That they ascribe partiality to God.
3. That they are inconsistent with the sincerity of God. Distinction between the love of complacency and the love of benevolence. Distinction between the decretive or secret and the perceptive or revealed will of God. Examination of Scripture passages adduced by Arminians.
4. That they are inconsistent with the liberty and responsibility of man. That no violence is done to these elements of human agency appears from the nature of effectual calling. Its elements enumerated.
5. That they destroy all solicitude about personal holiness. Graces which election encourages.
6. That they render the use of the means of grace nugatory.

    IV. *Inferences from the doctrine of Election.*
1. It pre-eminently glorifies God.
   (1) The independence and omnipotence of His will.
   (2) His grace.
   (3) His justice.
2. It necessitates the perseverance of the saints.
3. It establishes the doctrine of limited atonement. Distinction between the sufficiency and extent of the atonement. The offer of Gospel universal.

CONTENTS

V. THE NECESSITY OF THE ATONEMENT. -205

Paul's argument in the Epistle to the Romans.
Its fundamental postulate the inseparable connection between guilt and punishment.
The Gospel God's power to save, because it provides a vicarious righteousness.
The Gospel not simply a republication of natural religion.
It provides atonement. Two principles on which atonement rests—the inseparable connection between guilt and punishment, and the admissibility of a competent substitution.
The necessity of atonement the necessity of a means to an end.
Atonement the effect, not the cause, of saving mercy.
The denial of unconditional pardon of guilt not inconsistent with God's perfections.
The proof of the necessity of atonement must consist in showing that the glory of God necessitates the punishment of sin.
The power to arrest the sentence of a judge not an essential element of sovereignty.
In human governments it arises from the imperfection of legal processes.
No real analogy between them the Divine government in this respect.
Discussion of the theory that atonement is demanded not by justice, but by wisdom; is expedient, not necessary.
Socinian and Hopkinsian views examined.
The good of the subjects not the primary design of the Divine government: that end the glory of God.
The end of the creation of the universe a moral one.
This necessitates moral rule over moral agents.
Three elements essential to moral government—competent authority, a rule of action and a suitable sanction.
These suppose necessary relations, and are consequently not dependent upon the suggestion of expediency.
Proof that the authority of the Ruler is inalienable.
Proof of the necessity of the law as a rule of action.
Proof of the necessity of a penal sanction.
The immutable necessity of the Divine government having been proved, the necessity of the punishment of sin is established.
The punishment of sin, however, does not take place according to the analogy of physical laws.
Sovereign discretion of God as to certain circumstances attending its infliction.

CONTENTS

Discussion of the theory that repentance secures pardon.
True repentance shown to be impossible to an unpardoned sinner.
The infinite ill-desert of sin.
The moral impossibility of annihilation.
No escape to the unpardoned sinner from the penal consequences of sin.
The substitution and atonement of Christ the only ground of the remission of guilt.
The glory of the cross.

VI. THE PRIESTHOOD OF CHRIST.   -265

The prominence given by the Scriptures to the priestly office of Christ.
The doctrine of the Epistle to the Romans the legal substitution of Christ.
That of the Epistle to the Hebrews the priesthood of Christ.
Question: why mediation was accomplished, not by legal representation simply, but also by priesthood.
The latter the method in which the law of substitution has been actually applied in the redemption of the race.
Reasons for the priestly functions of Christ.
1. Conceptions of the origin of salvation are rendered clearer and more impressive by Christ's priesthood.
2. The priesthood of Christ relieves His punishment of all appearance of inexorable rigour on the part of God.
3. The priesthood of Christ makes provision for the application of redemption.
4. The priesthood of Christ stimulates devotion by the provision it makes for the acceptance of the imperfect worship of sinners.
5. The priesthood of Christ is the form of mediation in which consolation is most effectually administered.
Inferences from the doctrine of Christ's priesthood.

VII. CHRIST TEMPTED AS THE SECOND ADAM.   - 293

The temptation a most important portion of our Saviour's history.
Rationalist objections to the narrative.
The credibility of the account vindicated.
The import of the temptation of Christ.
1. Christ is to be considered in His public character as the representative of men and unfallen angels.
2. The trial more severe and protracted than that of Adam for two reasons—

CONTENTS

(1) The magnitude of the results.

(2) As a vindication of the principle on which man had fallen.

3. The trial was public and conducted upon the same principles with that in Eden. The bitterness and intensity of the trial evinced by comparing it with that of Adam.

1) The place of the temptations.

2) The extent—that is, the points at which both might be assailed.

3) The thing to be tested and the mode of attack as adapted to the different circumstances of the parties.

The sum of all is, Christ as the Second Adam fulfills the second probation of the world. Inferences from the success of Christ—

1. The race had not been hardly dealt with in Adam.

2. The sublimity of Christ's virtue was illustrated.

3. Individual life, as to temptation, is an analogue of the dispensation which rules the history of the race.

VIII. THE GOSPEL, GOD'S POWER AND WISDOM. - 301

The Gospel as viewed by the Jew and the Greek.

Why it was a stumbling block to the Jew.

Why it was foolishness to the Greek.

"Christ crucified" a compendious phrase for the scheme of redemption.

The Gospel as proclaiming a crucified Saviour the highest exponent of God's power and wisdom.

Three forms in which God's power is displayed in the salvation of men—

1. In the exercise of naked strength, or of immediate causation, in producing new physical effects. To this kind of power must be referred the Incarnation, the Miracles of Jesus and His Resurrection.

2. In the secret and silent influence which is exerted upon the minds of men. The power which controls the mind is greater than that which creates and upholds matter. The regeneration and sanctification of sinners extraordinary effects of power.

3. In the adjustment of the legal relations of sinners under the Divine government to the conflicting claims of justice and mercy. The greatest moral difficulties overcome in making the salvation of the sinner consistent with the principles of justice.

The forms in which God's wisdom is displayed in redemption—

1. In the manifestation of the Divine glory. The ultimate end of God the glory of His name. His immediate end is redemption, the salvation of sinners.

(1) The attribute of mercy could not otherwise have been known.

CONTENTS

(2) The scheme of redemption proves the compatibility of the exercise of mercy with that of justice.

(3) Sin is made the occasion for the most striking and glorious manifestation of the Divine excellences.

2. Divine wisdom displayed in the adaptation of the means to the end in view. The employment of the principle of representation. The extraordinary constitution of Christ's person.

3. Divine wisdom displayed in redemption by so applying its blessing as to secure the distinct acknowledgement of grace. The repudiation of personal obedience as the ground of acceptance and the appointment of faith as the mere instrument of justification. Man becomes nothing, Christ is all. Representation and Imputation still employed as in man's first religion, and enforce our dependence on God's grace in Christ.

4. God's wisdom displayed in redemption by so arranging its provision as to allure human confidence and secure the interests of personal holiness. The humanity of Christ provides for sympathy between Him and men, and His Deity affords the surest ground of confidence. Divine love draws us to Christ, and repels us from sin.

Conclusion: the motives urging the subjects of grace to overflowing gratitude. They are introduced into a supernatural world—the world of grace. They are endued with supernatural vision—the vision of faith. They behold Christ crucified the power and wisdom of God.

IX. THE PERSONALITY OF THE HOLY GHOST. - 337

The defectiveness of the popular belief in regard to the nature, office and operations of the Spirit. The ministration of the Spirit the characteristic glory of the New Testament dispensation. The possession of the Spirit the true distinction of Christ's people.

The bearing of our views of the Spirit upon the whole of redemption.

The existence and functions of three Divine persons proved by the phenomena of grace, as the being of God is evinced by those of nature.

The proof of the Trinity as derived from Christian experience.

The experience which fails to recognize the personality of the Spirit essentially defective.

The admission of the personality of the Spirit, and of the supernatural character of faith, stand or fall together.

The formalist theory, which affirms a course of grace analogous to the course of nature, discussed.

CONTENTS

The operations of the Spirit supernatural, and imply a voluntary, sovereign agent. These operations analogous not to the fixed order of nature, but to those extraordinary exercises of power which produces miracles.

The means of grace are not laws, and the Spirit is not simply the invisible means connecting the spiritual cause with its effect.

The experimental processes of grace necessitate the acknowledgement of the direct personal agency of the Spirit.

The witness of the Spirit supposes the knowledge of a person who testifies, in contradistinction from our own spirit as a witness.

The objection met that, according to the author's theory, the means of grace, not having the efficacy of laws, are nugatory.

The true end subserved by the means of grace expounded.

The doctrine of supernatural grace vindicated from the charge of leading to fanatical enthusiasm.

Enthusiasm defined, and supernatural illumination discriminated from it.

Supernatural illumination and prophetic inspiration distinguished.

Relation of faith as a supernatural gift to the supernatural phenomena of grace. The argument from abuse refuted.

The importance of the doctrine of the Spirit's personality as a guard against formality on the one hand and fanaticism on the other.

X. THE NATURE OF SALVATION. - 371

The senses in which the term *Saviour* has been used.

The question is, In what does the salvation of Jesus consist?

The great end of the scheme of salvation is deliverance from sin and ruin, and the impartation of eternal life.

The difficulties to be overcome growing out of man's condition.

The depravity of man. The enmity of the carnal heart to God.

The removal of this enmity necessary for salvation.

This is done by removing its cause.

The cause of the enmity to God is the consciousness of sin and the dread of its consequences.

This state can only be removed by the exhibition of Divine love.

The principle of imputation furnishes the conditions upon which God's love can be shown to the sinner.

His guilt is transferred to Christ and Christ's righteousness to him.

Two results are secured: (1) The sinner's guilt being removed, God can show him love; and (2) the sense of guilt being destroyed, the sinner is able to love God. The final effect is that the sinner delivered from guilt is attracted to God by love manifested in the cross, and moved by the same cause to the hatred of sin.

XI. Antinomianism. - 383

Definition of the term. Account of the origin of Antinomian principles.
The circumstances which produced the Antinomianism of the Apostolic age.
The origin of the Antinomianism of the time of the Reformation.
Legalism the parent of Antinomianism.
Questions of Dr. Crisp's relation to Antinomianism.
The "Middle Way," a scheme originating with Vossius and Grotius, and maintained by Richard Baxter and Bishop Bull.
Arminian view of the relation between Calvinism and Antinomianism.
Traill's refutation of that view.
Vindication of the Calvinistic doctrine of justification from leading to Antinomianism by Robert Bragge.
Bishop Bull's elaborate effort to reconcile justification by works with the grace of God. Refutation of this and kindred schemes.
Exposure of the error that grace is whatever is opposed to merit.
In the Scriptures grace is not opposed to merit, but to legal obedience.
The true antithesis pointed out.
Important distinction between merit on the part of the moral agent and debt on the part of God. No connection between them.
Definition of a legal scheme. The scheme of Baxter and Bull legal.
No medium in principle between Pelagianism and Calvinism.
Salvation, as including deliverance from the guilt and dominion of sin alike, is the free gift of God in Christ.

XII. CHRISTIAN EFFORT. - 397

I. The leading objects of Christian effort.
    1. Personal holiness.
    2. The edification of the Church.
    3. The conversion of sinners.
II. The manner in which Christian effort should be put forth.
    1. Striving with earnestness.
    2. Unanimity; concert of action.
    3. Steadfastness and regularity.
    4. The adoption of those measures alone which the Gospel warrants.
    5. Deep and entire dependence upon God for success.
III. The necessity of striving in our Christian effort.
    1. Consider you are not your own, thus you must pursue the Master's call.
    2. Consider that the consequences of our effort are tremendous.
    3. Consider the value of the souls of men and the reality of eternity.

CONTENTS

XIII. THE SACRIFICE OF CHRIST, THE TYPE AND MODEL OF MISSIONARY EFFORT. - 411

The nature of the Father's commission to the Son to execute redemption.
The free consent of the Son.
His sovereign authority over His own life. He was Master of Himself.
The Son an independent, sovereign party to the covenant of redemption.
The death of Jesus a special ground of His Father's love to Him.
Jesus a free, heroic actor in His death.
His death a sacrifice rendered as a free-will offering.
The nature of sacrifice; its matter and form.
Considerations which evince the moral greatness of Jesus in His death—
1. It was an act of worship.
2. The moral elements which entered into that act of worship.
   (1) An intense zeal for the glory of God.
   (2) Tender compassion for man.
3. These two elements, love to God and love to man, constitute the essence of virtue.
The resurrection of Jesus as also furnishing a special ground of His Father's complacency in Him.
Application of the subject to the work of Missions as a calling out the priestly character of believers—
1. The zeal for God's glory which characterized Jesus in dying must be the dominant principle of action in the Christian heart.
2. The form which our zeal for the Divine glory is to take—that is, the works to which we should be impelled by it—is determined by the influence of the other motive which entered into the sacrifice of Christ, pity for man.
3. These two motives should not be transient emotions, but active and operative principles leading to sacrifice of self.
4. As there was a joy set before Jesus in dying, so there is a glorious reward to our sacrifices and labours of love.

PREFATORY NOTE.

The fragments which are here brought together seem to be too valuable to be omitted from this collection; and they likewise appear suitable to stand as a sort of Introduction to this Second Volume, into which are to be gathered all which Dr. Thornwell has left relating to the Covenant of Grace.

Outline of the Covenant of Grace

AND

TESTIMONY TO SUBLAPSARIANISM.

I. Outline of the Covenant of Grace.

IN the original distribution of the topics embraced in Theology they were reduced to three heads:

1. Those essential principles of moral government which are involved in the relations of a rational, responsible creature to its Creator and Ruler. These lie at the basis of all religion. There can be neither duty, sin, holiness nor worship without them. Under this head we consider man as he was created, and only in those aspects which belong to his nature as rational and moral, the product of supreme intelligence and righteousness. Here we discuss the question of his original endowments, his knowledge, righteousness and holiness; all that is implied in the notion of his being created in the image of God; the moral law; the nature of moral government, its responsibilities, promises and threatenings.

2. The second head includes the dispensation under which man was placed after his creation, commonly called the Covenant of Works. This dispensation involved the purpose on the part of God to bring man into closer relations with Himself. His natural position was that of a servant—God designs to make him a son. In his natural estate, his will was mutable; his obedience was contingent; he was

liable to fall—God designed to establish him in holiness for ever. The means through which this was to be done was a limited probation of the whole race in the person of one man—in other words, the justification of all through one. This purpose introduced several important modifications of moral government. The limitation of probation as to time introduces the idea of justification; the limitation as to persons introduces the idea of federal representation; and both together necessitate indefectibility of holiness. This dispensation had a threatening as well as a promise. Hence, to understand it fully, we must know the state to which its breach reduces us, that being the legal state in which the race now exists. Hence, we were led to a full consideration of Sin, its nature, its consequences, its origin in us.

3. The third great department of Theology is that which relates to redemption, and that is the topic on which we are to enter now. The scheme of redemption, otherwise called the Covenant of Grace, is the answer which God gives to the question, How shall a sinner be justified and established in holiness for ever? as the Covenant of Works was an answer to the question, How shall a moral creature be justified and confirmed? They are both evolutions of the same purpose, the same grace in God. The difference in the provisions is owing to a difference in the condition of the persons affected. The principle on which these provisions are granted is precisely the same—federal representation. But man's different state introduces three peculiarities in its application: (1.) It gives occasion for the exercise of sovereignty on the part of God in discriminating among the members of the human family. All need not be represented. There is a positive desert of punishment which may be respected and ought to be respected. Some must die that it may be clearly seen that all were ruined. (2.) In the next place, man's guilt requires a new element in righteousness—satisfaction to the justice of God. The penalty of the law must be borne, and borne as a matter of obedience. (3.) Man's nature

now requires a change in its whole inward state. Hence, the doctrine of sanctification is introduced. The federal Head must be one who is competent to these exigencies in His person, and in the offices which He undertakes to discharge.

According to this analysis the doctrine of Redemption involves the discussion of the following topics:

1. The persons embraced in the Divine purpose; that is, the doctrine of Election. This may also be placed last, as Calvin has done. If we look at the thing in the order of the Divine purpose, it is first; if in the order of execution, it is last. One advantage of making it first is to show its regulative influence upon the atonement. It is not an afterthought to save atonement from being a failure.

2. The nature of a sinner's justification; what is required in it; and upon what grounds it is possible.

3. The nature of sanctification, or the whole of that internal work by which holiness is produced and perfected in the heart.

4. The federal Headship of Christ, including the conditions to His becoming such; the qualifications necessary for the office; the duties He discharges in it; the work which He actually performed; His birth, His life, His death, His resurrection and ascension—that is, Christ in His person, His offices, and in both estates of humiliation and exaltation.

5. The bond of union, the tie betwixt us and Christ, involving the office of the Holy Spirit in the application of redemption, and the specific acts on our parts responsive to that office; effectual calling and faith.

6. The means: the Church, the ministry, the ordinances.

7. The actual result of all in the different periods of the soul's history; the Christian's life now, his condition hereafter.

8. The state of those not embraced in the Covenant of Grace.

This is an outline of the great and glorious topics which

fall under the scheme of redemption in their logical relations and dependence.

II. Sub- and Supra-lapsarians.

1. The distinction between these two parties has been represented as very unimportant, as a mere difference in their mode of viewing the same things. But the question concerning the order of the Divine decrees involves something more than a question of logical method. It is really a question of the highest moral significance. The order of a thing very frequently determines its righteousness and justice. Conviction and hanging are parts of the same process, but it is something more than a question of arrangement whether a man shall be hung before he is convicted.

2. It is admitted that the decrees, as they exist in the Divine mind, are not conditioned: this would be to limit the absolute freedom of the Divine will. But the things which those decrees relate to are conditioned, and these conditions are regarded in the decrees. The things sustain relations to each other of cause and effect, of antecedent and consequent, of means and end; they are subordinate or co-ordinate, and all those relations are contemplated and embraced in the decree. The determinations of God in regard to them are determinations about things so and so connected.

3. There are three general opinions as to the order of Divine decrees, founded on the condition in which man, in the purpose of election and reprobation, was contemplated as being.

(1.) There are those who maintain that the end being to glorify God's grace and justice, the destination to death and life was the first thing in the Divine mind, and creation and the fall were only means ordained for the execution of this purpose. Man is viewed as neither fallen nor created, but simply as capable of being and as fallible—simply as an instrument that may be made and adapted to the purpose. This is the Supralapsarian hypothesis. It is so called because in fixing the object of election it ascends beyond creation and the fall.

(2.) Others maintain that election and reprobation are conditioned upon creation and the fall—that is, that the purpose of salvation and grace contemplates man as lost and ruined, and proposes to deliver him out of this state. This is the Sublapsarian hypothesis, so called because in fixing the object of predestination it presupposes creation and the fall.

(3.) Others think that the decree contemplates man not only as created and fallen, but as redeemed by Christ, and as actually believing in Him and persevering in grace.

This scheme we shall discount for the present, and consider only the two first.

4. The state of the question betwixt the Supra- and Sublapsarians is compendiously expressed by Turrettin. It is not whether creation and the fall enter into the Divine decree—that is confessed on all hands; but, whether they stand related to salvation and damnation as means to an end—whether in the order of thought God first conceived the purpose of life or death, and then the purpose of giving being and fallibility.

Again, it is not the question whether in predestination sin is taken into the account, for even Supralapsarians admit that sin must precede condemnation; but the question is, whether sin is in the Divine thought antecedent to condemnation, the real ground of it, or only a providential means of executing the decree of reprobation formed irrespective of it.

The question, further, is not whether sin is the impulsive cause of predestination. All parties are agreed that the distinction in the final states of men must be referred to the sovereign pleasure of God; but the question is, whether sin must not be presupposed as a quality in the objects of predestination; whether it is not a state or condition in them, without which predestination could not exist; whether sin must not be presupposed in order that a being may be capable either of election or reprobation.

That the Sublapsarians are right in their answers to these questions is apparent from several considerations:

(1.) The general impression made by the other scheme is extremely revolting to our moral nature and to our conceptions of the goodness and mercy of God. It represents the universe as a vast clock of complicated machinery, wound up and set to going for no other purpose but to strike throughout Eternity the dismal sounds—*Damnation and Glory!* To these ends the hands point upon the dial-plate of creation and Providence, and for these ends alone God has stepped forth from the depths of His own immensity to create, to order and to people worlds.

(2.) The Supralapsarians proceed upon a hypothesis altogether groundless: What is last in execution is first in intention. This is true only of things that stand related directly as means and end. The man who constructs a particular kind of plough has first in view the effect to be produced on the soil. But in a co-ordinate series it does not hold. All men were not made for the last man. Now, the works of God are manifold—each has its independent sphere; and they are all connected by their common relation to the Divine glory. Creation is one work, Redemption another.

(3.) That the creation and fall are not means, but antecedent conditions, is plain from the nature of the case. Sin is not in order to damnation, but damnation in order to sin.

(4.) The decree of Election and Reprobation is unmeaning without the presupposition of sin. It is an act without an object.

5. The true order of the Decrees is—(1.) Creation; (2.) The Fall; (3.) Election; (4.) Redemption; (5.) Vocation.

The New School order is—(1.) Creation; (2.) Fall; (3.) Redemption; (4.) Election; (5.) Vocation.

III. Testimonies to Sublapsarianism.

1. The Helvetic Confession, Chapter X. Here the objects of election are said to be, "*Sanctos; quos vult salvos facere in Christo.*"

2. The Gallic Confession, Section XII. The language is very explicit: *Credimus ex hac corruptione et damnatione universali, in qua omnes homines natura sunt submersi, Deum alios quidem eripere, quos videlicet æterno et immutabili suo consilio sola sua bonitate et misericordia, nullo que operum ipsorum respectu, in Jesu Christo elegit; alios vero in ea corruptione et damnatione relinquere, in quibus nimirum juste suo tempore damnandis justitiam suam demonstret, sicut in aliis divitias misericordiæ suæ declarat.*

3. The Anglican Confession, Article XVII. They are chosen in Christ and to be delivered from the curse of the Fall.

4. The Scotch Confession, Section 8. The election is in Christ, and to grace and fraternity with Christ.

5. The Confession of Dort, Article XVI.

6. The Synod of Dort, Canons VI. to XI.

IV. PREDESTINATION AS HELD BY SUBLAPSARIANS.

Predestination, though sometimes used in a wide sense as synonymous with decrees in general, is, for the most part, restricted to the special decree concerning the final destiny of men and angels. In this aspect it is subdivided according to the nature of the destiny into Election and Reprobation. Election secures the everlasting happiness, and Reprobation the everlasting misery of its objects. Leaving angels out of view, we may resume the Scripture doctrine of Predestination in relation to man under the following heads:

1. Man is viewed in the decree as a *fallen being*. It is a purpose which contemplates him under the character and in the condition of a lost sinner. He could not be capable of election to life nor of reprobation to death unless he were in a state which justly exposes him to the Divine displeasure and to death. That cannot be *found* which is not lost, and that cannot be *saved* which is in no danger. An election to salvation or to deliverance from guilt and misery as necessarily presupposes guilt and misery in its objects as

healing implies a disease or cooling implies heat. The opposite theory, which makes the decree respect man not as fallen nor even as existing, but only as capable of both, makes the decree terminate upon an object which in relation to it is a nonentity. It makes the decree involve a palpable contradiction—a purpose to save what in the light of the decree is not lost, and is therefore not saveable.

Besides, that the Supralapsarians have no object corresponding to the nature of the decree, their system is liable to other and insurmountable objections:

(1.) It correlates things as means and end which actually sustain no such relations. Creation and the permission of the fall are made simply means for the execution of the purpose of election and reprobation. They have taken place *because* of that purpose. The truth is, these are co-ordinate and not subordinate works of God, and have their distinct and separate place in the Divine plan as manifestations of the Divine glory. All God's works are correlated to each as means for the expression of Himself. They all contain some letters and syllables of His great Name, and it is because of this relation to His glory that they all enter into the Divine decree.

(2.) The Supralapsarians, by their arbitrary reduction of creation and the fall to the category of means, really make sin the consequence of damnation and not its ground. Man is not condemned because he sins, but sins that he may be condemned.

(3.) Providence is the explicit manifestation of God's plan and counsels. Now in Providence we recognize the fact of creation, therefore we say that God decreed to create; the fact of the fall, therefore that God decreed to permit the fall; the fact of redemption, therefore that God decreed to redeem. In Providence these are connected not as *means* and *end*, but as successive developments, or rather as furnishing the occasions and conditions of successive developments of the Divine perfections. Creation glorified God in its sphere; the moral administration under which the fall occurred glorified Him in still another aspect of His being; and the fall furnished the occasion upon which a still more illustrious exhibition might be made. Here is a plan, a progressive plan, a plan in which each part prepares the way for something beyond, but in which each part has its own special and independent significancy.

(4.) The only support of this theory is a logical crotchet which will not bear examination. What is last in the execution is first in the intention. The maxim applies only to things connected as means and ends, but is not applicable to a co-ordinate series, or to a series in which the preceding is only a condition, but not the cause—a *sine qua non*, but not the ground—of the next.

(5.) The hypothesis is contrary to the Scriptures. They uniformly represent calling as the expression of election—the first articulate proof of it. But calling is *from* a state of sin and misery. Therefore, election must refer to the same condition. Historically, too, the doctrine has been developed in the Church from the experience of grace, and so connects itself necessarily with the transition from darkness to light. In so many words, we are said to be chosen out of the world.

(6.) The most matured Confessions of Faith represent election as presupposing sin and misery. The Gallican, the English, the Belgic, the Synod of Dort, may all be quoted.

This, then, is the first point. Man is contemplated in the decree of predestination as a fallen being.

2. The decree respecting man thus conditioned is absolutely sovereign. It is grounded exclusively in the good pleasure of God's will. It is not arbitrary and without reasons, but the reasons are all drawn from God Himself, and not from the creature. He chooses one and passes by another, not because one is better or worse than another, but because such is His sovereign will. Here we encounter the Arminians, who make election depend upon faith, and reprobation upon impenitence among men—that is, men

are chosen to life or ordained to death under the formal consideration of being believers or unbelievers. The ground of distinction is in the creature and not the sovereign will of God. The Arminian hypothesis is refuted by all those Scriptures which make faith, repentance and holiness the gifts of God and the *results* or *fruits* of election.

3. The election is to everlasting life and all the means of attaining it. It includes grace and glory. It is not an election to external privileges, but to the heavenly inheritance. If grace and glory are the end to which election looks, then election is prior in the order of thought to the scheme of redemption, and is the moving cause of its institution. Here we encounter a section of the orthodox, who undertook to conciliate the Arminians by postulating a general purpose of mercy to the whole race, in consequence of which Christ was given as the Saviour of the world and made a redemption intended for all under the condition of a true faith. According to this scheme, election is posterior to the introduction of the Gospel, and instead of contemplating man simply as fallen, contemplates him as *perverse* under the general call. It comes in, not as the impulsive cause of redemption, but as the means of saving redemption from being a failure. This scheme is the one to which all the advocates of general and indefinite atonement are logically driven. But it is contradicted by the whole tenor of Scripture. The elect are said to be given to Christ to *be* redeemed, not given *as* redeemed. Christ is distinctly affirmed to be the fruit of election. He is the head of the election of grace. Then again the whole doctrine of atonement must be given up in any just and proper sense of the term.

4. Election is eternal. This is admitted by all but Socinians. Others dispute about its nature and grounds, but admit that whatever it is, it is an eternal purpose.

5. The order of the Divine decrees according to these views is—(1.) Creation; (2.) Permission of the Fall; (3.) Predestination; (4.) Redemption; (5.) Vocation.

According to the Supralapsarians—(1.) Predestination; (2.) Creation; (3.) Fall; (4.) Redemption; (5.) Vocation.

According to general atonement Calvinists—(1.) Creation; (2.) Fall; (3.) Redemption; (4.) Predestination; (5.) Vocation.

Under redemption here must be included the general dispensation of mercy by the proposition of salvation.

PREFATORY NOTE.

THE following discussion appeared first in the "Southern Presbyterian Review" for October, 1859. It should come in here, notwithstanding that a considerable portion of it would be suitable for the Fourth Volume of this collection.

THEOLOGY AS A LIFE
IN
INDIVIDUALS AND IN THE CHURCH:

BEING A REVIEW OF BRECKINRIDGE'S SUBJECTIVE THEOLOGY.

THAT a second volume, so weighty in matter and so bulky in form, should have been written and prepared for the press within the time that has elapsed since the publication of the first, is a testimony to the diligence and industry of the author which vindicates him from all suspicion of making his professorship a sinecure. Dr. Breckinridge measures life by labour and not by years. A man of action, he finds no place for rest, he seeks no repose in this sublunary scene, where the Master's commission is only to work. The truth is, in every state the unimpeded exercise of energy is bliss; it is not action, but toil, not exertion, but drudgery, which constitutes the bitterness of labour. Soundness of mind is as inconsistent with torpor as soundness of body with lethargy. Motion is the sign of life, and delight in motion an unfailing symptom of health. It is an omen of good that our professors in all our seminaries seem to be working men. Princeton, year after year, is sending forth volumes of sacred criticism which are not surpassed in genius, scholarship and piety by the productions of any other school in Europe or America. She has taken her place as an authority abroad. Danville, in her infancy, has vindicated her claim to the title of a first-class institution by works which belong to the highest regions of thought. Allegheny is not idle; every Sunday-school and almost every Presbyterian family bear witness to the quiet and unostentatious labours which are prosecuted within her walls. Our friends at Union are notoriously indefatigable, and we have no doubt that the North-west will not be long in putting her light on a candlestick from which it may be radiated through the whole Church. It is perhaps enough for our humble selves to read what our brethren write; and if any man thinks that it is no labour to peruse their teeming works and occasionally sit in judgment upon them, we would say to him, as a certain minister said to his congregation when upon entering his pulpit he found his head prove truant to his tongue, "If any man thinks it easy to preach, let him come up here and try it." In reading Dr. Breckinridge's massive volumes we are reminded of an anecdote of himself when he was a pastor in Baltimore. On a certain Sunday his pulpit had been filled three times by ministers returning from the General Assembly, and at the close of the day he was asked in our presence by a member of his congregation how he felt. "Oh, very tired—very much exhausted!" "Tired! How on earth can that be when you have been resting the whole day?" "Resting! resting!" said the doctor; "do you call it *rest* to listen to such preaching, and then to be compelled to understand it? Why, sir, I never worked so hard in my life." If, upon going through the six hundred and ninety-seven pages which make up the volume before us, any one should be asked whether he had an easy time of it, he might answer— and if he were a spiritual man he certainly would answer— that he had had a most delightful time of it, most profitable and refreshing, but he would be far from saying that there had been no tax upon his intellectual energies. It is a work which has cost labour, and it exacts labour in order to master it. But the labour is not unrequited. Diligence here, as in the culture of the earth, maketh rich. Dr. Breckinridge—to use the beautiful simile of Milton—conducts us to a hillside, laborious indeed at the first ascent, but else so smooth, so green, so full of goodly prospects and melodious sounds on every side, that the harp of Orpheus was not more charming.

The book bears the image of its author; it is a faithful transcript of his mind. The tendency to seize the abstract in the concrete, to detect the law in the fact; intensity of energy manifested in a fervour of expression amounting not unfrequently to positive exaggeration; bursts of passion, often swelling into the highest eloquence, or breaking forth into terrible invective, or subsiding into the tenderest tones of pathos; sudden alternations from the most opposite extremes, from the gay to the grave, from the lion to the lamb, are as conspicuous in the book as in the man; and if his name had not been upon the title-page, albeit not gifted with any extraordinary power of guessing, we should have been at no loss in divining the author.

The general design of the book is to trace the history and progress of religion, whether personally considered as manifested in the individual or collectively considered as manifested in the Church. The first volume discussed Theology as a doctrine; the second treats it as a life. In the first volume, the science was purely speculative; in the second, it is wholly practical. In the first, the scheme of redemption and the great truths which it presupposes and involves were merely the object-matter of thought; in the second, they are living springs of energy, subjective laws and powers in the soul of man. The first volume aims simply to describe the theologian; the second portrays the Christian believer. It may, therefore, be regarded as a treatise of experimental religion; and its special province is to exhibit the work of the Holy Ghost in applying redemption to the hearts of men. The book falls into two general divisions—religion as produced and manifested in the individual, religion as produced and manifested in the Church; for Dr. Breckinridge considers the Church as subsequent in the order of thought to the individual—the outward organic expression of an inward spiritual life. With him the Church as naturally springs from the common relation of individual believers to Christ, as the family from the relation of children to the same parent. The following is his own summary of the general contents of the volume:

"The order of the general demonstration may be made intelligible by a brief statement. In the First Book I attempt to trace and to prove the manner in which the knowledge of God unto salvation passes over from being merely objective and becomes subjective. In the Second Book I endeavour to disclose and to demonstrate the whole work of God in man unto his personal salvation. In the Third Book the personal effects and results of this Divine, subjective work are sought to be explicated. This seems to me to exhaust the subject in its subjective personal aspect. But these individual Christians, by means of their union with Christ and their consequent communion with each other, are organized by God into a visible kingdom, which has a direct and precise relation to the subjective consideration of the knowledge of God. From this point, therefore, the social and organic aspect of the subject arises, and the Fourth Book is occupied with what is designed to be a demonstration of the Church of the living God. But just as the work of grace in individual men is necessarily followed by the Christian offices, and so the subject of the Third Book necessarily followed the subject of the Second, in like manner the consideration of the gifts of God to His Church, and of all the effects of these gifts, follows the organization and progress of the visible Church in a peculiar manner. And thus the subject of the Fourth Book leads directly to the subject of the Fifth, in which the life, action and organism of the Church are discussed with reference to the special gifts bestowed on it by God. And here the organic aspect of the knowledge of God unto salvation, subjectively considered, seems to terminate. What remains is the general conclusion of the whole subject, in a very brief attempt to estimate the progress and result of these Divine realities, and to disclose the revealed consummation of God's works of creation, providence and grace."

Dr. Breckinridge begins with a graphic description of the actual posture of the universe under the condemnation of sin as modified by the introduction of grace. He shows that the scriptural accounts of the fall and of redemption are the only facts which are competent to explain the mysteries of our present condition. The world is not what it would have been, and what it must have been, had there been no purpose of deliverance; it is not what it would have been, and what it must have been, had the deliverance been as universal as the curse. The election of grace modifies everything, so as to produce and to explain the precise dispensation of mingled good and evil which we daily experience. Our race is in ruins, but not hopelessly lost. God has a seed to be collected from it, and the whole career of Providence is but the evolution of the plan by which He displays His grace in the vessels of mercy, and gloriously vindicates His justice in the vessels of wrath fitted for destruction. We are neither in the incipient state of moral beings, probationers for life under law, nor in the final state of punishment or reward. We have been tried and have failed, but are not yet wholly abandoned to despair. Intermediate between the fall and its final issue is a dispensation of mercy, which looks to the full execution of the sentence or its complete remission, accordingly as the offered Saviour is received or rejected. In the mean time, the blessing and the curse are marvellously intermingled. Good and evil are in constant and terrible conflict, and the miseries of our lot are made the instruments of a wholesome discipline or the proofs of incorrigible impenitence.

Dr. Breckinridge next proceeds to unfold the nature and general provisions of that covenant through which this modifying grace has found its way into our world. The discussion of this topic, without being scholastic or technical, is logically complete. It is more—it is rich and scriptural; and in the sublime march of the principles which are successively evolved, the petty cavils of petty minds against the supremacy and sovereignty of God are felt to be contemptible. One of the most delightful features of this book is the conviction which everywhere pervades it that God's character needs no apology at the bar of sinners. Dr. Breckinridge never shrinks from the offensive truths of the Gospel. He brings them out plainly, fully, boldly and confidently. He opens his mouth wide and utters all that God has revealed. Election, particular redemption, efficacious grace—he scouts the notion of the possibility of salvation without recognizing these elements. Grace with him is real grace, and not an euphemistic name for a result actually dependent upon the will of the creature. Christ is a real Saviour, and not an instrument by which the sinner is enabled to gratify his pride. The Holy Ghost is a real sanctifier, and not an influence by which the energies of men are stimulated, and their better impulses roused into action. The Persons of the glorious Trinity have entered into a real covenant to redeem a Church from the lost multitude of the race, and are not the authors of paltry expedients or abortive efforts to coax men into what they find it impossible directly to effect. The problem of sin is a problem with which, according to Dr. Breckinridge, God is competent to deal. It is not something unexpected—not something which He could not have prevented, and which fills Him with regret as He looks upon the universe perverted from its end. It did not take Him by surprise. In the depths of eternity the fall of angels and of men was distinctly contemplated, and that eternal covenant established which, in its final evolution, was to bring infinite glory to the wisdom, goodness and power of God, from the whole manner in which He has dealt with, and manifested the infinite resources of His being in dealing with, this vast question. Dr. Breckinridge next shows that the provisions of the covenant are not arbitrary or capricious, but exactly adapted to the moral and intellectual nature of man. The plan of salvation is precisely such a plan as the exigencies of sinners demanded. It fits their case as the form of the key corresponds to the wards of the lock. Man is dealt with as a rational and accountable being, and every element of the constitution which God gave him is minutely respected in the method by which God saves him. And yet the plan, while it disturbs not the freedom of man, is so ordered that salvation is no contingency. The scheme is incapable of failure. So far from being a wonder that the elect are saved, the marvel would be how any of them could be lost. Here is the mystery of infinite wisdom and of infinite grace. How absurd, in the light of such provisions—provisions revealed in the Scriptures and realized in the hearts of thousands and tens of thousands of God's children—to represent sin as something too strong for the Almighty!

The next topics brought before us are the conditions with respect to the sinner upon which the promises of the covenant are suspended—that is, what God requires of us in order that we may be saved. Here Dr. Breckinridge concurs with that class of the Reformed divines who resolved them into *two*—repentance and faith. The double relation of these graces, as duties in themselves and as the means of other benefits, is carefully noted. They do not save as duties—that would be legalism—but as graces involving a peculiar relation to Christ and to God. Here we think the reduction unscriptural and the argument illusive. The term *condition*, if taken in the general sense of a preliminary requisite, is applicable to every grace which precedes the final result, as well as to faith and repentance. It is applicable to meditation, to prayer, to the reading of the Scriptures, to the diligent use of all the ordinances of the Gospel, as well as to every internal habit wrought by the Spirit preparatory to the great reward. This is only saying that there is an order in the communication of God's blessings by virtue of which one grace is prior to another. In the narrow sense of that which unites us to Christ and makes us actual partakers of redemption, the term *condition* is, in our judgment, applicable only to faith. It is clear that the ground of all personal interest in the blessings of the covenant is union with Christ.

This no one asserts more strongly than Dr. Breckinridge. Union with Christ secures justification, adoption, sanctification and the whole salvation of the Gospel. The condition, and the sole condition, of union with Christ is faith. The man who believes is saved. Now, if we understand Dr. Breckinridge, he seems to maintain that repentance sustains a relation to God analogous to that which faith sustains to the Lord Jesus Christ. Repentance he represents as the only means of our deliverance from sin, either outward or inward, either original or actual. "Nothing," he says, "can be more certain than that every benefit we derive from Christ is made to depend in some way on our faith in Him, while all pardon of sin is directly connected with repentance, and all increase in holiness is beyond our power, except as we see and hate sin on one side, and see and strive after holiness on the other." It is true that there is no pardon to the impenitent; but there is no pardon, not because repentance is a means of pardon, but because there is no union with Christ and consequently no possibility of being sprinkled with His blood. It is precisely because faith is the exercise of a renewed soul that it is incompetent to those who cherish the love of sin; true faith includes in it the renunciation of the flesh as well as the reception of the Saviour. The very purpose for which it receives Christ is, that it may be freed as well from the dominion as from the guilt of sin. Salvation, the blessing to be obtained, means nothing, unless it includes holiness. To state the thing in another form: What is the formal ground of pardon? It is certainly the blood of Christ which cancels our guilt. How is that blood applied to us? Just as certainly by the Holy Spirit. How does the Spirit apply it? By uniting us to Christ. How does He unite us to Christ? By that process of grace which terminates in the production of saving faith. United to Christ, we receive two classes of benefits—inward and outward; the inward all included under the generic name of *repentance*, and appertaining to the entire destruction of sin and the complete restoration of the image of God; the outward having reference to all those benefits which affect our relations to God as a Ruler and Judge. Both classes of blessings are equally the promise of the covenant. Both are treasured up in the Lord Jesus Christ. We obtain both by being in Him, and as we are in Him only by faith, faith must be the exclusive condition of the covenant. There can be no doubt that we are justified exclusively by faith, but justification includes pardon; therefore we are pardoned only through faith. It is clear, too, that the Spirit is received only by faith; and yet the Spirit is the Sanctifier, the Author of all penitence and of all real holiness. We think, therefore, that repentance, instead of being represented as a condition of the covenant, should be represented, as Calvin has done, as a compendious expression for one great class of its blessings, while justification and adoption should be referred to another, both classes sustaining the same relation to faith. The blood and the water flowed together from the Saviour's side. To be in Him is to have them both; and if we are in Him, as Dr. Breckinridge frequently admits, only by faith, then faith is the sole condition of the covenant. This seems to us to be the teaching of the Westminster Confession.

"The grace of God is manifested in the second covenant, in that He freely provides and offereth to sinners a Mediator, and life and salvation by Him; and requiring faith as the condition to interest them in Him, promiseth and giveth His Holy Spirit to all His elect, to work in them that faith with all other saving graces, and to enable them unto all holy obedience as the evidence of the truth of their faith and thankfulness to God, and as the way which He hath appointed them to salvation."[1]

We have but little sympathy with the fears of those theologians who have insisted upon repentance as a condition of the covenant in order to screen the Gospel from the imputation of licentiousness. The faith which justifies is no dead faith, but a faith which works by love. It admires the

[1] Larg. Cat., Q. 32.

beauty of holiness as well as the glory of the Saviour, and contains in it the very seeds of repentance. It never embraces Christ without renouncing sin, and the more lovely and adorable He appears, the more hateful and odious sin becomes. The truth is, Christ cannot be divided, and to receive Him at all is to receive Him in the fullness and integrity of His salvation. Faith, moreover, is the only grace which exactly responds to the nature of the Gospel as a complement of promises; therefore faith is the only grace which is suited to be the condition of the covenant. Our design, however, is not to argue the question, but to intimate the general grounds of our dissent from the author's mode of representation.

After the conditions, he next takes up the successive dispensations of the covenant, and in this chapter a rich mass of truth is condensed in a very brief compass. He shows conclusively that there never has been but one Gospel, and that though there have been diversities of administrations, and each illustrative of the manifold wisdom of God, there never has been but one Saviour. The first great promise has spanned the arch of time.

These five chapters, briefly recapitulated, constituting the First Book, have all been preliminary to the main design of the treatise—the exhibition of the work of grace upon the human soul. They have briefly illustrated our precise condition as under the curse of one covenant and the promise of the other; they have shown the origin, nature and exact provisions of that promise which compendiously includes all Divine grace; they have traced its nice and beautiful adaptations to our nature as men and our case as sinners, and marked the steps by which, to ages and generations past as well as in these latter days, God has revealed it as the ground of all human hope. We are brought at last to the Gospel as it comes to us in the new economy; and as that is the instrument through which all salvation is applied, we are now prepared to follow the wondrous path of the Spirit, as He calls the sinner from darkness to light, and translates him from Adam to Christ, and from the kingdom of Satan into the kingdom of God's dear Son. This work of grace upon the soul is contemplated in two distinct but inseparable aspects: First, with reference to the agency of the Holy Ghost, who accomplishes it; secondly, with reference to the agency of the new creature which it evokes; that is, we are first led to consider the graces, and then the offices or duties, of the Christian—his life as a habit divinely implanted, and as an energy actively manifested. To the first topic the Second Book is devoted; to the second, the Third. Union with Christ, effectual calling, regeneration, justification, adoption, sanctification and eternal blessedness, together with all the benefits incidentally connected now or hereafter with these august gifts, are the subjects which, under the first head, successively pass before us; while faith, repentance, new obedience, good works, the spiritual warfare—in fine, all the elements of holiness, together with the rule by which faith and duty are to be regulated—constitute the topics which exhaust the consideration of the second head. The reader will perceive at once that here is a rich table of contents; that if these subjects are adequately treated in the experimental relations in which they are contemplated, we have a work upon personal religion of the deepest interest and importance. We are happy to say that Dr. Breckinridge has fulfilled his task nobly and well. No child of God can lay down the book without being grateful to the author for the comfort and edification he has received; and no minister can take it up without feeling, as he passes through its closely-concatenated chapters, that Theology, as here exhibited, is not a dead abstraction, but a living reality, and that he is better prepared, by the pregnant discussions of these pages, to deal with the hearts and consciences of his people. Dr. Breckinridge has taken the two factors, the truth in the hands of the Spirit and the soul of man, and has shown the wonderful results produced by their joint action. Other qualifications besides learning were required to write such a book. The author must have felt the power which he describes, and been conscious of the life he delineates. He must likewise have been familiar with the exercises of others. It is evidently Christian experience, portrayed by a pastor who has conversed with many a sinner and comforted many a saint. We need not say that the work is thoroughly evangelical, exaggerating nothing to increase the offence of the cross, and extenuating nothing to conciliate the approbation of the carnal heart. The supernatural character of religion, the utter impotence of man, the resistless efficacy of grace, the all-pervading nature of the change implied in the new birth,—all these and kindred points are brought out with a freshness, an unction and a truth to life that make the book as delightful to the Christian as the last new novel to a girl in her teens. It is one instance of a work in these days of sophistical speculation in which there are no compromises with a shallow philosophy. Here are no evasive efforts to reconcile the justice of God's authority with the helplessness of man by distinctions which every converted heart instantly repels, and the only effect of which is to seduce the impenitent into the belief of a lie; no futile attempts, on the one hand, to strip God of His sovereignty under the pretext of saving His character, or to refine away, on the other, the depravity of man under the pretence of saving his responsibility. Dr. Breckinridge states the truth, and the whole truth, as God has revealed it, perfectly confident that the Divine glory has nothing to lose, and human guilt nothing to gain, from honest and faithful dealing.

Having in the Second and Third Books despatched the subject of personal religion in its graces and its duties, he next develops the doctrine of the Church as the necessary result of the communion of believers with each other in consequence of their union with Christ. Children of the same Father, they must constitute one family. The Church is considered in a twofold aspect, corresponding to the twofold aspect in which the individual believer was surveyed—first, in relation to its idea or essence, its fundamental principles, its aims and ends, and then in relation to the gifts of God to it in the ministry, the Word and the ordinances. The Fourth Book is devoted to the first, the Fifth to the second aspect of this subject. In the matter of church-polity, the exposition contained in this volume is the clearest and most scriptural of any with which we are acquainted. It is a disreputable truth that there are many Presbyterians, and Presbyterian ministers, who are very imperfectly acquainted with the characteristic principles of their own system. The ruling elder, even in decisions of the General Assembly, occupies a very anomalous position; and it is still disputed whether he is the proxy of the congregation, deriving all his rights and authority from a delegation of power on the part of the people, or whether he is an officer divinely appointed, deriving his authority from Christ the Lord. It is still disputed whether he belongs to the same order with the minister, or whether the minister alone is the presbyter of Scripture, and the ruling elder a subordinate assistant. It is still disputed whether he sits in presbytery as the deputy of the brotherhood, or whether he sits there by Divine right as a constituent element of the body; whether as a member of presbytery he can participate in all presbyterial acts, or is debarred from some by the low nature of his office. That all government is by councils; that these councils are representative and deliberative; that, *jure Divino*, they are all presbyteries, and as presbyteries composed exclusively of presbyters; that presbyters, though one in order and the right to rule, are subdivided into two classes; that all presbyteries, whether parochial, classical or synodical, are radically the same; that the Church in its germ and in its fullest development presents the same elements; that her whole polity is that of a free commonwealth;—these points are ably, scripturally, unanswerably established in the work before us. The only topic which Dr. Breckinridge has failed to elaborate, is one which all the Reformed theologians have evaded— the precise nature of the visible Church. Is it or is it not specifically a different thing from the communion of saints? Dr. Breckinridge treats it as the body of believers made apparent. He restricts the Church in its proper sense to the congregation of the faithful. None can be truly members of it but those who are members of Christ. He accordingly maintains with Calvin, with Luther, with Melancthon that hypocrites and unbelievers, though in it, are not of it. They are insolent intruders whom it is the office of discipline to expel. We do not say that this representation is not correct; but supposing it to be correct, we should like to have had it explained upon what principle the official acts of an unconverted minister become valid. Judas was a devil and the son of perdition, but was he not also an apostle, and did he not receive his commission directly from the Lord? Was he a mere intruder into an office to which he was divinely called? Our Book evidently makes the distinction between the visible Church and the invisible Church to be that in the one the profession, in the other the possession, of faith is the indispensable condition of membership. The two do not, therefore, seem to correspond. The one is not an imperfect exhibition of the other, but a different though a related institute. Where the specific difference is not the same there can be no identity of species. Then, again, the constitution of the visible Church, through families, many of whose members never become saints, would seem to intimate that the visible Church is something more than the communion of saints made apparent. The whole subject is encompassed with difficulties, and we should have been glad if Dr. Breckinridge had devoted to it a larger share of his attention. It is undergoing a warm and vigorous discussion in Germany, and we hope the result will be the clearing up of difficulties which still embarrass many earnest minds.

We cannot express too highly our approbation of those parts of the work in which Dr. Breckinridge has discussed the relations of the Church to the State, the world and the secular institutions of society. We are confident that the truths which he has had the grace to enunciate upon these topics are the only truths which can secure to the Church in this country the position of influence which she ought to occupy. If she undertakes to meddle with the things of Cæsar, she must expect to be crushed by the sword of Cæsar. If she condescends to put herself upon a level with the countless institutes which philanthropy or folly has contrived for the earthly good of the race, she must expect to share the fate of human devices and expedients. She is of God, and if she forgets that it is her Divine prerogative to speak in the name and by the authority of God—if she relinquishes the dialect of Canaan, and stoops to babble in the dialects of earth—she must expect to be treated as a babbler. Her strength lies in comprehending her spiritual vocation. She is different from all other societies among men. Though as a society she has ethical and political relations in common with the permanent organizations of the Family and the State, yet in her essence, her laws, and her ends she is diverse from every other institute. The ties which bind men together in other societies are only mediately from God and immediately from man; she is immediately from God and mediately from man. The laws of other societies are the dictates of reason or the instincts of prudence; her laws are express revelations from heaven. Other societies exist for the good of man as a moral, social, political being; she exists for the glory of God in the salvation of sinners. Her ends are supernatural and Divine. She knows man and God only in the awful and profound relations implied in the terms guilt, sin, pardon, penitence and eternal life. Existing in Christ, by Christ and for Christ, she has no other law but His will. She can only speak the words which He puts in her mouth. Founded upon Divine revelation and not in human nature, she has a Divine faith but no human opinion, and the only argument by which she authenticates either her doctrines or her precepts is, Thus saith the Lord. Her province is not to reason, but to testify. These principles, clear in themselves and as vital as they are clear, Dr. Breckinridge has unfolded with signal success; at the same time he has not overlooked the aspect of opposition in which her testimony must often place her to the institutions and customs of the world. Whenever earthly societies of any sort involve corrupt doctrines, it is her duty, in the name of God, to witness against the lie; but she can interfere no farther, except in relation to her own members, than to expose and rebuke the falsehood. When secular institutions involve no corrupt principles her position is one of silence in relation to them. As God has neither commanded nor prohibited them, she leaves them where He has left them—to the discretion of His children. The simple proposition that all Church-power is ministerial and declarative, consistently carried out, explains her whole duty. The meaning is, that the Church can only execute what God enjoins, and can teach as faith or duty only what God reveals. When, therefore, she is requested to recommend some human contrivance, she has only to ask herself, Has God made it the duty of His people to engage in it? Has He anywhere commanded them to join this, that or the other society? If not, what right has she to require it? If the thing is wrong she has a right to condemn it; if liable to no moral objections on the score of principle, she must be silent; and the reason of the distinction is obvious. All wickedness is contradictory to the law of God, and she has a right to declare that law. In the other case the question is one of the fitness of means and ends, and that is a question of opinion. God has given no revelation about it, and therefore she has nothing to declare. She may say, if she chooses, that the principles involved are not objectionable, but she cannot say that the given application of the principles is ordained of God. In other words, in the case of evil she has the positive right to condemn; in every other she has only the negative right not to disapprove.

It may be said that this conception of the province of the Church has never been adequately realized. This is only saying that she has never fully comprehended the liberty wherewith Christ has made her free. It was a slow process to cleanse off all the slime of the Papacy. The purest churches in Europe are still bungling about the question, perfectly simple to us, concerning the relations of the Church to the State. It is not strange that we should be perplexed about problems growing out of her peculiar posture in America as in one aspect a purely voluntary institution. In the mean time, God has been teaching us by disastrous examples. We have seen the experiment tried in certain quarters of reducing the Church to the condition of a voluntary society, aiming at the promotion of universal good. We have seen her treated as a contrivance for every species of reform—individual, social, political. We have seen her foremost, under the plea of philanthropy, in every species of moral knight-errantry, from the harmless project of organizing the girls of a township into a pin-cushion club, to the formation of conspiracies for convulsing governments to their very centre. The result has been precisely what might have been expected. Christ has been expelled from these pulpits, and almost the only Gospel which is left them is the gospel of the Age of Reason. Extreme cases prove principles. If we would avoid a similar condemnation, we must hate even the garments spotted by the flesh; we must crush the serpent in the egg; we must rigidly restrain the Church within her own proper sphere; and as she refines and exalts the spiritual nature of man, we may expect her to purify the whole moral atmosphere, and indirectly, through the life which she imparts to the soul, to contribute to the prosperity of every human interest. Her power in the secular sphere is that of a sanction and not a rule. As pre-eminently suited to the present time, when this subject is beginning to awaken the interest which its importance deserves, we commend the twentieth and twenty-second chapters of the treatise before us.

The future of the kingdom of God—that is, the dispensations of the covenant of grace beyond the economy of the Gospel under which we live—Dr. Breckinridge has reserved for a few modest and cautious suggestions at the close of the book. He thinks that there are two dispensations yet to come—the dispensation of millennial glory to be inaugurated by the second advent of the Redeemer, and the dispensation of heavenly blessedness to be inaugurated by the delivery up of the Lamb's Book of Life. We are delighted with the spirit which pervades the exposition of these topics, and equally delighted that though Dr. Breckinridge coincides in some of the leading views of the Millennarians, he repudiates the crudities—we had almost said the monstrosities—which disfigure the publications of that sect. He has no idea of a period in which Christ is to become subordinate to Moses, and in which it shall be the highest glory of the Gentiles to turn Jews. We may differ from Dr. Breckinridge as to the competency of the Gospel dispensation, under augmented measures of the Spirit, to subdue the world to Christ, but we are heartily at one with him as to the duty of the Church to preach the Gospel to every creature. We may differ from him as to the state of things preceding and introduced by the second advent of Christ, but we are at one with him as to the necessity of watching and praying and struggling for His coming. It is the great hope of the future, as universal evangelization is the great duty of the present. If the Church could be aroused to a deeper sense of the glory that awaits her, she would enter with a warmer spirit into the struggles that are before her. Hope would inspire ardour. She would even now rise from the dust, and like the eagle plume her pinions for loftier flights than she has yet taken. What she wants, and what every individual Christian wants, is faith—faith in her sublime vocation, in her Divine resources, in the presence and efficacy of the Spirit that dwells in her—faith in the truth, faith in Jesus, and faith in God. With such a faith there would be no need to speculate about the future. That would speedily reveal itself. It is our unfaithfulness, our negligence and unbelief, our low and carnal aims, that retard the chariot of the Redeemer. The Bridegroom cannot come until the Bride has made herself ready. Let the Church be in earnest after greater holiness in her own members, and in faith and love undertake the conquest of the world, and she will soon settle the question whether her resources are competent to change the face of the earth. We are content to await the progress of events. In the mean time, who that has ever reflected upon these great realities, and groaned in spirit at the clouds and darkness which beset them, can withhold his sympathy from the man who writes the following lines?—

"In every point of view, therefore, the glory of the Messiah seems to be immediately and transcendently involved in His second coming and millennial reign. And His loving and trusting children ought to beware of dishonouring him and deadening their own high and spiritual hopes by low and carnal allegorizing about these sublime mysteries, as well as of deluding themselves by vain and shallow dogmatizing concerning them, as if they were perfectly simple and elemental. For myself I speak concerning them, after many years of anxious meditation, as one who would prefer not to speak, and who feels assuredly that they who will follow us will get a clearer insight as they draw nearer to them. The grand and leading ideas which belong to the future progress and glorious consummation of God's eternal covenant seem to me to be perfectly clear. Around these are other ideas, carrying with them, apparently, the highest probability of truth, but not a satisfying assurance that we comprehend them justly. And then around these, in circles perpetually enlarging, are topics vast and numerous, involving God and man and the universe, and questions the most intricate and overwhelming concerning them all, in which a single inspired word misunderstood, or even a shade of thought wrongly conceived, may involve us far beyond our scanty knowledge and feeble powers. And how could it be otherwise? It is the infinite and eternal thought of God, not yet realized in its actual accomplishment, which mortals are striving to penetrate and disclose."—Page 681.

In the conclusion of the meagre and imperfect sketch which we have attempted to give of the contents of this volume it only remains to form a general estimate of its merits, and of the place which it is likely to occupy in our religious literature. Accepting Theology as a science of positive truth—that is, of truth which can be certainly and infallibly known—the author has attempted to construct the system in such a manner that each particular proposition should not only authenticate itself by its own light, but command conviction by its manifest relation to the whole. The autopistic power of the truth is more prominent in the second than in the first volume. In the first, which is purely speculative, the theory charms by its consistency, clearness and coherence—the temple which is reared is a grand thing to look on and a noble thing to contemplate; but in the second another element is added, the element of experience. The Holy Ghost bears witness in the human soul, and man is no longer a spectator, but a worshipper, and actually beholds the glory of God as He displays His grace above the mercy-seat. That a work whose aim was to make Divine truth speak for itself, first to the understanding as a matter of speculation and then to the heart as a spiritual power, if executed with even tolerable ability, must be entitled to respectful consideration, is obvious from the nature of the case. That a book on experimental religion, professing to trace it, not in the light of philosophy, but in the light of the written Word—which compares the impression with the stamp, the life with the doctrine—that such a work, if executed by one who has any real insight into the mysteries of grace, must be pre-eminently useful to the children of God, is equally clear. All this might have been said if these books had been written by feebler hands. The second volume we think in all respects superior to the first. It touches a chord which vibrates in every Christian heart, and though specially prepared with reference to the training of ministers of the Gospel, it is equally adapted to the edification and comfort of the humblest child of God. "The penitent and believing followers of the Saviour of sinners," "they who fervently desire life after death," will "find light and consolation" in what the author has written, and that which he "has done will live." We have received the most grateful testimonies to its worth. Unsophisticated believers, who knew nothing of Theology except what God had taught them, have spoken of the book to us in terms which showed how much good they had gotten from it; and we have before us the case of a young minister of more than ordinary promise who professed to have derived more benefit from it than from all the treatises he had read. It not only warmed his own heart, but taught him how to warm the hearts of others. We do not say that the book is free from faults—it has faults, faults of method and faults of expression—but they do not seriously impair its sterling merits. We have already intimated that the separation of the objective, subjective, and relative—or, as we should prefer to express it, the speculative, practical, and polemical—strikes us as arbitrary and little suited to the successful culture of the science. Theology is one; it is either wholly speculative, wholly practical, or mixed. In our judgment the mode of treatment should correspond to its own essence, and should not be successively adapted to the single elements which constitute that essence. If Theology is purely speculative, it should be expounded exclusively in the light of theory; if it is wholly practical, it should be taught with a special reference to the activities it is intended to call into play; if mixed, it should be treated as a combination in which these elements are jointly and not successively found. For our own part, we dislike the phrase *mixed* as applied to the manner in which speculation and practice enter into the religious life. There is no mixture, but these phases of our being are blended into the unity of a higher energy. Spiritual energy is one, but it includes every lower intellectual and moral energy. To explain: We have one form of mental energy in the mere assent to truth; this is the lowest exercise of reason. Then we have another form of mental activity in the perception of the beautiful. Here there is combined with assent a feeling or an emotion. The combination is what we mean by the sense of the beautiful. So in the sense of duty or obligation there is also an intellectual and an emotional element, but they constitute one energy. In the religious life we have a combination of the purely intellectual, the æsthetic, and the moral into a still higher energy; and the science of Theology should be treated according to this characteristic of true religion. Hence it leads to a needless repetition to represent successively what the nature of the thing presents in combination, and we cannot but think that Dr. Breckinridge is occasionally hampered by the restraints of his method. Still, whatever defects the book may have they are only blemishes. Its solid worth is hardly affected at all. He has not written in vain. There are thousands of hearts that bless him, of which he will never know until he meets them before that throne where he and they will better understand and appreciate the infinite grace of a glorious Saviour which he has so lovingly described. His book is a noble testimony to truths which, but for his exertions in concert with those of a congenial band of confessors, would have been almost forgotten in the present generation. It well deserves to be the crowning labour of a life which has been zealously devoted to the vindication of the grace of God against fraudulent suppressions on the one hand, and sophistical evasions on the other; and long, long may he continue to speak through these refreshing pages!

PREFATORY NOTE.

THE NECESSITY AND NATURE OF CHRISTIANITY is taken from the "Southern Presbyterian Review," for March, 1849. It constituted the substance of a sermon preached to the students of the South Carolina College, its author being Chaplain and Professor of Moral Philosophy and the Evidences of Christianity in that institution.

THE NECESSITY
AND
NATURE OF CHRISTIANITY.

THE first public conflict, as Milman properly remarks,[1] betwixt Christianity and Paganism took place at Athens. The champion on the one side was Paul, the distinguished Apostle of the Gentiles, who had himself been a relentless persecutor of the Gospel, and who had been graciously honoured with supernatural evidence of its truth. He was prepared to speak what he knew and to testify what he had seen. On the other side were certain philosophers of the Epicureans and Stoics, impelled partly by curiosity and partly by vanity of contest to encounter one whom their philosophic pride prompted them to stigmatize as a babbler, and their settled indifference to truth to receive as a setter-forth of strange gods.

The loss of Athenian independence had removed the checks which, in ancient times, political considerations had arbitrarily imposed upon freedom of debate and liberty of discussion in regard to the popular religion; and though this renowned city was still the headquarters of the reigning superstitions of the world, no philosopher was likely, for the sake of his opinions, however apparently licentious or heretical, to be exposed to the fate of Socrates, Stilpo or Diagoras. In the schools of Athens, no subjects were too sacred for discussion, too profound for inquiry, or too sublime and mysterious to awe the efforts of vain curiosity. The stubborn doctrines of the Stoics, the polite, accommodating

[1] History of Christianity, Book II., chap. iii., p. 178. Amer. Ed.

principles of the Epicureans, the sentimental refinements of Plato and the practical methods of the illustrious Stagirite, the claims of the popular worship, the superstitions of the mass, and the hidden mysteries disclosed to a chosen few,—were matters of free, open, unrebuked debate. In such a city, the long-chosen abode of philosophy, science and the arts, the literary metropolis of the world, rendered holy to a freeman by the mute memorials of Independence eloquent in ruins,—in such a city, and among such a people, the Apostle of the Gentiles appears the champion of the Gospel, against philosophy, science, idolatry, superstition—all the wisdom of this world arrayed in enmity to God. To the eye of sense the odds were fearfully against him. His name and country were identified, among the Pagan nations around him, with all that was little, contracted and mean. A Jew by birth, exclusive in his religion, and a reputed bigot in his opinions, he presented, in his national associations, those features of disgust which provoked the satire of Juvenal, the contempt of Gallio and the raillery of Martial. It is true Paul was a scholar skilled in Grecian models; but all his pretensions to refinement and elegance were sunk in the fact that he was a *Jew*, as the valour and courtly influence of Naaman were nothing to the damning consideration that after all he was a leper. But curiosity was too strong for either prejudice or contempt. His disputes in the synagogue with his own brethren, his instructions to those whom he found seriously intent upon the duties of religion, and his public discussions in the marketplace with all whom the providence of God threw in his way, had made him the object of attention to the leading sects of philosophy. *Then certain philosophers of the Epicureans and of the Stoics encountered him.*[1]

We may here pause to contemplate the contrast in their motives and aims and those of the servant of Jesus. He had come to Athens as a stranger. Driven from Thessalonica by a popular tumult excited by religious bigotry, he

[1] Acts xvii. 18.

sought safety and quiet in this mart of learning, elegance and Paganism; and while tarrying for his brethren, his spirit was stirred in him when he saw the city wholly given to idolatry. He looked not upon its statues and temples, its altars and sacrifices, with the eye of poetry or taste. These ornaments of art, these imposing monuments of genius and skill, however they might adorn the names and perpetuate the memories of Phidias and Praxiteles, were an insult to God; and, like Elijah, the prophet of another dispensation, he was very jealous for the Lord God of Hosts. His imagination could not expatiate in rapture upon scenes which proclaimed too plainly to the ear of faith that the curse of the Almighty was there. What signified the beauty of the work when the end was death? While he mused and saw, the fire burned; the love of Christ, an emotion felt for the first time, perhaps, upon that classic soil—zeal for the glory of God, intense desires for the salvation of the lost, the terrific sanctions of the law,—all pressed upon him and roused his noble spirit to lift up his voice like a trumpet, to cry aloud and spare not. He was a man of God, and the word of the Lord was like fire in his bones. His position was indeed sublime, and though the object of contempt, ridicule or idle curiosity to others, he was raised by the grandeur of his mission and a Tenant in his heart whom the world knew not yet, above all the petty desires which vanity, pride or ambition could suggest, and like his Divine Master prayed in spirit for those who despised him. He had no doubtful disputations to propose, but a message to proclaim in the name of God. He was no dialectician from the Schools, but an ambassador of the skies; he preached not the wisdom of men, but the wisdom of God in a mystery. He spake with the confidence of one whose feet rested upon the rock of eternal truth, and with the persuasiveness of one who was not a lord of the faith, but a helper of the joy of his hearers. The zeal, devotion and deep convictions which glowed in his soul made him earnest, but neither an enthusiast nor fanatic. His discourse is managed with consummate skill, and while the Word of the Lord is plainly declared, it is studiously framed with a reference to the state, prejudices and opinions of the assembly. Paul had seen, among the monuments of Athens, an altar to the Unknown God. This furnishes the Apostle with a text. He begins with the statement of a general fact, true of all men, but pre-eminently true of the Athenians, that the interests of religion, in some form or other, must and will exact attention. Man is essentially a religious animal. His nature calls for religious worship. He must have a God to pray to, as well as a God to swear by, and while the true God is unknown the heart will be filled with idols in His place. All idolatry consists essentially in the false worship of the true, or a superstitious worship of the unknown, God. Having paved his way to the favourable attention of his hearers, Paul proceeds to recapitulate the leading doctrines of Natural Religion, to some of which, with more or less modification, the Stoics might assent, and to others the Epicureans.[1] The doctrines of providence, of human responsibility, of a moral government, are not only announced, but are pressed as formal arguments against a false worship, and urged as motives for seeking to be ascertained of the truth. The obvious dictates of nature, if properly heeded, are sufficient to condemn idolatry. The fall of man, his present depravity, and the necessity of repentance, are briefly and compendiously stated, and then the peculiar doctrines of the Gospel are summarily discussed under the heads of Jesus and the resurrection.

The effects of this sermon are briefly detailed by the historian.[2] Some of them treated the matter with downright scorn; others were afraid that it might be true, but were not prepared to make the sacrifices which a full assent would obviously require. Still there were a few, a select and noble band, consisting alike of plebeians and philosophers, who clave to the Apostle and believed his doctrines. It is re-

---

[1] Milman's History of Christ, Book II., chap. iii., p. 179. Amer. Ed.
[2] Acts xvii. 32–34.

markable that these effects were produced, not by Paul's dissertations upon natural religion, upon the being and providence of God, the accountability of man, and the strict moral government which has been established in the world. He seems to have been heard with patience as long as he insisted upon these and kindred topics. Even his denunciations of idolatry, though a direct rebuke of their practice, and a tacit imputation upon their understanding or integrity, awakened no visible displeasure. But the very moment that the Apostle entered upon the territory of grace, and proceeded to expound those mysteries of the Gospel which eye had not seen nor ear heard, neither had it entered into the heart of man to conceive, the effect was striking and characteristic; some mocked, others said, We will hear thee again of this matter, and only here and there an auditor received the engrafted Word and lived.

This sermon of Paul at Athens deserves our serious attention, as it sets forth, in brief and pregnant heads, the whole contents of revelation, and the essential doctrines in particular of what is properly and exclusively Christianity. Revelation and Christianity are not convertible terms. Everything that even the Bible contains is not a part of Christianity. There have been at least three dispensations of this religion, distinguished from each other by outward form and accidental circumstances; and each of these is described in the Bible, and the peculiarities of each throw light upon the general scheme to which they all pertain.

Everything in revelation is subsidiary to Christianity, but is not necessarily part and parcel of its being. Some things are presupposed in it—their truth is essential to its arrangements; and other things belong to the age, people and country of its first introduction. All these subsidiary and incidental circumstances are to us the subjects of revelation, and therefore to be received with undoubting faith, but much may be received and the Gospel in its essence not be embraced, and many revealed facts may be unknown and yet the salvation of the Gospel imparted. It is, therefore, a profoundly interesting question, What is Christianity? What are the essential features of that system which Jesus introduced into the world, and which without His interposition would not only have been unknown, but would not and could not have been true? What are those peculiarities which, wherever they have been proclaimed, whether on the Areopagus of Athens, in the seats of modern learning, the halls of science, the church, the market-place or meeting-house, have uniformly made some mock, and staggered others, until God by His Spirit gave them a lodgment in the heart? The solution of this question is of fundamental importance. Our lives depend upon it. True, the Gospel is a simple system; but notwithstanding its simplicity multitudes perish with a lie in their right hands, fondly dreaming that they are in the ark, when they are only sheltered by bulrushes. Thousands mistake what Christianity is and die; they kindle a fire and walk in its light, and receive the punishment at God's hand that they shall lie down in sorrow. Let us, therefore, address ourselves to this question with the solemnity and earnestness the nature of the subject demands.

The course of thought pursued by the Apostle in this celebrated sermon, the disposition and arrangement of his topics, and the obvious relations which they sustain to each other, will correct many prevalent errors, and conduct us by an easy process to the precise views which ought to be entertained. Paul first insists upon the *necessity* of the Gospel, and then announces its doctrines in their adaptation to the wants they were designed to relieve.

1. First, then, what is the *necessity* of Christianity? What is the call for it in the circumstances of our race? And what end, consequently, was it designed to answer? The necessity of *revelation* is a point upon which Christian apologists are accustomed to insist as establishing the antecedent credibility of the fact; and though their arguments are, for the most part, conclusive, as showing the likelihood of some interposition to mitigate our ignorance, they fail to

present the peculiar need of such a dispensation as that of the Gospel. It is too frequently taken for granted that "the supposition of sin does not bring in any new religion, but only makes new circumstances and names of old things, and requires new helps and advantages to improve our powers, and to encourage our endeavours; and thus the law of grace is nothing but a restitution of the law of nature."[1] The ground ordinarily assumed is the ignorance of man and the goodness of God; and this ignorance, which seems to be regarded as the principal injury of the fall, has reference to the great facts of natural religion, which, if known, would have sufficient efficacy to secure amendment of life and everlasting happiness. The controversy has been, in many instances, so conducted with the Deists as to convey the impression that the doctrines of nature were sufficient to constitute the complete religion of a sinner; the sole point in dispute being the competency of reason to discover these doctrines without supernatural aid.[2] We are represented as creatures destined for another life, and needing information in reference to its character and its connection with the present, which cannot be derived from the light of nature. In this view Christianity is no new religion; it is only a new publication of that which subsisted from the beginning of our race. It is a *revelation*, strictly and properly so called, and nothing more; and its whole relation to us is exhausted when we receive and submit to it as a Divine teacher.[3] We

---

[1] This extraordinary statement is quoted by Halyburton from one who, he says, "wore a mitre."—Nat. Rel. Insuf., chap. 1, p. 279—Works in one volume.

[2] This is the impression left by Paley; and it is clearly the doctrine of Mr. Locke. His Christianity is nothing but *Revealed Deism*.

[3] It is very unfortunate that the distinctions between Christianity and natural religion have been expressed by the terms natural and revealed religion. The idea obviously suggested by this phraseology is that their difference lies in the sources whence we derive our knowledge of them. Nothing, however, has been more clearly proved by Christian writers— among whom we may especially refer to Halyburton and to Norris— than that we are as much indebted to revelation for any adequate knowledge of natural religion as for the mysteries of the Gospel. They are

are ignorant, for example, of a future life; or if we have, from the operations of conscience or the spontaneous desires of the soul, vague convictions or indistinct impressions of continued existence in another state or among other scenes, the evidence is too feeble and shadowy to furnish the grounds of a steady belief. Christianity, accordingly, relieves our blindness and brings life and immortality to light. The apprehensions of nature it reduces to realities; its vague impressions to the certainty of facts. So, again, without revelation we are represented as uncertain whether our conduct here shall affect our destinies hereafter, or what is the nature of the connection which subsists between the present and the future. Christianity comes to our assistance and teaches us that this present world is a school for eternity; and that according to our characters and conduct here will be our destiny hereafter. This is the method in which the apologists for Christianity have too often conducted the argument with the Deists. There has been no dispute between them as to *what* religion is sufficient to secure the happiness of a sinner. They are, for the most part, agreed in its nature and principles; but it has been keenly debated whether reason, since the fall, is capable of discovering this religion without supernatural assistance, or of authenticating it with sufficient evidence to make it of practical importance. We may admit that the argument is conclusive as conducted by the friends of revelation. Natural religion is certainly not the offspring of natural light. In the present condition of our race, whatever may be the evidences which exist within us and around us of the being, perfection and character of God, of the condition of man, and the relation he sustains to his Creator, his darkened faculties are incompetent to gather from them the conceptions which make up the

---

both *revealed*. The difference between them is radical and essential, and not accidental or contingent. They are different *religions*. One is the religion of our nature before the fall; the other the religion of grace after the fall. The one contemplates God simply as a moral Governor; the other as a Saviour and Redeemer.

fabric of natural religion, however he may prove its truth from these sources after the ideas have been suggested to the mind. We confidently believe that if natural religion were the *sole* religion of a sinner, revelation would still be necessary to teach us what it is, to republish it with light and power, to free it from corruption, superstition and abuse, and present it in the symmetry of its parts and the integrity of its combination. But then this, although a *revelation*, would not be Christianity. It might remove the veil from the eye of ignorance, and unfold realities of tremendous power to alarm the guilty and stimulate the righteous; but all its truths would be independent of the mission of the Saviour, except in so far as he was the instrument in the hands of Providence to unfold them. That this whole theory is fundamentally wrong—though sustained by the splendid names of Locke and Paley, though the favourite and cherished hypothesis, during the dynasty of the Stuarts, defended alike by mitred prelates and humble curates—that Christianity is something more, immeasurably more than a *revelation* of truths, which in themselves were independent of the mission of Christ, may be inferred from the order and connection in which Paul has here introduced the mysteries of the Gospel. It is not a little remarkable that every solitary element of the system which those who take this view of the subject make it the object of Jesus to communicate, was insisted on by the Apostle before he gets to the Gospel. The great doctrines of natural religion which constituted the faith and the worship of man before the fall, are treated as preliminary to the distinctive peculiarities of Christianity. The creed of Herbert—the most liberal of the Deists, as good a Christian as many who have defended miracles and prophecy—so far as this creed is natural religion, is recapitulated by the Apostle as introductory to the Gospel. The unity of God; His absolute independence and universal sovereignty; the relation in which He stands to men; the necessity of religious worship, and the guilt and folly of idolatry; the perfection of His moral government, and the essential, unchangeable distinctions of right and wrong,—these are all eloquently enforced, but these are not the Gospel. We do not say that they are not revealed truths—we do not say that any religion is the offspring of mere natural light; but we do say, and the method of the Apostle justifies us in saying it, that although these are truths of revelation, and truths which must be recognized in order to understand the Gospel, yet they are not Christianity. We will go a step farther and assert that the natural religion which Paul preached on Mars' Hill contained propositions which unassisted reason is utterly, under any circumstances, incompetent to discover; and which yet, from the beginning, must have been parts of the primitive religion of the race. He insists upon the Federal Headship of Adam. This is the fundamental truth in nature's system. We are of *one* blood. There is a mysterious unity in our race, indicated by a common descent and a common nature, in consequence of which we sustain different relations to each other from those which we would have sustained if we had been separate, independent, isolated beings. In our world there is not only *society*, but *kindred*—not only similarity, but identity of nature; and our religion proceeds upon a principle which recognizes this unity, and in its great charter of hope treated with the race in one man. So, also, the doctrine of the Trinity is a doctrine of natural religion. But there might have been imparted to us a knowledge of the object of worship, the great federal dispensation under which our race was created, and the consequent condemnation and ruin of mankind in the first man, who was of the earth, earthy,—and yet not a single doctrine of the Gospel, as connected with the mission of Jesus, be known. Nay, all these things, whether known or not, would have been true had Jesus never been born or never died. Paul's Christianity, therefore, was something more than a republication of natural religion, even in its true form and perfect proportions, as adoring the Trinity and binding the race in a federal compact with a common head. The Apostle virtually admits that in our present state we cannot discover the true system under which we were born, and which attaches to our natures as moral and as human. There was a season of ignorance in which all who had no revelation were permitted to walk. But the removal of this ignorance is not all that the Gospel proposes; it is a new dispensation, out of which new duties and new relations to God spontaneously grow. God *now* commandeth all men everywhere to repent, because He hath appointed a day in the which He will judge the world in righteousness by that Man whom He hath ordained; whereof He hath given assurance unto all men, in that He hath raised Him from the dead. It is plain that Paul regarded Jesus as introducing a religion whose distinctive law, so far as it respected human conduct and obedience, was the law of repentance. We shall not stop to inquire whether repentance is a duty of nature; but as here unfolded by the Apostle it depends upon principles supernatural and Divine. But the argument which we would frame from this passage, against the supposition that the prime necessity of our nature arises from our ignorance, and is therefore to be relieved simply by revelation, is drawn from the importance which the Apostle attaches to the resurrection of Jesus and the consequent resurrection of the dead. The religion which Paul preached at Athens, and which the necessities of all men require, is a religion into which this fact must enter. We must bear in mind that the resurrection, neither of Jesus nor His followers, is ever treated in the Christian Scriptures as a *proof* of Christianity; it is always made a *part* of it—an essential, indispensable element of the scheme. It is not presented to us simply as a *miracle*, authenticating the Divine mission of Christ, though of course this must be an incidental result, but it is treated as being as really, and truly, and necessarily a component part of the Gospel as the death or incarnation of the Saviour. Paul[1] sums up the whole of Christianity in Jesus and the resurrection: For I delivered unto you, first of all, that which I also received; how that

[1] Acts xvii. 18; 1 Cor. xv. 3.

Christ died for our sins according to the Scriptures, and that He was buried, and that He rose again the third day, according to the Scriptures. The death, burial, resurrection of Christ,—these were the facts upon which the Gospel depended that Paul preached at Athens and Corinth. To represent the resurrection as a mere proof of Christianity, resting upon the same footing with the other miracles of the New Testament, and authenticating Christ's supernatural commission in the same way, is without sanction from the Scriptures. It is never treated simply as a credential—a motive to belief, but not the thing to be believed. On the contrary, Paul affirms that if Jesus be not risen our preaching is vain, and your faith is also vain—the Gospel is absolutely worthless. This cannot be said of any single miracle of the Saviour or His apostles. They might have wrought more, they might have wrought fewer; the Gospel would have been the same. But if Jesus had not *risen*, there would have been no Gospel, and we should *have been in our sins.*

The passage in Romans which seems to make the resurrection a proof of the Sonship of Christ has a much wider sweep than interpreters have been accustomed to give to it. The ordinary view is, that as Christ before His death had declared Himself to be the Son of God, and as He was condemned by the Jewish courts upon the ground of His supernatural pretensions to a Divine generation alone, His resurrection from the dead was the endorsement by the Father of the veracity of His own testimony. But, according to this view, any other miracle would have answered the same purpose. The darkened heavens, the yawning earth, the cleaving rocks and the rising dead had already proclaimed His Sonship as truly as the resurrection—proclaimed it so loudly and powerfully that the centurion confessed the stupendous truth, while all the people that came together to that sight, beholding the things which were done, smote their breasts and returned.[1] The impressions of that scene were as awful and convincing as any mere miracles could

[1] Luke xxiii. 47–49.

possibly have made. Every previous miracle had as much authenticated the Divine mission of Jesus, and, of course, the Divine truth of all that He had uttered, as this final one of His resurrection from the dead. And that God never intended it as a *mere proof* is evident from the fact that He did not show Himself openly to all the people, but to witnesses chosen beforehand.

The whole reasoning of the Apostle goes upon the supposition that His resurrection *directly* declared His Sonship; it did not simply declare that he spoke the truth when he affirmed it, but it attested the fact independently of any such connection. The Psalmist, looking to this great event, represents the Almighty as proclaiming by it, Thou art my Son, this day have I begotten Thee;[1] and when He ascended into heaven the joyful acclamation was heard, "God is gone up with a shout, Jehovah with the sound of a trumpet."[2]

It is, therefore, evident that both the Old Testament and the New represent the resurrection not only as an integral part of Christianity, but as a pregnant proof of the eternal Sonship of Christ, and consequently every scheme must be false in which this great fact is not obviously possessed of this distinction. Whatever the Gospel is, it must be something into which the resurrection essentially enters, and so enters as to establish the Sonship of Jesus; and as neither the one nor the other can be affirmed of His office as a Prophet, it is very certain that the necessity which Paul contemplated must lie much deeper than the natural ignorance of man in regard to truths which are independent of the mission of Jesus. It is obvious that whatever the Gospel is, its truths must have been *created* by the mission of Jesus. They would not have existed at all if He had not been born, crucified, buried, and if He had not risen from the dead.

Enough has been said to show that Paul contemplated Christianity as something more than a *revelation*. This proposition may strike our readers as hardly worth the

[1] Ps. ii. 7; Acts xiii. 33.   [2] Ps. xlvii. 5.

labour we have expended upon it, but those who have been brought most in contact with the educated minds of the country must be sensible that the difficulties which they experience in Christianity are largely owing to this low view.

The principles of natural religion seem so reasonable, when once they are fairly proposed, that it is hard to get quit of the conviction that what so obviously commends itself to the understandings and consciences of men might have been discovered without supernatural light. The presumption against *revelation* is increased by confining its scope to a department of truths which were certainly the original furniture of reason, and which, when once they are announced, reason, apart from the influence of prejudice and passion, does not hesitate to recognize. To tell us that nature and Christianity embrace exactly the same religion, that Christianity is distinguished by nothing but the source from which it springs, that its sole object is to publish with clearness and enforce with authority the doctrines of nature, is to put its necessity on a footing which, however successfully it may be maintained, will seldom produce that deep and earnest conviction of need which hails the Gospel with joy, and detects in its provisions an adequate reason for the interposition of God. This low view of the subject has not only to encounter the supposed presumption against revelation in general, but an additional presumption against that species of revelation which, with an immense apparatus of means, does little more than enlarge the territory of knowledge and dispel a few floating clouds from the atmosphere of truth. The great bell of the universe is rung to preach a sermon of which nature was previously in possession of the heads.

Lord Herbert's difficulties with Christianity arose, for the most part, from an utter misconception of its principal design. The question could never be raised concerning the sufficiency of reason if the proper end of the Gospel were kept steadily in view. Deism was comparatively unknown in England until a style of preaching was adopted which confounded morality with holiness, habits with the Spirit of God, and faith with a general conviction of truth—which discarding all its distinctive doctrines, reduced Christianity to a frozen system of heathenism, and made the ministers of Jesus little better than the "miserable apes of Epictetus." When the prelate and the curate were equally anxious to have the world believe that their Gospel had exploded the antiquated notions of spirituality and grace, that such uncouth phrases as justification, adoption, regeneration and redemption were stripped of their repulsiveness, and adjusted as well to the notions as the dialect of fashionable life, it is not to be wondered at that men should stare at the pomp of preparation with which *such* a religion had been announced to the world. The affluence of means and the poverty of result were so conspicuously in contrast that the question seems to have been naturally suggested, whether, if *this* were all, reason might not have been left to itself. We can sympathize with such difficulties; and though we are far from asserting—for we by no means believe—that unassisted reason since the fall would ever have discovered the whole system of natural religion, yet we are as far from asserting that Christianity is the form in which a revelation designed chiefly to assist reason would have been given. To this inadequate conception of its office, as a mere handmaid to nature, is owing in some degree the fact that the whole current of modern philosophy, under the pretext of great veneration for religion, is fatal in its tendencies to the claim of inspiration. The sufficiency of reason has been defended, not on historical but psychological grounds, and the excellency of Christianity is represented as consisting in the distinctness and fullness with which it echoes the voice of nature. This is to betray the Saviour with a kiss. These insidious assaults may indeed be repelled by direct arguments, but we can only reach the source of the evil by placing the necessity of the Gospel on its true basis. The change which sin has introduced in the relations of our race to God, and the glorious provisions of the new covenant, must be set in the light in which the Scriptures uniformly put them, if we would not judge of Divine revelation by a false standard. To show that ignorance is not the great evil which Christ came to dispel, that the scheme of redemption is a vast and mighty dispensation of grace, a stupendous work which our exigencies demanded and God was glorious in doing, is to remove one of the leading difficulties which press upon educated men when they first turn their attention to the subject. They often hesitate because they do not understand the case.

2. Others, unable to escape from the pervading testimony of Scripture that the mission of Jesus contemplated a work to be done as well as truths to be revealed—that Christianity is a grand dispensation of providence and grace, involving a series of supernatural acts directed to the salvation of the sinner, the history of which in their origin, relations and results is the principal instruction it imparts—while they discard the low conceptions of an earth-born philosophy which can detect in the Gospel nothing but a republication of natural religion, fail yet to rise to an adequate apprehension of the real nature of Christ's mediation. Whether it be owing to a fastidious modesty which perverts a just dread of presumption and a becoming sense of ignorance into a refusal to be wise up to what is written, or whether there be a lurking dislike of the principle upon which a consistent explanation can be given of the method of redemption—whatever be the cause, there are men who admit an apparent necessity of the interposition of the Mediator, and yet fail to present in their account of His work any correspondence discoverable by us to the necessity they acknowledge. They very justly represent natural religion as unsuited to the condition of a sinner; it makes no provision for the pardon of the guilty; it knows nothing of mercy, nothing of restoration to the favour of God. Conducted upon the principle of distributive justice, it promises life to the obedient, denounces death to transgressors, but opens no door of hope to the wretch who has incurred its curse. It *must*

render to every man according to his works—"to them who by patient continuance in well-doing seek for glory and honour and immortality, eternal life; but unto them that are contentious and do not obey the truth, but obey unrighteousness, indignation and wrath, tribulation and anguish upon every soul of man that doeth evil, of the Jew first and also of the Gentile." With these representations—not so strongly and emphatically made, we confess, as the nature of the case seems to us to warrant—of the necessity of justification to the salvation of a sinner and the hopelessness of any justification by personal obedience, it is not a little remarkable that the persons we have in view should miss of the precise nature of redemption in its relations to man, and make it the great purpose of the Saviour to introduce a new principle of government or a new method of administration, which has the effect of mitigating the severity of law, putting the guilty in a capacity of salvation, and furnishing them with facilities for turning to account the advantages of their new condition. This principle is the pardon of sin upon repentance. Jesus has made it possible that God should receive penitent transgressors into favour, and has rendered penitence itself less difficult and arduous than it is found to be under the regular and ordinary course of nature. How this capacity of salvation has been introduced by Him the advocates of the system do not pretend to explain; it is due, in some way mysterious to us and unrevealed in Scriptures, to His humiliation, sufferings and death. It is enough for us to know the fact that repentance has the efficacy ascribed to it, without presuming to inquire how it came to be possessed of it.[1]

[1] "Some have endeavoured to explain the efficacy of what Christ has done and suffered for us beyond what the Scripture hath authorized; others, probably because they could not explain it, have been for taking it away, and confining His office as Redeemer of the world to His instruction, example and government of the Church; whereas, the doctrine of the Gospel appears to be, not only that He taught the efficacy of repentance, but rendered it of the efficacy which it is by what He did and suffered for us; that He obtained for us the benefit of having our

None can censure more severely than ourselves that arrogance of understanding which refuses to recognize any dispensation as Divine which cannot be adjusted to the measures of human probability. We are too sensible of the ignorance of man and the greatness of God to dream for a moment of making our finite reason the standard of the counsels of infinite wisdom; and we sympathize profoundly with the humility of mind, always characteristic of exalted attainments, that shrinks in reverence from the clouds and darkness which surround the throne of the Eternal. It is the glory of God to conceal a thing; and where He has drawn a veil over the operations of His hand it is presumption in us to pry into His secrets or speculate with confidence on the mysteries He has not thought fit to reveal. But it is neither piety nor modesty—it is unbelief, however speciously disguised—which makes darkness where God has given light; mystery, where all things are plain. To say that we are left in ignorance as to the method by which the mediation of Christ achieves the salvation of a sinner, is to contradict all those passages of Scripture which directly teach, as well as indirectly imply, that the wisdom of God is conspicuously displayed in the scheme of redemption, and in which it is made the duty of the saints to admire it. "We preach Christ crucified," says the Apostle, "unto the Jews a stumbling-block and unto the Greeks foolishness; but unto them which are called, both Jews and Greeks, Christ the power of God and the wisdom of God." "Howbeit we speak wisdom among them that are perfect." The lowest conception of wisdom involves the idea that the means should be adapted to the end, and it is displayed only in so far as the correspondence betwixt them is capable of

repentance accepted unto eternal life, not only that He revealed to sinners that they were in a capacity of salvation, and how they might obtain it, but, moreover, that He put them in this capacity of salvation by what He did and suffered for them—put us into a capacity of escaping future punishments and obtaining future happiness. And it is our wisdom thankfully to accept the benefit by performing conditions upon which it is offered on our part without disputing how it was procured on His."—*Butler's Analogy*, Pt. ii., chap. v., § 6.

being discerned. Where the adaptation of means to an end is not perceived, wisdom may indeed exist, but it is absurd to say that it can be an object of admiration. That emotion can be elicited only by an actual contemplation of the fitness upon which the wisdom depends. It is, accordingly, impossible that believers should be expected to glorify that attribute of God to which, as much as to His power and grace, we are indebted for the economy of redemption, if they are not permitted to see how the mediation of Christ is adapted to effect their salvation. They can no more be filled with admiration at the contemplation of a wisdom which is concealed from their understandings than they can be filled with love at the contemplation of a beauty which is hidden from their eyes. We are very far from asserting that we, or any other finite intelligence, can comprehend the whole mystery of godliness: there are facts in redemption, such as the incarnation, and the subsistence of two natures in one person, and there may be designs in reference to other worlds, and perhaps also in relation to our own, proposed by it in the infinite counsels of God, which shall for ever transcend the capacities of creatures. We do not pretend to know the whole case. We hardly presume that we ever shall know it. Throughout the countless cycles of eternity we expect to occupy the anxious position of the angels, who, previous to the advent, are represented as earnestly inquiring into these things. The glories of redemption are as boundless, the depths of its wisdom as fathomless, as the infinite perfections of the Godhead. But, though there be heights which the loftiest genius cannot climb, and depths which no finite line can sound, still we maintain that there *is* a wisdom which we can discover and a wisdom we are required to adore. In so far as our own personal acceptance is involved we can see the fitness of Jesus for His work and the fitness of His work to the necessities of man. If we cannot comprehend all the fullness of meaning in which Christ crucified is the wisdom of God, we can at least receive that portion of light which irradiates our own *salvation;* and we dare not brand as delusion all that joy in Him which flows not simply from the faith that He is a Saviour, but from the felt conviction that He is a Saviour peculiarly adapted to our wants. We must therefore protest against any hypothesis which discards as presumptuous all efforts to explain how the sacrifice of Christ contributes to our pardon. Whatever other mysteries surround the cross, this point is not left to the hazard of conjecture or the uncertainty of speculation. It is *revealed*, or words have lost their meaning, and the Bible is a book of riddles.

But the most serious objection to the theory in question is, that it represents Christ as introducing by His work a new principle in the moral government of God, or a new method of administration, which cannot be conceived without confusion of ideas nor expressed without a contradiction in terms. The patrons of the scheme, studious to put in its true light the inadequacy of natural religion, are not wanting in proofs that whatever intimations the facts of experience may give of the possibility of mercy under the general government of God, they all point to mediation as the channel of compassion, and furnish no ground to suppose that any arbitrary purpose on the part of our Judge, or any penitence or amendment on our part, could have arrested the execution of the curse. Between penitence and pardon they are unable to trace any natural or necessary connection; but a mediator may cause to be instituted, and in the case of Christ has caused to be instituted, a dispensation of leniency under which repentance may be followed by forgiveness. The defect of natural religion to which Christianity is a remedy is not that nature admits of no repentance, but that repentance is incapable of securing pardon. The design of mediation is to establish a connection between them; not to make one or the other possible or certain, but, supposing them to exist or to be capable of existing, to bind them in a new relation unknown to nature.

Now we take leave to say that Christianity has instituted no connection between penitence and pardon which is not founded in the very nature of things. Their relation to each other is not contingent, but necessary; not derived from the interposition of a Mediator, but from their essential relations to God. There never was a case, and there never will be a case in all the history of the universe, of a penitent sinner's being damned. What is repentance in its full development but a restoration to that state of integrity and holiness, of knowledge, righteousness and communion with God, from which Adam by transgression fell? And can we entertain the thought, without horror, that He whose nature is in sympathy with the righteous should banish into outer darkness those who are devoted to His law, who love His name and rejoice in His glory? A penitent sinner is one who has been a transgressor, but is now just; the laws of God are now put within his mind and written on his heart, and his moral condition is evidently one which renders the supposition of punishment incongruous and contradictory. Such a man is as unfit for the atmosphere of hell as an impenitent transgressor is unfit for the atmosphere of heaven. There is obviously, therefore, no principle of reason or nature, as there is unquestionably none of revelation, which teaches that a man may be penitent and perish—that he may be driven into final banishment with the love of God in his heart and the praise of God upon his tongue. On the contrary, we are expressly taught that "if the wicked will turn from all his sins that he hath committed, and keep all my statutes, and do that which is lawful and right, he shall surely live, he shall not die; all his transgressions that he hath committed, they shall not be mentioned unto him: in his righteousness that he hath done he shall live."[1] This seems to be the dictate of right reason. The incongruity is so palpable and revolting of dooming to destruction one who at the time is possessed of every element of character that puts him in harmony with the perfections of God, that writers[2] are by no means wanting who

[1] Ezek. xviii. 21, 22.
[2] Locke and Warburton may be particularly mentioned. Of course.

are as confident in asserting a natural, as those whom we have more immediately in view an instituted, connection betwixt penitence and pardon. The difficulty of natural religion is, not that it excludes the penitent from hope, but that it precludes the possibility of repentance itself. Upon the hypothesis that the thorough and radical change of heart and character implied in the Scripture doctrine of sanctification could take place under its administration—that a man could be delivered from his moral degradation and reinstated into that condition of righteousness to which its promises of life are directed—we see no harm in asserting that in his righteousness that he hath done he shall live. The question under the law of nature in regard to such a case is precisely analogous to the question under the law of grace whether an apostate saint can be damned. The true answer is that the case can never occur. Nature shuts us up in despair because it shuts us up in *impenitence*. The least transgression contracts guilt; guilt calls for punishment; and this punishment consists in that banishment from God which is attended, in every dependent being, with spiritual death and the unbroken dominion of sin. To be a sinner therefore once, is to be a sinner for ever, unless some agency should be interposed to arrest the natural and ordinary course of justice and law. Hence the office of a Mediator must be, not to make repentance efficacious of pardon, but to make repentance possible. It is, accordingly, the great blessing which is promised, as well as the paramount duty enjoined under the dispensation of the Gospel. In other words, it is the great end of Christianity to restore and secure to man the holiness he has lost.

The first step, it is obvious, which must be taken in this

however, what they mean by *repentance* is no real repentance at all. That is a change of heart effected by the power which originally formed it, and a man thus renewed is evidently in a state of salvation already. Holiness is salvation, or there is nothing which deserves the name. But the case is very different in relation to those changes which are wrought in our characters by the law of habit under the influence of convictions and of fear. Such repentance is no preparation for heaven, and such penitents are worthy of death.

work of renovation is the removal of guilt. In the only sense in which it can be conceived that repentance is likely to be acceptable to God, all its appropriate exercises are the results of His favour and of the communication of His grace. If the least degree of sin entails spiritual death, if death must continue as long as guilt abides, and repentance is a resurrection from this state, the guilt, in some way or other, must be effaced before life can be imparted. There must be pardon before there can be that union with God which is the foundation of all holiness as contradistinguished from morality. It is guilt which seals the soul in impotence, and that guilt must cease to be imputed before a renovation of the nature can be effected. To say that an unpardoned sinner can repent, is to affirm that he may be under the curse and in the favour of God at one and the same time—that he is both dead and alive, active and senseless, free and a slave, at the same moment and in the same relations. There is no method of escaping from these palpable contradictions but by making pardon prior in the order of nature to repentance, and resolving both into a state of reconciliation, for which we are indebted to the gracious interference of a Mediator. The same work, whatever it may be, which removes our guilt and propitiates the favour of the Father of our spirits, entitles us to those communications of love which render us meet to enjoy the blessedness of His smile. We must be pardoned that we may live; and we must live in order to repent; so that repentance and pardon are indeed indissolubly connected; not, however, as cause and effect, nor in the order in which they are too commonly presented, but as the joint results of a common grace arranged in the relation of means to an end, pardon being in order to repentance.[1]

[1] In what we have said about the priority of pardon to repentance, we do not mean that the sense of pardon is experienced, or that the thing itself formally takes place, antecedently to regeneration. In the actual communication of grace, the heart must be changed before faith can exist, and faith must be exerted before justification can be had. But the *grounds* of pardon in the work and intercession of Christ are presupposed in any provisions for the renewal and the sanctification of the

That these were the doctrines which Paul preached on the Areopagus at Athens cannot of course be directly collected from the brief record of his sermon which has come down to us; but that he could not have taught any different theory seems to us plain from the nature of the arguments he employed: "And the times of this ignorance God winked at, but now commandeth all men everywhere to repent, because He hath appointed a day in the which He will judge the world in righteousness by that Man whom He hath ordained; whereof He hath given assurance unto all men, in that He hath raised Him from the dead." The Apostle here makes it the great design of the Gospel, in contradistinction from the law of nature, to inculcate the duty of repentance. As long as men were left to the light of their own eyes, without any adequate revelations of the method of redemption, the doctrine of repentance was not promulgated, because the grace of it was not yet to be imparted. The dead were not commanded to live, because He had not arrived whose voice could penetrate their graves and quicken the pulse of immortality. It is only in connection with the kingdom of heaven that the Scriptures ever insist upon repentance, because it is in that kingdom alone that repentance can possibly exist. Had not Jesus appeared, no eye would ever have wept a tear, no heart ever heaved a sigh of godly sorrow for sin. When we attend to the steps by which Paul reaches the conclusion that God now commandeth all men everywhere to repent—that the generation of holiness and the destruction of sin are the characteristic ends of the Gospel—the inference is inevitable that his views of repentance must have been very different from that which makes it the

sinner, and the mission of the Spirit through which he is made a partaker of Christ is in consequence of that mediation which could effect nothing if it did not remove guilt. We mean nothing more in what we have said than the absolution in heaven and the imputation of Christ, of which Owen speaks in his Death of Christ and Vindiciæ Evangelicæ. See also Witsius, Dissert. Ireni. and Halyburton's Inquiry into the Nature of Regeneration, etc. But see particularly chaps. xi. and xii. of Owen on the Death of Christ.

condition of pardon. It will be recollected that the general judgment is not presented as a *motive* to amendment, but as a proof that it is commanded. He does not say that men *ought* to repent because they will be judged, but that they are *commanded* to do it. He first collects the command from a general judgment in righteousness, and then proves, not that there will be a judgment, but that it will be in righteousness, because Jesus has been raised from the dead. The sum of his reasoning is briefly this: Men are required to be holy, because God will hereafter deal with them upon the principle of distributive justice; and that this is the method of His government is put beyond doubt by the resurrection of His Son from the dead.

There are two aspects in which this inspired argument is inconsistent with the doctrines we have been combatting. In the first place, if we are ignorant of the nature of the Saviour's mediation, and know not the principles on which it contributes to our pardon, it is impossible to detect any logical connection betwixt His resurrection and ascension and the final judgment of the world in righteousness. If we know not what relations to the law He sustained in His death, we must be incompetent to perceive how His resurrection secures its supremacy. Paul does not adduce the resurrection as a proof of His Divine mission, and through it a proof of what He had asserted in regard to the proceedings of the last day, but he appeals to it as a fact, which in itself contained an infallible assurance from God that the world should be judged in righteousness. It is a fact which, as soon as it is understood, proclaims this awful truth.

In the next place, if repentance is the appointed precursor of pardon, then it is either a principle of natural justice that the penitent should be pardoned, or under the mediation of Christ the government of God is not one of distributive justice. To assert that repentance and pardon are connected as antecedent and consequent, under the dispensation of nature, is to set aside all those arguments by which the divines of this school are accustomed to establish the necessity of mediation. To say that under the mediation of Christ the government of God is not strictly and properly just, is to contradict the Apostle, who affirms a general judgment in righteousness, of which this very mediation is the clearest and most convincing proof. Hence, they must be either inconsistent with themselves or inconsistent with the apostle in making it the end of Christianity to put men in a capacity of salvation, by dissolving, through the work of Christ, the natural connection between guilt and punishment when a moral change has taken place in ourselves.

3. There is another class of divines possessing many points of resemblance to the one whose opinions we have just been considering. They differ, however, in the circumstance that they profess to understand the principle on which the efficacy of what they denominate *atonement* depends. They are unwilling to assert the absolute necessity of the death of Christ, not from the modesty which shrinks from the presumption of pronouncing with confidence upon what the Almighty might or might not do, but from the principle, plainly avowed and elaborately defended, that public policy is the only necessity to be admitted. Those very considerations of expediency by which others have been accustomed to repel objections, and which are in felt disproportion to the importance and magnitude of the event, are received by them as a complete explanation of the case. The great problem to be solved by the death of the Redeemer was the consistency of pardon with the honour of the Divine Name, and the dignity of the Divine administration, and the general prosperity of the universe. It was a terrible tragedy enacted before the eyes of all creatures to display the holiness of God and illustrate the transcendent enormity of sin. It was intended to give emphasis and depth of impression to truths which might have been obscured or undervalued if sin had been absolutely pardoned, or pardoned upon mere repentance. The divines of this school do not hesitate to assert that, according to their scheme, the method of salvation involves an inversion of the principles

of strict retribution. "Neither Christ nor the sinner"—we use the very words of Dr. Wardlaw—"neither Christ nor the sinner has his own due. The guilty who, according to these principles, should suffer, escapes, and the innocent, who should escape, suffers. In no strict and proper sense, then, can distributive justice be *satisfied* by substitution, when its demands, instead of being adhered to and fulfilled, are, for a special purpose and by an act of Divine sovereignty, suspended, superseded, overruled." These men, whatever they may affirm to the contrary, regard the distinctions betwixt right and wrong, not as final and ultimate, but as means to an end. The great purpose of God in the government of His creatures is the production of the largest amount of happiness, and His laws are nothing but the expedients of His prudence and wisdom to accomplish the ends of His benevolence. When, accordingly, the public good can be promoted without these laws, there is nothing in the nature of rectitude, the perfections of the Deity, or the relations of man to his Creator which prevents them from being suspended, superseded or overruled. They are binding because they are necessary to the well-being of the universe; and when a larger amount of happiness can be produced without them, the same reason which induced the Deity to prescribe them induces Him to set them aside. Policy is superior to right, or rather right is nothing but policy under another name. Experience, however, and the obvious fitness of things concur to demonstrate that the principles of morality are, for the most part, the highest expediency; that truth, justice, benevolence are the surest means of private felicity and public prosperity, and that the interests of the universe accordingly require that all the Divine proceedings should be distinguished by the tendency to impress an awful sense of them upon the minds of intelligent creatures. When, therefore, the Divine administration in any degree departs from them, the general result should be a stronger commendation of them than if they had been faithfully and punctiliously observed. Whenever God, in other words, breaks His own law, the design should be to make that law more sacredly and solemnly impressive upon the minds of His subjects. It is seen to be "more honoured in the breach than in the observance."

That we have not misrepresented the theory in question, nor the reasoning by which it is supported, however inconsistent that reasoning appears in our account of it, will be obvious to any one who will take the trouble to analyze and compare the following statements from a work of confessed ability: "*Distributive*, or, as others designate it, *retributive* justice, according to its strict requirements, admits not of substitution. It issues a righteous law with a righteous sanction. It passes its sentence of condemnation against the transgressor of that law. It makes no mention of any possible satisfaction but the punishment of the guilty themselves, the endurance by them of the penal sanction in their own persons. It is only by the death of the sinner himself that the proper demand of the law can be fulfilled, that the principles of distributive justice can have their due application, and that under this aspect of it, consequently, justice, can be satisfied. According to the requisition of justice in its distributive sense, every man personally must have *his own due*. But in substitution it is otherwise. There is an inversion of the principles of strict retribution. Neither Christ nor the sinner has his own due. The guilty who, according to those principles, should suffer, escapes, and the innocent, who should escape, suffers. In no strict and proper sense, then, can distributive justice be *satisfied* by substitution, when its demands, instead of being adhered to and fulfilled, are for a special purpose and by an act of Divine sovereignty suspended, superseded, overruled. It is well to remark, however, that in another sense it was satisfied, all its ends being virtually and to the full effected by other means. And this leads me to the true end of atonement. It is to *public justice*, as we have before defined it, that in substitution and propitiation the satisfaction is made. The grand design is to preserve unsullied the glory of the great principles of eternal rectitude; to show the impossibility of the claims of equity founded in these principles and essential to the government of the universe being dispensed with; to settle in the minds of God's intelligent creatures, as the subjects of His moral administration, the paramount obligation and immutable permanence of their claims; to give such a manifestation of the Divine regard to these elements of His immaculate administration as to preclude the possibility of any the remotest surmise that in the pardon of sin they have been at all overlooked or placed in abeyance, and thus to render it consistent with Divine propriety, or, in other words, honourable to the whole character as well as to the law and the government of Jehovah, to extend pardoning mercy to the guilty, and to reinstate them in His favour according to the provisions of the Gospel. It is thus that, in so pardoning, His regard to righteousness is as conspicuous as His delight in mercy, and, in the minds of the pardoned, the impression of the claims of the one as deep as that of their obligations to the other. In this view of it the scheme possesses a Divine grandeur. The glory of God and the good of His universal empire, the two great ends of *public justice*, are with 'all wisdom and prudence' admirably combined in it. It is as essential to the latter of these ends as it is to the former (they can never indeed be separated) that the authority of the Divine government be maintained in its awful and inviolable sacredness; that the demands of the law be upheld without one jot or tittle of abatement; that no sin appear as venial; and that if any sinner is pardoned, the mercy shown to the offender be shown in such way, on such a ground, through such a medium, as shall at once manifest the Divine reprobation of his offences, and, at the same time, secure the restitution of the guilty perpetrator of them to the principles, affections and practice of holy allegiance. Such are the purposes and such the effects of the Christian atonement."[1]

The plain meaning of all this smooth and beautiful decla-

[1] Wardlaw on Atonement, pp. 58–60.

mation is, that God may do evil that good may come. He may do a thing which confessedly is not just. He may invert the principles of strict retribution, suspend, supersede, overrule the operation of His own law, provided in so doing He make His creatures feel the paramount obligation and immutable permanence of the claims that are set aside. Rectitude is essentially eternal and unchangeable,[1] but God need not observe it if by occasional departures from its rules He can make the universe more scrupulous and punctilious. The death of Christ was, accordingly, a grand expedient by which the Deity in all wisdom and prudence has successfully contrived to impress with commanding emphasis the eternal principles of truth and justice upon the minds of every other intelligent being, while He Himself, in this awful dispensation, confessedly disregards them. Such is the theory as expounded by one of its ablest advocates.

Our business at present is not with the merits of it, but simply with the question whether the historian has not furnished reasons for believing that, whether true or false, this was not the scheme of atonement which Paul preached in the metropolis of Paganism. Paul's gospel is compendiously expressed in Jesus and the *resurrection*. But so far as we can discover, the resurrection is no necessary part of the Gospel upon this scheme, which resolves the death of Christ into considerations of expediency, and explains its efficacy by the moral impression against sin it is suited to produce. The two great ends of public justice, we are told in the passage just quoted, are the glory of God and the good of His universal empire, and these ends, according to the patrons of the scheme, are adequately secured by a dispensation which shows that God *hates* while He pardons iniquity. All that would seem to be essential, therefore, is the sufferings and death of the Redeemer. The resurrection is not an element of the work of redemption; it is simply a necessary fact springing from the divinity of the sufferer,

---

[1] Upon this subject Dr. Wardlaw has expressed himself very strongly, both in his Christian Ethics and his work on Atonement.

and no more conducive to the expiation of our guilt than the eating and drinking which pertained to His humanity, or the alternations of activity and repose which were inseparable from His sublunary state. As Jesus was God, it was certain that He could not be holden of the bands of death. He had power to lay down His life, He had power to take it up again; but if we could conceive the possibility of His permanent subjection to the dominion of the grave, the impression, for aught that appears, of the transcendent enormity of sin, would have been more awful than is likely to be produced by temporary suffering followed by unutterable glory. To say that such a doom would have been a revolting exhibition of cruelty is either to deny that the principle on which His sufferings were inflicted was just, and then any degree of them would have been a measure of cruelty, or to affirm that there is a point beyond which justice cannot push the punishment of sin, and then it ceases to be the mighty evil they represent it. Upon any view of the case, therefore, the resurrection is an immaterial circumstance in this scheme of redemption. Suffering, the visible and palpable endurance of it, this is what is required to the manifestation of the righteousness of God—this is what is needed for the purpose of salutary impression.[1]

It deserves further to be remarked that according to this scheme the resurrection of Christ furnishes no proof that God will judge the world in righteousness. If by righteousness we are to understand the principle of distributive jus-

---

[1] "Meanwhile it is enough to remind you how the idea of *manifestation* is associated with the atonement. There is not only a provision for the exercise of the Divine righteousness in man's salvation, but there is the *declaration* of that righteousness. Now, in order to this, there is required not suffering merely, but the palpable and visible endurance of it. It would not otherwise have the necessary impression and effect. . . . And without vain and presumptuous speculations we are, every one of us, sensible that the spectacle of a Saviour *thus* dignified, *thus* suffering, is enough for the purpose of salutary impression—impression deep, solemn, awful, of the Divine righteousness, and impression amply and delightfully encouraging of the Divine mercy."—*Wardlaw on Atonement*, Dis. II., pp. 45, 46.

tice—and such, in all similar connections, seems to be its meaning—*that*, according to this hypothesis, is inverted. Neither man nor the Saviour receives his due. If we are to understand the Public Justice to which so much importance is attached, *that* may be illustrated by the *death*, but we cannot perceive its relation to the *resurrection*, of Christ, which becomes, upon this hypothesis, a necessary adjunct of the *person*, but no part of the *work*, of the Redeemer.

There is another objection to this theory suggested by the sermon at Athens, which, if we can make it as clear to our readers as it is to ourselves, will, we apprehend, be conclusive against it. The whole discourse seems to have been conducted on the principle that the Gospel is its own witness—that the facts of redemption authenticate themselves; that we can reason from its phenomena as effects to their origin in the mind of God, as we ascend from nature up to nature's Cause. Paul has evidently taken it for granted—for there is no allusion to any external proofs of the Divine mission of Jesus, and no intimation that he himself wrought any miracles at Athens—that as the heavens proclaim the glory of God and the firmament showeth His handiwork, so the death and resurrection of Jesus, when properly apprehended, are their own proofs that He is the power of God to salvation to every one that believeth. The work itself proves its divinity. That work cannot be acknowledged without prompting the confession of Peter, Thou hast the words of eternal life, and we believe and are sure that Thou art the Christ, the Son of the living God. Now there is one branch of this *a posteriori* argument which is absolutely impossible upon the theory of Public Justice. The resurrection furnishes no direct proof of the Deity and Sonship of Christ. There is nothing in the nature of the sufferings which He underwent which requires that the sufferer should be a Divine Person. As to their amount, for aught that appears, they might have been endured by a creature; and as to their design, we could not have pronounced beforehand that a very solemn and awful display of the holiness of God and the malignity of sin, fitted to inspire with a salutary fear the minds of the guilty, might not have been made by one who was less than Jehovah's fellow.[1] Hence the mere fact that He died the death which He died, and triumphed over it in His resurrection from the grave, is no necessary proof of what Paul affirms it to demonstrate with power—that He was the true and proper Son of God. He died—He rose. These are the facts. Now, if there be not something in the nature of His death which imperatively demanded that the sufferer should be Divine, there can be nothing in the nature of the resurrection to declare His Deity. If we know beforehand that He was God, we can account for His resurrection upon that hypothesis, but there is nothing in the circumstance itself which, independently of any other proofs, demonstrates His eternal Sonship as well as His kindred to man. It deserves further to be remarked that, according to this hypothesis, the connection between the death of Christ and the salvation of His people is a matter of arbitrary appointment, and the entire efficacy of His work is resolved into the dignity of His person. In the Epistle to the Corinthians the Apostle teaches us that there is a species of death which if *any one* endures in the name and for the sake of others, they shall be acquitted, renewed and sanctified. Because we thus judge, says he, that if one died for all, then all died. The death of the substitute is, in law and justice, the death of the principal; it delivers him from guilt. The effect depends not upon the *person* dying, but upon the nature and relations of the death itself. If any other being could have been found who was capable of dying the death which Christ died, the same glorious results would have followed. His Deity was essential, not to establish the connection between His death and the salvation of His people, but to create the possibility of the death itself. There was

---

[1] Dr. Wardlaw admits as much in attempting to prove the necessity of Christ's death from the fact that He *did* die, which, no doubt, is very sound reasoning from cause to effect, but it cannot be reversed.—P. 14. Cf. p. 46.

a peculiarity about it which absolutely demanded the strength of Omnipotence to undergo it. None but God could have shed the blood which Jesus poured out. When it is said that the value of Christ's sufferings depends upon His person, it is not intended that a fictitious importance is to be attached to something inherently and essentially worthless, in consequence of its association with a Divine being—which is the only sense of the terms consistent with the theory of Public Justice. The meaning is that they were fully and completely the *death* which the exigencies of the case required, and which they could not possibly have been if the sufferer had been less than Divine. Redemption is glorious, not because God achieves it, but because none but God *could* achieve it. The death of Jesus was glorious, not because it was His death, but because it *could* be the death of no other. A creature might as well have undertaken to *create* as to *save* a world. The work itself demands the interposition of God; and any theory which fails to represent the death of Christ as an event which, in its own nature, as clearly proclaims His Divinity as His superintending care and preservation of all things, cannot be the Gospel which Paul preached at Rome, at Corinth, at Athens, and which extorted from Thomas, upon beholding the risen Saviour, the memorable confession, My Lord and my God!

4. If the necessity of the Gospel is not founded in the ignorance of man, nor the want of a natural connection between penitence and pardon, nor the policy of government, the question recurs, What is the *nature* of it and what peculiarities must distinguish the provisions that are intended to relieve it? It is obvious that Paul, in his recapitulation of the great principles of natural religion, designed to produce in the minds of his hearers a deep and pungent conviction that sin had occasioned an emergency in the government of God which rendered salvation, independently of Jesus and the resurrection, hopelessly impossible. These very principles created the difficulty. They represent God as a just judge and a righteous governor; dispensing rewards and

punishments according to the rule of distributive justice; dealing with every man according to his works. The first great necessity of man, therefore, as a sinner, arises from his guilt—an obligation to punishment which, according to the eternal principles of rectitude, cannot be set aside. The government of the world is not prudential, but moral; and under a strict and proper moral government the wicked cannot be received into favour; they *must* be punished. There can consequently be no hope to a sinner until the problem is solved how God can be *just;* not simply wise, discreet or prudent—this is not the difficulty which a sense of guilt presses upon the conscience of a sinner, but how God can be *just;* can maintain the principle upon which His administration is conducted, and yet receive transgressors into favour. There appears to be an impossibility in the pardon of sin under the law of nature. This first and paramount necessity, springing from guilt under a righteous government, it is the design of Christianity to relieve. It is accordingly an amazing dispensation of Providence and Grace which proposes to reconcile the pardon of the guilty with the strictest principles of justice; which, while it opens a door of hope to the guilty and removes the apprehensions which conscience awakens in the breast of transgressors, demonstrates, at the same time, in the clearest and brightest light, that God will judge the world in righteousness by that man whom He hath ordained. The more clearly the doctrines of natural religion are understood, the more hopeless becomes the condition of a sinner. The imperfect knowledge of them which can be gathered from the dictates of our own consciousness, the crude and mouldering remains which may yet be detected of the law originally written on the heart, are enough to arouse our fears and fill the mind with anxiety and suspense as to the possibility of final acceptance upon any terms. As the light increases, and revelation pours in upon us its discoveries of our former state, of our present ruin, of God's immutable holiness and inflexible justice, despair thickens upon us. Our hearts condemn us, and God is greater than our hearts and knoweth all things. The anxious question is wrung from us, "Wherewith shall I come before the Lord and bow before the High God? Shall I come before Him with burnt-offerings, with calves of a year old? Will the Lord be pleased with thousands of rams, or with ten thousands of rivers of oil? Shall I give my first-born for my transgression, the fruit of my body for the sin of my soul?" Now, guilt is only another name for a conviction of *ill desert*. It is the response of the human soul to the justice of punishment, and is utterly independent, as all human experience testifies, of all calculations of expediency. The burden upon the conscience is not simply that we shall suffer, for suffering may be a calamity as well as a punishment; not that the interests of the universe and the safety of God's throne demand our misery; these are considerations which never enter into the bitterness of remorse. The burden which presses with intolerable weight upon the soul is the terrible conviction, wrung from the depths of our moral nature, that we have done wrong and *deserve* to die. It is this feeling that we *deserve* our doom which kindles the hell within us. If we could strip ourselves of the burning consciousness of this fact, no amount of evil could ever be regarded in the light of punishment. Whatever was inflicted for the general good we might nerve ourselves to bear, from lofty considerations of benevolence and self-sacrifice; and to whatever was inevitable we might bow with patience, if not with resignation. But energy and resolution avail nothing against a sense of guilt; the feeling of ill desert drinks up the spirits, and "conscience makes cowards of us all." This, then, is the peculiarity which distinguishes guilt—it is a conviction that punishment is due, that it ought to be inflicted, and that under a righteous government, sooner or later, it *will* be inflicted; and it is precisely this sense of guilt which the truths of natural religion are adapted to produce within us. It is the echo of our own hearts to the fearful condemnation of a holy God.

If guilt is the response of the soul to the justice of punishment, the only way in which its sting can be extracted is by an arrangement which shall make the punishment cease to be just, and give the sinner a right to escape from the evils which conscience forecasts. By no other conceivable method can peace and tranquillity, in conformity with the principles of eternal rectitude, be imparted to the mind. The source of all its fear is the conviction that it *ought* to die, and unless a contrary conviction can be produced that the same justice which doomed to death now exempts from the curse, guilt will continue to agitate the heart with dismal forebodings which cannot be dismissed as phantoms, because they are founded in the very nature of the soul. This *obligation* to punishment, this *righteousness* of condemnation, must cease to press, or the need which guilt creates cannot be relieved. The sinner feels, in other words, that the justice which calls for his blood must be satisfied, or that blood be yielded to its demand. It is, accordingly, the glory of the Gospel that the blood of Christ who, through the eternal Spirit, offered Himself without spot to God, purges the conscience, dispels all its distracting fears, and imparts peace and serenity where despair and guilt had held their troubled reign. Availing itself of a principle which in every dispensation of religion has been fundamental in the Divine dealings with our race, which belongs to natural as well as supernatural religion, and which, in some form or other, has always commended itself to the moral judgments of mankind, it reveals to us a work in consequence of which the pardon of sin on the part of God becomes not merely a dictate of mercy, but a matter of right. Jesus, in the name of His people and as their federal head and representative, has endured the curse, and the justice of God is now solemnly pledged to Him to exempt them from personal subjection to its woes. He has died the death of the law, and, upon an obvious principle of justice from the relations in which they stand to Him, His death is their death. If one died for all, then all died. We are baptized into His death. I am crucified with Christ, nevertheless I live; yet not I, but Christ liveth in me.

No scheme of atonement that fails to represent Christ as submitting to the proper penalty of the law which the sins of His people had provoked, and in such relations to them that His sufferings can be justly charged as their own, can be regarded as adapted to the exigencies of *guilt*. It does not relieve that condition of the conscience which apprehends punishment as a matter of right. It does not meet the prime necessity of the sinner. He is still left *guilty*,[1] under *obligation* to punishment; and if his iniquities are pardoned, law and justice are defrauded of their due. Hence, if the principles of natural religion are immutable, there can be no peace to the transgressor until he is placed in a position in which it is no longer *right* to remember his offences against him. When God can be just and faithful in blotting out his transgressions, then, and not till then, is his conscience sprinkled with clean water and purged from dead works. Christianity must take away our *guilt*, or it leaves us under the curse of nature. This, we maintain, is precisely what the Gospel achieves. The Lamb of God bore away our guilt. He became a curse for us, sin for us, though He Himself knew no sin, that we might be made the righteousness of God in Him. He was wounded for our transgressions, He was bruised for our iniquities, the chastisement of our peace was upon Him, and with His stripes we are healed. All we like sheep have gone astray, but the Lord hath laid on Him the iniquities of us all. It is in reference to this aspect of the work of Christ as expiating guilt that the eternal covenant which He came to ratify and seal is styled The counsel of peace. The kingdom which He came to establish consists in joy and peace, and the great blessing which He communicates to all who are sprinkled with His blood is that peace which passeth all understanding, and which abides unshaken amid the agitations and tumults, the glooms and convulsions of the world. Through

[1] This is admitted by Dr. Wardlaw and divines of the same school.

Him God becomes the God of peace, the Gospel the message of peace, preachers of righteousness the heralds of peace, and the two great results of His work, according to the rapturous song of the angels, are glory to God in the highest and peace on earth. We see no alternative, but an open denial that the Gospel is the religion of a sinner, adapted to those moral necessities of his nature which spring from the immutable principles of natural religion, or a cordial admission of the fact that Christ by His sufferings and death completely satisfied the justice of God in regard to the sins of His people. They, through Him, either cease to be guilty or they must die; their consciences are either purged by His blood or they have no peace. They are still under the law and its curse, or they are delivered from its condemnation. It is idle to speak of the ends of punishment being answered by anything but punishment itself, of costly and imposing expedients by which a salutary impression is made on the universe, and the righteousness of God illustriously displayed and the malignity of sin unfolded; this may be true, but all this does not reach the malady within, the plague of the sinner's conscience. That is seized by the strong hand of justice, and until its iron grasp is relaxed, until right as well as policy ceases to demand his blood, he cannot be at ease. Hence it is, and must be, an indispensable element in anything which deserves the name of *atonement* that it satisfies the justice of God, or lays the foundation of a claim of right to exemption from punishment.[1]

But guilt is not the only need a sense of which is awakened by those truths of nature which Paul proclaimed at Athens. To be delivered from guilt is to be put in the moral position of the innocent without obstructions to the

---

[1] "Even the commender and publisher of Grotius' Book of 'Satisfaction,' the learned Vossius himself, affirmeth, that Christ by His death purchased for us a double right: First, a right of escaping punishment, and then a right of obtaining the reward."—*Owen's Death of Christ*, chap. x.

free communication of Divine favour, and without a right to any good but the exemption from ill.¹ Such persons might be made alive to God, but they could have no claims to His favour, and no security for whatever integrity might be graciously imparted. It is only to the *just* that the confirmed state of blessedness which the Scriptures mean by *life* is infallibly promised. Obedience to the law, *righteousness*, is the indispensable condition of God's everlasting favour. If, therefore, the scheme of redemption had done nothing more than deliver us from the curse of the law, though it would have conferred an incalculable benefit upon us, an unutterably great salvation, it would not have done all, that the necessities of the case required, to secure the perfection and blessedness of our nature. If it had gone so far as to remove spiritual death and re-establish the communion of the soul with God, the life which it imparted might still have been contingent. It might be forfeited by disobedience; and in the actual circumstances of our race, surrounded with temptations, encompassed with infirmities, ensnared alike by the world and the Devil, if our first father under much greater advantages failed when left to himself, it is morally certain that all of us would have come short of the glory of God. A contingent life would have been a cruel mockery of our hopes. Hence, the Gospel proposes not merely to deliver us from the condemnation

---

[1] "The satisfaction of Christ tends, in all that it is, to the honour and reparation of the justice of God. This, then, in its utmost extent and efficacy, cannot give ground to build such a right upon. The ultimate effect of satisfaction may be accomplished, and yet not the least right to any good thing communicated to them for whom this satisfaction is made. The good things attending the death of Christ may be referred unto two heads, the amotion of evil and the collation of good. For the first, the amotion of evil, the taking that from us that it may not grieve us, and subducting us from the power and presence thereof, it is immediately aimed at by satisfaction. That the curse of the law be not executed, that the wrath to come be not poured out, is the utmost reach of the death of Christ considered as satisfactory. . . . For positive good things in grace and glory, by satisfaction alone, they are not at all respected."—*Owen's Death of Christ*, chap. xi.

of sin, to put us into a state in which it is no longer right to damn us, but to introduce us into a state in which it is right to *bless* us. It proposes to give us a title to life—a title founded on the same eternal principle of rectitude which would have confirmed Adam in holiness and bliss for ever if he had fulfilled the condition of his trial. The Gospel, in other words, proposes to justify, and upon the broad principle of righteousness to open the kingdom of heaven to all believers. This righteousness secures our holiness, secures life, because it secures God's favour and gives a right, under the constitution of His own government, to the enjoyment of Him as the supreme portion of the soul. They who are justified must be glorified. The very end of justification is to take away the contingency of holiness. If Adam had maintained his integrity during the term of his probation, his justification would have imparted to him no element of character which he did not previously possess—the image of God was not half drawn upon him; but it would have put him in a *state* in which he could never lose his holiness nor be exposed to the risk of condemnation. And so the justification of a sinner introduces him into a state in which he can no more be left to the dominion of sin and the possibility of the curse than Christ can lose His glory or God be unfaithful to His promises and oath. "For whom He did foreknow He also did predestinate to be conformed to the image of His Son, that He might be the first-born among many brethren; moreover, whom He did predestinate them He also called, and whom He called them He also justified, and whom He justified them He also glorified."

Such, we apprehend, is the substance of that doctrine which Paul preached in his first open conflict with Paganism. The religion he proclaimed was pre-eminently that of a sinner—adapted, in all its provisions, to the spiritual necessities of a fallen being under the righteous government of God. The altars around him were dumb, yet pregnant, witnesses that the wants which the Gospel undertook to relieve were not the fictions of fancy nor the creatures of superstition, but the urgent demands of the soul. Under the imperfect light of heathenism there were still cases in which conscience asserted its supremacy, and summoned the guilty to the tribunal of the unknown God. The uncertainty which invested the doctrine of a future life was suited to quicken the apprehensions of guilt, while the utter darkness, into which the spirit seemed to retire, invited a disturbed imagination to people its shades with ministers of vengeance and executioners of justice. Amid all the ignorance of God and vagueness of conjecture which pertained to the condition of a thoughtful Pagan, the terrible impression would cleave to him that he was under a curse. It would haunt his dreams like the ghost of the murdered, embitter his waking hours, turn life itself into a burden, and make him long, yet dread, to die. He might endeavour to lay the flattering unction to his soul that the great Unknown in whose hands he was, and to whom he was responsible, was good and kind, and would be tender to his infirmities and failures; but the scenes of wretchedness around him, the frightful ravages of disease, pestilence and death; the stern and relentless judgments which scourge entire generations and in their progress sweep away nations; the cry of weeping, lamentation and woe which bursts from the smitten bosoms of the whole family of man; the portentous fact, written in blazing characters around him, stamped upon the cheek of the dying, the brow of the living, and even upon inanimate nature itself, that God has a controversy with men, and that though He is good He yet deals out to the trembling tribes of earth the vials of a fierce indignation,—considerations like these would thicken the blackness with which conscience had covered the future, and shroud the soul in the deepest night of despair. If the siren voice of hope should attempt to whisper that there yet might be peace, the monitor of God within would proclaim, in tones of thunder, There is no peace to the wicked. If there should still be an effort to prop the sinking spirit upon the mercy of its Author, Nature would cry aloud from her thousand chambers of suffering and anguish, Woe, woe, woe to the inhabitants of earth! Where could comfort be found? Where could peace be sought, except in that desperate hardihood of spirit which would sternly banish thought, and, like the beasts that perish, catch only the passing moment as it flies? And what is the religion which such a sinner, grappling with despair, burdened with life and afraid to die,—what is the religion which the necessities of his soul demand? Is it more of light in relation to God, His law, His justice and the stern retributions of eternity, when what he knows already presses on his conscience like a night-mare, and peoples the land of darkness with all that is awful in mysterious power, with all that is dreadful in insulted justice? Ah, no! He needs not light, but life—not philosophy and science, not new discoveries in heaven and earth, but a Saviour—a Saviour who can pluck him from the wrath to come, arrest the avenger of blood, seize the sword of justice, put it up into its scabbard, bid it rest and be still. The glory of Christianity is its Saviour, and His power to save is in the blood by which he extinguished the fires of the curse, and the righteousness by which He bought life for all His followers. Jesus made our curse, Jesus made our righteousness, this, this is the Gospel! All else is philosophy and vain deceit. This it is which gives Christianity its power. By this, and this alone, it subdues the ferocity of passion, disarms temptation of its violence, disrobes the world of its charms, changes the tiger into the lamb, and makes the lion eat straw like the ox. This constitutes the grand difference between the religion of Mohammed and the religion of Jesus, between the Koran and the Bible.

Upon this scheme, and this scheme alone, as it seems to us, the preaching of Paul at Athens can be reduced to consistency and method. It accounts for the importance which he attached to the doctrines of nature. He would acquaint the patient with his malady before he explained the character and application of the remedy, especially when it was likely to be sought just in the degree in which it was felt to be needed.

In the next place, it makes the resurrection an integral part of Christianity. That resurrection was the justification of Jesus as the Head of the Church, the discharge of the prisoner upon the satisfaction of the debt, as well as the passage of our great High Priest into the holiest of all. If Christ had remained under the power of death, the curse of the law could not have been removed from us; we should have died in our sins. He was delivered for our offences, and was raised again for our justification.

Upon this view we may add, further, that the resurrection of Christ becomes what Paul affirms it to be, a signal proof of His eternal Sonship, if by His eternal Sonship we understand that spirit of holiness according to which He is truly and properly God. None but Jehovah's fellow could have received the stroke of Jehovah's justice in His bosom and survived the blow. The penalty of the law was no vulgar ill, to be appeased by a few groans and tears, by agony, sweat and blood. It was the wrath of the infinite God, which, when it falls upon a creature, crushes him under the burden of eternal death. It is a blackness of darkness through which no ray of light or hope can ever penetrate the soul of a finite being; to all such it must be the blackness of darkness *for ever*. But Jesus endured it, Jesus satisfied it, Jesus bowed beneath that death which the law demanded, and which sinks angels and men to everlasting ruin, and came victorious from the conflict. If He had been a creature, He would have been crushed, sunk, lost; if He had been less than God, the bitterness of death could not have been passed; never, never could He have emerged from that thick darkness into which He entered when He made His soul an offering for sin. The morning of the third day—and a more glorious morn never dawned upon our earth—for ever settled, to all who understood the event, the Deity of Jesus. It was the crisis of all human hope. When our great Substitute had given up the ghost for us and descended into hell, the possibility of His return to us depended on His ability to meet the infinite wrath of the Infinite God. When the terrific cup was administered and He drank it and died, His slumbers in Joseph's tomb could never have been broken unless He could thunder with a voice like God, and bear the burden of infinite woe. The third day, which proclaimed His triumph, declared Him to be the Son of God with power, according to the spirit of holiness, by His resurrection from the dead. He had died a death which none could die but one who was Almighty.

But Paul teaches us that the resurrection is not only a proof of the Deity of Christ, but a proof, at the same time, that God will judge the world in righteousness by that Man whom He hath ordained; that His government, in other words, is conducted on the principle of distributive justice. This is an obvious inference from that representation of Christianity which makes the sufferings of Jesus a full and perfect satisfaction of the penalty of the law, and His life of spotless obedience the ground to all claim of everlasting bliss. No other scheme harmonizes the salvation of a sinner with the immutable principles of natural religion. This is its characteristic excellence; it rears the fabric of grace, not upon the ruins, but the fulfilment, of the law. God is never seen to be more gloriously just, nor the law more awfully sacred, than when He spared not His own Son, but delivered Him up for us all. The impression which this event makes is indeed solemn, awful, sublime. It was a wonder in heaven, a terror in hell, and is the grand instrument through which the rebellion of earth is subdued and the stout-hearted made to melt at the remembrance of sin. Upon the cross it is written in characters of blood that none can ever be pardoned who have not died, in their substitute, the death of the law—that none can ever be admitted into heaven who cannot present that obedience to which life is promised. Justice has its full demands upon the representative of the sinner, while grace abounds to the sinner himself. It may be said, however, that the admission of a substitute is itself a compromise of the strictness of justice. Without entering into the abstract question, it is sufficient for our present purpose to observe that God never contemplated any other justification of our race than through the obedience of a federal head. This was the fundamental principle of the covenant which contains the substance of natural religion. If Adam had stood, we should all have been justified by his obedience; as having fallen, we sinned in him, and fell with him in his first transgression. No promise of life has ever been made to man upon any other basis than that of imputed righteousness. It is nature's method, as well as the method of grace, and as natural law is admitted to be just, there is no concession nor compromise of the eternal principles of right in laying upon Christ the iniquities of us all.

From the exposition given of this noble monument of eloquence which inspiration has transmitted to us, it may be seen what constitutes the essence of the Gospel. It is Jesus and the resurrection—Jesus dying for our sins and raised again for our justification. Where these elements are wanting, whatever else may be found, there is no Christianity. A penal death and a perfect righteousness imputed, the one for pardon and the other for acceptance—these are things which make the Gospel glad tidings of great joy. To deny these is to deny Christ.

We may here see also that the most successful method of preaching is that which aims at thorough and radical *convictions* of sin. The law must be applied with power to the conscience, or the preciousness of grace will be very inadequately known. The superficial piety of the present day is owing, in a large degree, to feeble impressions of the malignity of sin. That complete breaking up of the fallow ground of the heart, that groaning under bondage, that deep sense of weakness and nothingness, which characterized the experience of the past generation, are unsuited to the haste and bustle of this stirring age. The transition from absolute indifference to cordial reliance upon

Christ must now be made in an instant. One gush of sorrow, one leap of joy, and the work must be done. Such converts can know little of the law, little of Christ, and less of themselves. Men must be soundly instructed by Moses if they would know the sweetness of the liberty in Christ.

PREFATORY NOTE.

IN 1840, Dr. Thornwell undertook to issue at Columbia a series of tracts on the fundamental doctrines of the Gospel, being impressed with the conviction that the errors opposed to those doctrines were then "propagated with an industry and zeal worthy of a better cause." One of the series was Traill's "Vindication of the Protestant Doctrine of Justification, and of its Preachers and Professors, from the unjust charge of Antinomianism," published first in 1692—to which he added an appendix, which appears in this collection.

Another of this series was the following discussion, from his own pen, of the Doctrines of Election and Reprobation. He was at that time about twenty-eight years old. His treatment of these subjects is vigorous and thorough, although it may not have the majestic sweep of his later productions. It manifests, however, very strikingly his critical acumen and sound judgment in expounding Scripture—talents which he undoubtedly possessed in an extraordinary degree. His subsequent studies not leading him to any special cultivation of these powers, his possession of them was not generally known.

ELECTION AND REPROBATION.

WHATSOEVER the Scriptures contain was designed by the Holy Spirit for our careful study and devout meditation, and we are required to search them habitually and prayerfully, since they contain the "words of eternal life." The doctrines of the Bible cannot prove hurtful unless they are perverted by ignorance or wrested by abuse. In examining, however, the more mysterious features of revealed truth, there are two extremes widely different, but perhaps equally dangerous, into which there is hazard of running—presumptuous curiosity on the one hand, and squeamish timidity on the other. Men of inquisitive and speculative minds are apt to forget that there are limits set to human investigation and research, beyond which it is impossible to pass with safety or satisfaction. To intrude with confidence into the unrevealed secrets of God's wisdom and purpose manifests an arrogance and haughtiness of intellect which cannot fail to incur the marked disapprobation of Heaven, and should always meet the prompt reprobation of the pious. Whatsoever is useful to be known God has kindly and graciously revealed, and it argues no less ingratitude than presumption to attempt to be "wise above what is written." Theology has already suffered greatly from the pride of human intellect. Men, anxious to know more than God has thought proper to communicate, or secretly dissatisfied with the form in which statements of Divine truth are made in the Bible, have recurred to philosophy and science to improve or to explain the doctrines of revelation. Sometimes the Scriptures stop too short, and then metaphysics and logic must be called in to trace their disclosures to the secret recesses of the Eternal mind. Sometimes the Scriptures and philosophy, "falsely so called," come into collision, and then the former must go through an exegetical transformation, so as to wear the shape which the latter would impress on them. All this is a wide departure from that simplicity of faith with which the Word of God should always be received. "All Scripture is given by inspiration of God," and to quarrel with it, or to attempt to push our investigations beyond it, is just to quarrel with the wisdom and goodness of the Deity Himself. It is tacitly charging the Holy Spirit with keeping back from men what it is important to their happiness to know. A deep conviction of the fullness and sufficiency of the Scriptures, combined with a hearty regard for their disclosures, is the only effectual check to this presumptuous pride of intellect.

But while some thus madly attempt to overleap the boundaries which God has set to their knowledge, others, through excessive caution, are afraid to know what the Lord has actually revealed. This squeamish timidity is no less dishonouring to God, as it supposes that He has communicated some truths, in a moment of unlucky forgetfulness, which it would have been better to conceal, and flatly and palpably contradicts the assertion of Paul that all Scripture is "profitable." If we suffer ourselves to be deterred from a fearless exposition of Divine truth by the cavils and perversions of profane minds, we may just surrender all that constitutes the Gospel a peculiar system, and make up our minds to be content with the flimsy disclosures of Deism or the cheerless darkness of Atheism. The doctrines of the Trinity, of the incarnation of the Son, of the covenants, of imputation, etc., are all made the scoff of the impudent and the jest of the vain. Paul's doctrines were perverted to unholy purposes by the false apostles, but all their defamation and reproach could not make Paul ashamed of the truth, nor afraid to preach it. "One hoof of Divine truth," says the venerable Erskine, "is not to be kept back, though a whole reprobate world should break their necks on it." "The Scripture," says Calvin, "is the school of the Holy Spirit, in which, as nothing useful or necessary to be known is omitted, so nothing is taught which it is not beneficial to know." While, then, a presumptuous curiosity, on the one hand, may not be allowed to carry us beyond the Scriptures, let not a sickly timidity, on the other, induce us to fall below them. "Let the Christian man," as Calvin again says, "open his heart and his ears to all the discourses addressed to him by God, only with this moderation, that as soon as the Lord closes His sacred mouth he also shall desist from further inquiry. This will be the best barrier of sobriety, if in learning we not only follow the leadings of God, but as soon as He ceases to teach we give up our desire of learning. It is a celebrated observation of Solomon, 'that it is the glory of God to conceal a thing.' But as both piety and common sense suggest that this is not to be understood generally of everything, we must seek for the proper distinction, lest we content ourselves with brutish ignorance under the pretext of modesty and sobriety. Now, this distinction is clearly expressed in a few words by Moses: 'The secret things belong unto the Lord our God, but those things which are revealed belong unto us and to our children, that we may do all the words of this law.' Deut. xxix. 29. For we see how he enforces on the people attention to the doctrine of the law, only by the celestial decree, because it pleased God to promulgate it; and restrains the same people within those limits with this single reason, that it is not lawful for mortals to intrude into the secrets of God."

These preliminary remarks will not be taken amiss by any who are even tolerably acquainted with the state of opinion in the theological world on the great doctrine of predestination. Instead of attending to the Scriptures as a rule of infallible truth, and receiving the instructions derived from them with implicit faith, we find some men boldly scrutinizing those secrets of infinite wisdom which God has concealed in Himself; while others of less adventurous dispositions seem to be filled with apprehension lest the Holy Spirit has spoken indiscreetly and inculcated absolutely what should be received only with cautions and limitations. We readily assent to the proposition in words, but the unsanctified heart makes no small opposition to it, that the Word of God is truth, and that we are bound to receive all that it contains on the authority of its Author, independently of all other considerations. We are neither to question nor to doubt, but simply to interpret and believe. Philosophy and prejudice and everything else are to yield to the voice of God speaking in His Word. It is owing to a neglect of this simple but obvious principle that views so contradictory have been held and published of the doctrine of predestination, and the necessary consequence of such inconsistency of opinion has been to involve the discussion of the subject in no little difficulty and perplexity. In maintaining the true doctrines of the Bible, as set forth in orthodox standards, we have not only to encounter the violent, unmitigated opposition of Pelagians and Arminians, but the no less unwarrantable excesses of the Supralapsarians and Hopkinsians. While the former explain the decrees of God in such a way as to amount to a downright denial of their certainty and sovereignty, the latter have pushed their inquiries with a censurable boldness into the hidden things which belong only to the Lord, and in their explanations of what is actually revealed have departed widely from the simplicity of the Bible. The Westminster Confession of Faith has happily avoided both these extremes of squeamish timidity and presumptuous boldness, and has exhibited, with its usual clearness and precision, the true doctrine of the Scriptures. The limits of a single tract will not allow me to enter into the broad and extensive field of the Divine decrees generally, and therefore I shall confine myself to the single feature of this great subject presented in the inseparable doctrines of Election and Reprobation. The fixing of the eternal destiny of men and angels is but a single link in the golden chain of "God's eternal purpose, by which, according to the counsel of His own will, He freely and unchangeably ordains whatsoever comes to pass." In the discussion of this subject I shall first endeavour to state clearly what the doctrines of Election and Reprobation are, as set forth in the Standards of the Presbyterian Church. I shall next attempt to vindicate these doctrines by a candid reference to the Word of God. I shall, in the third place, refute the cavils of those who reject them, and conclude the whole with a few practical inferences.

I. From the account given in the third chapter of the Confession of Faith we deduce the following propositions, which will be recognized at once as a correct statement of orthodox views: 1. Election is personal. "By the decree of God, for the manifestation of His glory, some *men* and angels are predestinated unto everlasting life, and others foreordained to everlasting death. These men and angels thus predestinated and foreordained are *particularly* and *unchangeably* designed, and their number is so *certain* and *definite* that it cannot be either increased or diminished." Sec. 3, 4. Hence, it is not an election of nations and communities to external privileges, but of men "particularly and unchangeably designed," and that to everlasting life, as we shall soon see more fully. 2. Man, in the decree of Election, is regarded as a *fallen* being. "Wherefore, they who are elected, *being fallen in Adam*, are redeemed by Christ," etc. Sec. 6. That this is the settled opinion of the orthodox will appear yet more clearly from the decision of the Synod of Dort on this very point: "Election is the unchangeable purpose of God by which, before the foundation of the world, He did from the whole human race, *fallen by their own fault from original righteousness* into a state of sin and misery, elect to salvation in Christ, according to the good pleasure of His own will, out of His mere free grace, a certain number of individuals, neither better than others nor more worthy of His favour, but involved with others in a common ruin."[1] This was likewise the opinion of Calvin and Turrettin and the leading divines of the Secession Church of Scotland, such as the Erskines and Fisher and Boston. 3. It is an election to *everlasting life,* and includes all the means which the Scriptures lay down for accomplishing this glorious end. "As God has appointed the elect unto glory, so hath He, by the eternal and most free purpose of His will, foreordained all the means thereunto. Wherefore, they who are elected, being fallen in Adam, are redeemed by Christ; are effectually called unto faith in Christ by His Spirit working in due season; are justified, adopted, sanctified, and kept by His power through faith unto salvation." Sec. 6. 4. This election of individuals of Adam's fallen race to everlasting life was made from *eternity.* In proof of this there needs no appeal to any particular portion of the chapter, for it is either definitely stated or clearly implied from the first section to the last. 5. It is absolute or wholly irrespective of works, having no other originating or impulsive cause than the mere good pleasure of God's will. "Those of mankind that are predestinated unto life, God, before the foundation of the world was laid, according to His eternal and immutable purpose, and the secret counsel and good pleasure of His will, hath chosen in Christ, unto everlasting glory, out of His mere free grace and love, without any foresight of faith or good works, or perseverance in either of them, or any other thing in the creature, as conditions or causes moving Him thereunto; and all to the praise of His glorious grace." Sec. 5. In regard to Reprobation, the Confession teaches the following particulars: 1. The individuals reprobated are guilty and polluted, "being by nature the children of wrath." This follows from the fact that the reprobate, equally with the elect, "are fallen in Adam;" and in Section 7th, God is said to "pass by and to ordain them to dishonour and wrath

[1] Article vii.

for their sin." 2. God passes them by or refuses to elect them, and leaves them in that state of misery and ruin into which, by their own fault, they had plunged themselves. 3. He dooms them to the deserved punishment of their sins in the world to come by a righteous act of vindicatory justice. 4. In the decree of reprobation God acts absolutely. He passes by one and elects another only from His own good pleasure; but in inflicting and pronouncing the sentence of death, He acts as a righteous Judge in consigning the wicked to deserved punishment. In other words, none but a sinner can be a suitable subject of reprobation, and men are reprobated only as sinners; but one man is passed by and another elected, not because one was a greater sinner than the other, but because God saw fit to do so. All these points are embraced in Section 7. "The rest of mankind God was pleased, according to the unsearchable counsel of His own will, whereby He extendeth or withholdeth mercy as He pleaseth, for the glory of His sovereign power over His creatures, to pass by, and to ordain them to dishonour and wrath for their sin, to the praise of His glorious justice."

Of this tremendous doctrine, therefore, which has been the prolific subject of so much vituperation and abuse—which has supplied a theme of ranting declamation to many a stripling theologian, who, when all other subjects failed him, could fill out his allotted time and entertain his hearers by running a tilt against Calvin's ghost—which has made the knees of many a strong man shake and blanched the cheek of many an ignorant zealot with terror,—of this tremendous, this "horrible" doctrine, which has been represented as so revolting to every thing like reason, Scripture or common sense, this then is the sum: Man, having by wilful and deliberate transgression sinned against God, justly fell under His wrath and curse. All men, regularly descended from Adam, became "children of wrath, alienated from the life of God," and utterly destitute of original righteousness. The consequence was that sentence of condemnation actually passed upon all men. Unless we are prepared to question or impugn the stainless justice of God, we must admit that this sentence, thus solemnly passed upon the race, was a *righteous* sentence. Out of this race of guilty and polluted sinners, thus justly condemned, God graciously and eternally elected some to life and happiness and glory, while He left the rest in their state of wretchedness and ruin, and determined to inflict upon them the punishment which they justly deserved. The reason why He elected some and passed by others, when all were equally undeserving, is to be referred wholly to Himself—to the counsel of His own will or to His mere good pleasure.

I have been thus particular in deducing a plain statement of this doctrine from the Standards of the Church, because it is so difficult to meet with any fair or consistent account of it from writers who oppose it. They indulge too freely in the merest caricatures, or deduce their whole views from dislocated and disjointed expressions of Calvinistic divines. It would be no hard matter to show, by quotations from Calvin and Turrettin and the published Confessions of the Reformed Churches, that the statement just given is a fair exposition of the views which have usually been regarded as orthodox from the period of the Reformation until now. That there have been men who have overleaped the bounds of sobriety and modesty, and have consequently lost themselves in the mists of Supralapsarian and Hopkinsian error, need not and will not be denied; but then their excesses are no more to be regarded as the genuine doctrines of Calvinistic churches than the wild speculations of Clarke on the Sonship of Christ and the omniscience of God as the genuine doctrines of the Wesleyan Methodists. In ascertaining the doctrines of a Church, we must appeal to her standards; and having done so in this instance, and given, in the words of the Confession, the precise position of the Presbyterian Church, I proceed to show that her views are scriptural.

II. Widely as men may differ in their views of predestination, it is generally conceded by all who profess any reverence for the Word of God that there is an election, of some sort, to eternal life made known in the Scriptures. But there is much violent and bitter opposition to that account of it which places a crown of absolute sovereignty on the head of Jehovah, and prostrates man in entire dependence upon His will. In deducing the scriptural argument, I shall endeavour to arrange the texts under the several heads, or rather upon the separate points, made out in the explanation or statement of the doctrine from the Confession of Faith.

1. First, then, election is *personal;* that is, it is a choice of *individuals,* from the corrupt mass of our fallen race, to everlasting life. I am far from intending to insinuate that in every instance in which words expressive of election are used in the Scriptures a personal election to eternal life must of course be understood. On the contrary, it is freely admitted that the Scriptures speak of the choice of nations to peculiar privileges, of the choice of individuals to particular offices, and of the choice of Christ to the mediatorial work. All this is fully conceded, but yet there are passages which cannot, without unwarrantable violence, be interpreted in any other way than as teaching the doctrine of personal election to eternal life. "According as He hath chosen us in Him before the foundation of the world, that we should be holy and without blame before Him in love." Eph. i. 4. Here election is expressly said to be personal—"*hath chosen us,*" that is, Paul himself and the Christians at Ephesus. The epistle is directed to "the saints which are at Ephesus, and the faithful in Christ Jesus." i. 1. Here then is not an election of nations or communities to external privileges, but an election of individuals to everlasting life. In verses 5, 6, 7, 11 we have a more particular view of the blessing which they received in consequence of their election, and which cannot, by any ingenuity of criticism, be plausibly distorted into national advantages. "Having predestinated us unto the adoption of children by Jesus Christ, to Himself," etc.; and again, "In whom we have redemption through His blood, the forgiveness of sins, according to the

riches of His grace." Those, therefore, to whom Paul was writing were "saints, faithful in Christ Jesus, adopted to be sons, redeemed and forgiven," and all these privileges he traced to the election of which he was speaking. Are there any so blind as not to see that these are saving blessings, and that those who were addressed as possessing them were *individuals* and not communities or nations? But it has been said that Paul could not know that the whole Church at Ephesus were elect. To this it may be readily replied that Paul does not say so. He sufficiently designates the individuals of whom he was speaking by the characteristics noticed above. Macknight, always anxious to fritter away the peculiar features of the Gospel, tells us in his note on the fourth verse that the election here spoken of is "that election which before the foundation of the world God made of holy persons of all nations to be His children and people, and to enjoy the blessing promised to such." Upon this singular note it is enough for my present purpose to remark—(1.) That it sufficiently admits the fact that the election here spoken of is personal. But (2.) that it was not, however, an election of "holy persons," but an election to be holy, "that we might be holy and without blame before Him in love." (3.) That these Ephesians, previously to their acceptance of the Gospel, were "dead in trespasses and sins, walked according to the prince of the power of the air, the spirit that now worketh in the children of disobedience," etc. ii. 1–3. They could not possibly, therefore, have been elected as "holy persons," seeing that they were utterly destitute of all pretensions to holiness.

I might here refer to the cases of Ishmael and Isaac and of Esau and Jacob adduced by the Apostle in the ninth chapter of Romans as examples, respectively, of personal election and righteous reprobation. These cases are conclusive on the point. The attempts of Socinian and Arminian writers to pervert that celebrated chapter from its natural and obvious meaning will be considered sufficiently in another part of this discussion.

2. The second point to be proved is, that man in the decree of election was regarded as a *fallen being*. Three opinions have been maintained by divines as to the light in which he was looked upon in this decree. The first is that of the Supralapsarians; the second, that of our Standards; and the third, that of the Arminians and Remonstrants at the Synod of Dort. The Supralapsarians take their name from the fact that in the decree of election and reprobation they suppose that God regarded man not even as yet created, or only as created and not as fallen. They, consequently, look upon the creation and fall as only intermediate steps through which man was to pass in accomplishing this great decree. To this scheme there are insuperable objections— (1.) The very ideas of election and reprobation suppose man to be involved already in a state of sin and misery. While in a state of holiness in their covenant head all men were regarded as equally righteous, and equally shared in their Maker's approbation. The fall, therefore, must take place before such a distinction could be made as this doctrine supposes; I mean that God in the counsels of eternity must have looked upon man as lost and ruined, since otherwise a determination to save some, and to leave others in their wretchedness and ruin, could not be expressed without a "solecism in language," and much less "conceived without confusion of thought." The very idea of salvation implies misery, and a determination to save implies a view or knowledge of that misery. It is plain, then, that sin and misery, in the individuals elected and reprobated, is an indispensable prerequisite. It might be objected here that in the case of the angels who stood election did not suppose a fall; but I would answer that the cases are not parallel. It was not a decree to save the angels from sin, but from sinning, and therefore they could be regarded only as liable to fall. But in the case immediately before us there is a decree to save men from a state of guilt and ruin, and

yet they are not involved in guilt and ruin! (2.) If it be maintained that man is not even regarded as created, we are thrown into still more perplexing absurdity. It is hard to conceive how a being not yet created can become the subject of such a decree at all. The decree of creation must be first in order of nature, or election and reprobation will be concerned not about men, but nonentities. (3.) What is said of this doctrine in the Scriptures is usually referred to the mercy and justice of God. The elect are monuments erected to the "praise of the glory of His grace," and the reprobate are "vessels of wrath," or of righteous and just displeasure; but how this could be said when man had not yet become obnoxious to God's justice, nor had yet been in a situation of wretchedness to require His mercy, it is hard to conceive. Sin is that alone which renders man a proper object of reprobation, and misery is the proper object of mercy. For these reasons—and many others might be adduced—I am led to regard the Supralapsarian scheme as untenable and false. The whole current of Scripture testimony is in favour of the doctrine of our Standards, commonly called Sublapsarianism. "I have chosen you out of the world, therefore the world hateth you." John xv. 19. The elect here are the objects of the Divine choice while belonging to the world, and the world means corrupt and fallen man, as is plain from its hating the righteous and godly. We are said to be "chosen in Christ"—that is, to be redeemed and saved by Him—which implies that when chosen we are guilty and polluted. Again: "Hath not the potter power over the clay, of the same lump to make one vessel unto honour and another unto dishonour?" Rom. ix. 21. That the lump here represents corrupt and ruined human nature is plain from the following considerations which I translate from Turrettin: "1. It is the lump from which vessels of mercy and wrath are formed—one for honour, the other for dishonour, but wrath and mercy necessarily suppose sin and misery. 2. It is the same lump from which Isaac and Ishmael, Jacob and Esau are taken, who are brought forward, respectively, as examples of gratuitous election and of righteous and free reprobation. This must be the corrupt mass of human nature, because the Apostle speaks of Jacob and Esau as twins conceived in the womb, and therefore as sinners." It is no valid objection that the children are represented as having done neither good nor evil, for this is manifestly to be understood comparatively. Jacob had done no good and Esau no evil which caused the one to be preferred and the other rejected. It was not Jacob's being better than Esau, nor Esau's being worse than Jacob, which induced God to elect the one and reject the other.

The "vessels of wrath" (Rom. ix. 23) are represented as being "fitted for destruction" during the time that God bears with them in great patience and long-suffering, which seems to be inconsistent with the idea that they could have been "vessels of wrath" before they yet became "fitted for destruction" by sin and depravity. But, probably, the most pointed and remarkable passage on this subject is Ezek. xvi. 6: "But when I passed by thee, and saw thee polluted in thine own blood, I said unto thee when thou wast in thy blood, Live; yea, I said unto thee when thou wast in thy blood, Live." Here the elect, of whom Jerusalem was a symbol, are represented by the figure of a filthy and outcast infant, finding from none either sympathy or aid, but so loathsome in its person as to be abandoned in the "open field" the very day on which it was born. Verses 4, 5. The Lord represents Himself as looking upon this wretched infant thus polluted in its blood with an eye of compassion, and commanding it to "live." Ver. 6. Effectual calling cannot be intended by the word "live" here, because in effectual calling the soul is married to Christ, but in this passage the elect are represented as not yet of a marriageable age. Therefore the word must denote only God's *purpose to save*, and the passage thus interpreted shows conclusively in what light the elect are regarded in the decree of election. This interpretation will probably be confirmed by considering this verse in connection with the two following. In verse 7, God describes the growth of this miserable infant until it became a marriageable woman. "I have caused thee to multiply as the bud of the field; thou hast increased and waxen great, and thou art come to excellent ornaments; thy breasts are fashioned, and thine hair is grown, whereas thou wast naked and bare." The infant, having thus become a young woman and of marriageable age, the marriage or the union of the elect with Christ in effectual calling is celebrated in verse 8: "Now when I passed by thee, and looked upon thee, behold thy time was the time of love, and I spread my skirt over thee, and covered thy nakedness; yea, I sware unto thee, and entered into a covenant with thee, saith the Lord God, and thou becamest mine." Here, then, we have much the same view of the inseparable connection between election and vocation which Paul gives us in the 8th of Romans, and here it is clearly demonstrated that men are elected in that state from which they are called, which is a state of sin, condemnation and misery. The views of the Arminians, who suppose that man is regarded as believing or unbelieving in the decree of election and reprobation, will be refuted in another part of this discussion.

3. It is an election to *everlasting life or salvation*. "But we are bound to give thanks always to God for you, brethren, beloved of the Lord, because God hath from the beginning chosen you to salvation through sanctification of the Spirit and belief of the truth." 2 Thess. ii. 13. "For God hath not appointed us to wrath, but to obtain salvation by our Lord Jesus Christ." 1 Thess. v. 9. In both these texts the word *salvation* is probably used in reference to the state of glory beyond the grave. The first text is peculiarly forcible. The Apostle had been giving a graphic and appalling account of the revelation of the "man of sin," through whose seductive influence many souls would be led to reject the truth and be given over to judicial blindness, and finally be damned. Such statements as these were well calculated to

alarm the faithful, especially weak believers. The Apostle therefore shows in the text cited that there is no ground of apprehension to the real children of God; they are chosen to salvation, and therefore cannot come short of it. In order that the Thessalonian Christians might be able to receive the comfort of this truth, that the elect are absolutely safe, he points out the marks of election or the evidences of it—"sanctification of the Spirit and belief of the truth." The second text is equally clear. The Apostle is exhorting the Thessalonians to a diligent discharge of Christian duty. He had urged the unexpectedness of the Lord's coming as one motive, and presents another in the text I have quoted, and that is the certainty of success. The Lord has destined us to salvation; we can therefore discharge our Christian duties in confidence and hope. The election of God is a sufficient security against disappointment. The word salvation, however, is not always used in this sense when applied to the elect. In fact, it is a word of extensive signification, including in the language of Scripture what we commonly mean by grace and glory. Many of the absurd consequences which have been rashly and intemperately charged upon the doctrine of election would vanish at once before a correct apprehension of the true nature of eternal life. It is a common but erroneous opinion that the happiness of heaven is that alone which the Scriptures designate by this phrase, and those who entertain this error generally have crude conceptions of what constitutes the blessedness of glory. A slight acquaintance with the Bible, however, will show us that all believers even in this world are in actual and irreversible possession of eternal life. "My sheep hear my voice, and I know them, and I give unto them *eternal life*." "He that hath the Son hath *life*." That life which is implanted in the soul in regeneration, which is developed in sanctification and completed in glory, is what the Scriptures call eternal life, and it is called eternal because by the grace of God it is absolutely imperishable. There are not wanting passages of Scripture in which the word *life* is used in its full latitude of meaning: "I am the living bread which came down from heaven; if any man eat of this bread he *shall live for ever.*" John vi. 51, 57.

The scriptural meaning of *salvation* is deliverance from the curse, power and love of sin. The word in general implies deliverance from evil, but it is always, in the Bible, positive as well as negative, and imports the bestowment of a corresponding good. The blind, when healed by our Saviour, are said to be saved—that is, they are delivered from the evil of blindness, and receive the corresponding blessing of sight. So sinners are said to be saved by Christ, because through "the faith of Him" they are delivered from the evils of their natural state, and receive the blessings of a gracious state. Were it possible that a man who had obtained the forgiveness of sin should afterward fail of the blessedness of heaven, there is no assignable sense in which it could be said that he was saved. If there be any difference in the spiritual import of the words *salvation* and *life*, it would seem to be this, that the former has a more pointed reference to the evils from which we are delivered by grace, and the latter to the benefits of which we become partakers. It is true that these words are not always used in their fullest latitude, but are sometimes confined to one and sometimes to another feature of the general meaning. This, however, is a strong proof of the inseparable connection between grace and glory. In accordance with these remarks it may be observed—(1.) That salvation implies pardon and gratuitous acceptance. Luke i. 77: "To give knowledge of salvation unto His people by the remission of their sins." The original is, "in the remission of their sins"—that is, when our sins are pardoned we become partakers of salvation. Luke xix. 9: "This day is salvation come to this house." Whatever else the word may mean here, pardon of sin must be one of the blessings which Jesus conferred on Zacchæus. The curse of the law is what the

Scriptures mean by the "wrath to come," and no one can doubt that deliverance from this forms an important element of salvation. But we are delivered from the curse and covenant claims of the law in our gratuitous justification and pardon. (2.) Salvation implies regeneration and progressive sanctification, or the production and development of the new nature. Titus iii. 5: "Not by works of righteousness which we have done, but according to His mercy, He saved us by the washing of regeneration and the renewing of the Holy Ghost." Here the washing or cleansing of regeneration, which is explained to be the renewing of the Holy Ghost, is in so many words stated to be an element of salvation. Jesus received His name by the express and solemn appointment of God, because He should "save His people from their sins." The spiritual life which the Holy Spirit communicates in regeneration, and fosters and strengthens in sanctification, is of the same nature, though different in degree and the circumstances of its exercise, with the life of glory at God's right hand. The one is represented as an earnest of the other, and an earnest must be of the same kind with that of which it is an earnest. If, then, eternal blessedness is a part of our salvation, the new nature here necessarily must be. All, therefore, who are elected to salvation are elected to sanctification in the full scriptural extent of that word. Hence, the Apostle says that we are chosen, "that we might be holy and without blame before Him in love." Eph. i. 4. Hence, the Thessalonians are said to be "chosen to salvation through sanctification of the Spirit and belief of the truth;" and hence, it is said, "We are His workmanship, created in Christ Jesus unto good works, which God hath before ordained that we should walk in them." Eph. ii. 10. (3.) Salvation implies the blessedness of heaven. This is such a common and familiar use of the term that we need not waste time in adducing texts.

From this short examination of the scriptural meaning of two words in very common use, we have seen that the

Standards of the Church have adhered closely to the Word of God in resolving election to salvation into election to all the privileges of redemption in this world as well as the world to come. Salvation is one great whole, and wherever it begins to exist it takes hold upon eternity. The blessedness of heaven is the result of election; so is personal holiness on earth—the grand preparative for glory; so is faith in the Lord Jesus—the great shield by which sin and Satan are effectually subdued. It would be a monstrous conception to suppose that men were elected to salvation, and yet not elected to a certain employment of the means by which alone salvation is secured. The Scriptures show conclusively—(1.) That effectual calling is the fruit of election. 2 Tim. i. 9: "Who hath saved us, and *called* us with an holy calling, not according to our works, but according to His own purpose and grace, which was given us in Christ Jesus before the world began." Rom. viii. 30: "Moreover, whom He did predestinate them He also called." (2.) As a matter of course, faith is the fruit of election. Eph. ii. 8: It is called the "gift of God." Phil. i. 29: "Unto you it is *given* to believe on Christ." Col. ii. 12: "Buried with Him in baptism, wherein also ye are risen with Him through the faith of the operation of God who hath raised Him from the dead." Heb. xii. 2: Jesus is regarded as "the Author and Finisher of our faith." 1 Cor. xii. 9: "To another, faith by the same Spirit," and saving faith is spoken of distinctively as the faith of "God's elect." (3.) But perhaps the most conclusive scriptural authority that all the blessings of redemption are included in election to eternal life is to be found in Romans viii. 29, 30: "For whom He did foreknow He also did predestinate to be conformed to the image of His Son, that he might be the firstborn among many brethren. Moreover, whom He did predestinate, them He also called, and whom He called, them He also justified, and whom He justified, them He also glorified." In these verses we have—1st, the election of God or His determination to save a chosen number: "Whom

He did foreknow." The connection of this verse with the preceding, and of this clause with the succeeding, sufficiently determines the meaning of the word "foreknow." Those who are said to be called in verse 29 are called according to God's "purpose," and in this verse their calling is coupled with God's foreknowledge. To foreknow, therefore, is to purpose or determine, or, what in this connection is just the same, to choose. This is a common and familiar meaning of the word. Rom. ii. 2; 1 Pet. i. 20. 2dly. We have the purpose of God to render them holy: "He also did predestinate to be conformed to the image of His Son," etc. Those whom He elected He determined to sanctify, to make holy even as Christ was holy. 3dly. We have the steps of the actual accomplishment of this decree: "Whom He did predestinate, them He also called;" that is, by the word of the Gospel, and the efficacious operation of the Spirit, He brings them into saving union with Christ, that so they may be conformed to His image. This is the common and familiar acceptation of the word in the writings of Paul. 1 Cor. i. 9, 24, etc. 4thly. We have the justification and final and complete salvation of those who were foreknown: "Whom He called, them He also justified, and whom He justified, them He also glorified." Being united to Christ in their effectual calling, they become partakers of His righteousness and grace, by which their justification, sanctification and glorification are infallibly secured. From this celebrated passage we see that "election, calling, justification and salvation are indissolubly united."

4. Election to everlasting life or salvation is *eternal*. Whatsoever purposes God now has, or ever will have, in regard to the destiny of men, He always has had. It would be a serious and dangerous detraction from the glory of the Divine unchangeableness to suppose that exigencies can arise in the government of the world calling for a change of the Divine purposes, or for a new and unexpected course of Providence. "Known unto God are all His works from the beginning of the world." Acts xv. 18. His all-seeing

eye brings all possible events within the light of a present and infallible omniscience. What He is now He was from all eternity, and will continue to be the same everlastingly. Succession of time can only be applied to Him in accommodation to our weak capacities, since all things past and future are "naked and opened to the eyes of Him with whom we have to do." But while, owing to the simplicity and eternity of the Divine nature, there cannot be conceived in God a succession of time, nor consequently various and successive decrees, yet we may justly speak of His decrees as prior or posterior in point of nature. Though they all constitute but one eternal act of the Divine will, the objects about which they are concerned are connected with each other by various relations, and the decrees themselves may be spoken of in a language accommodated to these diversified relations. In ordinary life we often see effects and causes coexistent in point of time, yet since a cause is prior to an effect in the order of nature, we usually speak of it as prior in point of time. Upon the same principle we speak of God's decrees in language borrowed from the relations which the objects of the decrees sustain to each other, though to His mind all things are "naked" and present. Hence, all the decrees of God are absolutely eternal, but the Scriptures speak of the eternity of election with marked and pointed emphasis: "According as He hath chosen us in Him before the foundation of the world," etc. Eph. i. 4. "According to His own purpose and grace which was given us in Christ Jesus before the world began." 2 Tim. i. 9. "Known unto God are all His works from the beginning of the world." Acts xv. 18.

5. The next point in the statement is the *sovereignty* of election, and here we enter upon that peculiar view of the doctrine which renders it so unpalatable to the carnal heart. There is, in all unrenewed minds, a scarcely acknowledged but secretly felt persuasion that God can be conciliated or brought under obligations to be propitious by their own legal performances. Men are unwilling to admit that their case is hope-

less without the intervention of sovereign mercy; they will not believe until persuaded to it by the Holy Spirit that they neither do nor can have any claims upon God, that they are just "vessels of wrath fitted for destruction," in themselves considered, and that the only ground of Divine favour is in the Divine Being Himself. But all our legal bias and propensities must be carefully dismissed while we attend with impartial ears to the testimony of Inspiration. What say the Scriptures? for whatever they say must be the truth. But before entering directly upon the Scripture testimony, it may be well to give a brief view of the sentiments of the Arminians, who, as Turrettin too justly remarks, "recall Popery and Pelagianism by the back door." They suspend the decree of personal election upon a foresight of faith and perseverance in holiness, and resolve both of these, in great measure, into a good use of the sinner's free will. "They make," says Turrettin, "the decree of election twofold: the first is general, being God's purpose to save all believers; the second is special, being His purpose to save such and such individuals who, He foresaw, would believe. The first they resolve entirely into the will of God; the second, though founded in the Divine will, attaches so much importance to faith as to make it the reason why one is elected and another not." The question between us and the Arminians respects simply the cause of election in the Divine mind—whether the decree is wholly unconditional, depending upon the mere good pleasure of God's will, or whether it is suspended upon a foresight of faith and perseverance in the creature. We do not deny that the decree of election includes the instrumentality of means in its accomplishment, and that faith and good works are indispensably necessary to its execution or fulfilment, but we do deny that faith, perseverance, good works, or any other thing in the creature, was the cause or reason why God elected one and passed by another; and we confidently appeal to the Scriptures of eternal truth to bear us out in our positions.

(1.) Faith is uniformly represented in the Bible as the

fruit or effect of election, and therefore cannot possibly be the cause of it. This point has already been fully established in the previous discussion of the nature of eternal life or salvation. It was there shown that a decree to save must mean a decree to bestow all the blessings of redemption, from the implantation of a new nature in regeneration to its full development in a state of glory. Having, then, already anticipated this point, I shall now dismiss it with only a few additional texts: "As many as were ordained to eternal life believed." Acts xiii. 48. It is the merest quibbling to interpret the *ordination* here of a disposition to believe, and it would probably puzzle those who do so to tell us whence the disposition arose. The word generally means "ordained or appointed," and accordingly these individuals are said to have believed because they were appointed to salvation. This is the natural and obvious meaning of the passage. "All that the Father giveth me shall come to me." John vi. 37. To come to Christ means to believe on Him, and faith is in this passage attributed by the Saviour Himself to election. Others did not believe because they were not of Christ's sheep; those who do believe must trace their faith to the sovereign goodness of God. The passage teaches us, moreover, that all who are given to Christ certainly shall believe, thus evidently throwing election farther back than faith. The truth then plainly is, that election is the cause of faith, and not faith of election.

(2.) This scheme, which suspends election upon foreseen faith and perseverance, amounts to a downright denial of the doctrine altogether, or, if there be any choice in the case at all, it is the sinner choosing God, and not God the sinner. Arminians represent faith and perseverance as prescribed conditions of salvation. The man, therefore, who complies with the conditions obtains the blessing promised upon a principle very different from that of election. It is an abuse of language to say that an individual under these circumstances is *chosen* to receive the blessing. The executive of the country issues a proclamation in which he offers a great reward to any individual who shall apprehend a notorious malefactor fleeing from justice. Some citizens do apprehend him and claim the reward. Is there any propriety in saying that they were elected to the reward? Nor would it affect the principle involved in the case at all to suppose that the executive knew beforehand precisely what individuals would apprehend the criminal. The Arminians, therefore, charge the Apostles and our Saviour Himself with an outrageous abuse and perversion of language when they represent them as using plain and familiar words in an acceptation which they cannot bear. There is much weight in the following remark of Turrettin: "If election depend upon foreseen faith, God cannot elect man, but man chooses God, and so predestination should rather be called post-destination—the first cause becomes the second, and God becomes dependent upon man, which is false and contrary to the nature of things, and Christ Himself testifies, 'ye have not chosen me, but I have chosen you.'" John xv. 16.

(3.) The Scriptures in so many words refer the cause of election to the sovereign pleasure of God, independently of any considerations derived from the creature. Eph. i. 5, 11: "Having predestinated us unto the adoption of children by Jesus Christ to Himself, *according to the good pleasure of His will;* in whom also we have obtained an inheritance, being predestinated according to the purpose of Him who worketh all things after *the counsel of His own will.*" 2 Tim. i. 9: "Who hath saved us and called us with an holy calling, not according to our works, but *according to His own purpose and grace,* which was given us in Christ Jesus before the world began." Titus iii. 5: "Not by works of righteousness which we have done, but according to His *mercy* He saved us," etc. These Scriptures require no comment; they are so plain and unambiguous that he who runs may read.

But the ninth chapter of the Epistle to the Romans is in a great measure a professed exposition of the absolute sovereignty of God in selecting the objects of His favour. Pelagians and Arminians have laboured diligently but unsuccessfully to neutralize the testimony of the Apostle in that chapter, and they have been somewhat encouraged by the partial concurrence of a few Calvinistic commentators in their views. They maintain that the Apostle is not speaking of a personal election to eternal life, but merely of a national election to external privileges—not of Jacob and Esau as individuals, but of their respective descendants as communities or nations. This interpretation rests principally upon the quotations from the Old Testament which Paul applies to the discussion, and upon a gratuitous assumption that Esau did not serve Jacob. The first passage of any great importance in the discussion is taken from Genesis xxv. 23: "Two nations are within thy womb, and the one people shall be stronger than the other people, and the elder shall serve the younger." Macknight, in his second note on Romans ix. 11, remarks: "The Apostle, according to his manner, cites only a few words of the passage on which his argument is founded, but I have inserted the whole in the commentary, to show that Jacob and Esau are not spoken of as individuals, but as representing the two nations springing from them—'Two nations are in thy womb,' etc.—and that the election of which the Apostle speaks is not an election of Jacob to eternal life, but of his posterity to be the visible Church and people of God on earth, and heirs of the promises in their first and literal meaning, agreeably to what Moses declared, Deut. vii. 6, 7, 8, and Paul preached, Acts. xiii. 17. That this is the election here spoken of appears from the following circumstances: 1. It is neither said, nor is it true of Jacob and Esau personally, that the elder served the younger. This is only true of their posterity. 2. Though Esau had served Jacob personally, and had been inferior to him in worldly greatness, it would have been no proof at all of Jacob's election to eternal life, nor of Esau's reprobation. As little was the subjection of the Edomites to the Israelites in David's days a proof of the election and reprobation of their progenitors. 3. The apostle's professed purpose in this discourse being to show that an election being bestowed on Jacob's posterity by God's free gift might either be taken from them, or others might be admitted to share therein with them, it is evidently not an election to eternal life, which is never taken away, but an election to external privileges only. 4. This being an election of the whole posterity of Jacob, and a reprobation of the whole descendants of Esau, it can only mean that the nation which was to spring from Esau should be subdued by the nation which was to spring from Jacob, and that it should not, like the nation springing from Jacob, be the Church and people of God, nor be entitled to the possession of Canaan, nor give birth to the Seed in whom all the families of the earth were to be blessed. 5. The circumstance of Esau's being older than Jacob was very properly taken notice of, to show that Jacob's election was contrary to the right of primogeniture, because this circumstance proved it to be from pure favour. But if his election had been to eternal life, the circumstance of his age ought not to have been mentioned, because it had no relation to that matter whatever." The next leading passage which Paul quotes is taken from Exodus xxxiii. 19: " And He said I will make all my goodness pass before thee, and I will proclaim the name of the Lord before thee, and will be gracious to whom I will be gracious, and will show mercy to whom I will show mercy." " Here," says Macknight, " mercy is not an eternal pardon granted to individuals, but the receiving of a nation into favour after being displeased with it; for these words were spoken to Moses after God had laid aside His purpose of consuming the Israelites for their sin in making and worshipping the golden calf." "It is a notorious fact," says Bishop Sumner,[1] "though often overlooked in argument, that the very passage, 'I will have mercy on whom I will have mercy, and I will have compassion on whom I will have compassion,' which is almost

[1] Apostolic Preaching, p. 36.

the only support claimed from St. Paul to the system of absolute decrees, is quoted from Exodus, and forms the assurance revealed by God Himself to Moses that He had *separated the Hebrew nation* from all the people on the face of the earth." The next quotation is from Exodus ix. 16: " And in very deed for this cause have I raised thee up, for to show in thee my power, and that my name may be declared throughout all the earth. In reference to this, Macknight observes: "Though Pharaoh alone was spoken to, it is evident that this and everything else spoken to him in the affair of the plague was designed for the Egyptian nation in general, as we learn from Exodus iv. 22: 'Say unto Pharaoh, thus saith the Lord, Israel is my son, even my first-born.' 23: 'And I say unto thee, let my son go that he may serve me, and if thou refusest to let him go, behold I will slay thy son, even thy first-born.' For, as Israel here signifies the nation of the Israelites, so Pharaoh signifies the nation of the Egyptians, and Pharaoh's son, even his first-born, is the first-born of Pharaoh and of the Egyptians. In like manner, Exodus ix. 15: 'I will stretch out my hand that I may smite thee and thy people with pestilence, and thou shalt be cut off from the earth;' that is, thou and thy people shall be cut off, for the pestilence was to fall on the people as well as on Pharaoh. Then follow the words quoted by the apostle, verse 16: 'And in very deed,' etc. Now, as no person can suppose that the power of God was to be shown in the destruction of Pharaoh singly, but in the destruction of him and his people, this that was spoken to Pharaoh was spoken to him and to the nation of which he was the head."

I have thus given above, and mostly in the words of Macknight, the very marrow and pith of the Arminian argument. The notes which I have quoted contain the sum and substance of the more expanded observations of Sumner and Adam Clarke, who have laboured in the perversion of this celebrated chapter with a diligence and zeal worthy of a better cause. It will be seen at once that the principle upon which their reasoning proceeds is wholly gratuitous and false. They settle what they suppose to be the meaning of a passage in the Old Testament, and then determine that it cannot be used in any other sense in the New. Let the principle be tested by a reference to Matt. ii. 15, where Joseph is said to have departed into Egypt, "that it might be fulfilled which was spoken of the Lord by the prophet saying, Out of Egypt have I called my son." This last clause is clearly a quotation from Hosea xi. 1, where it has a manifest allusion to the children of Israel as a people or nation: "When Israel was a child then I loved him, and called my son out of Egypt." Upon the principle of interpretation on which Macknight proceeds the 15th verse of the second chapter of Matthew cannot refer to the Lord Jesus Christ, because the passage in Hosea will not bear that meaning; but every one sees from the context that it must and does refer to Christ, no matter what may be the meaning of the original passage in the Prophet. And so, if the scope and drift of the Epistle to the Romans show that Paul is discussing the question of a personal election to eternal life, no matter what may be the meaning of the original passages in Genesis and Exodus, the Apostle applies them to the subject before him. It is true that where an appeal is made to the Old Testament to *confirm* a truth delivered by an Evangelist or an Apostle, the words cannot be accommodated, but must be quoted in their original sense; but it is equally true that the language of the Old Testament is often used by the writers of the New, just as we use the language of writers who have gone before us in the way of illustration and ornament. In such cases we may warrantably employ the language in a sense different from that in which it was originally used. It is certainly incumbent upon the Arminians therefore to show not only that the original passages quoted by Paul have reference to nations and not to individuals, but also to show that Paul has actually applied the passages in the identical sense of Moses. Their point is not gained by proving the first proposition without also proving the last. Besides all this, they must show that these passages are not referred to as containing undeniable proofs of a principle which was suited to the point in hand. So far from attempting to show this, Arminian commentators universally concede that God is sovereign in the distribution of national privileges; in other words, they admit the principle that God does distribute some blessings without respect to the character or works of individuals. May not Paul have been quoting the passages from the Old Testament merely because they teach this principle so peculiarly appropriate to the subject in hand? May not his reasoning have been something like this?—"We see that there is no injustice in God's bestowing peculiar blessings on some and rejecting others, because from His word that appears to be a principle of His government—a well-settled and established principle. He declares that He is not influenced by the merit of individuals, but by His own will. If this principle extend to the distribution of favours upon earth, there is no reason why it should not extend to the bestowment of eternal blessings. There are the same objections to the principle in the one case as in the other; and yet if God declares that He does act upon it in the one case, we infer from His unchangeableness that He must act upon it in the other. The difficulty lies, not against the character of the blessings bestowed, but against the sovereign nature of the choice." I can easily conceive that Paul might have applied the quotations from the Old Testament to the case of personal election, merely because they contain the *principle,* and the *whole principle,* upon which personal election depends. It is obvious, then, that even upon the supposition that the passages from Genesis and Exodus are correctly interpreted, it is not proved that Paul is not speaking in the ninth of Romans of personal election to eternal life. The point which Paul has in hand must be gathered, not from the writings of Moses, but from the scope and design of his own Epistle, and it only shows how hardly pressed the Arminians are when they overlook one of the simplest and most obvious rules of interpretation in order to avoid the truths which Paul so clearly teaches.

[1.] I am not prepared, however, to admit, though I believe Arminians would gain nothing by the admission, that the passages in the Old Testament refer exclusively to nations. On the contrary, I think that they manifestly teach a distinction between *individuals* as the ground of the distinction between nations. A careful examination of Genesis xxv. 23 will put this matter beyond all reasonable doubt. Rebecca, while pregnant, and probably somewhat advanced in pregnancy, seems to have felt a strange and unusual agitation in her womb, arising from the violent conflict of the twins, and, perplexed with a very natural anxiety, she consulted the Lord for instruction and relief. It is obvious that the contest of the brothers in the womb was altogether an extraordinary event, and was the certain presage of the future animosity which should distract and divide their descendants. The distinction between the nations, then, seems to have commenced in the womb. The answer of the Lord to Rebecca is decisive on this point: "Two nations are within thy womb;" that is, the children which are in thy womb shall become each the father of a nation. "And two manner of people shall be separated from thy bowels;" that is, two distinct and separate nations shall spring from the twins. Now, here the separation is said to take place from Rebecca's "bowels;" that is, from the children which were then in her womb. This teaches as plainly as language can teach that the distinction between the Edomites and Israelites supposed a previous distinction between Jacob and Esau as individuals. This again is confirmed by the unambiguous and pointed testimony of Malachi, who represents God's love to the Israelites as originating with God's love to Jacob as an individual. Besides, it is common in the Scriptures to trace the grace of God toward the Jews to His love for their fathers: "as touching the election, they are beloved for their fathers' sake." Rom. xi. 25. There is no violence, therefore, in applying this passage of Genesis to a distinction between Jacob and Esau as *individuals;* for it *does* teach such a distinction, and it is in this sense alone that Paul has quoted it: "For the *children* being not yet born," etc. v. 11. Here is nothing about *nations,* but *children*. But we are told that Esau never did serve Jacob, and therefore the passage cannot possibly apply to them as individuals. It may be answered that Jacob did obtain the birth-right, which was the blessing promised, and that Esau did upon several occasions acknowledge his inferiority to his brother. This was the spirit of the prophecy in regard to the individuals, though it had a fuller accomplishment in their respective descendants. But it is contended that if the prophecy did have a reference to the brothers as individuals, it would not follow that the distinction was that one was elected to eternal life, and the other reprobated and left to the sentence of eternal death. But if Paul is speaking of the brothers as individuals, it will follow that the ninth chapter of Romans has no reference to an election of nations to external privileges; it will overthrow the Arminian if it does not establish the Calvinistic interpretation. There are, however, good reasons for supposing that the birth-right was a type of spiritual blessings, as Canaan was a type of a heavenly country. Many of the events and personages of the Old Testament are certainly typical, and the Jewish people were constantly taught spiritual truths in the strong, impressive language of types. When we consider how little personal advantage Jacob gained in this world from obtaining the birth-right, it is natural to suppose that God's promise had reference to other and higher blessings. In fact, the election of the Jewish people themselves was a standing symbol of another and a nobler election. All the prominent transactions of God in reference to Canaan shadow forth the spiritual principles by which His Church is regulated and governed. The Exodus from Egypt, the Paschal Lamb, the journeyings in the wilderness, the crossing of Jordan, the settlement in Canaan and the expulsion of the Canaanites and surrounding tribes, are all typical of solemn and important spiritual events connected with the redemption of sinners by the Lord Jesus Christ. There is nothing unreasonable, therefore, in supposing that Jacob, under the type of the birth-right, *did* receive the gratuitous promise of eternal life, and that Esau was passed by and rejected. This certainly is the sense, as we shall presently see more fully, in which Paul quotes the passage, "the elder shall serve the younger." Macknight's third argument, in the first note quoted, is a mere begging of the question. He takes for granted what the Apostle's express design is, and then argues, from his own gratuitous assumption, against personal election to eternal life. The same is true of his fourth. In regard to the fifth, it may be remarked that the age of Jacob is mentioned to show how entirely free the election was—how completely independent of all considerations derived from the creature.

As to the passage in Exodus xxxiii. 19, it is wholly gratuitous to suppose that this was spoken in reference exclusively to the Jewish people. It is true that God spake these words after He had laid aside His purpose of consuming Israel for their idolatry, but this does not prove that the truth obtains only in particular circumstances. The immediate occasion of the words was the request of an individual. Moses said unto the Lord, "I beseech Thee, show me Thy glory." The 19th verse, which seems to be an answer to Moses' request, is a statement of the character of God considered in Himself: "I will make all my goodness pass before thee, and I will proclaim the name of the Lord before thee." This cannot mean God's goodness to *Israel*, but the goodness of the Divine character *generally*. It is not spoken to the nation, but to an individual, and that in answer to a particular request. The words are to be taken in their general sense, then, as expressive of Divine attributes. In fact, the whole verse is designed to state a proposition in regard to God which is always and universally true—that God is good and sovereign. God was showing Moses the "back parts" of His "glory," and it is all forced interpretation to confine the declarations to a particular form of the Divine goodness, as Macknight and Bishop Sumner have done. This is limiting what God has left absolute. There is no foundation for Sumner's remark, that this verse forms "the assurance revealed by God Himself to Moses that He had separated the Hebrew nation from all the people on the face of the earth;" for there is not a syllable about such a separation in the passage itself or in the immediate context.

The next quotation from Exodus (ix. 16) affords just as little ground for a national interpretation. It is manifest that the words themselves regard Pharaoh only as an individual: "And in very deed for this cause have I raised *thee* up for to show in *thee* my power," etc. It was Pharaoh's heart that was hardened, and the destruction of the Egyptians is represented as a punishment to Pharaoh himself. It was Pharaoh alone that could let Israel go, and Pharaoh is answerable for keeping them in bondage. Pharaoh is rejected from no national privileges; he is brought forward as a gross and flagitious sinner, stiffening his neck against God and setting at naught His authority. The whole transaction has not the remotest tendency to show that God elected Israel and passed by Egypt. God did not design to illustrate this principle in His dealings with Pharaoh, but to show His power and justice in casting down the proud and punishing the guilty; and for this purpose the case of this monarch is frequently alluded to in the sacred writings. True, Pharaoh was the head of his nation, and his guilt seriously affected his subjects; but how does this prove that God deals with him only as the representative of his people? The private sins of kings and emperors at the present day often involve their respective nations in sufferings and war, and yet their sins are personal and individual. Upon the whole, then, a correct view of the passages in the Old Testament does not bind us to believe that they have any necessary reference to the dealings of God with nations in respect to external privileges. Some necessarily apply to *individuals*, and all may be safely interpreted of them. The only possible foundation, therefore, on which a national interpretation of this chapter can rest is, to say the least, precarious and doubtful.

[2.] But should it be admitted that an election to the blessings or privileges of the external theocracy is all that is meant, the difficulty is by no means removed. "A choice," as Professor Hodge justly remarks, "to the blessings of the theocracy, that is, of a knowledge and worship of the true God, involved in a multitude of cases, at least, a choice to eternal life, as a choice to the means is a choice to the end. And it is only so far as these advantages were a means to this end that their value was worth considering." And again: "Is there any more objection to God's choosing men to a great than a small blessing on the ground of His own good pleasure? The foundation of the objection is not the character of the blessings we are chosen to inherit, but the sovereign nature of the choice. Of course it is not met by making these blessings greater or less."

[3.] The whole scope of the Epistle goes to show that the Apostle is not speaking of a choice to external privileges. The first eight chapters are occupied in the doctrinal discussion of justification—the guilt and depravity which it supposes in our race, and the glorious blessings which are inseparably connected with it. These blessings are not mere outward privileges, but are *saving graces*—purity, holiness, peace with God and the certain hope of eternal life. These blessings are not bestowed on *nations*, but on *individuals*. It had, however, been a favourite prejudice of the Jewish nation that all the blessings of the Messiah's kingdom were to be exclusively confined to them, in virtue of God's covenant with Abraham. The Apostle, therefore, in the ninth chapter, begins the discussion of the question, Who are to be the subjects of Christ's kingdom? Who are to be partakers of that "pardon, peace, and eternal life" which are found only in Jesus? All the previous parts of the Epistle have been speaking of only one kind of privileges, and that the saving blessings of the Gospel. It is a violent presumption to suppose that Paul here drops all consideration of them, and begins a discussion about national advantages which have no conceivable connection with the scope and design of the Epistle. Unconnected as Paul is thought by many to be in his writings, such a transition would be altogether unpardonable. The question plainly before him was, Who shall be saved? Who shall be recipients of the hopes of the Gospel? This question is very naturally and obviously connected with the previous discussion. As in the solution of this question he was about to announce a very unwelcome truth to his brethren, he commences the chapter with cordial professions of attachment and love, manifested by the deep interest which he took in their spiritual welfare. He then delicately approaches the main point by anticipating an objection, verse 6: "Not as though the Word of God had taken none effect." That is, God was not bound by His promises to Abraham to bestow the blessings of the Gospel on the Jews, considered merely as natural descendants of the patriarch. Why? "They are not all Israel which are of Israel;" that is, the promises were made only to the spiritual seed, but all the natural descendants of Israel are not the spiritual seed. He then proves that natural descent did not entitle to the saving blessings of the Gospel, by a reference to the cases of Ishmael and Isaac, and of Esau and Jacob. The question then recurs, Who are the recipients of the promises? The answer is given in verse 8, which amounts to this: "Those who are born by a special interposition of God are the true individuals to whom the promises are effectual." But are these individuals confined to any particular nation, or found among any particular people? No. Ver. 24: They are those "whom He hath called, not of the Jews only, but also of the Gentiles." And here he begins the full disclosure of the solemn fact that many of his own countrymen, in spite of their privileges, would fail of eternal life, while many of the Gentiles would be admitted to the blessings of Messiah's kingdom. The observation of the Apostle in verse 24 is utterly inconsistent with the idea of a national election to external privileges, for he pointedly declares that the blessings of which he was then speaking are confined to no nation, but are extended to called or chosen ones in every nation: "Those whom He hath called, not of the Jews only, but also of the Gentiles"—those *persons* or *individuals* in every nation whom He hath chosen to eternal life. The Apostle here, as elsewhere, tells us that "there is no difference," no distinction in Christ's kingdom, of Jew and Greek—that "neither circumcision availeth anything, nor uncircumcision, but a new creature." To illustrate this great principle, that the recipients of the blessings of the Gospel are just those whom God chooses in His sovereign pleasure, is the design of the ninth chapter and the two following. In applying it to the Jews, he was obliged to reveal the rejection of many of his countrymen, and to establish, contrary to their prejudices, the calling and conversion of the Gentiles.

To any candid reader of this Epistle the evidence is cumulative that Paul does not refer to the choice of nations to peculiar privileges. In verse 3 he says: "For I could wish that myself were accursed from Christ for my brethren, my kinsmen according to the flesh." Now could the "heaviness" of Paul's heart on account of his brethren have been so great as to prompt such language as this, if his brethren after all were losing nothing but the privilege of being the exclusive people of God? Would Paul grieve so seriously and deeply because the Gentiles were admitted to equal privileges with the Jews? Can it be supposed for a moment that such language was or could have been penned by the inspired Apostle, when the whole grievance was that the middle wall of partition between Jew and Gentile was broken down, and that God was dispensing His Gospel to the ends of the earth? No! Paul saw a cloud filled with wrath—a black cloud of vindicatory justice affecting the eternal interests of his countrymen—ready to burst upon their heads; he saw many of them sealed up under the terrible judgment of judicial blindness, and in spite of their privileges going down to hell; and this it was which racked his heart with agony, and drew forth his thrilling expressions of sympathy and grief. He envied not the Gentiles; on the contrary, he makes their calling and conversion matters of solemn doxology and thanksgiving to God; but he did lament, deeply and sorely lament, that so many of his countrymen were cut off from the hopes of eternal life.

"The choice, moreover, is between vessels of mercy and vessels of wrath—vessels of mercy chosen unto '*glory*,' not unto church privileges, and vessels of wrath who were made the example of God's displeasure against sin."

In verses 30, 31, Paul states definitely the privileges which this election respected—justification by faith and its attendant blessings. "What shall we say then? That the Gentiles, which followed not after righteousness, have attained to righteousness, even the righteousness which is of faith. But Israel, which followed after the law of righteousness, hath not attained to the law of righteousness." It would certainly be a gross abuse of language to apply the phrases "righteousness which is of faith, law of righteousness," to mere external privileges; these phrases manifestly refer to the saving blessings of the Gospel, and yet it is this righteousness which a majority of the Jews forfeited, and which the Gentiles obtained by election.

The tenth chapter shows that the rejection of the Jews implied the loss of saving privileges. Paul commences it with a prayer that they "might be *saved*"—not that their national privileges might be retained, but that they might receive the gift of eternal life. He shows that they lose *justification*, not church privileges, by rejecting Christ and clinging to their own righteousness. Much of the chapter is taken up in discussing the plan of salvation and the nature and grounds of saving faith, but not a word concerns national privileges. The eleventh chapter bears a plain testimony to the fact that Paul was discussing matters of eternal life and eternal death. I shall just refer to the first verse. Here Paul denies that God has rejected the whole Jewish nation, and brings himself forward as an instance of a Jew who was not rejected. If the question respected only national privileges, an argument drawn from the case of an individual would be sheer nonsense. How could Paul possess *national* privileges? But Paul means to say that some of the Jews will be *saved*, or that all will not be lost, and in proof of this proposition he brings himself forward as an example of a converted Jew. That this is his meaning will appear from a comparison of verses 5 and 6, in which he asserts that there is a chosen remnant who will be saved, while the great majority of the nation was blinded. And in the conclusion of this protracted discussion, I would only observe that the interpretation for which I contend derives no small support from the objections which the Apostle considers against his own doctrines. They are those which in all ages have been urged against personal election to eternal life, but I do not know that they have ever been applied to the cases of nations or communities blessed above others with peculiar privileges.

These considerations are sufficient, it would seem, to satisfy any candid mind that in the ninth of Romans the Apostle is treating of a personal election to eternal life, and if so the texts are in point, and render it absolutely certain that election is wholly unconditional and sovereign. In fact, Arminians are aware of this, and therefore labour so strenuously to distort these Scriptures from their obvious application. In verse 11 it is said: "For the children being not yet born, neither having done any good or evil, that the purpose of God according to election might stand, not of works, but of Him that calleth, it was said unto her, The elder shall serve the younger." If language has any meaning at all, these verses teach that there is no other foundation of election than the mere mercy and goodness of God, which embrace whom He chooses of Adam's ruined race, without paying the least regard to works. Again, verse 15, it is said: "I will have mercy on whom I will have mercy, and I will have compassion on whom I will have compassion." "God," says Calvin, "proved by this very declaration that He is debtor to none; that every blessing bestowed upon the elect flows from gratuitous kindness, and is freely granted to whom He pleases; that no cause which is superior to His own will can be conceived or devised why He entertains kind feelings or manifests kind actions to some of the children of Adam and not to all." "So, then, it is not of him that willeth nor of him that runneth, but of God that showeth mercy." Verse 16. "These words," says Professor Hodge, "are not intended to teach that the efforts of men for the attainment of salvation are useless, much less do they teach that such efforts should not be made. They simply declare that the result is not to be attributed to them—that the reason why one man secures the blessing and another does not is not to be found in the greater ardour of desire or intensity of effort in the one than in the other, but the reason is in God."

The last passage which I shall quote to sustain the gratuitous election of God is found in Romans xi. 5-7: "Even so then at this present time also there is a remnant according to the election of grace. And if by grace then it is no more of works, otherwise grace is no more grace. But if it be of works, then it is no more grace; otherwise work is no more work. What then? Israel hath not obtained that which he seeketh for, but the election hath obtained it, and the rest were blinded." In order to avoid the force of this passage an interpretation has been devised utterly at war with all the principles of language. The gratuitous election here spoken of has been twisted to mean an election of *faith* as the condition of salvation rather than works. Out of all the possible plans which God might have adopted, He has selected that which makes faith in Christ the medium of justification, and this choice of faith is entirely gratuitous, faith having no more claims upon God's favour than works. "*Risum teneatis amici?*" It is sufficiently plain that the Apostle is not discussing the election of a principle, but of men; "the election"—that is, the elect or chosen ones—"have obtained it, and the rest were blinded." Can he mean that all the other possible schemes of salvation which God might have laid down instead of faith were blinded? And what strange jargon is it to talk of electing a principle! These pitiful subterfuges show how hard it is to close the eyes against a truth which Paul so plainly teaches—the solemn truth that God is free and sovereign in the distribution of His favours.

The separate points in the doctrine of election having been thus discussed, it may be well to make a few remarks on the inseparable doctrine of *reprobation*. The very fact that all men were not elected shows that some were passed by. This passing them by, or refusing to elect them, and leaving them under a righteous sentence of condemnation, constitutes reprobation. If election is personal, eternal and absolute, reprobation must possess these qualities also. There is this difference between them, however: election finds the objects of mercy unfit for eternal life, and puts forth a positive agency in preparing them for glory; reprobation finds the objects of wrath already fitted for destruction, and only withholds that influence which alone can transform them. It is not intended to deny here that cases of judicial blindness occur in which the sinner's heart is hardened. The example of Pharaoh is a case in point. But judicial blindness is a *punishment* inflicted in which God acts as a righteous Judge dealing with men for their obstinacy; whereas reprobation is strictly an act of sovereignty in which God refuses to save, and leaves the sinner to the free course of law. Our Standards afford no sort of shelter to the Hopkinsian error that the decree of reprobation consists in God's determining to fit a certain number of mankind for eternal damnation, and that the Divine agency is as positively employed in men's bad volitions and actions as in their good. These doctrines, we know, have been frequently charged upon us with no little violence and acrimony, but we have always adhered to the position of the Bible, that God is not the author of evil; and we believe that there is no inconsistency in supposing that

God may determine an action as a natural event, and yet be unstained with its sin and pollution. That the Scriptures teach the doctrine of reprobation, as depending on the sovereignty and good pleasure of God, is manifest from the following passages—Matt. xi. 25: "At that time Jesus answered and said, I thank thee, O Father, Lord of heaven and earth, because Thou hast hid these things from the wise and prudent, and hast revealed them unto babes." Here our blessed Saviour addresses the Father by a word highly expressive of sovereignty, and refers the illumination of some and the blindness of others to His Father's will alone: "Even so, Father, for so it seemed good in Thy sight." Rom. ix. 18: "Therefore hath He mercy on whom He will have mercy, and whom He will He hardeneth." If it be said that this refers to the judicial blindness with which Pharaoh was struck, let it be remembered that no punishment of any sort would or could be inflicted on the wicked, if they were not left under the sentence of condemnation originally pronounced upon the race. The fact of their reprobation leaves them in that state to which punishment was justly due, and the argument of Paul is that some are left in that state and others not by the sovereign pleasure of God. Verse 21: "Hath not the potter power over the clay, of the same lump to make one vessel unto honour and another to dishonour?" Jude 4: "For there are certain men crept in unawares, who were before of old ordained to this condemnation—ungodly men, turning the grace of our God into lasciviousness, and denying the only Lord God and our Lord Jesus Christ." In fact, every passage of Scripture which teaches that any will be finally lost, teaches at the same time, by necessary implication, if the doctrine of election be true, that they were eternally reprobated or left out of the number of the elect. The two doctrines stand or fall together.

Independently of the direct and immediate testimony which the Scriptures bear in support of eternal and unconditional election and reprobation, there is an indirect teaching of them by the inculcation of doctrines in which they are necessarily involved—such as the foreknowledge, providence and independence of God, and the total depravity of man. There is no way in which these truths can be reconciled with the Arminian or Semi-Pelagian scheme. Foreknowledge of a future event means, if it mean anything, that the event is regarded as absolutely certain in the Divine mind, and that it cannot possibly happen otherwise than as God foresees it will happen. How the absolute certainty of events is consistent with contingency, which necessarily implies uncertainty, I leave it to the advocates of that strange hypothesis to determine. The Scripture account of foreknowledge is simple and consistent: God foreknows all things because He decrees them, and hence the terms are frequently interchanged. Peter says that Christ was delivered to death "by the determinate counsel and foreknowledge of God;" that is, by the purpose and appointment of God. The doctrine of providence, by which God is represented as acting upon a plan of which He knew the end from the beginning, cannot be conceived at all if we deny the existence of a fixed and definite purpose in the Divine mind. In fact, the denial of an eternal purpose is a virtual dethronement of God in His own dominions; and the voice of reason remonstrates, as loudly as the voice of revelation, against the ruinous results to which such a denial must lead. The will of God becomes fearfully dependent upon the will of man, and the counsel of God must be formed and modelled upon the wisdom of the creature. The truth is, Arminianism declares an open war upon the essential attributes of God, and, if carried out into all its necessary consequences, it would lead at once to blank and cheerless Atheism.

The account which the Bible gives us of human corruption and depravity is utterly inconsistent with the scheme which makes election, in any measure, dependent upon the faith or perseverance of man. Sinners, in their natural state, are said to be "dead in trespasses and sins." "Every imagination of man's heart is only evil, and that continually." The necessary consequence of depravity is an utter inability to think a good thought or to perform a good action. The understanding is darkened, the affections alienated, the will bent on evil; in short, the man is dead, spiritually dead, and therefore cannot believe or do any holy action until quickened and renewed by the supernatural grace of God. Hence our Saviour says, "No man can come to Me, except the Father which hath sent Me draw him." If this, then, be the true state of the case, all who believe are drawn by the Father, being utterly unable to do it of themselves. Why does God draw one and not another?—for it is manifest that all are not believers. Every Christian will promptly ascribe his calling and conversion to the mere grace of God, and this is election. The man who rejects election is bound to reject the scriptural account of human depravity if he would maintain consistency of opinion. He may resort to the superficial theory of common grace, but that will not relieve him of his difficulty. The Scriptures attribute *every* good disposition to God, and so the disposition not to resist common grace must after all be referred to special grace. No Christian would ever have dreamed of Arminianism if he had been guided only by his own experience; hence, when the love of system is laid aside, we find all pious Arminians sober and honest-hearted Calvinists, as their earnest prayers for grace and assistance unequivocally declare.

Another source of argument on this subject is the whole course of Divine Providence, which shows that God is absolutely sovereign in the distribution of His favours. The Lord does not deal with all men alike. The election of the Jews to church privileges, and to their relation to God as His peculiar people, was founded solely on His gratuitous mercy. Moses again and again admonishes them that their exaltation was due to God's unmerited love, and the more effectually to check their pride and humble their hearts, "he reproaches them with having deserved no favour, but as being a stiff-necked and rebellious people." At this day millions of our fellow-men, no worse by nature than we, and no more unworthy of Divine compassion, are sunk in idolatry, degradation and ruin, while we enjoy the light of the Gospel and the privileges of the sanctuary. Why is this? It can only be resolved into the sovereign pleasure of God. Even amongst us some are born to affluence, honour and distinction, while others by the sweat of their brow can hardly procure a scanty subsistence for themselves and their families. Some are endowed with extraordinary powers of intellect, while others exhibit the melancholy spectacle of drivelling idiotcy. Why these distinctions among men whose moral characters are naturally the same? No other answer can be given but the sovereign pleasure of God. The Divine sovereignty in the distribution of favours is written in broad and palpable characters upon all His dealings with men and nations in the present course of His providence, and shall it be thought a thing incredible that the same principle should extend to their eternal interests? Has God the right to bestow or withhold temporal blessings, and not the right to bestow eternal blessings? The very same objections which may be raised against an election to life lie with all their force against the inequalities of Providence. The very same arguments which are adduced to prove that one man cannot be chosen to spiritual privileges while another is rejected, apply just as strongly to the point that one man cannot be born rich and another poor. The objections are raised to the nature of the choice, and not to the character of the blessings bestowed or withheld.

There is no other scheme which can be reconciled with the doctrine of salvation by free grace. If anything be left for the sinner to do, no matter how slight or insignificant the work may be, the blessing ceases to be the *gift* of God and becomes a matter of pactional debt. The Apostle testifies, however, that eternal life is the gift of God through the righteousness of Christ. Arminians endeavour to avoid the difficulty by maintaining that the intrinsic value of salvation far exceeds the merit of our works, so that the latter cannot be regarded as deserving the former; and inasmuch as our faith and repentance are not a strict equivalent for the blessings of life, in a comparative sense our works are not meritorious. But suppose a man should expose for sale an article worth a thousand dollars at the small price of one cent; the man who pays the one cent becomes entitled to the article on the score of debt just as completely as though he had paid the full value. The principle of debt is just this: a reward in consideration of something done. It matters not how slight that something may be. Now, when salvation is said to be by grace in opposition to works or debt, it excludes everything in the sinner himself as the ground of his title to it, and leaves it to the mere disposal of God, so that it shall not be of him that willeth nor of him that runneth, but of God that showeth mercy; and this is the very principle upon which election turns.

III. When the doctrines of absolute and unconditional election and reprobation are proclaimed, the perverse and rebellious hearts of the children of men are ready to conjure up a thousand objections against them. There is seldom any attempt made to overthrow the mass of positive, direct testimony in their favour, drawn alike from the Scriptures of truth, the character of God, the experience of the Christian and the uniform course of Divine Providence, because this is felt to be absolutely impossible. A less ingenuous method is resorted to. The prejudices of the carnal heart against the truth are diligently fostered; horrible consequences, revolting alike to reason and common sense, are perversely deduced; hobgoblin terrors are excited; bold and reckless assertion is substituted for argument; and all this miserable artifice is passed off as a refutation of Calvinism. Take away from many Arminian writers their gross misrepresentations and disgraceful personal abuse, their pompous rhodomontade against the " horrible decree," and their fiery declamation against consequences which exist nowhere but in their own brains, and what is left will be but a small portion compared with the whole. It seems to be forgotten that mere *objections,* which constitute at best but a negative testimony, cannot destroy positive evidence. If the truth is to be sacrificed to difficulties, what will become of the doctrines of the Trinity, of the incarnation of the Son, and of the residence of the Spirit in the hearts of believers? A thousand objections have been raised against these glorious truths just as plausible and fully as forcible as the objections of the Arminians against the doctrine of election; and yet no Christian would think of doubting them, because, though encumbered with difficulties, they are sustained by adequate testimony and confirmed by positive evidence.

The great source of error in regard to Divine things is ignorance. We are ignorant of God as He is in Himself, and ignorant of the full economy of His government. "Ye do err, not knowing the Scriptures nor the power of God," was the reply of our Saviour to the captious Sadducees when they brought forward what they conceived to be an unanswerable argument against the resurrection of the dead. The same reply may be justly given to those who are rebellious against the sovereignty of God, and it ought to be sufficient. If the Scriptures teach the doctrine, we may rest satisfied that all our difficulties arise from our ignorance; not from the subject itself in its own intrinsic nature, but from our limited faculties and still more limited knowledge. With this general observation the whole subject might be dismissed; but as a mode so summary of treating objections might have a tendency to magnify them in the minds of some beyond their just importance, it will probably be well to give the more prominent and common ones a fuller discussion. Let it not be supposed, however, that objections lie exclusively against the Calvinistic system. Men make but a poor exchange in the way of difficulties when they renounce the good old doctrines of the Reformation for the superficial schemes which depend essentially upon the sinner's free will. Arminians talk as confidently of the difficulties of Calvinism as if their own system were perfectly disencumbered of all objection, when the truth is that it has many difficulties in common with Calvinism, besides others peculiar to itself.

The leading objections to the doctrine of election are drawn from the moral character of God and from the moral agency of man. We shall consider them in order.

First. The attributes of God which are supposed to be injured by this doctrine are, His *justice,* His *impartiality,* and His *truth.* It is enough to make the blood run cold to read the terms of shocking and revolting blasphemy in which these objections are sometimes brought forward; and, I must believe, in many instances only for effect.

1. It is a standing theme of Arminian declamation that election and reprobation are utterly inconsistent with the justice of God; in other words, that God cannot be sovereign in fixing the destinies of men without ceasing to be just. It seems to be forgotten that there are two recorded notices in Scripture of this very objection: (1.) "What shall we say then? Is there unrighteousness with God? God forbid." Rom. ix. 14. Paul had, as we have already seen, been asserting in unlimited terms the very doctrine for which we are contending, and here, in verse 14, notices an objection which he was sure the flesh would bring up: "Is there unrighteousness with God?" "How prodigious," says Calvin, "is the frenzy of the human mind, which rather accuses God of injustice than convicts itself of being influenced by blindness!" It is observable that Paul, in answering this objection, simply appeals to the Scriptures of eternal truth. He shows that God, in so many words, claimed to be sovereign in the distribution of His favours, and appeals to a celebrated instance in which that sovereignty, in the withholding of favours, was actually exercised. He takes it for granted that the Scriptures are true, and that whatever God does must necessarily be right. No matter in what difficulties or obscurity the Divine dispensations may seem to be involved, yet God is essentially *just,* and therefore cannot do an unrighteous act. Now, the Scriptures *do* declare that God " hath mercy

on whom He will have mercy, and whom He will He hardeneth;" therefore such a procedure cannot possibly be *unjust.* God does it, *and on that account* it must be right. This is the sum and substance of Paul's answer to the objection, and it ought to be satisfactory to every pious mind. "The thought," as Calvin well observes in explaining the answer of Paul, "deserves the utmost execration which believes injustice to exist in the Fountain of all righteousness." And again: "The apology produced by Paul to show that God was not unjust, because He is merciful to whom He thinks fit, might appear cold; but because God's own authority, as it requires the aid and support of no other, is abundantly sufficient of itself, Paul was content to leave the Judge of quick and dead to avenge His own right." I cannot forbear to notice here how conclusively this objection evinces that Paul's doctrine and ours are precisely the same. "It clearly proves that the cause of God's rejecting some and electing others is to be sought for merely in His will and purpose; for if the difference between these two characters depended upon a regard to their works, Paul would have discussed the question concerning God's injustice in a very unnecessary manner, since no suspicion could possibly arise against the perfect justice of the Disposer of all things if He treats every son and daughter of Adam according to their works." If the Scriptures do really teach this doctrine, it cannot injure the justice of God, for the same Scriptures as clearly teach that God is *just.* If we have any regard for the authority of inspiration, we are bound to believe *both* truths. Suppose we cannot reconcile them or understand how they are reconciled, what then? It only follows that we are blind and short-sighted, and "cannot see afar off." The objection, then, according to the showing of an inspired Apostle, is good for nothing. But (2.) we have another authority on this subject. The Son of God Himself has condescended to notice this objection, and, in effect, to pronounce it utterly worthless. He put forth a parable, recorded in the twentieth chapter of Matthew, for the purpose of showing that God might distribute peculiar and special favours to some, without being guilty of any sort of injustice to others.

The scope of this whole parable is definitely stated in the sixteenth verse: "So the last shall be first, and the first last; for many be called, but few chosen." The terms *first* and *last*, in a spiritual sense, are applied to those who, in the judgment of men, would naturally be expected to be first or last in receiving the blessings of the Gospel. The "*first*" are those who, in consequence of peculiar endowments or adventitious circumstances, would seem to have the fairest claims upon the Divine clemency. They are sober, intelligent, respectable moral men. The "*last*" are those who notoriously have no shadow of claim, even in the carnal judgment of men, upon the compassion of God. They are decidedly and openly wicked. The moral and scrupulous but yet self-righteous Jews may be taken as a fair specimen of those whom our Saviour meant by the "first;" the abandoned publicans and harlots may be regarded as appropriate examples of those whom He intended by the "last." We should have expected *a priori* that the rigid descendants of Abraham would give a more ready and welcome reception to the Gospel than the profligate publicans or abandoned harlots; but yet facts, and the positive assertion of the Saviour, show that the last were first, and the first last. The same general truth is taught by Paul, 1 Cor. i. 26, 27: "For ye see your calling, brethren, how that not many wise men after the flesh, not many mighty, not many noble are called; but God has chosen the foolish things of the world to confound the wise, and God has chosen the weak things of the world to confound the things which are mighty," etc. Here Paul's wise men after the flesh, his noble and mighty, are the same with our Saviour's first, while his foolish and weak are the same with our Saviour's last. What is the reason that the first are last and the last first? "Many are called, but few chosen." "God hath *chosen*," etc., says Paul. The meaning, then, of verse 16, which contains the scope of the whole parable, is simply this: While all are freely invited to partake of the blessings of the Gospel, yet the sovereign choice of God applies them effectually, not to those who, according to the carnal judgment of men, would seem to have the greatest claim on the Divine mercy, but to those whose utter destitution of all shadow of claim would render God's grace the more remarkably conspicuous. To illustrate this principle, which has been frequently exemplified in the history of the Church, and to show that it is by no means inconsistent with the Divine justice, seems to be the special purpose of the parable. Our Saviour begins: "For the kingdom of heaven is like unto a man that is an householder, which went out early in the morning to hire labourers into his vineyard." Ver. 1. That is, the principle on which the saving blessings of the Gospel are conferred on men may be illustrated by the case of a householder in employing and rewarding labourers in his vineyard. "And when he had agreed with the labourers for a penny a day, he sent them into his vineyard. And he went out about the third hour, and saw others standing idle in the market-place, and said unto them, Go ye also into the vineyard, and whatsoever is right I will give you; and they went their way. Again he went out about the sixth and ninth hour and did likewise. And about the eleventh hour he went out and found others standing idle, and saith unto them, Why stand ye here all the day idle? They say unto him, Because no man hath hired us. He saith unto them, Go ye also into the vineyard, and whatsoever is right that shall ye receive." Verses 2-7. The circumstances of standing in the market-place and hiring labourers are merely ornamental, being designed to give life and costume to the narrative, but they have no immediate connection with its scope. It is idle, therefore, to attempt to seek, in our spiritual relations to God, anything to correspond with these minute particulars. The general truth designed to be conveyed is that the Lord is our common Master, and that we have no claims whatever upon Him except those to which He gives rise by His own gratuitous promise. The labourers had no claim to the patronage and bounty of the householder, and after he had employed them they had no right to expect a liberality from him beyond the terms of their engagement. Their relations to him required on his part nothing more than *sheer justice*. This was all they could ask. It may be asked here, What is meant by labouring in the vineyard? I answer that our Saviour by this meant simply to designate the relations in which men stand to God. These are twofold—legal or gracious, according to the covenant under which men are. As the labourers in the vineyard were dealt with on the principles of justice or mercy, according to the light or relationship in which the householder chose to regard them, so men are dealt with by God upon the same principles, according to the relations in which they stand to Him. The labouring in the vineyard is a circumstance in the narrative designed to teach only a relationship, without specifying precisely what it is, or at all intimating that it was the same in all. This is most obvious from the sequel of the narrative. Suffice it to say, that we all stand to God in the general relationship of subjects to a sovereign, without having any right or title to clemency and grace. "So when the even was come, the Lord of the vineyard said unto his steward, Call the labourers and give them their hire, beginning from the last unto the first. And when they came that were hired about the eleventh hour, they received every man a penny. But when the first came they supposed that they should have received more, but they likewise received every man a penny." Verses 8–10. Here the point of resemblance between the kingdom of heaven and the householder is introduced, and here the *principle* on which the destinies of men are determined is clearly developed. That principle is simply this: God does injustice to none, while He is peculiarly merciful to some. The householder gave the labourers first employed their *due*. He was just to them, he withheld nothing to which they had any claim. So God will eventually give reprobate sinners their *due;* "the wages of sin is death;" they virtually agreed for this, for they knew the necessary consequence of guilt, and therefore God does them no injustice. On the other hand, the labourers last employed, who represent the elect, are treated far beyond their deserts; they are dealt with on a principle of mercy, and through grace receive what they have no personal right to expect. It will be observed here that the labourers first employed answer, in the spiritual sense of the narrative, to those who seem to have some claims to the clemency and grace of God, while the labourers last employed answer to those who are notoriously destitute of all shadow of claim. It will be further observed that the penny simply denotes the idea of *wages*, for that was the customary hire of a day-labourer. From the fact that all received a penny we are simply to understand that all were fairly and honourably reckoned with. Some were dealt with on the principle of justice, receiving the stipulated wages of day-labourers; others on the principle of mercy, receiving what they had no right to expect. In a spiritual sense the penny in one case would be death, the stipulated wages of sin; in the other, eternal life, the stipulated reward of grace. "And when they had received it, they murmured against the good man of the house, saying, These last have wrought but one hour, and thou hast made them equal unto us, which have borne the burden and heat of the day." Verses 11, 12. The force of this objection is this: We have greater claims upon your kindness than the others; we have been moral, upright men, and in many cases had a zeal for God, while these others have in too many instances been mere publicans and harlots, the ignorant and abandoned of society. Our claim is as much greater than theirs as the claim of labourers who have "borne the burden and heat of the day" is greater than the claim of idlers who have laboured only one hour. They no more compare with us in the qualifications suited to recommend them to God than such an idler can compare with such a labourer.

The men, it will be observed, who had laboured longest in the vineyard were literally first, and so had, it would seem, the fairest claim on the favour of the householder, but he judged differently, and consequently made the last first: "But he answered one of them and said, Friend, I do thee no wrong. Didst thou not agree with me for a penny? Take that thine is and go thy way. I will give unto this last even as unto thee. Is it not lawful for me to do what I will with mine own? Is thine eye evil because I am good? So the last shall be first, and the first last; for many be called, but few chosen." Verses 13–16. Here the proposition is flatly maintained that goodness to one implies no injustice to another in the case supposed. The reasons are—(1.) Because God is absolutely sovereign, and can do as He pleases in perfect consistency with justice. (2.) Because sinners have no claims upon God whatever. (3.) Because they are actually dealt with according to the demands of justice—just as much so as if they had stipulated with God for the punishment which they will ultimately receive.

To say nothing of the first, the two last points of our Saviour's answer contain a triumphant refutation of this vaunting objection, and therefore we shall consider them a little more particularly. The *first* position is that sinners have no sort of claim upon the Divine clemency. It has been already shown sufficiently that men in the decree of election and reprobation were regarded as fallen in Adam. The fall, being a breach of the covenant of law, brought the whole race under the sentence of condemnation and death. "By the offence of one judgment came upon all men to condemnation." Rom. v. 18. "And were by nature the children of wrath even as others." Eph. ii. 3. The only question of any importance here is, Was this a *righteous* sentence? The fact that God pronounced it is a sufficient answer. Now if the whole race were righteously condemned in the first instance, there could be no injustice in leaving them under the sentence and in actually inflicting the curse.

If the sentence itself was right, the execution of it cannot be wrong. God might, then, most justly and righteously have left every son and daughter of Adam to the terrible course of law, and if He could have left all indiscriminately, surely He can leave some, and yet be just and righteous still. But the sinner is not only legally and righteously condemned, but he is also desperately corrupt. His heart is deceitful above all things, being wholly alienated from God, and holiness, and heaven. He is absolutely *fit* by native depravity for nothing but banishment and eternal separation from his Maker. His mind is *enmity* against God, and therefore if introduced into heaven without a moral renovation he would be supremely miserable. His deep and malignant depravity is an object of abhorrence to God and to all holy beings, and the fact that he has destroyed himself cuts him off from all claim to the sympathy and compassion of the Being whom he has so grievously offended. The following remarks of Calvin deserve a serious and attentive consideration, and they are purposely introduced because that great and good man has been egregiously calumniated on this point: "Therefore, if any one attack us with such an inquiry as this, Why God has from the beginning predestinated some men to death who, not yet being brought into existence, could not yet deserve the sentence of death, we will reply by asking them in return, What they suppose God owes to man if He chooses to judge of him from his own nature? As we are all corrupted by sin, we must necessarily be odious to God, and that not from tyrannical cruelty, but in the most equitable estimation of justice. If all whom the Lord predestinates to death are in their natural condition liable to the sentence of death, what injustice do they complain of receiving from him? Let all the sons of Adam come forward; let them all contend and dispute with their Creator because by His eternal providence they were previously to their birth adjudged to endless misery. What murmur will they be able to raise against this vindication when God, on the other hand, shall call them to a review of themselves? If they have all been taken from a corrupt mass, it is no wonder that they are subject to condemnation. Let them not, therefore, accuse God of injustice if His eternal decree has destined them to death, to which they feel themselves, whatever be their desire or aversion, spontaneously led forward by their own nature. Hence appears the perverseness of their disposition to murmur, because they intentionally suppress the cause of condemnation which they are constrained to acknowledge in themselves, hoping to excuse themselves by charging it upon God." These two facts—that sinners are by nature odious and loathsome to God, and are under a righteous sentence of condemnation and death—establish beyond all doubt the position of the Saviour that none have any claims upon the Divine clemency or mercy. The *second* position is, that reprobate sinners are actually dealt with according to the demands of justice. God withholds nothing from them to which they have any claim, and He inflicts a punishment no more severe than they had every reason to expect. They are doomed to hell, but is not that the righteous allotment of the wicked? They are banished everlastingly from the presence of God, but did they not despise His authority, and were they not alienated in heart and affection from Him? Where is or can be the injustice of punishing the wicked? It is true that God withholds from them saving grace, because they have no right to expect it and He is under no obligation to bestow it. There is no *injustice* here—no more than there is *injustice* in my withholding alms from a beggar who despises me and calumniates my family.

Such seem to be the sentiments contained in the reply of our adorable Redeemer. But it may be said that justice is violated in the case of the elect, because they do not receive the punishment which is due to them. The answer is obvious: their glorious Substitute and Surety became a curse for them in order to redeem them from the curse of the law. Jesus suffered in their name and stead, and completely satisfied the demands of justice, so that God can be just and yet the justifier of all who believe on His Son. In neither case, then, is the justice of God violated. Upon the reprobate it has free course, and they endure in their own proper persons the tremendous penalty of the law. Upon the elect it has free course in the person of their adorable Head, and He endured the unutterable curse of the law. May we not, therefore, triumphantly ask with Paul, " Is there unrighteousness with God ? God forbid."

I know that there are caricatures of Calvinism which represent God as having made man for the specific purpose of damnation, and as putting forth a positive agency in fitting him for hell. The reprobate are represented as poor, helpless, dependent creatures in the hands of a bloodthirsty tyrant, who, in the first instance, makes them sinners contrary to their own will, absolutely forcing them into transgression, and then, in spite of all their efforts, drives them to hell, that he may delight himself with their torments; and in such caricatures the reprobate are often represented as most *amiable* and *lovely* creatures, suited by their excellencies to soften a heart of stone; but yet the cruel God of the Calvinists frowns upon them and sends them down to hell. These gross and slanderous caricatures might pass unnoticed if they were not palmed off upon the ignorant and unthinking as the genuine doctrines of Presbyterianism. And the worst part of the whole is, that when Presbyterians disavow them, instead of being believed or regarded as fair judges of their own principles, they are only charged with disgraceful cowardice, or taunted with being ashamed of their doctrines. If it is to such caricatures that the charge of injustice is so confidently brought up, I have no motive to attempt an answer. It is enough that the charge cannot be sustained against the genuine doctrines of the Church.

2. Another very common but groundless objection to Calvinism is, that it imputes partiality to God, or makes Him a respecter of persons, while the Scriptures, on the other hand,

declare that God is "no respecter of persons." Now, there is no inconsistency at all in God's appointing some to life and others to death of His own sovereign will, and at the same time being "no respecter of persons," in the scriptural sense of the phrase. "By the word *person* the Scripture signifies not a man, but those things in a man which, being conspicuous to the eyes, usually conciliate favour, honour and dignity, or attract hatred, contempt and disgrace. Such are riches, wealth, power, nobility, magistracy, country, elegance of form, on the one hand; and on the other hand, poverty, necessity, ignoble birth, slovenliness, contempt and the like. Thus Peter and Paul declare that God is not a respecter of persons, because He makes no difference between the Jew and the Greek, to reject one and receive the other merely on account of his nation. So James uses the same language when he means to assert that God in His judgment pays no regard to riches. And Paul, in another place, declares that, in judging, God has no respect to liberty or bondage." According to this definition or explanation of the phrase, God cannot be regarded as a respecter of persons, unless His choice of some and rejection of others turn upon something in the individuals themselves. But we have already seen that God in this matter is wholly uninfluenced by anything in man—He acts according to His *own will*. The motives to favour are derived solely from *His mere mercy*. If the motives of Divine action are derived entirely from the Divine Being Himself, He has manifestly no respect to persons, but only to His own will. The Scriptures declare that God loved Jacob and hated Esau, but they declare at the same time that there was nothing in Jacob to conciliate Divine favour more than in his brother. Now, if God were determined in bestowing His favours by the birth, or blood, or rank, or respectability, or station of men, He would be a respecter of persons; but we have already seen that not many wise or noble or honourable are called. So far is His favour from being regulated by respect to persons. But it may be asked, Why does He not treat all alike? I would answer this question by asking a few others. Has not God an unquestionable right to manifest His mercy? or is mercy wholly denied to Him? Has He not an equal right to exercise His justice? or is that attribute also denied to Him? If He has a right to exercise both attributes, may He not do it upon any subjects that in their own nature are fit to display them? If man is guilty, may not God exercise His justice in punishing? if miserable, may not God exercise His mercy in saving? If man is a fit subject for the display of both attributes, may not God choose some men for the manifestation of His mercy, and others for the manifestation of His justice? An affirmative answer cannot be withheld without denying one of the following propositions: Man is not a fit subject either of wrath or mercy; or, God cannot manifest His justice and grace. Men must take one horn of this dilemma, or confess that the Lord's ways are equal, even though He has mercy on whom He will have mercy, and whom He will He hardeneth. Calvin, with his usual ability, observes: "The Lord, therefore, may give grace to whom He will, because He is merciful; and yet not give it to all, because He is a just Judge; may manifest His free grace by giving to some what they never deserve, while by not giving to all He declares the demerit of all."

3. The doctrine of election is supposed to be inconsistent with the sincerity of God in the general invitations and call of the Gospel, and with His professions of willingness that all should be saved. It is true that this doctrine is wholly irreconcilable with the idea of a fixed determination on the part of God to save, indiscriminately, the whole human race. The plain doctrine of the Presbyterian Church is that God has no purpose of salvation for all, and that He has not decreed that faith, repentance and holiness, and the eternal blessings of the Gospel, should be efficaciously applied to all. The necessary consequence of such a decree would be universal salvation. The Scriptures, which are supposed to prove that God sent His Son into the world with the specific intention of saving all without exception or limitation, it is

confidently believed, teach, when correctly interpreted, no such doctrine. It is often forgotten that *love* is ascribed to God under two or three different aspects. Sometimes it expresses the complacency and approbation with which He views the graces which His own Spirit has produced in the hearts of His children; and in this sense it is plain that God can be said to love only the saints. It is probably in this sense that the term *love* is to be understood in Jude's exhortation: "Keep yourselves in the love of God." Sometimes God's *benevolence* or general mercy is intended, such as He bestows upon the just and the unjust, the evil and the good, as in Psalms cxlv. 9: "The Lord is good to all, and His tender mercies are over all His works." The common bounties of Providence may be referred to this head. Sometimes it expresses that peculiar and distinguishing favour with which He regarded His elect from all eternity. In this sense, the love of God is always connected with the purpose of salvation. Again, the word sometimes denotes nothing more than God's willingness to be reconciled to sinners in and through Christ. In regard to the love of complacency or approbation, it is manifest at once that unconverted sinners have no lot nor part in it. God is angry with them every day; "He hateth all workers of iniquity." The special love of God is confined exclusively to the elect. The general benevolence of God is common, but it implies no purpose of salvation at all; and therefore, in that sense, God may be said to love the reprobate and disobedient. Even the vessels of wrath fitted to destruction are borne with in much long-suffering and patience. In reference to the last, it is plain that God may be heartily willing to save sinners in and through Christ—may determine to save all, in other words, who receive the Saviour—without positively decreeing to create in all men the necessary faith. In this sense, therefore, God may be said to love sinners, for whom, however, He has no purpose of salvation. Having established an inseparable connection between faith and salvation, He will infallibly save all that believe; but it by no means follows that He will certainly bestow faith on all to whom the Gospel is preached. Hence, another important distinction, to be borne in mind, is between what is technically called by divines the εὐαρεστία of God and His εὐδοκία. By the first is meant that which God commands and is agreeable to His precept—in other words, what He requires His creatures to do; by the other is meant His own fixed purpose or decree, or what He actually intends to do Himself. The distinction is sometimes expressed by the terms *preceptive* and *decretive*, applied to the will of God. It was the preceptive will of God that the Jews should not crucify the Lord Jesus Christ. They acted in this matter contrary to God's command, and were therefore guilty; still, it was His decretive will that the Saviour should be crucified, for the Jews and Roman soldiers did only what "His hand and His counsel determined before to be done." The preceptive will of God is the rule of duty to us; the decretive will, the plan of operations to Himself. The distinction is plainly just, natural and scriptural.

The preceptive will of God is sometimes called His *revealed* will, and His decretive called His *secret* will. This distinction does not suppose that the will of God in itself is compound or divisible; on the contrary, it is one and most simple, and comprehends all things in one simple act. But as this most simple will of God is employed about a variety of objects, we are obliged, in accommodation to our weak capacities, to recur to distinctions which exist not in the will itself, but in the objects of volition. It is therefore an objective and not a subjective distinction, which we have already stated. I said that the distinction was scriptural. This appears from the fact that both decrees and precepts are called the will of God. Thus the precept is called God's will in Psalm cxliii. 10: "Teach me to do Thy will"—that is, to obey Thy precept. The decree is called God's will in Rom. ix. 19: "Who hath resisted His will?"—that is, Who has frustrated His decree? "Though the precept," says Turrettin, "may fall under the decree, as to the proposition or prescribing of it, yet it does not fall under it as to the fulfilment or execution"—that is, to give or prescribe the precept is a part of God's decree, but to secure obedience forms no necessary part of it at all. "Hence," continues Turrettin, "the distinction is a just one—the decretive will being that which determines the certainty of events; and the preceptive will, that which simply prescribes duty to men. If this distinction be just, God may, without contradiction, be said to *will* preceptively, or in the way of command, what He does not will decretively, or purpose to effect." "Thus it was His preceptive will that Pharaoh should let the Israelites go, that Abraham should sacrifice his son, and that Peter should not deny Christ;" but yet none of these things were decreed. It was not the efficient purpose of God to cause them be done, as is plain from the event. Yet we are not to suppose that there is any contrariety in these wills, if I may so speak. They are different, being employed about different objects, but are not therefore contrary.

God cannot be said without absurdity to will and not will the same thing in the same sense; but God may be said to command a thing which He does not decree shall be done. He decrees to give the command and to prescribe the rule of duty, but He does not decree to give or secure obedience. There is no contradiction here. God commanded Abraham to offer up his son Isaac: this is God's preceptive will. He wills to give this precept as a trial of Abraham's faith. But God decreed that Isaac should not be offered up, as the event manifestly proved: this is God's decretive will. Is there any contradiction between them? Is there any inconsistency in supposing that God should *will* to try Abraham's faith by such a command, and yet *will* at the same time that Isaac should not be slain? I would just remark, in concluding this point, that the preceptive will is the sole rule of duty to man, as its name shows; and fearful guilt is always incurred when the commands of God are disregarded or despised. It is not my business to inquire whether God has a secret decree—that I shall or shall not, in point of fact, comply with

His injunctions; it is enough that I am bound to do so, and am justly held punishable if I do not obey. Whatever rule of operations He may prescribe to Himself, the one which He has given to me is plain and intelligible, and His unrevealed purposes will afford me no shelter if I neglect or disregard it.

Another important truth, which is necessary in this discussion, is, that man is now just as much under the authority of God as he was previously to his fall. He is just as much the subject of command and law as ever he was, and is consequently as much bound to render perfect and entire obedience to all the Divine precepts. It would be preposterous to suppose that his own wilful sin had cancelled moral obligation. If, then, God still continues to be man's rightful sovereign, and man God's lawful subject, if the Lord still possesses the power to command, and man is still under obligation to obey, it should not be thought strange that God deals with man according to this relation, and actually enjoins upon him an obedience to law which He has no determinate purpose to give. This can be regarded as nothing more than the rightful exercise of lawful authority on the part of God; and to deny that He can consistently do this without giving man the necessary grace to obey, is just flatly to deny that God is a sovereign or that man is a subject.

Let these few preliminary remarks be distinctly borne in mind—(1.) That there are various senses in which love, or similar affections, are attributable to God; (2.) that there is a just, natural and scriptural distinction of the will of God into preceptive and decretive; (3.) that the relation of sovereign and subject still remains unchanged between God and man—and I apprehend that there will be very little difficulty in refuting the Arminian hypothesis, that God actually wills or seriously intends the salvation of all men. The passages to which they most confidently appeal for support may be ranged under two classes: First, those which contain statements of general love or mercy; secondly, those in which they suppose an unlimited purpose of salvation is actually revealed.

In regard to the passages of the first class, it is manifest that where the universal epithets are to be taken in their full latitude—which, however, is not always the case—nothing more can be fairly deduced than God's benevolence, which leads Him to bestow blessings upon all men. There is nothing specific about the character or nature of the blessings, or whenever anything specific is stated it is found to be only the common bounties of Providence that the sacred writer had immediately in view. How preposterous, therefore, from such texts to deduce a purpose of universal salvation, as though God could not send rain upon the wicked and unjust without designing to save them! It is vain to allege that such general goodness is never referred to God's love. The Saviour settles the point in Matthew v. 44, 45. There He commands His disciples to love their enemies, to bless them that curse them, to do good to them that hate them, etc. Why? "That ye may be the children of your Father which is in heaven; for He maketh His sun to rise on the evil and on the good, and sendeth rain on the just and on the unjust." Here the disciples are commanded to *love* their enemies, that they might be *like* God. But how does it appear that God loves His enemies? "He maketh His sun to rise on the evil and on the good, and sendeth rain on the just and on the unjust;" in other words, from the *common bounties of Providence*. With such a plain illustration of the fact that God can be said to love without intending to save, it is amazing that such passages as the following should ever have been adduced to prove a purpose of universal salvation: "The Lord is good to all, and His tender mercies are over all His works." I would as soon think of appealing to Romans ix. 22, because God is there said to have endured the vessels of wrath fitted to destruction with much long-suffering.

The second class of passages will be found to involve no more difficulty than the first. We shall consider the most forcible, or those to which Arminians most frequently appeal. The first which I shall notice is found in 2 Peter iii. 9: "Not willing that any should perish, but that all should come to repentance." I think it exceedingly doubtful whether the words *any* and *all* have an indiscriminate application in this passage. The context would seem to confine them within the limits of the "us" spoken of just above. This will appear by taking the whole verse in its connection: "The Lord is not slack concerning His promise"—that is, the promise of His second coming—"as some men count slackness, but is long-suffering to usward." To whom? We cannot refer the "us" to any but those who in the eighth verse are addressed as "*beloved.*" It would seem, then, to designate only God's elect. Now, why is God long-suffering to His elect? Because He is "not willing that any"—that is, any *of them*—"should perish," but that all—that is, *all of them*—"should come to repentance." In other words, Christ delays His second coming, and will continue to delay it, until all His elect are savingly gathered into His kingdom and His mystical body completed. This, I confess, appears to me to be the most natural and obvious interpretation of the passage. It certainly is grammatical, and harmonizes well with the context. I am aware that Calvin and other respectable writers have given a different interpretation. They make the latter clause epexegetical of the first, and resolve the willingness of God into His precept. The force of the passage in this view would be, "God has commanded men everywhere to repent." This interpretation does no violence to the words of the passage, for they will certainly bear this meaning, but it seems to me to violate the grammatical connection. The next passage occurs in 1 Timothy ii. 4: "Who will have all men to be saved and to come unto the knowledge of the truth." It is difficult to conceive how this passage can be supposed to prove a purpose of universal salvation. It expresses simply the inseparable connection between salvation and the knowledge of the truth, together with the solemn fact that God enjoins it upon all to receive the truth. It is manifestly God's preceptive will as revealed in the offers and invitations of the Gospel which is here meant; there is not a syllable about any purpose or decree to save all men. Notice the expression: it is, "*who will have;*" it expresses what God is willing or commands that *men should do*, not what he *intends to do Himself*. If the latter had been the meaning, the passage would be, "who *will save* all men," not "who will *have* all men to be saved." The simple distinction of the will of God into preceptive and decretive divests this passage of all its difficulty.

The next which I shall notice is Ezek. xxxiii. 11: "As I live, saith the Lord God, I have no pleasure in the death of the wicked, but that the wicked turn from his ways and live; turn ye, turn ye, from your evil ways, for why will ye die, O house of Israel?" The remarks of Turrettin on this passage are so just and appropriate that I cannot forbear to translate them: "Although God here protests that He has no pleasure in the death of the wicked, but rather that the wicked should turn from his ways and live, it does not follow that God willed or intended, upon any condition, the conversion and life of each and every man. For, besides that conversion cannot be conditional, it being the condition of life itself, it is certain that the prophet is here speaking of God's preceptive and not His decretive will. The word חפץ, which is here used, always denotes complacency or delight. The passage then simply teaches that God is pleased with, or approves, the conversion and life of the sinner, as a thing in itself grateful to Him and suited to His merciful nature. God is pleased with this rather than the death of the sinner, and therefore enjoins it as a duty that men be converted if they expect to be saved. But although God takes no delight in the death of the sinner, considered merely as the destruction of the creature, it does not follow that He does not will and intend it as an exercise of His own justice and as an occasion of manifesting His glory. A pious magistrate takes no delight in the death of the guilty, but still he justly decrees the punishment demanded by the laws. The interrogatory, 'Why will ye die?' is added because God would show to them in these words how death was to be avoided, and that they, by voluntary impenitence, were the sole authors of their own ruin."

The passages, however, which are most confidently relied on as teaching a purpose of universal salvation are those which relate to the atonement of Christ, and which seem to give it an unlimited extent. It is freely admitted that the doctrine of election falls to the ground if an universal atonement—that is, a full *satisfaction* to law and justice for all the sins of every individual—can be fairly demonstrated. There are multiplied passages of Scripture in which the atonement is confined to the elect. Christ, the Good Shepherd, lays down His life only for the sheep. The song of the redeemed in glory seems to proceed upon no other supposition but that of a limited redemption: "Thou wast slain and hast redeemed us unto God by thy blood, *out of* every kindred, and tongue, and people, and nation." The general current of Scripture appears to represent the incarnation and death of the Redeemer as the grand means by which the great purpose of electing love was gloriously accomplished. Hence we are said to be "chosen in Christ." The texts which are supposed to favour the doctrine of universal atonement admit an explanation which does no violence to the laws of language or the analogy of faith. Many of the passages adduced to prove an unlimited design to save each and every individual prove nothing more than an universal offer. No one doubts that the Gospel offer is indiscriminate and general, but this only supposes an all-sufficiency in Christ, without at all implying that Christ actually *intends* to save all to whom the Gospel is preached. The universal epithets in other passages must be restricted by the immediate connection or scope of the passage. Having made these preliminary remarks, I proceed to examine the most prominent passages. 1 Tim. ii. 6: "Who gave Himself a ransom for all, to be testified in due time." The common and familiar application of the word *gave* to the Gospel offer sufficiently determines the meaning of this passage. It teaches only that Christ is offered to the whole world as an abundant and all-sufficient Saviour. The word *testified*, which has a manifest allusion to the proclamation of the Gospel or the public and indiscriminate exhibition of Christ as the Saviour of sinners, who in "due time" should be preached to "every creature," seems to me to confirm this interpretation. Not a word does this passage then contain about the *design* of Christ to satisfy for the sins of each and every individual. 1 John ii. 2: "He is the propitiation for our sins, and not for ours only, but also for the sins of the whole world." A reference to Romans iii. 25 explains sufficiently the meaning of John: "Whom *God* hath set forth to be a propitiation," etc. That is, Christ is held up to the acceptance of sinners indiscriminately as the only medium of reconciliation with God. He is "set forth," placed before them as "the way, the truth, and the life." Here then is nothing but the indiscriminate offer again. Hebrews ii. 9: "That He by the grace of God should taste death for every man." The phrase here is limited by the context. In the next verse they are called "many sons," whom Christ intended to bring to glory; and in the eleventh verse they are spoken of as one with Him, and therefore "He is not ashamed to call them brethren." "Every man," therefore, must mean each of these "many sons and brethren," of whose salvation Christ is "the Captain." Such a limitation of the word *every* is common in the Scriptures; compare Gen. vii. 21, Luke iv. 37, Psalms cxix. 101; Prov. vii. 12. In all these passages —and multitudes of others might be mentioned—the word *every* is limited by the context or the necessity of the case. In Romans v. 18, Christ and Adam are spoken of as *covenant heads*. The Apostle is establishing the principle of imputation, and illustrates our justification on account of Christ's merits by our condemnation on account of Adam's sin. The principle in both cases was the same—they were both federal representatives. The "all men," then, in one case means all who were represented by Adam in the covenant of works; in the other, all who were represented by Christ in the covenant of grace. The same may be said of 1 Cor. xv. 22.

The next passage may be found in 2 Cor. v. 14, 15: "For the love of Christ constraineth us; because we thus judge that if one died for all, then were all dead; and that He died for all, that they which live should not henceforth live unto themselves, but unto Him which died for them and rose again." To a candid mind this passage can present no serious difficulty. Two facts are stated which serve mutually to explain and interpret each other—1. Christ died for "all." 2. The "all" for whom He died do not "henceforth live unto themselves, but unto Him which died for them and rose again." The result or end of Christ's death, as stated in the last verse, actually determines the meaning of the "all" in the fourteenth. Even Doddridge, one of the most cautious and timid interpreters of contested passages, has given substantially this interpretation in his paraphrase upon these verses: "For the love of Christ, so illustriously displayed in that redemption He hath wrought, constraineth us; it bears us away like a strong and resistless torrent, while we thus judge, and in our calmest and most rational moments draw it as a certain consequence, from the important principles which we assuredly know to be true, that if one, even Christ, died for the redemption and salvation of *all who should sincerely believe in Him and obey Him*, then were all dead. And now we know that He died for all, that they who live only in consequence of His dying love should not henceforth from this remarkable period and end of their lives, whatever they have formerly done, live to themselves, but that they should all agree that they will live to the honour, glory and interest of Him who died for them, and when He rose again from the dead retained the same affection for them, and is continually improving His recovered life for their security and happiness." I have quoted this long paraphrase merely to show the mutual connection and dependence of the different parts of the passage, which require that the universal epithet should necessarily be limited.[1]

The nineteenth verse of this same chapter is frequently pressed into the service of an unlimited atonement, but by a dreadful distortion of its real meaning. "God was in Christ reconciling the world unto Himself, not imputing their trespasses unto them, and hath committed unto us the word of reconciliation." Two circumstances in the context show that the Apostle is here speaking only of the Gospel offer, or the grant of Christ to sinners indefinitely as an all-sufficient Saviour. The phrase, "God was in Christ," etc., means that God, *for the sake of Christ,* is willing to pardon all who appropriate the Saviour's merits. In other words, all who come to God in Christ—that is, by receiving Jesus as their mediator and intercessor—will find God a reconciled Father. This is the substance of the Gospel offer. Now, that this is the meaning of the Apostle appears plainly from the connection of this verse with the preceding, in which it is said that God "hath given to us the *ministry of reconciliation*—to wit, that God was in Christ," etc. The ministry of reconciliation, then, or the mere preaching of the Gospel, or the offer of salvation in and through Christ, is the Apostle's own explanation of the passage in question. This appears still more evident from the latter part of the nineteenth verse itself: "And hath committed unto us the *word of reconciliation.*" Hence the Apostle in the twentieth verse presses the Gospel invitation. The whole difficulty of the passage will disappear by simply recollecting that God is never a God in Christ to any but a believing sinner. To apprehend Him as a God in Christ is to apprehend Him by saving faith in the merits of His Son. Hence God in Christ, reconciling the world unto Himself, can mean noth-

---

[1] [NOTE BY EDITOR.—In the discussion on the Necessity and Nature of Christianity immediately preceding the present, there may be found (pp. 87, 91) a fuller explanation by the author of this passage.]

ing but God urging it upon sinners to believe. This passage, therefore, lends no support whatever to the dogma of universal atonement. It states only the universality of the external call of the Word, and the solemn duty of sinners to obey it.

The next and last passage which I shall consider is John iii. 16: "For God so loved the world that He gave His only-begotten Son, that whosoever believeth in Him should not perish, but have eternal life." The idea which our Saviour here intended to convey is, that the indefinite offer of salvation in the Gospel is a testimony to the whole world of God's amazing love or grace. The offer of Christ and salvation in Him is often expressed by words which convey the general idea of an unconditional gift or grant.[1] "My Father *giveth* you the true bread from heaven"—that is, sets before you and invites you to partake. "I will also *give* Thee for a light to the Gentiles, that thou mayest be my salvation unto the ends of the earth." "I will *give* Thee for a covenant of the people." Both of these passages seem to refer to the universal publication of the Gospel. The offer of Christ is called a *gift*, because it conveys to sinners a fair, revealed right to receive and rest upon Him for all the purposes of salvation. Such an offer of a Saviour is a standing testimony to the whole world of God's unmerited grace. But there is not a word in this passage about a purpose or decree to save all indefinitely. On the contrary, the limitation of salvation in the close of the verse to believers only is a striking proof that God did not intend to save all. That the giving spoken of in the verse relates only to the Gospel offer is manifest from its being held out as the ground and warrant of faith; the object of the gift is, "that whosoever *believeth* should not perish, but have eternal life." Now, as saving faith receives Christ "*as He*

---

[1] [NOTE BY EDITOR.—Dr. Thornwell, in after life, expressly condemned the view of the "Marrow men," that God the Father makes a "grant" of Christ as by a "deed of gift" to all men. Justice to him, therefore, might warrant the excision of this sentence.]

is offered" in the Gospel, it is manifest that this gift and the Gospel offer must be the same.

The examination which has just been made of the favourite texts of the Arminian writers is sufficient, it is believed, to refute the dogma that God has any purpose, either conditional or unconditional, of saving all men indiscriminately. There is no revelation of any such intention in the Bible, so that it becomes frivolous and absurd to oppose election with any arguments whatever derived from this source.

The next point in the objection is, that if God has no purpose of salvation toward all men, the invitations of the Gospel become only a mockery. God cannot possibly be sincere in the indiscriminate offer of salvation if He does not intend to bestow it upon each and every individual. This specious objection proceeds upon a gratuitous assumption that the external call of the Word conveys to every sinner to whom it is directed a specific intimation that God designs his own salvation in particular. But this is far from the truth. The Gospel offer is not an expression of *God's* purposes or decrees, but a plain and intelligible ground of duty to *man*. It comes to no one and says, "You individually and particularly are included in God's purpose of saving mercy." If this were the nature of it, none could pretend to reconcile its acknowledged universality with the doctrines of election and reprobation. But this is so far from being the case that it simply gives to sinners a *right* to believe; it gives them an adequate foundation, a warrantable ground for the exercise of faith. In other words, it is such a general, indefinite, unconditional grant of Christ in all His plenitude of grace as conveys to each and every sinner who hears the joyful sound an unquestionable right to appropriate and apply the Saviour in all His fullness to his own individual case without presumption or blasphemy. God, in the Gospel, holds up a Saviour in all respects suited to the fallen condition of man, and abundantly able to heal the diseases and relieve the miseries of every son and daughter of Adam. The Divine nature of the adorable Redeemer stamps an *infinite value* upon His doings and sufferings, so that there can be no possible limitation of the all-sufficiency of Christ. Holding up this Saviour to sinners in the outward dispensation of the Gospel, God conveys to all indiscriminately a plain right to appropriate Christ for all the purposes of salvation, and at the same time solemnly assures men that all who do appropriate Him shall infallibly be saved. From all this the general object of the Gospel offer is sufficiently obvious: it is to afford a *lawful ground* for *faith*. Saving faith is measured by the offer of Christ in the Gospel, and no man could possibly be required to believe if he had no lawful right to believe. The command of God is positive that all men should believe; the Gospel offer comes in as a handmaid to the command, and gives all men adequate authority for believing. Now, in all this God may be perfectly sincere, while He has no purpose of actual salvation for all. He is sincere in giving the sinner a warrant to believe on Christ, and God may certainly give such a warrant without giving the sinner a disposition to make use of it. God is sincere in all the promises of the Gospel, because He will assuredly fulfil them to all who scripturally embrace them—that is, embrace them as yea and amen in Christ, the great Trustee of the Covenant, for no promise is made separate and apart from Him. God is sincere in His invitations and entreaties, because He is only urging the sinner to the faithful discharge of solemn and imperative duty. And surely God as a Sovereign may require of man and urge upon him the performance of duty without duplicity or deceit, and yet withhold that strength which man has basely forfeited, and is now guilty for needing. If God gave sinners a right to believe on Christ, and then by creating a positive inability should debar them from believing, the Gospel offer would clearly be a mockery. But this is not the case. God makes no man an unbeliever. He commands and urges it upon *all to believe*, and *debars* none from an access to the throne of grace. They wickedly debar themselves, and the decree of reprobation leaves them to walk in the sight of their own eyes and the pride of their own hearts. The Gospel offer, combined with the positive command of God, renders the duty of believing imperative upon all, and therefore leaves every unbeliever utterly without excuse in the sight of God. An all-sufficient Saviour has been held up before him, abundantly able to save all that were ever invited to come; a door of access has been opened to the throne of grace, so that he might have gone with boldness and sought for the mercy which he needed, with the certain prospect of obtaining it. His duty was plainly declared and solemnly enforced, and God put forth no influence upon him to hold him from Christ, had he felt a disposition to go. He is therefore without excuse. But yet the doctrine of reprobation remains unaffected. God withheld grace which He was under no obligation to bestow, and left the sinner to perish in his sins. He opened the eyes of others to see the Saviour in His glory, and to read their own right to receive and appropriate Him in the record of the Word. Thus is election equally unaffected by the nature and design of the Gospel offer.

Let it be borne in mind that the external call of the Gospel simply points out a ground of duty, and all difficulty is removed. This call merely represents God as a sovereign Legislator and man a dependent subject—a truth with which the doctrines of election and reprobation by no means interfere. This external call says not a syllable about the purposes of God in giving or withholding the grace of faith. But when the call is proclaimed among men indefinitely, then comes in election and persuades some to receive and obey it, while others are left utterly without excuse for refusing to do what they had a plain and unquestionable right to do, and were moreover solemnly bound to do.

Secondly. The next leading class of objections to the sovereignty of God comprehends those which are derived from the moral agency of man. They may be reduced to the following heads: 1. Election is inconsistent with liberty, and consequently with accountability. 2. It destroys all solicitude about personal holiness. 3. It renders the means of grace entirely nugatory. These, I believe, are the most prominent; at least, they are more frequently reiterated than any others of this class. I will answer them in order.

1. Election is inconsistent with the moral agency and accountability of man. It will be remembered that this is one of the objections which the Apostle Paul notices in the ninth of Romans: "Thou wilt then say unto me, Why doth He yet find fault? for who hath resisted His will?" Ver. 19.

That the decrees of God do render events absolutely certain is beyond all doubt, but that they change the nature of second causes can never be made out. All that is necessary to constitute moral agency is to be a rational, intelligent being; to possess the faculties and affections which invariably belong to spirit, and without which it would cease to be spirit. Now, election or Divine sovereignty, in its fullest extent, does not destroy the spiritual or intelligent nature of man, and consequently does not destroy what alone is essential to moral agency. Again, the decree of God does not force men to act contrary to their wills. They are conscious of pursuing the bent of their own thoughts and of prosecuting their own plans. No man is dragged or reluctantly driven by the purpose of God into a course of conduct which he does not choose to pursue. How then does the Divine decree make man a mere machine? It is wholly a gratuitous assumption that the *nature* of second causes is at all changed by the purposes of God. Events are certain, the concurrence of causes in producing them is certain; these things are determined, they *must* take place, there is no possibility of failure, but man still continues to be man notwithstanding the decree.

In relation to the reprobate it is constantly denied by Calvinists that God puts forth a positive agency in creating their sinfulness. He does not make them sinners. He does not infuse into their hearts that moral turpitude and carnal enmity from which their actual rebellion proceeds. He ordains their actions as natural events by decreeing to permit them, or by positively appointing them, but He does not originate the sinner's malignity and desperate aversion to holiness. He finds them in the decree of reprobation under the curse of a righteous law, and determines to leave them in their ruin and depravity. He finds them sinners and He leaves them sinners, with the settled purpose of inflicting upon them the merited penalty of death. Where is there any violence offered to their wills? There is manifestly none. They have all the freedom which their corruption and depravity will permit them to possess. They walk in the "sight of their own eyes." "They kindle a fire and walk in the light of their own sparks." They love sin, and freely indulge in it because they love it.

In reference to the elect, it is freely admitted that God by a positive and direct influence is the author of every holy affection in their hearts. It is freely admitted that they are passive in effectual calling until being quickened by His grace they are enabled and inclined to answer the call. But still it is denied that any violence whatever is offered to their wills. This will appear by considering the separate elements of effectual calling. (1.) "The minds of the elect are enlightened spiritually and savingly to understand the things of God." But surely the infusion of light into the soul does not destroy its nature, does not make that a slave which was free before. A new discernment of things does not affect the accountability of man which grows necessarily out of his relations to God. There is no reason why spiritual knowledge, any more than natural knowledge, should affect man's moral agency considered in its own intrinsic nature. Light in no sense can alter the spiritual constitution of the subject enlightened. How preposterous, then, the idea that because man has spiritual light he ceases to be a moral agent!

(2.) The next element of effectual calling is, "taking away their heart of stone, and giving them a heart of flesh." This sentiment in Scripture is variously expressed, but the influence which the Holy Spirit here puts forth is a *creating* influence. A new heart is *created.* Holy susceptibilities are originated which did not exist before. But surely creation involves no contradiction to moral agency, otherwise no created being could be a moral agent. If the mere fact of creation destroyed moral agency, it would be impossible for God to make a moral agent. Besides, the new heart does not change the *essence* of the soul.

(3.) The third element is "renewing their wills, and by His Almighty power determining them to that which is good." Nor is man's liberty at all infringed in this. Previously to the operations of the Spirit man *could* will nothing but sin; but his will is now renewed by an Almighty power, and determined to that which is good. Does the fact that man is inclined to good by a power which he has *no disposition* to resist prove that he is not an accountable and moral being? If man were reluctantly driven to the choice of good, he would cease to act freely—that is, in conformity with existing dispositions; but when man delights in what is good, no matter from what cause this delight may have originated, he acts freely in choosing it.

(4.) The last element is, "effectually drawing them to Jesus Christ, yet so as they come most freely, being made willing by His grace." To this no objection can be raised, as it flatly asserts man's freeness and willingness in receiving Christ. I apprehend that the cause of difficulty with many lies in an oversight of the fact that man is passive in regeneration, though active in believing. He is the *subject* of a Divine influence; and therefore it is no more reasonable to suppose that his *essential* constitution is changed by being acted upon by God than in any other case of external influence. It is true that the influence which God puts forth is efficient; it secures the intended result, but it is just as true that man acts freely and spontaneously, since the result intended was to determine the will to good. Previously to the operations of the Spirit, the man was *dead;* he could perform no spiritual action at all. God infuses into him spiritual life. Now this implies no violence. In consequence of this life being infused into his soul, he now freely chooses and embraces that which is good. And here there is no violence. Where, then, is the inconsistency between Divine influence and moral agency?

There is a sense in which moral agency is attributed to man which, I freely confess, is irreconcilable with election. It consists in making man's will the sole originating cause of his actions, without any regard to existing dispositions or extraneous influences. The theory is, that the will can and does determine itself; that the only reason why man adopts one mode of action and not another is that his will, in consequence of its own inherent power, so determined itself. There is no such thing on this scheme as choice, deliberation, disposition; the will is arbitrary and sovereign, and submits to no influence out of itself. To this theory there are insuperable objections: 1st. It makes man wholly independent of God. The Supreme Being has no more control over the actions of His creatures, according to this system, than if He did not exist. The only dependence which they can feel upon Him is simply for *preservation.* 2dly. It is inconsistent with accountability. As well might a weather-cock be held responsible for its lawless motions as a being whose arbitrary, uncontrollable will is his only law. What can the man account for? His actions have arisen from no moral considerations whatever; he acted because he acted; and this is the only account he can give. 3dly. It makes man the author of his own spiritual renovation. Divine grace, on this scheme, is not efficient; it does nothing. Everything depends upon the sinner's arbitrary will. God may expostulate, and warn, and send His Spirit to operate on the heart, but all in vain unless the sinner's will should determine itself to Christ and salvation; in other words, unless the sinner should convert himself. These are a specimen of the difficulties involved in this absurd theory of moral agency, which strictly implies only that man is not a fit subject for a government of laws.

The Scriptures are explicit in stating the unconditional

decrees of God in connection with the responsibility and moral agency of men. There was a plain decree in regard to the death and sufferings of the Lord Jesus Christ, and yet under that decree the agency of man was exerted in deeds of darkness. So far was this decree from annulling human responsibility that fearful guilt was incurred by the Jews, and tremendous sufferings inflicted upon them. "Him, being delivered by the determinate counsel and foreknowledge of God, ye have taken, and by wicked hands have crucified and slain." Acts ii. 23. "For, of a truth, against Thy holy child Jesus, whom Thou hast anointed, both Herod and Pontius Pilate, with the Gentiles and people of Israel, were gathered together for to do whatsoever Thy hand and Thy counsel determined before to be done." Acts iv. 27, 28. Now here it is expressly said that the enemies of our Lord acted only "according to the determinate counsel and foreknowledge of God," and did only what His "hand and His counsel determined before to be done," and yet they are charged with guilt and wickedness: "ye have taken, and by *wicked* hands have crucified and slain." Hence, the Apostle was clearly of opinion that the absolute and sovereign predestination of God did not take away responsibility from man or remove the guilt of his transgressions. All the difficulties involved in the doctrine, or that have ever been charged upon it, are involved in, and with equal propriety may be charged upon, this particular case. Election to grace is no stronger a feature of the absolute predestination of God than the death and sufferings of Christ; and if all the circumstances connected with the one could be positively decreed and rendered absolutely certain, consistently with the liberty of moral and rational agents, then all the circumstances connected with the other may also be determined without the destruction or infringement of the agency of man.

If efficient Divine influence is inconsistent with moral agency, then men can never be confirmed in holiness beyond the grave without ceasing to be moral agents. God cannot secure their holiness in heaven consistently with their liberty, any more than He can determine their actions here. The difficulty grows out of the sinner's own mind—his own liberty of moral action; and so long as that liberty continues, the same difficulty must continue. Upon the Arminian hypothesis, then, it is a possible, if not a probable, case, that a soul may have basked for myriads and myriads of years in the rays of eternal glory, and then fall, and fall like Lucifer, never to rise again—suddenly exchanging its shouts of praise and alleluia for the wail of the damned, and dropping the song of redeeming love for the gnashing of teeth and the fiend-like yell of despair. These monstrous results necessarily grow out of the position that election and moral agency are incompatible, and carry along with them so complete a denial of many promises of Scripture as at once to overthrow the fundamental position on which they depend. What then? We are compelled to receive election with its inevitable concomitant, moral necessity, or resort to wild and revolting theories of free-will with their cumbrous train of absurdity and nonsense. We are compelled to receive a moral agency which is consistent with a moral necessity, or adopt a hypothesis which destroys accountability at once. I cannot forbear to mention here that the difficulty presses just as hard in another form against the Arminians. They deny the Divine decrees, but admit the essential omniscience of God. Events, therefore, are certain; they must happen just as God knows that they will happen; they cannot possibly happen otherwise. Here, then, is a moral necessity just as strong as the moral necessity of the Calvinists. But they reply that God does not *produce* the events. It is a question of no manner of importance how the events are produced; the difficulty lies in this, that they are *necessarily* produced. Arminians cannot evade it; their system involves moral necessity as much as ours; and it is as much their business as ours to reconcile this necessity with moral agency.

2. The next objection of this class is that election destroys all solicitude about personal holiness. It reduces men to a

system of such stern necessity that there is no reason at all why they should be concerned about their personal salvation. It will be seen that this difficulty grows out of the former. I shall make but two or three remarks upon it— (1.) As the nature of second causes is not at all changed by the Divine decree, the duties of man to God are just the same that they would be if there were no election in the case. Man's relations to his Maker are the same; he is still a creature and a subject. The connection of obedience and life is the same, and all the motives to activity and diligence remain unchanged. With none of these things do the decrees of God interfere. How then can election destroy solicitude about personal salvation? It cannot justly do it without destroying the inseparable connection between holiness and happiness, and the duty of man to obey his sovereign. Exhortations are useful and proper, because man *ought* to obey, and will be abundantly rewarded if he does. (2.) It would contradict the very nature and design of election if it made men careless and indifferent. The end contemplated by election is holiness. The decree is that the chosen ones shall believe, repent, be humble and exemplary in their walk and conversation, and yet this has a tendency to make them stupid, unconcerned and indifferent! Because it is decreed that a man shall believe, *therefore* he will *not* believe; because it is decreed that he shall be *holy, therefore* he will be profligate and abandoned. What absurdity! So long as holiness continues to be an indispensable element of salvation, the election to grace cannot be an election to sin. Election as much involves the certainty of personal holiness as it does the certainty of heaven. (3.) My third remark is, that it has directly a contrary tendency, and that in several respects. It is an acknowledged principle of human nature that when great interests are at stake deep solicitude is felt by men, if there is only a bare possibility that they may be personally concerned. If the means of knowing whether or not they are in fact concerned be within their power, they will resort to them with eager avidity.

This is a plain principle of human nature. Apply this to the case in hand. Here are solemn and commanding interests at stake. Heaven or hell will infallibly be the lot of every child of Adam. Here are the means of knowing, in the inspired volume, with certainty whether I am predestinated to eternal life. If I really *believed* all this, I would shake heaven and earth in the great commotion; I would give no sleep to my eyes nor slumber to my eyelids till I had settled this solemn point. Just let me realize the *certainty* that heaven or hell is my portion, and I could no more fold my arms under the bare possibility of going to hell, while there was a prospect of escape, than I could take my ease on a burning volcano. The certainty of *one* doom, but the uncertainty in regard to *which*, has a natural tendency to rouse the soul into vigorous efforts to throw off the pangs of suspense.

If the Scriptures pointed out by name and surname the individuals elected and reprobated, there would be some foundation for the objection, but they do no such thing. They simply tell men that they belong to one class or the other, and add as an encouragement to effort that those who comply with the prescribed plan of salvation are certainly elected. Hence they call upon us to make our "calling and election sure" by receiving the Saviour and walking in the way of His commandments. None know that they are reprobates, and therefore none can know that their efforts will be useless. I am fully satisfied that if men had a deeper and more impressive sense of the truth of this doctrine, there would be more earnest inquiry and serious alarm among the careless and impenitent. But the misfortune is that they do not *feel* the astounding certainty that heaven or hell is theirs. They are radically Arminians; they have the keys of both kingdoms in the pocket of their own free-will, and rest satisfied under the full but delusive impression that *they* can determine the matter just when they please.

In reference to those who know that they are elected, it cannot be maintained that election has a tendency to lull them into carnal security, unless it is also maintained that a deep and clear sense of God's love to us has a tendency to call forth only hatred to Him. This would be to make a Christian not only depraved, but unnatural in consequence of conversion. The biography of the saints furnishes a running commentary upon the happy moral influence of Calvinism in quickening and invigorating the graces of the Spirit, and some Arminians have been candid enough to confess that the charge of licentiousness is the offspring of ignorance. It is obvious, in fact, that there are some graces of the Christian character which a cordial belief of election is wonderfully suited to cherish.

(1.) "We love Him because He first loved us." "Without the doctrine of predestination," says Zanchius, "we cannot enjoy a lively sight and experience of God's special love and mercy towards us in Christ Jesus. Blessings not peculiar, but conferred indiscriminately on every man without distinction or exception, would neither be a proof of peculiar love in the donor, nor calculated to excite peculiar wonder and gratitude in the receiver. For instance, rain from heaven, though an invaluable benefit, is not considered as an argument of God's special and peculiar favour to some individuals above others, because it falls on all alike, as much on the rude wilderness and the barren rock as on the cultivated garden and fruitful field. But the blessing of election, somewhat like the Sibylline books, rises in value proportionably to the fewness of its objects. From a sense of God's peculiar, eternal and unchangeable love to His people their hearts are inflamed to love Him in return. Slender indeed will be my motives to the love of God on the supposition that my love to *Him* is beforehand with *His* to me, and that the very continuance of His favour is suspended on the weather-cock of my variable will, or on the flimsy thread of my imperfect affection. Such a precarious, dependent love were unworthy of God, and fitted to produce but scanty and cold reciprocation of love from man. Would you know what it is to love God as your Father,

Friend and Saviour, you must fall down before His electing mercy. Till then you are only hovering about in quest of true felicity. But you will never find the door, much less can you enter into rest, till you are enabled to love Him because He hath first loved you." It is manifest that a doctrine so friendly to the love of God cannot be unfriendly to universal obedience, "for love is the fulfilling of the Law." The man who sincerely loves God, as a matter of course, will desire conformity to His image, and as "electing goodness is the very life and soul of love to God, good works must flourish or decline in proportion as election is glorified or obscured."

(2.) This doctrine is peculiarly favourable to the cultivation of humility, and that in two respects. 1st. It lays the axe at the root of all human merit, and ascribes to sovereign, unmerited grace the whole glory of our salvation. It is found from experience that the legality of the heart presents a formidable barrier to the reception of the Gospel. Men's performances are so essential to their own self-complacency that it is hard to persuade them that all their righteousnesses are as filthy rags, and that salvation is not the reward of debt, but the gift of grace. This very natural pride of the carnal heart can be humbled or removed by no truth so effectually as the doctrine of election. When this is brought home upon their minds, men can then understand that "it is not of him that willeth, nor of him that runneth, but of God that showeth mercy." It strips them of all pretensions to merit, shows them their deep and loathsome unworthiness, and prostrates their souls in the very dust of self-abasement. The following remarks of Zanchius are forcible and appropriate: "Conversion and salvation must, in the very nature of the things, be wrought and effected either by ourselves alone, or by ourselves and God together, or solely by God Himself. Pelagians were for the first, the Arminians are for the second, true believers are for the last, because the last hypothesis, and that only, is built on the strongest evidence of reason, Scripture, and experience. It most effectually hides pride from man, and sets the crown of undivided praise upon the head—or, rather, casts it at the feet—of that glorious Triune God 'who worketh all in all.' But this is a crown which no sinners ever yet cast before the throne of God who were not first led into the transporting views of His gracious decree to save freely, and of His own will, the people of His eternal love." 2dly. This doctrine is not only favourable to humility by counteracting a legal spirit, but it is the very soul of dependence on Divine influence. The importance which the Scriptures attach to an uniform, habitual dependence on the grace of God sufficiently appears from the frequent and earnest exhortations to cultivate such a disposition; and if indeed it be so that the Holy Spirit is the source of all pious and devout affections, this dependent temper is the only one which is consistent with a Christian's true condition or his relations to God. Emptied as we are by election of all that cannot abide the scrutiny of heaven, we are pointed to inexhaustible treasures at God's right hand, which are bestowed only upon those who habitually depend upon His grace. Blind, naked and miserable in ourselves, we take the counsel of the Holy Spirit and lean upon the Lord for all that we need. Self-annihilation, as Luther calls it, is the mainspring of uniform dependence upon grace; and whatever has a tendency to drive us out of ourselves has likewise a tendency to drive us to God.

(3.) The doctrine of election affords great encouragement to prayer. 1st. Because prayer is the natural expression of dependence upon Divine influences. 2dly. Because election represents the grace of God as efficient. There would be no motive to pray for spiritual blessings if our growth in grace depended upon our own free wills and not upon the Spirit of God. If Divine grace exerted no invincible efficacy in subduing sin, mortifying lust and invigorating the principles of piety, it would be hard to determine why the life of a Christian should be a life of habitual, unceasing prayer. 3dly. Election is favourable to prayer, because it represents it as a *gift* of God, and as the appointed medium of receiving Divine blessings. When God decrees to bestow a blessing upon His people, He decrees also to give them the Spirit of prayer and supplication, so that when they find this Spirit poured out upon them they have every encouragement from the usual order of Divine providence to "ask in faith, nothing doubting."

(4.) This doctrine is the sole foundation of a full assurance of faith. It is the duty and privilege of Christians not only to be assured of their present acceptance with God, but also of their future, everlasting salvation. But this assurance they never could possess if justification, sanctification and glorification were not inseparably connected in the Divine decree. That such an assurance is in the highest degree friendly to piety is manifest from the fact that faith itself, even in its lowest exercises, works by love and purifies the heart.

Such are some of the obvious tendencies of election. I have said nothing of the support which it yields in affliction and distress, the patience and submission with which it inspires the soul in the gloomiest hours of adversity, and the strong consolation it administers to the dying saint when struggling in the pangs of death. Enough has been said, however, to show that its tendencies are all in favour of godliness, and I regard it as no proof of the spirituality of the present age that amid our bustle and excitement so little is said of this precious doctrine of the Gospel.

That wicked and profane persons have perverted it to their own eternal undoing I have no disposition to deny. So has every doctrine of the Gospel been perverted. The difficulty is not in the doctrine, but in the heart; swine will trample on a jewel be it ever so precious.

3. The last objection under this head is that election renders the means of grace perfectly nugatory. If the elect are to be saved they will be saved, let them do what they will; if the reprobate are to be damned they will be damned, let them do what they may. This objection involves a contradiction. Salvation implies faith, and repentance, and

holiness, and it is perfect nonsense to say that men may believe and repent let them be as skeptical and profligate as they may. Faith necessarily supposes the *Word*, which is the only ground of faith, and the Word is usually dispensed by preaching, and hence the indispensable necessity of an instituted ministry. God's decrees are accomplished through the medium of second causes, and the means of grace are the appointed channels through which He dispenses the blessings of the Gospel. They are a necessary part of the decree. When God determines to save He determines to send His Word and ordinances, and to render them efficacious by the mighty operation of His Spirit. There is no inconsistency in this. God decrees to send rain upon the earth, but He first collects the vapours into clouds. A caviller might say, if it is to rain it will rain, whether there be any clouds or not.

The means of grace in themselves have no efficiency. They cannot convert a single soul; all their efficacy is derived from God and from His electing grace. They are valuable only because He has decreed them as the medium of His blessings. But yet it would seem as if the objectors supposed that the means of grace possess in themselves an inherent efficacy, for how else can election be opposed to them? I shall conclude this head with two extracts from Zanchius: "They who are predestinated to life are likewise predestinated to all those means which are indispensably necessary in order to their meetness for entrance upon and enjoyment of that life, such as repentance, faith, sanctification and perseverance in these to the end. Now, though faith and holiness are not represented as the cause wherefore the elect are saved, yet these are constantly represented as the means through which they are saved, or as the appointed way wherein God leads His elect to glory, these blessings being always bestowed previously to that. Agreeable to all which is that of Austin: 'Whatsoever persons are, through the riches of Divine grace, exempted from the original sentence of condemnation are undoubtedly brought *to hear the Gospel*, and when heard, they are caused to believe.'" The next extract is more to the point: "That absolute predestination does not set aside nor render superfluous the use of preaching, exhortation, etc., we prove from the examples of Christ Himself and His apostles, who all taught and insisted upon the article of predestination, and yet took every opportunity of preaching to sinners, and enforced their ministry with proper rebukes, invitations and exhortations as occasion required. Though they showed unanswerably that salvation is the free gift of God and lies entirely at His sovereign disposal, that men can of themselves do nothing spiritually good, and that it is God who of His own pleasure works in them both to will and to do, yet they did not neglect to address their auditors as being possessed of reason and conscience, nor omit to remind them of their duties as such. Our Saviour Himself expressly and *in terminis* assures us that no man *can* come to Him except the Father draw him, and yet He says, Come unto me, all ye that labour. St. Paul declares it is not of him that willeth nor of him that runneth, and yet exhorts the Corinthians so to run as to obtain the prize. He assures us that we know not what to pray for as we ought, and yet directs us to pray without ceasing. St. James, in like manner, says that every good and perfect gift cometh down from above, and exhorts those who want wisdom to ask it of God. So, then, all these being means whereby the elect are frequently enlightened into the knowledge of Christ, and by which they are, after they have believed through grace, built up in Him, and being means of their perseverance in grace to the end, they are so far from being vain and insignificant that they are highly useful and necessary, and answer many valuable and important ends without in the least shaking the doctrine of predestination in particular or the analogy of faith in general."

We have now given what was promised at the outset: 1. A plain statement of the doctrine of Election as held by the Presbyterian Church. 2. A vindication of its truth by an appeal to the Scriptures. And, 3. We have answered, as we hope satisfactorily, the leading and prominent objections of those who are opposed to Calvinism. The Essay must now stand or fall by its own merits. If it maintains the doctrines of the Bible, it is a comfort to think that God will take care of His own truth, whatever may become of this feeble effort to defend it; if the doctrines here advanced are false, the sooner they fall to the ground the better. Nothing now remains to complete our design but the deduction of a few obvious inferences.

1. This doctrine pre-eminently glorifies God, and that in several respects. (1.) It glorifies the independence and omnipotence of the Divine will. Every other scheme renders the plans and purposes of God in some measure dependent upon the conduct and determinations of his creatures, and Arminians have no hesitation in avowing that the designs of God are susceptible of failure, although He solemnly declares, "My counsel shall stand, and I will do all my pleasure." It is the will of God, we are told, that each and every man should be saved. The fact that all are not, and will not be, saved, shows one of two things—either that God *could not* accomplish His own design, or that the Divine will is dependent on the will of the creature. Hence God either has no settled purpose of His own, or is unable to carry it out as He would wish. This is the necessary and unavoidable consequence of conditional decrees; they virtually dethrone God by making the volitions of man of equal importance in the government of the world with His own. They destroy at once His independence and omnipotence. But the doctrine of predestination ascribes to God that which unquestionably belongs to Him, the supreme disposal of all events "according to the counsel of His own will." "Our God is in the heavens, He hath done whatsoever He hath pleased. There is none that can stay His hand or say unto him, What doest Thou?" Creation and Providence are nothing but the actual evolutions in time of the secret purpose which lay in the bosom of God from

all eternity. There is nothing fortuitous, nothing accidental, nothing unexpected, because nothing does or can take place which has not been previously determined by "the counsel and foreknowledge of God." While God as yet existed alone, supremely glorious in Himself, before one particle of matter had been called into being or a solitary soul was found to adore and reverence the perfection of Deity, He scanned in the light of an infallible omniscience and fixed by the power of an immutable decree all objects and events, whether small or great, whether grand or minute. He simply *wills*, and emptiness and desolation become peopled with a thousand inhabitants of a thousand ranks and gradations of being, the wheels of Providence begin to roll, and every creature, whether small or great, organic or inorganic, material or intelligent, walks in the track which an eternal purpose had settled and arranged. "According, therefore, to the Scripture representation," says Toplady, "Providence neither acts vaguely and *at random*, like a blind archer who shoots uncertainly in the dark as well as he can, nor yet *pro re nata*, or as the unforeseen exigence of affairs may require; like some blundering statesman who plunges, it may be, his country and himself into difficulties, and then is forced to unravel his cobweb and reverse his plan of operations as the best remedy for those disasters which the court-spider had not the wisdom to foresee. But shall we say this of God? 'Twere blasphemy! He that dwelleth in the heavens laugheth all these miserable afterthoughts to scorn. God who can neither be overreached nor overpowered has all these post-expedients in derision. He is incapable of mistake. He knows no levity of will. He cannot be surprised with any unforeseen inconveniences. 'His throne is in heaven, and His kingdom ruleth over all.' Whatever, therefore, comes to pass, comes to pass as a part of the original plan, and is the offspring of that prolific series of causes and effects which owes its birth to the ordaining and permissive will of Him in whom 'we all live, and move, and have our being.'

Providence in time is the hand that delivers God's purpose of those beings and events with which that purpose was pregnant from everlasting." All events hang upon the nod of Jehovah, while His purposes and plans are dependent upon nothing but the "unsearchable counsel of His own will." He is the mighty Ruler of the universe, and His *will, His eternal purpose*, is supreme and irresistible through all the boundless ranges of existence. Amid the seeming irregularity and confusion which distract the world, amid all the failures in human schemes and calculations which are daily taking place, amid the horrors of war, the fall of kingdoms and the ruins of empire, there is one grand, unchangeable purpose which never fails, but which meets its accomplishment alike in the frustration or success of all other purposes. Every event in nature or in grace is simply an evolution of that grand purpose; and could the thread of this purpose be traced by the limited intellect of man in all its bearings and relations, chaos would exhibit regularity, and order and harmony would rise from confusion. In fact, the *glory* of the Divine independence and omnipotence is so inseparably connected with predestination that even Unitarians when describing the Divine majesty forget their system and substantially acknowledge the fundamental principles of Calvinism. They cannot portray the majesty of God without it. Hence the following extract from Buckminster's Sermon on Providence need not surprise us: "How inexpressibly great is that Being who penetrates at once the recesses and circumscribes within Himself the boundless ranges of Creation; who pierces into the profound meditations of the most sublime intelligence above with the same ease that He discerns the wayward projects of the child; who knows equally the abortive imaginations and the wisest plans of every creature that ever has thought or ever will think throughout the realms of intellect! How wonderful is that power which wields with equal ease the mightiest and the feeblest agents, directs the resistless thunder-bolt, or wafts a feather through the air; bursts out in the imprisoned lava, or rests on the peaceful bosom of the lake; rides on the rapid whirlwind, or whispers in the evening air! Think, I pray you, of that wisdom which conducts at the same moment the innumerable purposes of all His creatures, and whose own grand purpose is equally accomplished by the failure or success of all the plans of all His creatures. Think of Him under whom all agents operate, because by Him all beings exist. Think of Him who has but to will it, and all moving Nature pauses in her course, chaos succeeds to the harmony of innumerable spheres and eternal darkness overwhelms this universe of light. Yet in the midst of darkness His throne is stable and all is light about the seat of God!" It is really amazing that any one who has correct apprehensions of the moral character of God should be at all opposed to the supremacy and independence of His righteous will. Supremely just, and wise, and holy, it ought to be a matter of thanksgiving and joy that such a Being controls the armies of heaven and the hosts of earth, and all should join the shout of the redeemed in glory, "Hallelujah, the Lord God Omnipotent reigneth!"

(2.) This doctrine not only glorifies the omnipotence and independence of God's will, but furnishes an illustrious display of His grace. The Scriptures represent the grace and mercy of God as the only sources from which all our blessings are derived, and particularly the saving blessings of the Gospel. We are everywhere described in the Bible as having no claim upon God, but as being justly exposed to His wrath and curse. Polluted and defiled by nature, we are under a righteous sentence of condemnation, and all holy beings would approve the severity of the Divine judgment, if we, like the devils, were eternally cut off from all hope of pardon or acceptance. This is the natural state of every soul of man, and this is the light in which God saw us when the purpose of salvation went forth in favour of His elect. He saw them in their *blood*, and when nothing could have been justly expected but vengeance and death, He said unto them, " *Live.*" Here was *grace*—pure, unmerited favour—breaking through all the barriers of their depravity and guilt, and yearning toward them with an amazing purpose of redemption and life. But the questions might well have been asked, "How shall I put thee among the children?" "How shall I reconcile the conflicting claims of grace and justice and prepare my elect for an inheritance among them that are holy?" Here *grace* becomes still more wonderful. It pitches upon the eternal Son, the second person of the adorable Trinity, and enters into a solemn covenant transaction with Him to redeem, and sanctify, and save. He undertakes, as the Substitute and Surety of the elect, in the fullness of time to become their kinsman by being born of a woman; to humble Himself by being found in fashion as a man; to obey the law as a covenant in their name, and to bring in an everlasting righteousness; to redeem them from its awful curse by being made a curse for them; and to satisfy completely in their behalf all the claims of justice and of law, so that God consistently with His adorable perfections could regard them with an eye of favour and acceptance. The next step in this glorious economy of grace is the mission of the Holy Spirit to apply the purchased redemption to the hearts of the elect by His efficient, almighty operations. Here, then, is an astonishing display of grace, such as can consist with no other doctrine but that of election. Here is a chain of Divine love reaching from the great decree of salvation in the counsels of eternity to its full accomplishment in the regions of glory. Not one link of this golden chain hangs upon human merit—all, all from first to last is pure, unmerited grace. No wonder that the Apostle, in speaking of election, breaks forth into doxologies, for that doctrine erects an eternal monument to the glory of God's grace. It brings down every lofty imagination, abases every high thought that exalts itself against God, and issues forth the solemn and peremptory edict that "no flesh shall glory in His presence." "But of Him are ye in Christ Jesus who of God is made unto us wisdom, and righteousness, and sanctification, and redemption, that according as it is written, he that glorieth let him glory in the Lord." "Blessed be the God and Father of our Lord Jesus Christ, who hath blessed us with all spiritual blessings in heavenly places in Christ Jesus, according as He hath chosen us in Him before the foundation of the world, to the *praise of the glory of His grace*, wherein He hath made us accepted in the Beloved." This grace becomes remarkably conspicuous, because it is confined to the elect. Such a limitation of its objects shows in the light of undeniable reality its utter undeservedness. Had it been promiscuously extended to all, its freeness could not have been so remarkably displayed, but by being withheld from some the demerit of all is unanswerably established, and just in proportion as that is established the freeness of Divine grace is exalted. It is a flimsy cavil that grace to be infinite must include every possible object; then, verily, the devils would be saved. The plain truth is that the Divine attributes are all infinite only as they exist in God, and not in relation to the number or extent of the objects on which they are exercised.

(3.) This doctrine glorifies God's justice. "But what if God, willing to show His wrath and to make His power known, endured with much long-suffering the vessels of wrath fitted to destruction?" Romans ix. 22. "The two objects," says Professor Hodge, "which Paul here specifies as designed to be answered by the punishment of the wicked, are the manifestation of the wrath of God and the exhibition of His power. The word *wrath* is used here as in chapter i. 18, for the Divine displeasure against sin, the calm and holy disapprobation of evil, joined with the determination to punish those who commit it. Though the inherent ill desert of sin must ever be regarded as the primary ground of the infliction of punishment—a ground which would remain in full force were no beneficial results anticipated from the misery of the wicked—yet God has so ordered His government that the evils which sinners incur shall result in the manifestation of His character, and the consequent promotion of the holiness and happiness of His intelligent creatures throughout eternity." I would only add that if sin be an infinite evil, the Divine displeasure against it must be signal and conspicuous; but if God had included the whole human race in His gracious purpose of salvation, it might be a question whether mercy had not eclipsed justice. But by graciously electing some and passing by others the Divine justice is doubly manifested: First, in the sufferings and death of Christ as the Substitute of the elect; and, secondly, in the persons of the reprobate themselves. But be this as it may, the punishment of the wicked can never be regarded as otherwise than just; and so long as God continues to be supremely holy and opposed to sin, it cannot be thought strange that the terrors of His wrath should overtake the guilty.

I have now shown, in these few and simple observations, that the doctrine of Election glorifies God, particularly His independence, omnipotence, grace and justice. But I do not mean to insinuate that God elected one and rejected another for the purpose of merely displaying His character. This is the natural and obvious result, but it by no means follows that this was the cause. On the contrary, it is the plain and undeniable doctrine of the Scriptures that "His counsels are unsearchable, and His ways past finding out." The reasons of the Divine procedure are the secret things which are known only to Himself. We know facts, and in many cases we can trace results; but we "know not the mind of the Lord," and cannot, without arrogance and presumption, undertake to inquire into the why and the wherefore of the Divine administration. He simply declares that He "worketh all things according to the counsel of His own will." This is all that He has revealed, and it is all that we are able to ascertain. When we reach the will of God we must stop; we can go no farther. Why He wills so and so is a question which we are utterly unable to solve, and it is darkening counsel by words without knowledge when we presume to prate about the general good of the universe and the greatest happiness of the greatest number. No doubt God has reasons for the conduct of His government, but we know them not; His *will* is law to us and the utmost boundary of our knowledge. Manifestly, the efficient cause of election and reprobation, in the Scriptures, is referred only to the sovereign will of Jehovah, as has been proved already at considerable length. But we should by no means confound this with the final cause or natural result which is certainly the manifestation of His glory; or, as the Confession of Faith expresses it, election is "to the praise of His glorious grace," and reprobation "to the praise of His glorious justice." By observing this necessary distinction between efficient and final causes we shall sail clear of the dangerous quicksands of Hopkinsian error.

2. The second inference which I would deduce from this doctrine is the infallible perseverance of the saints. This results necessarily from the immutability of God. His counsel shall stand—His will cannot be defeated, and therefore all the objects of His special love must necessarily be saved. The certainty of election is the ground of Paul's triumphant assurance in the eighth of Romans: "Who shall separate us from the love of Christ? Shall tribulation, or distress, or persecution, or famine, or nakedness, or peril, or sword? Nay, in all these things we are more than conquerors through Him that loved us. For I am persuaded that neither death, nor life, nor angels, nor principalities, nor powers, nor things present, nor things to come, nor height, nor depth, nor any other creature, shall be able to separate us from the love of God which is in Christ Jesus our Lord."

3. The next inference which may safely be drawn is the doctrine of limited atonement. We have seen that God has no purpose of salvation to all—that He has no design whatever of saving the whole human race; and, therefore, it is preposterous to suppose that the satisfaction of His Son was specifically intended for each and every individual. No doubt it is sufficient, because, in consequence of the union of

the two natures in the person of Christ, His sufferings possess an *infinite* value. No one denies the abundant sufficiency of Christ's merits to save this world and ten thousand others; but the question is, whether or not the satisfaction of the Saviour was designed for any but His own elect—whether it was rendered in the name of any others, or was intended to be available to their salvation? Now, if the doctrine of election and reprobation be true, such an unlimited design would appear to be impossible. How can God intend to save those toward whom He has no purpose of salvation? The two doctrines are wholly irreconcilable,—if election and reprobation be true, universal atonement must fall to the ground; if universal atonement be true, then election must be blotted from the pages of the Bible. As a matter of course, I speak of the work of Christ in the light of a *satisfaction* to Divine justice—the only light in which it is regarded in the word of God. As to that refined system of error which makes the atonement of Christ nothing but a pompous pageant, to amaze and astonish a gazing universe, this is not the place to refute its vapouring pretensions. It is at best a mere creature of the fancy, and entitled to no more respect than the mad ravings of a sick man's dream. Now, if the atonement of Christ is a strict satisfaction to the law and justice of God, in the name and place of every sinner, it is impossible to conceive how God, without manifest injustice, can pass any by and doom them to punishment in their own proper persons. They have already satisfied the law in the person of Christ. How can they then be possibly condemned? Does justice require two satisfactions? We may safely say, then, that universal atonement is not only inconsistent with the doctrine of election, but absolutely incompatible with the ultimate damnation of a single sinner; it is, in other words, when legitimately carried out, nothing but the plain, unvarnished doctrine of universal salvation. It is not necessary, in order to give a warrant of faith and to render it the duty of every sinner to believe on Christ. The offer of the Saviour in the Gospel, which has no reference on its face to the secret designs of God, is the only legitimate ground of faith, and the command of God would render it binding upon every soul to believe on the Saviour, even though He had died for only one solitary sinner. The right of men to receive and rest upon Christ depends not upon the unrevealed purposes of God in regard to His death, but upon the broad and unlimited grant which is contained in the Gospel record, with its cheering invitations and pressing injunctions. In other words, faith fastens on the preceptive and not the decretive will of God. It would certainly imply a defect of some sort in the economy of grace to suppose that Christ died indiscriminately for all men; that is, with the specific design of saving each and every individual, when, in point of fact, it is generally conceded that all men will not be saved. It is much more honourable to the Divine character to limit the design to the number that will actually be redeemed, and to maintain with the advocates of this scheme that the all-sufficiency of the atonement is an adequate ground of a general offer, and the sovereign authority of God an adequate ground of a general obligation to believe.

I have now completed my original design. It is unnecessary to say that consequences of momentous importance, involving the fundamental principles of the Gospel, hang upon the reception or rejection of this doctrine. To the humble Christian, who has been taught it by the Spirit of God—who has been emptied of self in every form and shape, and brought in deep prostration of soul to bow at the footstool of sovereign mercy—it is inexpressibly precious; and he knows something of the spirit in which that song, so often in his mouth, was dictated: "Not unto us, O Lord, not unto us, but unto Thy Name give the glory." In this precious doctrine he finds constant food for humility, gratitude and love; and when tempted to flag in his Christian course, nothing affords a stronger stimulant to duty than a deep sense of God's eternal, unmerited grace—"Lo, I have loved thee with an everlasting love." This doctrine is emphatically children's bread. They are often supported by the nourishment it contains, and strengthened for the race set before them, when they can give no connected, metaphysical account of their experiences or feelings. It is eminently devotional in its tendencies; and it is to be regretted that we are so often compelled to chastise the feelings which it naturally excites, in order to enter the lists of cold-blood argument with those who would rob us of this jewel which our Master has given us. We are often compelled to *reason* when the heart would prompt us to *adore*. It is a scriptural duty to *contend*, and contend *earnestly*, for the faith once delivered to the saints. "Now, unto the King, eternal, immortal, invisible, the only wise God, be honour and glory for ever and ever. AMEN."

PREFATORY NOTE.

THIS treatise on the "Necessity of the Atonement" was delivered as a sermon in the chapel of the South Carolina College on the first day of December, 1844, the text being Romans i. 16. The author was requested to give it to the press, and it was published in 1845 by Samuel Weir, at Columbia.

THE NECESSITY OF THE ATONEMENT.

IN the introductory portion of the Epistle to the Romans the Apostle expresses himself as being not ashamed of the Gospel of Christ, because it was the power of God unto salvation to every believer of it. The exultation and triumph with which he was accustomed to contemplate the provisions of the Gospel show that to his mind the scheme of redemption unfolded the perfections of the Divine character in an aspect of benignity to sinners equally unexpected and glorious. The freshness of interest and intensity of enthusiasm with which he habitually dwelt upon the cross were such as are wont to be elicited by a combination, in objects, of novelty and importance. From it he had received full satisfaction upon questions which had awakened a deep curiosity and baffled the resources of his wisdom to resolve. A light had been reflected from the Person and Offices of Christ which dissipated doubts that had painfully perplexed him, and revealed a prospect which might well endear to him a crucified Redeemer and change the current of his life. Discarding the refined system of licentiousness which renders the happiness of man a more important object than the moral government of God, and makes the distinctions between right and wrong mutable and arbitrary to save the guilty from despair, he assumes, in the masterly exposition which in that Epistle he gives us of the economy of grace, for the fundamental principle of his whole argument, the inseparable connection between punishment and guilt. "The wrath of God," he informs us, "is revealed from heaven against all ungodliness and unrighteousness of men," "who will render to every man according to his deeds; unto them that are contentious and do not obey the truth, but obey unrighteousness, indignation and wrath, tribulation and anguish upon every soul of man that doeth evil, of the Jew first and also of the Gentile."

If sin be in every instance the object of Divine indignation—and such we perceive is the statement of the Apostle—it would seem to be impossible even for God consistently with the perfections of His own nature to save the guilty from its doom. If *every* man must receive according to his deeds, and the wrath of God is revealed from heaven against *all* ungodliness and unrighteousness of men, the universality of guilt would seem to close the door upon every prospect of hope. Nature, at least, left to the resources of her own strength, must always entertain distressing apprehensions that perfection of government and the power of pardon are mutually destructive of each other, and that whatever consequently might be the mercy of God, He could hardly be expected to yield to its impulse at the expense of justice, holiness and truth. To the mind which has been impressed with the magnitude of sin, the purity of God and the stern inflexibility of the Divine law, the possibility of pardon is a question fraught with the profoundest interest and veiled in impenetrable gloom. It is the glory of the Gospel to remove the perplexities of unaided reason, and to explain the method by which God can be just and at the same time justify those who are ungodly. On this account it is styled by the Apostle the *power of God unto salvation*. This expression he seems to have employed as an exact definition of the scheme of redemption. The Gospel is not to be regarded as a simple *revelation* of the mercy of God and His ability to pardon; it is itself His *power* as a Saviour. The implication is irresistible that by the rich provisions of its grace, and by them alone, can the Lord deliver from going down to the pit; that apart from the righteousness revealed to faith, Jehovah Himself has not the *power* to receive the guilty into favour; that the mediation of Christ was the wonderful device of infinite wisdom to *enable* the Almighty in consistency with justice to save the lost. The phraseology of the text is a favourite mode in which the Apostle describes the mystery of the cross. "For the preaching of the cross," he declares in his First Epistle to the Corinthians, "is to them that perish foolishness, but unto us which are saved it is the *power* of God. The Jews require a sign and the Greeks seek after wisdom, but we preach Christ crucified, unto the Jews a stumbling-block, and unto the Greeks foolishness; but unto them which are called, both Jews and Greeks, Christ the *power* of God and the wisdom of God." To the same purport is a passage in Isaiah, in which Jehovah Himself solemnly refers to the grace of the Gospel as constituting His strength to save from death. The disobedient and unprofitable, addressed under the symbol of briers and thorns, are exhorted to make their peace with God, and, what is remarkable, they are directed to do so by taking hold of "His strength." Now as faith in the Divine Redeemer is the only means to tranquillity of conscience, as there is no peace to those who are strangers to the blood of the covenant, Jehovah's *strength* is evidently the same as the atonement of His Son. There lay His power to save, and independently of that He could only be as a devouring flame to briers and thorns. "Who would set the briers and thorns against me in battle? I would go through them, I would burn them together; or let him take hold of my strength that he may make peace with me, and he shall make peace with me."

The Apostle, in his Epistle to the Galatians, seems to me directly to assert that no scheme *could have been* devised, independently of the work of the Son of God, by which salvation could have been effected: "If there had been a law given which could have given life, verily righteousness should have been by the law, but the Scripture hath concluded all under sin, that the promise by faith of Jesus Christ might be given to them that believe." No method, in other words, could have been adopted, even in the plenitude of infinite power, by which God could acquit the guilty without the righteousness which His law demands; and as such a righteousness is wholly impossible to human obedience, it must be secured by the mediation of a substitute. God cannot dispense with the claims of justice. His power to save is moral in its nature, and cannot be exerted—cannot, in truth, be said to exist—while the law pronounces the sentence of death. The reasoning here is precisely analogous to that which succeeds the declaration of the text. The Gospel he pronounces to be the power of God unto salvation, because "therein the righteousness of God is revealed from faith to faith, as it is written, The just shall live by faith."

Such language must appear strange and enigmatical to those who view Christianity as little better than a republication of Natural Religion. Unaccustomed to the awful convictions of the malignity of sin and the holiness of God which the enlightened understanding, through the pressure of conscience, is driven to adopt, they can perceive no difficulty in absolute forgiveness, and cannot consequently comprehend the mystery that restraints should be taken from the power of God by the incarnation and death of the Redeemer. The necessity of atonement, as assumed by the Apostle, is to them inexplicable jargon. The low views in which they indulge themselves of the whole work and offices of the Saviour are to be ascribed to imperfect apprehensions of the government of God. Their fundamental error consists in denying the *need* of satisfaction—in contemplating the Gospel in any other light than as "the power of God unto salvation." It is but a single step more, and the atonement itself is either formally discarded or else frittered away through the subtle distinctions of philosophy and vain deceit. To appreciate aright the death and sufferings of Christ we must have a proper if not an adequate conception of the "needs be" into which He Himself resolved His undertaking—a "needs be" which extended much farther than the fulfilment of prophecy—which had itself given rise to the predictions in having given rise in the depths of eternity to the "counsel of peace." We must enter into the meaning of the great Apostle when he measures the ability of God as a Saviour by His power to provide a justifying righteousness.

The two great principles on which the doctrine of atonement rests are—the inseparable connection between punishment and guilt, and the admissibility under proper restrictions of a surety to endure the curse of the law. The unpardonable nature of sin, the practicability of legal substitution, these are the pillars of the Christian fabric. In the first we acknowledge the indispensable necessity, in the other the glorious possibility, of an atoning Priest. In the first we are taught the wages of sin, in the other that they need not be reaped by ourselves. If the first were true to the exclusion of the second, eternal darkness would settle on the minds of the guilty; it is the second which opened the door of hope and furnished a field, magnificent and ample, in which God might display the resources of His wisdom and unfold the riches of His grace—be at once a just God and a Saviour.

The contemptuous confidence with which sophists and skeptics have denied the propriety of vicarious punishment has evidently proceeded from the foolish apprehension that God, like ourselves, is bound to forgive upon a confession of the fault. If these arrogant disputers of this world could be brought to feel the truth and severity of the first great principle on which the atonement has been stated to rest, they would cling to the second as the only anchor of hope; and instead of expending ingenuity in abortive efforts to undermine its strength, they would probably lay their learning under tribute to defend its fitness, while they permitted their hearts to rejoice in its benignant aspect on the family of man. Let the position be firmly established that God can by no means clear the guilty, that sin must necessarily be punished, and all objections to the doctrine of suretyship would be given to the winds. To cling to them under such circumstances would be with deliberate malice "to despise our own mercies." The expectation of an easy pardon, secretly cherished if not openly avowed, is the real source of pretended difficulties with "the righteousness of faith." Hence, in discussing the doctrine of atonement the foundations should be deeply and securely laid in developing the scriptural account of its necessity. Clear apprehensions upon this point would serve at once to define its nature, determine its extent and put an end to cavils against its reality and truth.

The necessity of the atonement, it may be well to remark, is only the necessity of a means to an end. The end itself, the salvation of the sinner, is in no sense necessary; that is the free and spontaneous purpose of Divine grace. Had all the tribes of men been permitted to sink into hopeless perdition, no violence would have been done to the nature of God, no breach been made in the integrity of His government. But the end having been determined, the death and obedience of Christ were indispensably necessary to carry it into execution. God could not receive the guilty into favour while the demands of His law were unsatisfied against them.

That the design of the atonement was to generate mercy in the Divine Being, to beget the purpose as well as the power to save, is the gratuitous caricature of those who have assailed the work, in order to deny the Divinity, of the Redeemer. As well might it be pretended that the channel which the torrent forces for itself among the rocks and declivities of the mountain, is itself the source of the impetuous current it conducts, or that the air which daily transmits to us light and heat from the sun is therefore the parent of these invaluable gifts. The mediation of Christ and the mercy of God are related to each other as cause and effect, but in an inverse order from that which is stated by Socinians; it is mercy that gives rise to atonement, and not atonement that gives rise to mercy. The scriptural statement is: "God so loved the world that He gave His only-begotten Son, that whosoever believeth in Him should not perish, but have everlasting life." "God commendeth

His love toward us, in that while we were yet sinners Christ died for us." "In this was manifested the love of God toward us, because that God sent His only-begotten Son into the world, that we might live through Him. Herein is love, not that we loved God, but that He loved us, and sent His Son to be the propitiation for our sins." It was not, therefore, the design of the atonement to *make* God merciful—He was merciful before; it was not to generate the *purpose* of salvation—that had existed in the bosom of Deity from all eternity. It was to render the exercise of mercy consistent with righteousness, to maintain the stability of the Divine throne and preserve the integrity of the Divine government, while outlaws and rebels were saved from the fate which their transgressions deserved. It is not in the nature of God to take pleasure in the death of the wicked; it is equally remote from His nature to disregard the distinctions of moral conduct and treat the wicked as the righteous. The atonement, therefore, was necessary—not, as Socinians slanderously report that we affirm, to touch the Divine mind with compassion for the miserable, but, supposing the compassion to exist, to prepare the way by which it might be freely indulged with honour to God and safety to His law, as well as blessedness to man. The Gospel springs from mercy, and all its mysterious arrangements are only the contrivances of infinite wisdom, incited by infinite grace, to acquire the power to save.

It is no impeachment of the perfections of Jehovah to deny the possibility of unconditional remission. On the contrary, a full investigation of the whole subject will conduct, I apprehend, to the firm conviction that under all circumstances of the case it is infinitely more glorious not to be able to forgive without a satisfaction than to relax the severity of law. The *power* of God is only an expression for the *will* of God, and to say that there are things which cannot be the objects of Divine volition may, in one view, be as much to His honour as in another it would detract from His supremacy. The purposes of Deity are not lawless and arbitrary. His will is determined by the perfections of His nature. To say, therefore, that there are things which He cannot *do* is simply to affirm that He cannot *will* them, and to say that He cannot will them is just to assert that they are inconsistent with the perfections of His being. In such cases, consequently, we do not limit, we only define, the power of God; all things are possible which He wills. His will is the measure of His power, but as moral excellence is the measure of His will, it is only to vindicate His character from the charge of weakness and ascribe to Him the highest conceivable praise to deny that He can will what comes into collision with justice, holiness, wisdom or truth. When we speak of impossibilities in reference to God, the impression is likely to be made upon the minds of the thoughtless that there is a limit to what may be called physical omnipotence—that there are purposes which God may desire to accomplish, and yet find Himself unable to effect them. This, however, is a gross mistake. He can do whatsoever He pleases in the armies of heaven and among the inhabitants of earth. His pleasure is nothing different from His might. His volitions are always followed by corresponding operations of His hands. So inseparable is the idea of power from the will of the Almighty that it may, without extravagance, be asserted that the only efficient cause which exists in the universe is the fiat of the Deity. All other phenomena are produced—they are strictly and properly effects; this alone produces, speaks and it is done, commands and it stands fast. Physical causes are only dependent events in the great chain of contingencies fastened to the throne of God, and differ from the appearances which are usually described as their effects in nothing but the order of time. Both alike are destitute of power, and we can never detect the presence of that mysterious and undefinable agent until we ascend to the throne of the Eternal. His will is the spring of universal motion, the cause of every effect.[1] If he should will the unconditional pardon of a sinner, the pardon would not only be possible, but would most certainly and infallibly take place. Whatever He can will is possible—whatever He does will is fact. His will is power.

When it is affirmed, consequently, that God cannot receive the sinner into favour without satisfaction to His justice, the meaning is that He will not; that, however true it is that He hath no pleasure in the death of the wicked, there are qualities of His being, moral perfections of His nature, which make it as incongruous that He should will an unconditional pardon as that He should deny Himself or forfeit His veracity. The impossibility is of the same sort as that which is asserted when it is declared that "He cannot lie."

The proof, therefore, of the necessity of atonement must consist in showing that the glory of God, especially the integrity of His moral character, indispensably demands that sin should be punished. To make it appear that any essential attribute of Deity would be seriously, or even at all, infringed by remitting the penalty, apart from the righteousness of the law, is to furnish a complete demonstration that arbitrary pardon can never be the object of the Divine volition; that whatever purposes of salvation may be cherished in the bosom of God include the design of exacting the demands of justice from the person of a substitute; and that any other course, under the peculiar circumstances of the case, would involve as gross a contradiction as that the Strength of Israel should repent or lay aside His supremacy.

The common delusion that the power of arresting the sentence of a judge is an essential element of sovereignty has arisen, perhaps, from the deceptive analogy of human institutions. The chief magistrate of every nation possesses the prerogative, in a certain department of cases, to commute,

---

[1] [This should be understood in consistency with those views which elsewhere the author has expressed of the spontaneity and responsibility of the human will. See particularly the *addendum* to Lecture X., Vol. I.—EDITOR.]

relax, or at discretion dispense with, the punishment which the laws of the land have pronounced. This feature of human governments is nothing more than a contrivance to mitigate the evils which, under peculiar circumstances that may often happen, and yet that could not be defined in the terms of a statute, might result from the inflexible operation of general rules. To foresee the countless contingencies which control human conduct, to adjust the law to all the modifications of which crime is susceptible, to estimate beforehand the varieties of motives, of palliating and aggravating circumstances which determine the malignity of guilt, is evidently a task which, however important for the strict administration of justice, it is beyond the compass of human sagacity to achieve. The laws of men must consequently be general and extensive, grouping crimes by compendious descriptions into large classes, and affixing the same penalty to each separate species, without respect to the individual differences that must necessarily obtain among them. Human legislation, for the most part, must confine its view to the external expressions, and not to the real character, of motives themselves. The outward acts being the same, but little allowance can be made for constitutional infirmities, violence of temptation, and the delicate shades of feeling in the inner man which may impart very different degrees of malignity to the same action as perpetrated by different individuals. The consequence is, that civil punishments must sometimes transcend the sense of justice and the conviction of expediency which should regulate the severity of the penal code. The imperfection, too, of human tribunals may sometimes pervert the law through prejudice, weakness or corruption, and involve the innocent in the doom of the guilty. To correct these evils, arising from the necessary defect of human legislation, the power of pardon, as it is commonly denominated, though it is more properly a check upon injustice, is generally lodged with the chief executive officer of the state. It does not belong to him as a prerogative of sovereignty, but simply as he is the guardian of the laws, who is bound to enforce them according to the letter, with an occasional discretion according to their spirit when the letter would kill and the spirit would spare. The object is not that he may pardon at discretion, but that, under circumstances which could not have been foreseen by any human legislature, and which, in the moral sense of the community, essentially modify the crime, he might prevent a result which was never really intended, but which, from the general terms of the law, seems to have been contemplated. If human governments were perfect, if rules could be framed with an exact adjustment to all the varieties of individual cases that could possibly come under them, if those appointed to administer them could be exempted from prejudice, partiality, weakness and corruption, no injustice could ever exist to be corrected. The dispensing power would be felt to be an evil, the moral sentiments of the community would in every case sustain the law, nothing could plead for mercy —if indeed that can be called mercy which, in the disguise of pity to an individual, is often the bitterest cruelty to the State—nothing could plead for mercy but a squeamish tenderness, which it is effeminate to cherish and to which it would be wicked to yield. As the probabilities of occasional injustice under the inflexible operation of general rules constitute the true ground of arrangements for pardon in the State, no argument can be drawn from analogy in favour of a similar provision in the moral government of God. There, error, mistake, partiality and corruption can have no place; there, every case is determined upon its own individual merits, and each man is rewarded or punished according to his conduct under laws adapted to all the varieties of motive and temptation. Such, in fact, is the consummate perfection of the Divine administration that actions are never tried in the mass, but estimated according to their minutest details.

The checks and balances which experience has suggested to adjust the inequalities of human constitutions are more than supplied, the need of them is completely obviated, by the knowledge, wisdom, integrity and foresight which belong in infinite and unchanging proportions to the great Monarch of the universe. The very reason, that justice may be done or injustice prevented, which mitigates the sternness of human law, renders it equally important that the decisions of the Almighty should stand. Our laws are flexible, because we are liable to error; God's laws are inflexible, because, as Judge of all the earth, He must infallibly and always do right. The power of dispensing with the law is no part of the conception of sovereignty. To rule by arbitrary will without reference to a fixed standard of moral distinctions; to change the law or its sanctions at pleasure, according to the dictates of caprice, prejudice, partiality or expediency; to infuse uncertainty into the administration of justice, exciting expectations to-day which shall be mocked to-morrow, and awakening imaginary fears only in sport,—is the description of a despotism and not of a government; and he who sits supreme at the head of such a moral chaos or anarchy is not a sovereign, but a tyrant. The true idea of sovereignty is that of power which is responsible to none—whose decisions must stand on the simple ground that there is no tribunal to reverse them. God is sovereign, not because He rules without law or can set it aside at discretion, but because He is supreme and irresponsible, giving none account of His matters to any above Him. In the fact that He accomplishes His pleasure among the armies of heaven and the inhabitants of earth—that none can say unto Him, What doest Thou? or demand the reasons of any of His dispensations—lies the true ground of His sovereignty. His counsel must stand; from His decrees there is no appeal. He sits supreme at the head of the universe, and therefore is truly and properly a Sovereign. To say that the power of pardon—that is, the power of changing the operation of the law—is an essential element of such a supremacy, is equivalent to saying that He cannot be sovereign without being fickle; it is, in other words, to degrade His perfections in order to make Him the Disposer of events. The error has arisen from partial attention to the fact that the prerogative of mercy in human institutions is generally committed to the representative of sovereignty. The ground, however, of this arrangement is convenience and despatch. There is no reason in the nature of things why it might not be entrusted to an officer selected for the sole purpose of possessing it. To the chief magistrate it belongs, not in virtue of his office as a ruler, but as it is a solemn trust from the community, which, for obvious reasons, can be more available in his hands than in any other depository.

The doctrine of the atonement has been defended upon principles which, according to my apprehensions—and I would speak with profound respect of the opinions of such men as Grotius, Rutherford, Twiss and Magee—are not strictly applicable to Divine institutions. They have represented satisfaction as demanded, not so much by the justice of God as the wisdom of the measure, and have made it a matter rather of expediency than imperative necessity.[1]

[1] The following extract from the Lectures of Hill, who has professedly followed Grotius, may be taken as a fair specimen of the sentiments of all those divines who are mentioned in the text:

"The first principle upon which a fair statement of the doctrine of the atonement proceeds is this, that sin is a violation of law, and that the Almighty, in requiring an atonement in order to the pardon of sin, acts as the supreme lawgiver. . . . . If the Almighty, then, is to be regarded as a lawgiver, we must endeavour to rise to the most exalted conceptions which we are able to form of the plan of His moral government; and for this purpose it is necessary that we should abstract from it every kind of weakness which is incident to the administration of human governments, and lay hold of those principles and maxims which reason and experience teach us to consider as essential to a good government, and without which it does not appear to us that that expression has any meaning. Now, it is the first principle of every good government that laws are enacted for the benefit of the community. The happiness of the whole body depends upon their being observed, for they would not have been enacted if the observance of them had been a matter of indifference to the public. Hence, every person who violates the laws, besides the disrespect which he shows to that authority by which they were enacted, besides the hurt which individuals may sustain by his action, does an injury to the public, because he disturbs that order and security which the laws establish. It is therefore essential to the excellence of government that there succeeds, immediately after disobedience, what is

They tacitly assume, if they do not positively assert, as the basis of their argument, the cardinal principle of modern politics, that the ultimate end of government is the good of the governed, and that the primary design of punishment is to inspire a salutary fear in the breasts of the subjects. It is, in other words, a moral expedient to save the law from contempt. To pardon the guilty upon a profession of repentance, however sincere, would be to destroy the dignity of government, to weaken the bands of authority and afford a premium to crime. As a measure of impolicy, therefore, likely to be dangerous to the interests of virtue, no wise ruler would resort to it. The efficacy of law depends so much upon the certainty of its sanctions, that no consideracalled guilt—*i. e.*, the desert of punishment, an obligation to suffer that which the law prescribes. Accordingly, in the code of laws of many northern nations, who were accustomed to estimate all crimes at certain rates, a murderer not only paid a sum to the relations of the deceased as a compensation for their loss, but he paid a sum to the king for the breach of the peace. And in all countries that which is properly called punishment does not mean the putting the rights of a private party, who may have been immediately injured, in the same state in which they were before the trespass was committed, but it means the reparation made to the public by the suffering of the criminal for the disorder arising from his breach of the laws. The law generally defines what the measure of this suffering shall be, and it is applied to particular cases by criminal judges, who, being only interpreters of the law, have no power to remit the punishment. It is true that in most human governments a power is lodged somewhere of granting pardon, because, from the imperfection which necessarily adheres to them, it may often be inexpedient or even unjust that a person who has been legally condemned should suffer; and there are times when the legislature sees meet to pass acts of indemnity. But it is only in very particular circumstances that the safety of the state admits the escape of a criminal; and in most cases the supreme authority proceeds, not with wrath, but from a calm and fixed regard to the essential interests of the community, to deter other subjects from violating the laws, by exhibiting to their view punishment as the consequence of transgression. If we apply these maxims and principles, which appear to us implied in the very nature of good government, we shall find it impossible to conceive of God as a lawgiver, without thinking it essential to His character to punish transgression; and the perfection of His government, far from superseding this exercise of that character, seems to render it the more becoming and the more indispensable."—*Lectures*, Book iv., c. iii., sec. 1.

tions which can occur in the government of God should be permitted to arrest its operation. Severity to individuals is a public benefit. The character of the Ruler, too, might suffer in the eyes of his subjects from the appearance of vacillation, inconsistency and weakness, which a neglect to execute his threatenings, would perhaps present. To maintain, therefore, the stability of government, to prevent rebellion, and to preserve respect for the person of the Lawgiver, it is highly proper that unconditional pardons should never be admitted. This is an outline of the argument by which vicarious satisfaction has been commonly defended.

To say nothing here of what will afterward appear, that every single proposition in this chain of reasoning is false, it is evident that if the whole were true, the atonement is placed upon a basis too feeble to support so solid a fabric. Its necessity is not made out by showing that it is conducive to the ends of government. Government itself may be contingent and arbitrary, susceptible of change, relaxation or amendment. Unless the law be immutable and necessary, unconditional pardon, however inexpedient, would conflict with no principle of moral rectitude. It might be unwise, but would not be unjust—unsafe, but not essentially wrong. There are, besides, serious objections to resting the atonement on the basis of expediency.

If it is to be resolved into reasons of State, and treated as an expedient to prevent the evils of absolute forgiveness, then it produces no direct effect upon the mind of God, but reaches the Ruler through the medium of the subject. If its leading object is to render it possible to pardon with safety, then its operation is primarily upon the objects of favour, and not upon the Author. Though it is a satisfaction, yet its value depends not immediately upon its relation to the law, but upon its tendency to deter from disobedience and to check the contagion of evil example. Just in proportion as it creates the conviction that transgression is dangerous and obedience safe, does it answer its primary end. Its being a satisfaction to justice is not necessary on the score of justice itself, but on account of the moral impression which as a satisfaction it is suited to enstamp. Now, if the production of such an impression were the grand result which God intended to achieve by the sufferings and death of His Son, the question naturally arises whether it could not have been compassed by a less expensive and imposing arrangement. Expediency opens a boundless field of possibilities from which the wisdom of God might have chosen other contrivances suited to signalize His hatred of sin and to deter from rebellion, without subjecting the innocent to the shame and agony of an awful crucifixion. It might indeed be a question, if the government of God depends upon no higher principles than those of expediency, whether any considerations of policy could justify an act so extraordinary in its character as the humiliation and death of God's eternal Son. The obvious impression under such circumstances would seem to be that the happiness of man was a more important end than the glory and blessedness of the Second Person in the adorable Godhead. Expediency holds the scales; it is settled that the law cannot be sacrificed, and the real question is, whether on the score of public advantage it is better that the guilty should suffer or that the Son should die. Accordingly, we find that those who have been most deeply imbued with utilitarian views of the Divine government have not scrupled to deny the reality of the penal sufferings of our Lord.[1] They

[1] "Thus far we have been examining and attempting to ascertain precisely the nature of the difficulty which it was the business of the atonement to remove. The difficulty, it appears, consists wholly in the second ground of punishment—that is, in the necessity of distributive justice to the well-being of the universe. To remove this difficulty, or to enable God righteously to pardon the repenting sinner, the atonement must give the same support to law, or must display as impressively the perfect holiness and justice of God, as the execution of the law on transgressors would. It must be something different from the execution of the law itself, because it is to be a substitute for it, something which will render it safe and proper to suspend the regular course of distributive justice. If such an expedient can be found, then an adequate atonement is possible, otherwise it is not. Now such an expedient the text represents the

deny that He made a satisfaction to justice, since the moral impression which according to this scheme constitutes the end of the atonement could be as easily effected by a sym-

sacrifice of Christ to be. It is 'a declaration of the righteousness of God, so that he might be just,' might secure the objects of distributive justice as it becomes a righteous moral governor to do, 'and yet might justify,' or acquit and exempt from punishment, him that believeth in Jesus. It was, in the nature of it, an exhibition or proof of the righteousness of God. It did not consist in an execution of the law on any being whatever, for it was a substitute for an execution of it. It did not annihilate the guilt of transgressors, or cause them to be either really or apparently innocent, for this was impossible; it rather proclaimed the atrocity of the guilt. It did not fulfil the law, or satisfy its demands on transgressors, for then their acquittal would have been an act of justice, not of grace, and the atonement would have been but another mode of executing the law itself, not a substitute for it. Its immediate influence was not on the characters and relations of men as transgressors, nor on the claims of the law upon them. Its direct operation was on the feelings and the apprehensions of the beings at large who are under the moral government of God. In two respects it coincided precisely with a public execution of the law itself; its immediate influence was on the same persons, and that influence was produced in the same way, by means of a public exhibition. For what is a public execution of the law on culprits but a public exhibition? and an exhibition which is intended to affect the feelings and the apprehensions of the community, to impress them all with high respect and reverence for the law, that stern guardian of the public weal? The atonement, to be a proper substitute for the execution of the law, ought to be a public exhibition, and such an exhibition as would impress all the creatures of God with a deep and awful sense of the majesty and sanctity of His law, of the criminality of disobedience to it, and of the holy, unbending rectitude of God as a moral governor. And such, according to the text, the atonement really was. It was an exhibition or manifestation of the righteousness of God, and an exhibition of such a nature as must strike every intelligent beholder with astonishment. It was a transaction without a parallel in the history of the Divine government. The Son of God, the Lord of glory, Himself descended to this lower world. He veiled His Godhead in a human body, and humbled Himself to dwell with men. He toiled and bore reproach, and suffered from pain and weariness and hunger. He condescended to instruct men, to be their Physician, their Friend, their very Servant; He washed His disciples' feet. He was obedient to every ordinance of God and man; He fulfilled all righteousness. He suffered Himself to be reviled and persecuted, to be arraigned, condemned and crucified. He expired amidst the mockery of Jews and the insults of a Roman soldiery. That this was an astonishing exhibition—an exhibition bolical display. The sentiments of Murdock and those of Grotius diverge at this point. The Hopkinsian divine discards satisfaction, because he supposes that the ends of

calculated to fill the mind with wonder and amazement—every one feels instantly. The only difficulty is to understand how this exhibition was a display of the righteousness of God. To solve it, some have resorted to the supposition that the Son of God became our sponsor, and satisfied the demands of the law on us by suffering in our stead. But to this hypothesis there are strong objections. To suppose that Christ was really and truly our sponsor, and that He suffered in this character, would involve such a transfer of legal obligations and liabilities and merits as is inadmissible, and to suppose anything short of this will not explain the difficulty. For if, while we call Him a sponsor, we deny that He was legally holden or responsible for us, and liable in equity to suffer in our stead, we assign no intelligible reason why His sufferings should avail anything for our benefit, or display at all the righteousness of God. Besides, this hypothesis, like all the others which suppose the Son of God to have first entered into a close, legal connection with sinful men, and afterward to have redeemed them, would make the atonement to be a legal satisfaction for sin, and then the acquittal of the sinner would be no pardon at all, but would follow in the regular course of law. We must, therefore, resort to some other solution. And what is more simple and at the same time satisfactory than that which is suggested by the text? The atonement was an exhibition or display—that is, it was a symbolical transaction. It was a transaction in which God and His Son were the actors, and they acted in perfect harmony, though performing different parts in the august drama. The Son in particular passed voluntarily through various scenes of humiliation and sorrow and suffering, while the Father looked on with all that tenderness and deep concern which He, and none but He, could feel. The object of both in this affecting tragedy was to make an impression on the minds of rational beings everywhere and to the end of time. And the impression to be made was that God is a holy and righteous God, that while inclined to mercy He cannot forget the demands of justice, and the danger to His kingdom from the pardon of the guilty—that He must show His feelings on this subject, and show them so clearly and fully that all His rational creatures shall feel that he honours His law while suspending its operation as much as He would by the execution of it. But how, it may be asked, are these things expressed or represented by this transaction? The answer is, symbolically. The Son of God came down to our world to do and to suffer what He did, not merely for the sake of doing those acts and enduring those sorrows, but for the sake of the impression to be made on the minds of all beholders by His labouring and suffering in this manner. In this sense it was a symbolical transaction. And the import or meaning of it, as of every government could be accomplished without it; the Semi-socinian admits satisfaction, because he felt that vicarious suffering was the only basis for the desired impression. They reason upon the same general principle, although their conclusions are flatly contradictory. The Hopkinsian, to my mind, has the advantage in the argument. We can evidently see no wisdom in an arrangement in which the means are vastly disproportioned to the end. Even to finite creatures like ourselves it is possible to conceive of other plans beside the penal death of the Redeemer, by which sin might have been rebuked and the government of God maintained, if the only purpose had been to devise a scheme for dispensing mercy with safety. The strong language of the Apostle, however, which represents this as the *only* means by which God could accomplish the end He had in view, is utterly inexplicable if the atonement were nothing but a stroke of policy; and those who adopt this view, it deserves to be remarked, are not willing to assert that the mediation of Christ was in such a sense necessary as that God *could* not, consistently with His glory, pardon without it. They speak of it as wise, fit and proper, but not as absolutely necessary.[1] The difficulty of pardon, according to

other symbol, is to be learned either from the circumstances and occasion of it, or from the explanation that accompanies it."—*Murdock's Sermon on Nature of the Atonement*, pp. 20, 24.

[1] "When, therefore, Grotius, Stillingfleet and Clarke are charged (as they are in H. Taylor's B. Mord., Let. 5) with contending for 'the necessity of a vindication of God's honour, either by the suffering of the offenders or by that of Christ in their room,' they are by no means to be considered as contending that it was impossible for God to have established such a dispensation as might enable Him to forgive the sinner without some satisfaction to his justice (which is the sense forcibly put upon their words), but that, according to the method and dispensation which God's wisdom *has* chosen, there results a *moral necessity* of such vindication founded in the *wisdom* and *prudence* of a Being who has announced Himself to mankind as an upright Governor, resolved to maintain the observance of His laws. That by the *necessity* spoken of is meant but a *moral necessity*, or, in other words, a *fitness* and propriety, Dr. Clarke himself informs us, for he tells us (Sermon 137, vol. ii., p. 142, fol. ed.), that 'when the honour of God's laws had been diminished by sin, it was *reasonable* and *necessary*,

their view, does not spring from the essential attributes of God, but from the views of His government likely to be taken by His subjects, and the result of the Saviour's sacrifice has been, not that God might be *just*, though that is true, but that He might be *safe* in justifying those who believe on Jesus. The fundamental error of this whole scheme is an inadequate conception of the origin and nature of the Divine government, and of the principal end of Divine punishments. Correct apprehensions upon these points will furnish a triumphant vindication of the indis-

in respect of God's *wisdom in governing* the world, that there should be a vindication,' etc. And again, (Sermon 138, vol. ii., p. 150), in answer to the question, 'Could not God, if He had pleased, absolutely and of His supreme authority, without any sufferings at all, have pardoned the sins of those whose repentance He thought fit to accept?' he says, 'It becomes not us to presume to say He had not *power* so to do,' but that there seems a *fitness* in His testifying His indignation against sin, and 'the death of Christ was *necessary* to make the pardon of sin reconcilable, not perhaps absolutely with *strict justice* (for we cannot presume to say that God might not consistently with mere *justice* have remitted as much of His own right as He pleased), but it is *necessary*, at least in *this* respect, to make the pardon of sin consistent with the *wisdom* of God in His good government of the world, and to be a *proper attestation* of His irreconcilable hatred against all unrighteousness.' That the word *necessary* is imprudently used by Dr. Clarke and others, I readily admit, as it is liable to be misunderstood, and furnishes matter of cavil to those who would misrepresent the whole of the doctrine. But it is evident from the passages I have cited that so far from considering the sacrifice of Christ as a *debt* paid to, because rigorously exacted by, the Divine *justice*, it is represented by Dr. Clarke, and generally understood, merely as a fit expedient, demanded by the *wisdom* of God, whereby mercy might be safely administered to sinful man. Now, it is curious to remark, that H. Taylor, who so warmly objects to this notion of a necessity of vindicating God's honour, as maintained by Dr. Clarke, etc., when he comes to reply to the Deist in defence of the scheme of Christ's mediation, uses a mode of reasoning that seems exactly similar: 'God (B. Mord., Let. 5) was not *made* placable by intercession, but was ready and willing to forgive before as well as after, and only waited to do it *in such a manner as might best show His regard to righteousness.*' Is not this, in other words, saying there was a *fitness*, and consequently a *moral necessity*, that God should forgive sins through the intercession and meritorious obedience of Christ, for the purpose of *vindicating His glory as a righteous Governor?*"—*Magee's Discourses.* vol. i., p. 187.

pensable necessity of vicarious satisfaction in order to the exercise of grace.

Plausible and common as the doctrine is, it seems to me to be unquestionably false that the primary design of the Divine government is the good of the subjects. This is to confound the ultimate end with an incidental advantage, the final cause with a collateral effect. Happiness, having no separate and independent existence of its own, can never be made a separate and independent object of pursuit; it is a state of mind resulting from the possession of that which is suited to extinguish pain and to gratify desire. As there is no philosopher's stone for transmuting vulgar materials into gold, and for supplying men with wealth without diligence, activity and industry in the lucrative pursuits of life, so there are no means of imparting to them happiness, without imparting to them the objects which, from their relations to the state and affections of the heart, are usually denominated good. The highest felicity, it is true, accrues to the creature from uniform obedience to the law of God; but the law was not established on account of its tendencies to promote the enjoyment of the subject; these tendencies, on the other hand, result from the adaptation of the subject to the law. The government of God was not adjusted with reference to man, but man was constituted with reference to it. To make the creature an end to the Creator, and not the Creator an end to the creature, is to reverse the natural order, making that supreme which is only subordinate, and that subordinate which is truly supreme. From the nice and beautiful proportions which exist, in an unfallen state, between the moral capacities of the creature and the circumstances in which he is placed, he finds, with the Psalmist, that the statutes of the Lord are right, rejoicing the heart, and that perfect peace is the inheritance of those who love the testimonies of God. The affections of the subject, while yet a stranger to sin, move in such perfect harmony with the wheels of government that the rarest beatitude is the inseparable fruit of obedience. Still, the production of happiness was not the end which God proposed in the promulgation of His law; it was contemplated as an effect, a subordinate and incidental effect, which would infallibly take place upon the accomplishment of the nobler purposes which determined the decisions of His will. The true end of the Divine government, as of all the institutions of the Almighty, must be sought, not in the good of the creature, however certainly promoted, but in the GLORY OF GOD. This is the only object which is worth the attention of the Eternal Mind, and as it includes in itself all that is exalted in excellence, illustrious in truth, charming in beauty and delightful in goodness, the steady prosecution of it is an unfailing pledge of the ultimate prosperity and triumph of whatever can adorn, dignify or please. No danger can be apprehended to the universe while He, who sits supreme at its head, is the Father of truth, the fountain of purity and the patron of right. It is His glory to be what He is. The possession of infinite perfections and the enjoyment within Himself of unchanging blessedness, independence and self-sufficiency, are characteristics of the Deity which render it impossible that His manifold works should spring from any other motive but the counsel of His own will. To reveal Himself, to declare what He is, to make known the properties of His being, to manifest His glory by inscribing His character upon the achievements of His hand, is the great design with which He spread the heavens above us, adorned the earth beneath us, and peopled it with plants, animals and men. What are called the natural or physical attributes of God are displayed by His works, as passive recipients of the impressions of knowledge, power and wisdom which He has enstamped upon them. The heavens declare God's glory and the firmament showeth His handiwork, not because they are conscious themselves of the high destiny they fulfil but because the intelligent beholder traces the Divine providence, wisdom and power in their being, harmony and motions.

The moral perfections of God, which constitute pre-eminently His glory, cannot be *passively* displayed. Traces of justice, fidelity and truth cannot be detected in inanimate objects nor impressed upon involuntary agents. If the Deity should blot from existence every moral creature and suffer every other portion of His works to stand, there would not, in all the compass of the universe, be a single object to reflect the beauty of His holiness! Nature would be dumb in reference to the very characteristics of the Godhead which render it supremely and ineffably blessed. It is hard to conceive that a creation destitute of moral intelligences, incapable of love, gratitude or truth, could be an object of complacent contemplation to God. His own blessedness is unquestionably derived from the moral perfections of His being. Wisdom, knowledge and power possess no inherent and essential glory apart from their subserviency to the interests of holiness. Invest a being with unlimited might, sagacity and knowledge, and deprive him at the same time of integrity of character, and you make him an object of detestation to others and a burden to himself. Severed from goodness, knowledge is craft, power is violence, and sagacity is fraud. Taking *life* as a compendious expression for all the elements which constitute felicity, it may be truly said that the life of God is His HOLINESS.

We are accustomed to take quite too limited a view of the material universe of God. In its relations to us, it may perhaps be true that it rises no higher in the scale of dignity than to reveal the natural perfections of its Author. But the ground of the complacency with which He beholds it, and on which He pronounced it very good, is probably the part which it is appointed to play in that grand and comprehensive economy of things whose final scope is to manifest His glory as a Being of eternal rectitude. No doubt unity of purpose pervades all the works of the Almighty. The scheme of His government is one; and though there be wheels within wheels, plans within plans, all move on in unbroken harmony and tend to a common result. There is a subordination of parts,—the inanimate to the living, the material to the spiritual, the spiritual to the moral, and all to the glory of God; and when He casts the eye of His omniscience upon any portion of His works, He delights not in it as an isolated fragment, however perfect in its kind or however clearly displaying any single perfection of His nature, but as a means tending, in its proper place, to the development of the great result which the whole was designed to accomplish. The columns, arches and canopy of the temple are not admired upon their own account, but on account of their relations to the magnificent structure which they support, cement and adorn.

Such being the pre-eminence of moral distinctions, it is evidently no extravagance to assert that the subordination of its parts to a moral end is the probable cause of the creation of the universe and the measure of God's complacency in it. But as His moral perfections cannot be passively displayed—as they are essentially active, and require active elements to receive the impressions of them—there must be creatures endowed with understanding, conscience, affections and will, capable of bearing the image of His holiness, of appreciating the distinctions of right and wrong, and of feeling the supremacy of moral truth. While the habitations to which they are assigned display the natural perfections of Deity, they themselves, in their moral constitution, are mirrors to reflect His rectitude. Such creatures God not only can contemplate with pleasure, as He does every other portion of His works—He can even enter into communion with them; a foundation is laid for sympathy of affection and reciprocity of love.

To such beings God must sustain the relation of a Ruler. It is through His law that a permanent and faithful exhibition is made of the eternal principles of holiness which belong to the essence of the Godhead. His government is not a matter of expediency; it is indispensably necessary—springs spontaneously from the bosom of God, and can only cease with the cessation of His being.

Where the elements which constitute the adequate idea of government—competent authority, a rule of action and a suitable sanction—all arise from necessary relations, it cannot be a question whether the regiment itself is a contingent result, due to the dictates of benevolence and policy, or a natural event, the offspring of unchanging truth and morality.

In the present case the authority which prescribes the law is an inalienable right. The relation in which the Creator stands to His creatures makes them, in the strictest sense, His property. It is a settled principle of political philosophy that labour, in some form, either intellectual or physical, producing new combinations or changing existing materials, is the ultimate foundation among men of the right to appropriate. The product of one's own industry and skill sustains a relation to himself which it bears to no other being; and as *they* are *his own*, part and parcel of his own existence, that on which they have been expended becomes, in some sense, a portion of himself and subject to the control of his will. But the production of value by the application of labour is a feeble image of the power of creation; and if society instinctively recognizes the claims of its members to the operations of their hands, how much higher and more absolute is the right of the Almighty to appropriate, control and govern the offspring of His own omnipotence and will! "In Him we live and move and have our being." "It is He that hath made us, and not we ourselves; we are His people and the sheep of His pasture." The Psalmist accordingly traces the supremacy of God to the dependence of all things upon Him for their original existence. "For the Lord is a great God, and a great King above all gods. In His hand are the deep places of the earth: the strength of the hills is His also. The sea is His, and He made it: and His hands formed the dry land. O come, let us worship and bow down: let us kneel before the Lord, our Maker. For He is our God; and we are the people of His pasture, and the sheep of His hand." But if creation vests in the Almighty an absolute right to the disposal of His creatures, His constant preservation of man and beast is a continual augmentation of His title. To keep in being is no less a stretch of power than to create out of nothing. To God as a creator we are all indebted for original existence; to God as a preserver we are equally indebted for present existence; and therefore preservation, from its uniformity and constancy, gives a perfect title to each successive moment in the history of every individual. It is, indeed, a question whether preservation be anything distinct from a continued creation—whether the tendency to nothing which the one resists does not require the exercise of the same power, in the same degree, as the original nihility which the other destroys.

If, then, upon the solid basis of creation and preservation, God possesses an unquestionable propriety in all His creatures, they are under a corresponding obligation to acknowledge His dominion. Their dependence upon Him for past, present and continued existence makes it a matter of imperative duty to submit to His authority. The very confession that they are His property is a confession that His will is their law. Shall the thing formed say to Him that formed it, Why hast Thou made me thus? The right to govern, therefore, is not a contingent and accidental privilege, but a necessary result of the mutual relations of creature and Creator.

The dependence of the creature and the independence of God give rise to a radical and important difference in the sources respectively of their moral actions. God's holiness, justice, fidelity and truth spring from necessity of nature. He is under no obligation to do right, because He acknowledges no superior whose will can be law to Him: still, He can never fail to do right, because the perfections of His nature are more certain and necessary in producing unchanging rectitude of conduct than the operation of a law. He does right, in other words, because such is His nature that He cannot do wrong; not because He is bound to give account of any of His matters to any tribunal above Him. Now, the authority of God stands to the actions of a creature in the same relation which necessity of nature sustains to

His own. Hence, a moral creature is necessarily the subject of obligation. It must seek the law of its being beyond itself; the reasons, the ultimate standard of its conduct, must be found in a superior will to which it is responsible. The fundamental principle in the moral code of all created intelligences is, and must be, that the authority of their Creator is absolute, final and complete. Hence, the will of God, in whatever way expressed, is to them the sole standard of moral obligation. To deny this principle would be to make the creature independent. The confirmation in holiness, which is a large ingredient in the blessedness of angels and of saints, does not imply holiness by absolute necessity of nature, but such a continued communication of the grace of God as cherishes in their hearts an uniform conviction of dependence, and an uniform regard to the glory and will of the Creator. The perfection of the just is, in no proper sense, a law to them; it does not constitute their standard of conduct; they cannot make it the measure of their actions. It is the prerogative of God alone to be a law of rectitude to Himself; and the most exalted spirits must ever continue to venerate His will as the source of their duty, the fountain of their blessedness, and the medium of sympathy with His goodness.

As the relationship which subsists between God and His creatures is such as to invest Him with an absolute right to exact obedience from them, the question upon which the *necessity* of government must turn is, whether or not it is a matter of arbitrary discretion to prescribe a law. It would seem to be impossible but that a rule of some sort, either formally or virtually expressed, must be imparted. As dependence is the very condition of its being, the creature would possess no authority to move, to exert a single faculty or to love a single quality without some manifestation of the Divine pleasure. There must be some indication, direct or indirect, negative or positive, of the will of God, or the powers of a moral agent could be no more employed nor its susceptibilities developed than a stock or a stone be set in motion without the impression of an external force. The creature is the absolute property of its Maker, and has no right to think its own thoughts or indulge its own inclinations. To say that the constitution of its nature would necessarily impel it to some form of action is only to assert that the will of God, to which the peculiar tendencies of its constitution must be ultimately traced, has been indirectly communicated. Any expression of the Divine will is law. It is not the mode of expressing it that determines the obligation of the creature; it is the reality of the fact. That mode may be by extraordinary signs, by written communications, by an authorized ambassador, or by the constitution of the mind. But the will of the Creator, once known, is law to the creature. When, therefore, we inquire into the *necessity* of government, the single question is whether or not God possesses any will at all in regard to the conduct of intelligent agents. If He possesses any, be it of what character it may, that will is their rule, and necessarily places them under a government. To assert that He is totally destitute of any will in relation to their conduct involves a palpable contradiction. To express no will by external signs is to leave them to their own discretion, making it right for them to do what under other circumstances would be grossly censurable. To mark out no particular line of conduct by positive commandment is to commit them to the desires, affections and impulses of their own nature; it is indirectly to declare that the will of their Maker accords with the propensities and bias of their own minds. According to the very terms of the hypothesis they are agents, they must act. Now, if the will of God is indifferent to the course of conduct to be pursued, that is equivalent to saying that it is His will that they should act precisely as they pleased. To follow nature, the old Stoical maxim, would be, under such circumstances, as truly the law of their being as it was the expression of the Divine will in the original constitution of their minds. It is true that in such a condition they could do no wrong, because the will of God is supposed to tolerate everything without distinction of qualities. Government, then, in some form or other, must exist. A creature has no more right to act than it has power to be, without the consent of the Almighty. Dependence, absolute, complete, inalienable, is the law of its existence. Whatever it performs must be in the way of obedience; there can be no obedience without an indication of the will of a ruler, and no such indication without a government. It is, therefore, undeniably necessary that to justify a creature in acting at all there must be some expression, more or less distinct, direct or indirect, of the will of its Creator. As, then, the Almighty, from the very necessity of the case, must will to establish some rule, we are prepared to inquire what kind of government the perfections of His nature would impel Him to institute.

It should not be forgotten that the great end in all His works, and especially in the creation and support of intelligent agents, is to declare the glory of His name—to manifest particularly the moral attributes which adorn and exalt His character. The specific end for which conscience, understanding and will were imparted to them was that they might love, venerate and praise the ineffable holiness of their Maker, and exemplify in the state of their own minds the moral perfections of the Deity. It was the purpose of their being that they might be " imitators of God as dear children." To suppose that the object of their existence should be disregarded by Himself, that He would abandon the end which he proposed to achieve in the noblest specimens of His power, or adopt no efficient measures to secure it, is to attribute an inconsistency, weakness and folly to the Supreme Disposer of events which would disgrace the humblest subject of His law. The immutability of His counsel is a firm guarantee that He would institute a government and prescribe a rule which should stand as a memorial to all generations of those eternal principles of rectitude which spring from His essence and regulate all the decisions of His will. The nature of the Divine Being as imperatively demands that the law of His dominions should be *moral* as the dependence of the creature requires that a law should exist. That the distinctions between right and wrong are not the arbitrary creatures of the Divine will, but essential emanations from the holiness of God, is a proposition which lies at the basis of immutable morality. To say that God is the author of virtue, in such a sense as to deny to it a standard apart from the decisions of the Divine will, is virtually to affirm that His own perfections are the contingent acquisitions of choice, and not the unchangeable properties of His being. How God could be pre-eminently glorious on account of His holiness, when holiness itself was only an accidental accomplishment and no essential element of a just definition of the Deity, it is impossible for us to comprehend.

That moral distinctions are eternal, necessary and immutable, results, beyond a possibility of doubt, from what we are taught in the Scriptures concerning the Divine existence. If the unity of God implied unity of Person, it would be hard, perhaps impossible, to conceive how He could have been a moral being when as yet there existed no object but Himself on which His affections might be placed. The terms which, in every language, are expressive of moral perfections seem to point us to the existence of society as the only theatre in which they can be developed or expanded. Truth, justice, benevolence, fidelity and love are as obviously social affections as they are moral accomplishments; and if there was ever a period when God was a solitary Being in the depths of eternity, how could benevolence, fidelity or love have existed in Him except as susceptibilities dormant in His nature, ready to be unfolded whenever an opportunity should offer? Where was the field for the unceasing activity of His high and glorious perfections? I confess that, to my mind, absolute solitude of Being is wholly incompatible with the actual exercise of moral qualities. Society is the element of virtue, and hence I turn with delight to those representations of the Scriptures in which it is implied that God is necessarily social as well as holy—that such is the nature of His essence that while absolutely one it exists eternally in a threefold distinction of Persons. The social relations of the Trinity—the mysterious intercourse of the Father, the Son and the Spirit—springing from the inscrutable nature of the Godhead, involve the existence of moral accomplishments on a magnificent and splendid scale. Whether, however, the personal distinctions of the Godhead are the foundation of its moral perfections or not, it is certain that its social relations must have been the source of eternal confusion and disorder, unless they had been marked by the strictest integrity, fidelity and truth.

If we are not permitted to assert that God is holy because He is social, and necessarily holy because necessarily social, we may yet with confidence maintain that being social He *must* be holy, since to deny to Him moral distinctions would be to attribute to His nature elements destructive of society. It may be disputed whether moral relations presuppose social relations as the necessary condition of their existence, but it cannot be denied that social relations imperatively demand the exercise of moral perfections in order to harmony, perpetuity and peace. If then, as the Scriptures assert, God is by necessity of nature a social Being, the conclusion inevitably follows that He is by the same necessity a moral Being. The expressions of His will must, therefore, be in conformity with the holiness of His essence. The law which He prescribes as the standard of duty to His creatures must be a transcript of those perfections which He cannot disregard without ceasing to be God. The necessity of His nature determines the decisions of His will, and as He Himself is holy the law must be holy, just and good.

The confusion of the grounds of obligation and the nature of virtue has involved the discussion of the immutability of moral distinctions in no little perplexity. There is no doubt, from the necessary dependence of its being, that the creature is bound to be holy because its Creator commands it. The Divine will is the only standard of moral obligation. But there must be reasons for the command itself. To attribute a self-determining power to the will of the Almighty when it is acknowledged to be an imperfection among men; to suppose that His approbation of virtue is the result of choice, and that He might be indifferent or even opposed to it, would contradict our most exalted conceptions of His character. The motives, whatever they are, which operate on the mind of the Eternal in prescribing the command determine the nature of virtue. The reasons of His making it a duty define its essence. Still, that it *is* a duty is owing exclusively to the expression of His will. Our obligation does not depend upon abstract speculations on its origin, qualities or fitness; be its nature what it may, it is law to us, because the Creator, who possesses an absolute propriety in us, has marked it out as the rule of our conduct. Hence we by no means, as some have supposed, derogate from the authority of the Divine will as the standard of obligation when we go beyond it and attempt to discover in the essential perfections of the Deity the grounds of it. These, in a modified sense, are a law to Himself, the standard of His own decrees, the ultimate source of His purposes and acts.

Two principal elements of government—competent authority on the part of the governor, and a rule of life for the guidance of the governed—having been shown to spring necessarily from the mutual relations of God and the creature; the character of the law as moral, reflecting the beauty of the Divine perfections, in opposition to a system of arbitrary precepts, having been also evinced; it remains to be inquired whether the third and last element—the penal sanction—is likewise necessary, or is merely the dictate of public policy.

If the most important object of punishment, as civilians generally assert, is the prevention of crime, the question is settled. It becomes, then, a choice of expedients, and no reasons exist in the nature of things why this particular method should be adopted in preference to any other scheme promising equal success. If it be nothing but a means to an end, it falls within the province of wisdom, to be settled by considerations of fitness and expediency, and is therefore not to be discussed upon those eternal principles of rectitude which constitute the glory of God. According to this view, punishment is the demand, not of justice, but of public good, was instituted by policy and not by right—a conclusion so abhorrent to the instinctive sentiments of man that the premises, however plausible, must be false from which it is deduced.

Even in human governments, which contemplate the injury rather than the wickedness of actions, penal laws cannot be sustained upon the sole basis of expediency. Nothing can be punished as hurtful which is not felt to be vicious. The moral sympathies of the people must be in harmony with the considerations of policy which determine the objects and severity of punishment, or the government will come to be regarded as an odious and intolerable tyranny. It is a strong proof of God's disapprobation of sin that it carries stamped upon its face a character of mischief to the State which leagues society against it as a common nuisance, and makes its expulsion or restraint a public benefit as well as the satisfaction of a moral impulse. Such is the inseparable connection of social and moral order that whatever is hurtful to the one is prejudicial to the other; and as it is the purpose of God that men should live in a condition of society, He has made interest exactly to coincide with duty, so that the patronage of virtue is the surest safeguard of public prosperity; and as nothing can be really pernicious which is not also morally wrong, He has so tempered the social constitution that all punishments must be founded in moral principles. It is the viciousness of actions that renders them punishable. Expediency may regulate the measure and extent of the punishment, but something higher must settle the preliminary question whether they shall be punished at all or not.

The principle, therefore, is not true, even in reference to human institutions, that the penalty of the law is the mere creature of expediency. Punishment in the State always presupposes crime as well as injury, and though the State chiefly aims to prevent the injury, yet it is the crime which justifies the remedy to the moral sense of the community. Hence the origin of penal laws must ultimately be traced to convictions of justice, and not to calculations of policy.

That this is pre-eminently true of the Divine administration is obvious from the fact that punishments are inflicted, and that with the intensest severity, when no motives of expediency could be conceived to operate. Where will be the need when the just shall be exempt from the contingency of rebellion, when angels shall be confirmed in holiness, and when both together, united under a common Head, shall enjoy the security of grace,—where will be the need of stimulating diligence by the terrors of example, of torturing the guilty for the good of the innocent? What are the motives of expediency that shall then doom the disobedient to the regions of despair, and expose them a prey to the undying worm and the fire that shall never be quenched?

The perpetuity of its torments long after it has ceased to inspire a salutary fear, the continuance of its horrors when none are in danger of transgression—when absolute security prevails in every loyal province of God's empire, when the grace of the Redeemer has for ever placed angels and just men beyond the possibility of temptation and of sin—is a conclusive proof that the fires of hell were never kindled by the breath of expediency, that its shame and agony and anguish are owing to principles eternal as its own darkness, immutable as its own despair. That the eternity of future punishment, by operating as a perpetual motive upon the minds of the saints, is subservient to their stability, may possibly be true; but to say that this is the only account which can be given of it, or that the only reason of the second death is to preserve the living from its woe, is to shock every generous impulse of humanity. That would indeed be a terrible administration which purchased an incidental good at so transcendent a sacrifice of individual felicity. It would be an awful exhibition of benevolence to promote happiness by the spectacle of miseries which human language is incompetent to express and the human understanding unable to conceive; a strange doctrine, that hell was reared to display God's mercy, and that the groans of the damned and the wailings of the pit are songs of praise to the goodness of God!

It is no trivial objection to the doctrine that the primary end of punishment is the public good—that upon the supposition of the existence of only a single moral agent no provision is made for punishment as distinct from discipline. The eternal banishment of such an individual from God would be wholly inexplicable; and yet the Scriptures unquestionably inculcate the doctrine that all unrighteousness of every transgressor, apart from his relations to other moral creatures, is the object of God's abhorrence and the everlasting visitations of His wrath. Extreme cases, however improbable, are a test of the accuracy of principles.

As the government of God is founded in His right to exact obedience from His creatures, and as His law expresses the eternal rectitude of His nature, the characteristic end of punishment must evidently be, not the promotion of the public good—this, though a certain, is only an incidental result—but to enforce the authority of the Ruler and to illustrate the estimate He puts upon His law, or the light in which He regards disobedience. As the primary design of all His institutions is to glorify Himself, we must seek for the object of each of the elements which characterize His law in its relations to the peculiar perfections of His own nature, and not to the interests of man. Taking our departure from this point, it is easy to show that in the government of God penal sanctions are indispensably necessary. Without them a sense of obligation cannot be produced, and God's hatred of sin cannot be expressed. The moral conduct of a creature must be regulated with a specific reference to the authority of its Maker; there must be a distinct recognition of His right to command. Whatever may be the matter of its actions, their form must be derived from a sense of obligation corresponding to the right which exists to rule. They must be done specifically as something due. Now there can be no such sense of obligation when a law is not enforced by a penal sanction. In that case the obedience of the creature must be the result, not of authority, but of persuasion. A precept without a penalty is only advice, or, in the strongest view, is simply a request; rewards without punishments are nothing but inducements; and a dispensation conducted upon such principles is evidently a system of persuasion and not of authoritative government. Obedience is, in that case, compliance with the impulse of our own minds, and not submission to the rightful demands of another; we act right to please ourselves, and not to please the Almighty. We recognize not His will, but our own gratification. Such absolute sovereignty of the creature, even in doing what is materially right, is inconsistent with its dependence. The essential principle of all its morality must be compliance with the will of God, not because it is grateful to our nature or adapted to our impulses, but because it is His will. It belongs to the Deity alone to follow nature; all the creatures of His power are creatures of obligation. The constitution of our minds may be a medium through which the will of the Almighty is revealed, but we are required to yield to its propensities, not because we are so constituted, but because our Creator demands it. In all instances in which the frame and temper of our minds are inconsistent with the precepts of His mouth we are to crucify nature and follow God. His will, however communicated, is our only law. Now, in order that it may be felt as law and produce a corresponding sense of obligation, it must be enforced by a penal sanction. This upholds and supports the authority of the Creator; it keeps prominently in view the dependence of the creature, and contrasts the just supremacy of the one with the proper subordination of the other. It is remarkable that in all languages the term which expresses a conviction of duty is drawn from the analogy of physical violence; showing the universal sentiment of the race that moral obligation is a species of force, a sort of bondage or constraint—a necessity laid upon the subject which he dares not resist. If I may be allowed to repeat what I have formerly uttered from this desk, the least attention to our moral emotions, and the language by which the universal consent of the race has uniformly described them, must convince us that conscience is a prospective principle—that its decisions are by no means final, but only the preludes of a higher sentence to be pronounced by a higher court. It derives all its authority from anticipations of the future. It brings before us the dread tribunal of eternal justice and almighty power; it summons us to the awful presence of God; it wields His thunder and wears His smiles. When a man of principle braves calumny, reproach and persecution, when he stands unshaken in the discharge of duty amid public opposition and private treachery, when no machinations of malice or seductions of flattery can cause him to bend from the path of integrity,—that must be a powerful support through which he can bid defiance to the "storms of fate." He must feel that a strong arm is underneath him; and though the eye of sense can perceive nothing in his circumstances but terror, confusion and dismay, he sees his mountain surrounded by "chariots of fire and horses of fire," which sustain his soul in unbroken tranquillity. In the approbation of his conscience there is lifted up the light of the Divine countenance upon him, and he feels the strongest assurance that all things shall work together for his ultimate good. Conscience anticipates the rewards of the just, and in the conviction which it inspires of Divine protection lays the foundation of heroic fortitude. When, on the contrary, the remembrance of some fatal crime rankles in the breast, the sinner's dreams are disturbed by invisible ministers of vengeance and the fall of a leaf can strike him with horror; in every shadow he sees a ghost, in every tread he hears an avenger of blood, and in every sound the trump of doom. What is it that invests his conscience with such terrible power to torment? Is there nothing here but the natural operation of a simple and original instinct?. Who does not see that " wickedness, condemned by her own witness, and being pressed with conscience, always forecasteth grievous things?"—that the alarm and agitation and fearful forebodings of the sinner arise from the terrors of an offended Judge and insulted Lawgiver? An approving conscience is the consciousness of right, of having done what has been commanded, and of being now entitled to the favour of the Judge. Remorse is the sense of ill desert. The criminal does not feel that his present pangs are his punishment; it is the future, the unknown and portentous future, that fills him with consternation. He deserves ill, and the dread of receiving it makes him tremble.

To remove the penalty from the Divine law is to wrest the sceptre from the hands of the Deity, to pluck from His brow the crown which adorns it, to deprive Him of the essential dignity of His character, and to present Him before His creatures in the debasing posture of a suppliant at their feet. He ceases to be the august and glorious Monarch of the skies, doing His pleasure among the armies of heaven and the inhabitants of earth; disrobed of His majesty, He no longer thunders with a voice at which nature shakes and the guilty tremble, but dwindles down into a feeble petitioner, whose prayers and entreaties may be despised with impunity. Such degradation of the Supreme Being cannot be tolerated even in thought. He must be able to enforce His will or He ceases to be God. He must speak with a voice of authority; resistless power must stand ready to support His commands. They must be uttered in a tone which impresses the conviction that they must be obeyed—that disobedience is certain and infallible destruction. They must, in other words, oblige.

But whether a penal sanction be necessary to create a sense of obligation or not, it is the inevitable result of the Divine disapprobation of sin. God is of purer eyes than to behold iniquity. Such is the transcendent purity of His nature that even the heavens are not clean in His sight, and

He charges His angels with folly. The unutterable blessedness which accrues to the Persons of the Trinity from their mysterious communion with each other is to be ascribed to the confidence, harmony and love, the immaculate holiness and truth, which belong essentially to the nature of the Godhead. As the essential beatitude of the Deity is the result, the necessary result, of His moral perfections—as it is the prerogative of holiness alone to be surrounded with light and to be the parent of joy—an indissoluble connection must subsist between wretchedness and guilt. The favour of God is the only source of enjoyment to the creature. Whatever is beautiful or attractive in subordinate objects, whatever can adorn, dignify or please, the embellishments of life and the charms of friendship, are but feeble emanations from Him who concentrates in Himself all these scattered perfections, and without whose permission they would in vain be sought to adminster comfort to the heart. God has reserved it to Himself as His distinguishing privilege to be the satisfying portion of the soul, and apart from Him all sublunary materials will prove as dust and ashes to the wretch who is famishing for food. Now, if the essential holiness of God is such that He cannot tolerate iniquity nor look upon transgression without the utmost abhorrence, it is evident that the "ungodly shall not stand in the judgment, nor sinners in the congregation of the righteous." The least taint of impurity must debar its victim from communion with Him, expel it from the source of all joy and felicity, and doom it consequently to solitude and sorrow as the ancient leper was banished from the society of men. To be driven from the presence of God is to be rendered miserable. The negation of delight in an active creature is, in its effects, a positive and bitter calamity. It is a penal evil, the legitimate consequence of transgression. Hence a penalty is necessarily connected with a violation of the law. Every step in this reasoning is intuitively evident. God is essentially holy; communion with Him is the fountain of happiness; none can enjoy it but those who are holy; therefore the disobedient cannot be happy; and, as to an active being there is no condition of absolute indifference, the negation of happiness is equivalent to the infliction of misery.

There is another view of the subject, which shows that something more awful than negative ills ought to be expected as the wages of sin. The light in which God looks upon rebellion it is exceedingly proper, for the glory of His name, to make known unto His creatures. His holiness is declared by banishing the guilty from His presence—His hatred of sin by pouring out upon them the vials of His wrath. The extent to which He disapproves of transgression cannot be revealed by negative penalties. It is not enough to dry up the fountain of felicity, to say to the rebel that he shall have no more to do with peace; the waters of bitterness and death must also be let loose to desolate his soul; Tophet must be ordained, the pile thereof juniper and much wood, while the breath of the Lord as a stream of brimstone doth kindle it for ever and ever. In the penal fires of hell we contemplate the inextinguishable hatred of God to all the forms of iniquity. They result from the purity of infinite holiness in terrible collision with guilt.[1]

This brief discussion of the elements of government has

[1] The same view of the subject is taken by Owen in his Treatise of Divine Justice and in his Commentary on the Epistle to the Hebrews. The following extract may serve as a specimen of his reasoning:

"It will be granted by some that there is such a natural property in God as that which we contend for, but it doth not thence follow, they say, that it is necessary that God should punish all sin, but He doth it and may do it by an absolute and free act of His will. There is, therefore, no cogent argument to be taken from the consideration hereof for the necessity of the suffering of Christ. The heads of some few arguments, to the contrary, shall put a close to this whole discourse. First, God hateth sin, He hateth every sin; He cannot otherwise do. Let any man assert the contrary—namely, that God doth not hate sin, or that it is not necessary to Him on account of His own nature that He should hate sin—and the consequence thereof will quickly be discerned. For to say that God may not hate sin is at once to take away all natural and necessary difference between moral good and evil. For if He may not hate it, He may been sufficient, I apprehend, to establish its necessity and to correct prevailing errors in relation to its origin. While it is true that the highest felicity accrues to the creature from love it. The mere acts of God's will which are not regulated by anything in His nature, but only wisdom and liberty, are not determined to this or that object, but He may so will anything, or the contrary. And then if God may love sin, He may approve it, and if He approve sin, it is not a sin, which is a plain contradiction. That God hateth sin, see Ps. v. 4, 5; xi. 5; xiv. 1; liii. 2; Lev. xxvi. 30; Deut. xvi. 22; 1 Kings xxi. 26; Prov. xv. 5; Hab. i. 13. And this hatred of sin in God can be nothing but the displicency in, or contrariety of, His nature to it, with an immutable will of punishing it thence arising. For to have a natural displicency against sin, and not an immutable will of punishing it, is unworthy of God, for it must arise from impotency. To punish sin therefore according to its demerit is necessary to Him. Secondly, God with respect unto sin and sinners is called a consuming fire. Heb. xii. 19; Deut. iv. 24; Isa. xxxiii. 15; and v. 24, and xiii. 14. Something we are taught by the allusion in this expression. This is not the *manner* of God's operation. God worketh freely, the fire burns necessarily. God, I say, always worketh freely with a freedom accompanying His operation, though in some cases, on some suppositions, it is necessary that He should work as He doth. It is free to Him to speak unto us or not, but on supposition that He will do so it is necessary that He speak truly, for God cannot lie. Fire, therefore, acts by brute inclination according to its form and principle; God acts by His understanding and will with a freedom accompanying all His operations. This, therefore, we are not taught by this allusion. The comparison, therefore, must hold with respect unto the *event*, or we are deceived, not instructed by it. As, therefore, the fire necessarily burneth and consumeth all combustible things whereunto it is applied, in its way of operation which is natural, so doth God necessarily punish sin when it lies before Him in judgment, in His way of operation which is free and intellectual. Thirdly, it is necessary that God should do everything that is requisite unto His own glory. This the perfection of His nature and existence do require. So He doth all things for Himself. It is necessary, therefore, that nothing fall out in the universe which should absolutely impeach the glory of God or contradict the design of its manifestation. Now suppose that God would and should let sin go unpunished, where would be the glory of His righteousness as He is the Supreme Ruler over all? For to omit what justice requireth is no less a disparagement unto it than to do what it forbids. Prov. xvii. 15. And where would be the glory of His holiness, supposing the description given of it, Hab. i. 13? Where would be that fear and reverence which is due unto Him? Where that sense of His terribleness? Where that secret awe of Him which ought to be in the hearts and thoughts of men, if once He were looked on as such a God, as such a Governor, as unto whom it is a uniform obedience to the law of its Creator, it is in no sense true that the design of government in reference to God is to secure the happiness of His subjects. It is intended, as we have seen, to express His supremacy, and springs from the relations He sustains to His creatures. Punishment in the Divine administration is not an expedient to prevent the progress of rebellion, but a necessary emanation from the holiness of God and a just expression of His hatred to iniquity. The inflexibility of the law does not result from

matter of mere freedom, choice and liberty whether He will punish sin or not, as being not concerned in point of righteousness or holiness so to do? Nothing can tend more than such a persuasion to ingenerate an apprehension in men that God is such an One as themselves, and that He is so little concerned in their sins that they need not themselves be much concerned in them.

"Such thoughts they are apt to conceive if He do but hold His peace for a season, and not reprove them in their sins. Ps. l. 21. And if their hearts are fully set in them to do evil, because in some signal instances judgment is not speedily executed (Eccles. viii. 11), how much more will such pernicious consequents ensue if they are persuaded that it may be God will never punish them for their sins, seeing it is absolutely at His pleasure whether He will do so or not; neither His righteousness nor His holiness nor His glory require any such thing at His hands. This is not the language of the law—no, nor yet of the consciences of men unless they are debauched. Is it not with most Christians certain that eventually God lets no sinner go unpunished? Do they not believe that all who are not interested by faith in the sufferings of Christ, or at least that are not saved on the account of His undergoing the punishment due to sin, must perish eternally? And if this be the absolute rule of God's proceeding toward sinners, if He never went out of the way of it in any one instance, whence should it proceed but from what His nature doth require? Lastly, God is, as we have shown, the righteous Judge of all the world. What law is unto another judge who is to proceed by it, that is the infinite rectitude of His own nature unto Him. And it is necessary to a judge to punish where the law requires him so to do, and if he do not he is not just. And because God is righteous by an essential righteousness, it is necessary for Him to punish sin as it is contrary thereunto, and not to acquit the guilty. And what is sin cannot but be sin, neither can God order it otherwise. For what is contrary to His nature cannot by any act of His will be rendered otherwise. And if sin be sin necessarily, because of its contrariety to the nature of God, on the supposition of the order of all things by Himself created, the punishment of it is on the same ground necessary also."—Hebrews, vol. i., p. 504, *Tegg's Edition.*

a desire to promote the safety of the governed, but from its own essential character as founded in the immutable distinctions of morality, as arising from the essential perfections of the Godhead, and as holy, just and good. The glory of God is the ultimate end, and the perfections of God the primary source, of all the arrangements of His government; they rest upon principles grand as His nature, enduring as truth and immutable as holiness. He is the great centre at which, wherever they begin, all our inquiries must terminate. "For of Him and through Him and to Him are all things, to whom be glory for ever. Amen."

If, then, the government of God is founded in principles of immutable necessity, it is perfectly preposterous to dream of the unconditional pardon of sin. Its punishment is fixed as immovably as the law, and the law is as permanent as those perfections of the Deity of which it is a transcript. Until the Deity can be subject to change, or holiness made a contingent acquisition, the wages of sin must, in every instance, be death.

There is no principle on which unconditional remission can be justified. If the Deity should yield to the impulse of compassion and retract the penalty of His own law, He would evidently manifest a higher regard for the interests of a sinner than for the glory of His own name. He would receive a being into favour with whom His holiness precludes communion, and would, consequently, veil His moral perfections to compass a subordinate end. This would be to debase the dignity of moral distinctions, to degrade the majesty of virtue, to cast a reproach upon the goodness of law, in order to save the guilty from a doom to which justice has consigned them. It would be, in short, to resolve government into motives of expediency, and to deny its *necessity* as an enduring memorial of the moral character of God.

When the punishment of sin is affirmed to be necessary and therefore inevitable, it is not intended to inculcate the idea that it takes place according to the analogy of physical laws. While the essential holiness of God renders it absolutely certain that it must take place, there is yet a liberty in God as to the mode, time and measure of its infliction. He is not restrained to a single method or a single period. He is free to regulate severity by the dictates of wisdom—to administer justice according to the counsel of His will. All that is fixed and immutable is, that He should not forego the glory of His character, disregard His right to the allegiance of the creature, and suffer the rebel to escape from His hands. He cannot change the law any more than He can change His perfections, nor remit its penalty any more than He can relax His opposition to sin. The principles of His government are fixed, immutable and eternal; the details of its administration belong to His sovereign discretion; and are to be settled by the decisions of His will. In the selection, adjustment and arrangement of them there is full liberty; but all else is founded in His nature, and is certain, uniform, unvarying as fate.

The incongruity is so obvious between the character of God and communion with a sinner, that the most extravagant advocates of the right to pardon without a satisfaction have not scrupled to insist upon the need of repentance as an essential condition for procuring absolution. By repentance they maintain that the moral qualities of the transgressor are changed; and though he is substantially the same being, yet in regard to the condition of his heart, for which alone he was deserving of punishment, he is essentially different from what he was when he drank in iniquity like water. It has been usual to reply to reasoning of this sort by arguments drawn from the analogy of nature or considerations of expediency,[1] but the true answer is that repentance is impossible. If the government of God be necessary, the first act of transgression effects a separation between God and the creature; the spiritual life of the sinner is destroyed, and he can no more restore himself to his original position than the dead can return from the darkness of the tomb. The

[1] For specimens of such arguments see Butler's Analogy, Pt. ii., c. 5.—Magee's 1st Discourse, p. 5.

union of the creature with God, which, in an unfallen state, depends upon uniform obedience to the law, is the source of its purity, happiness and strength. The very moment in which it fails to recognize its absolute dependence and the consequent supremacy of the Divine will, it breaks the tie which binds it to its Maker, is treated at once as an alien and an outcast, passes under the condemnation of the law, and becomes for ever estranged from good. The slightest sin, like a puncture of the heart, is attended with death. The penalty is incurred by the first act of disobedience. Now that penalty, in its mildest and lowest form, implies banishment from God. But repentance involves a restoration to holiness and communion with God, from which the transgressor is debarred. Repentance and the curse are consequently contradictory; and hence to suppose that a condemned sinner can repent is to suppose that, at the same time, he can be and not be under the curse. The condemnation of the sinner, therefore, for ever precludes the possibility of repentance; it places him beyond the pale of communion with his Maker and consigns him to everlasting despair. The one transgression of the one man undid the race. To suppose that apostasy from God is a result accomplished by a course of disobedience is as unphilosophical as it is unscriptural. The separation from God is instantaneous; the entire disruption of the moral constitution, the total desolation of the character, may, however, be slow and progressive. Life may be suddenly extinguished, but the decay of the lifeless body may be the work of years.

Repentance, consequently, without a satisfaction would involve the same difficulties with absolute remission. It would be to the same extent an impeachment of the essential perfections of God; it implies pardon as its basis, and can never take place where a satisfaction has not been previously rendered. It is an inseparable element of the curse that the sinner cannot repent. All the affections and moral exercises which it includes presuppose that the exile is recalled from banishment; that the anger of God is removed; that a reunion with his Maker has taken place; and that the curse of the law is revoked.

By repentance is intended a thorough and radical change of the moral character of the sinner—all that is involved in the Christian doctrines of the new birth and sanctification. Remorse, shame, anguish and despair, the agony and horror of great darkness, which were experienced by such men as Cain and Judas, are not the ingredients of true repentance; these terrors of conscience reign with unbroken dominion in hell—they are the constant companions of devils and lost men, and are rather the belchings of guilt than expressions of sorrow for sin. They who are most keenly tortured by them, so far from reforming or even attempting to reform, blaspheme the God of heaven with increased malignity, and cherish a deeper hate to all that is holy, pure and good. Such repentance is, indeed, possible to the most abandoned fiend, but it is as worthless as it is easy.

As the true amendment of the heart and life is beyond the capacity of the sinner, so it is equally above his strength to render a full satisfaction to the violated law. The penalty must necessarily be infinite. It is the measure of God's authority, of the holiness of His nature and of His hatred to sin; it is designed to show the wrath of the Deity and to make His power known. It is a conspicuous exhibition of the extent to which the Divine nature is opposed to transgression.

It is a ruinous mistake that the malignity of guilt is determined by a standard drawn from the resources and capacities of the rebel. Though finite himself, he may yet perpetrate an evil of such desperate enormity as to involve, upon the strictest principles of justice, everlasting consequences; as a feeble impulse may set a ball in motion which the hand that impressed the original force shall find it impossible to resist. The true view of the subject is that, as the perfections of God are the ultimate standard of rectitude, and His will, supported by His power, the ultimate standard of obligation, so the discrepancy between Him and sin is the exact measure of its demerit, and the resources of His might the only limit to the actual severity of punishment. His glory is the true criterion of all that is good, venerable or lovely; and a just definition of virtue fixes necessarily an accurate conception of vice. We know the one by its repugnance to the other. Hence every sin—God being infinitely holy and cherishing an infinite detestation of all that is wrong—every sin entails after it the terrible necessity of eternal punishment; it fastens upon its victim a worm which can never die, and kindles around him a fire which can never be quenched.[1]

[1] The following argument of that great man, President Edwards, deserves to be seriously pondered by those who are disposed to make a mock of sin:

"I shall briefly show that it is not inconsistent with the justice of God to inflict an eternal punishment. To evince this, I shall use only one argument—viz.: that sin is heinous enough to deserve such a punishment, and such a punishment is no more than proportionable to the evil or demerit of sin. If the evil of sin be infinite, as the punishment is, then it is manifest that the punishment is no more than proportionable to the sin punished, and is no more than sin deserves. And if the obligation to love, honour and obey God be infinite, then sin, which is the violation of this obligation, is a violation of infinite obligation, and so is an infinite evil. Again, if God be infinitely worthy of love, honour and obedience, then our obligation to love, honour and obey Him is infinitely great. So that God being infinitely glorious, or infinitely worthy of our love, honour and obedience, our obligation to love, honour and obey Him, and so to avoid all sin, is infinitely great. Again, our obligation to love, honour and obey God being infinitely great, sin is the violation of infinite obligation, and so is an infinite evil. Once more, sin, being an infinite evil, deserves an infinite punishment—an infinite punishment is no more than it deserves: Therefore such punishment is just, which was the thing to be proved. There is no evading the force of this reasoning, but by denying that God, the Sovereign of the universe, is infinitely glorious, which I presume none of my hearers will venture to do.

"This appears as it is not only not unsuitable that sin should be thus punished, but it is positively suitable, decent and proper. If this be made to appear, that it is positively suitable that sin should be thus punished, then it will follow that the perfections of God require it, for certainly the perfections of God require what is proper to be done. The perfection and excellency of God require that to take place which is perfect, excellent and proper in its own nature. But that sin should be punished eternally is such a thing, which appears by the following considerations: 1. It is suitable that God should infinitely hate sin and be an infinite enemy to it. Sin, as I have before shown, is an infinite evil, and therefore is infinitely odious and detestable. It is proper that God should hate every evil, and

Annihilation, at any period of his woe, would be as grossly inconsistent with the claims of justice as to assist a culprit in escaping from his prison in order to screen him from the shame of the gibbet. It would be a violent arresting of the course of the law. Justice could as much tolerate that the sinner should be taken to heaven, as that he should be totally destroyed; in either case it would lose its victim. An infinite penalty can only be inflicted upon a finite creature by eternity of torment. Whatever freedom there may be in the Supreme Ruler to delay, modify or adjust the ingredients of anguish which constitute the cup of trembling administered to the lips of the damned, the unchanging principles of rectitude imperatively demand that eternity should be the measure of their woe; that the darkness to which they are consigned should be the blackness of darkness for ever; that the smoke of their torment should ascend for ever and ever. The severest penances, the most painful privations, the costliest oblations and the richest sacrifices are incompetent to remove the sentence or to cancel the handwriting of ordinances against them. What proportions can the tortures of the body—the keenest agonies of which it is susceptible, inflicted and endured in this sublunary state—bear to the infinite load of wretchedness which is due to the smallest sin? What can haircloth and rags avail—laceration of the flesh,

hate it according to its odious and detestable nature. And sin being infinitely evil and odious, it is proper that God should hate it infinitely. 2. If infinite hatred of sin be suitable to the Divine character, then the *expressions* of such hatred are also suitable to His character. Because that which is suitable to be is suitable to be expressed: that which is lovely in itself is lovely when it appears. If it be suitable that God should be an infinite enemy to sin, or that He should hate it infinitely, then it is suitable that He should *act* as such an enemy. If it be suitable that He should hate and have enmity against sin, then it is suitable for Him to express that hatred and enmity in that to which hatred and enmity by its own nature tends. But certainly hatred in its own nature tends to opposition, and to set itself against that which is hated, and to procure its evil and not its good; and that in proportion to the hatred. Great hatred naturally tends to the great evil, and infinite hatred to the infinite evil of its object."—*Sermon on the Eternity of Hell Torments*, Works, vol. vii., pp. 467–470.

penury and want, voluntary exile from home and friends, needless exposure to scorching suns or withering cold,—what signify all the devices of superstition and fear, when the real doom incurred is the wrath of God, and the just measure of its severity the omnipotence of His arm? Vain here is the help of man. To come before the Lord with thousands of rams and ten thousands of rivers of oil, to bring to His altar the fruit of the body for the sin of the soul, to mourn in bitterness and weep tears of blood, would be but a poor substitute for that eternity of horror, that endless night of despair, that hopeless banishment from God, which is the legitimate consequence of sin. The insulted justice of God is terrible beyond the power of mortal expression or of mortal thought. The collision of eternal rectitude with human guilt, the conflict of boundless power with the object of its inextinguishable hate, it belongs to eternity alone to disclose, since eternity alone is the theatre of the strife. But to dream of satisfying, by tears, penances and mortal blood, the awful justice of such an immaculately holy Being as God is to suppose that eternity can be swallowed up in time—the infinite lost in the finite.

Is there, then, no hope? Must the whole race of man perish beneath the frown of the Almighty? Shall none be found to ransom or to save?

To answer this question apart from Revelation is beyond the compass of created wisdom. The essential rectitude of God precludes the possibility of unconditional pardon; the principles of His government, springing necessarily from the perfections of His nature and His relations to the creature, are fixed, immutable, eternal. The glory of His own great Name is deeply and critically involved in the vindication of His justice, holiness and truth. He can by no means clear the guilty. The analogy of nature might indeed suggest the possibility of deliverance, as we find in the ordinary dispensations of Providence that the consequences of folly are not unfrequently averted by the agency of others. But where shall a fit mediator be found? It is certain as the immutability of God that no substitute could achieve our redemption who was not competent to bear the load of our guilt, to satisfy the insulted justice of our Ruler, to drain the cup of trembling to its dregs. The doctrine of substitution is unquestionably an ultimate principle in the moral government of God. Mediation pervades the arrangements of Providence as well as the economy of grace. But the grand difficulty is to find a representative who, without the entire destruction of himself, could exhaust the curse of the law.

Whatever glimmering of hope the doctrine of substitution might impart, it would seem, must be instantly extinguished when we call to mind the severe and arduous conditions under which alone it could be rendered available to sinners. The justice of God is too formidable to be encountered by created strength; it hangs like a dark cloud over the prospects of man and mocks his most anxious efforts to secure a Redeemer. Whither shall the sinner turn for help? Shall he look to his own brethren, the descendants of Adam's race? As each successive generation comes into being it passes under the curse; every man has iniquities of his own to bear, and none can by any means redeem his brother nor give to God a ransom for his soul. Shall he invoke the assistance of the angels above? The law might fitly turn aside from their proffered substitution, as it was man who had sinned and man who must die. Even if this difficulty were vanquished, and an angel should become incarnate, where is its power to contend with the justice of God? What created arm could meet the thunder of insulted holiness, and endure the storm of eternal wrath? Who can stand when Omnipotence wields the sword and sin provokes the blow? From the single element of substitution to work out the problem of human redemption is beyond the skill of angels and the archangel, of cherubim and seraphim. We might climb the loftiest heights and explore the utmost bounds of this widespread universe, every creature might be summoned in review before us, and heaven, earth and hell be laid under tribute, and still not a single being could be found *able* to endure the curse of the law; and yet this is the only conceivable condition on which salvation could be given. God cannot absolutely pardon. He can only transfer the punishment. He cannot set aside the sanction of His law, but only can give it a different direction. Who, then, can save from going down to the pit? It was reserved for the wisdom of the Eternal to answer this solemn question. The sublime idea of the incarnation and death of the Son could only have originated in the mind of Him who is wonderful in counsel and unsearchable in His judgments. In Jesus, the Mediator of the new covenant, we behold a kinsman, who, through the eternal Spirit, is able to endure the wrath of God—a man who can satisfy justice and yet recover from the stroke—a Being who could die and in dying conquer death. Great indeed is the mystery of godliness, but it is no less glorious than great. Through the infinite wisdom of God a suitable substitute is found who takes the place of the guilty, assumes their burden, and bears it away to a land uninhabited. In the scheme of redemption God visits the transgressions of sinners in the person of the Son, the law is executed in its utmost rigours, and God is just, perfectly and gloriously just, in justifying those who believe. Their sins have been as truly punished as if they themselves had been consigned to the darkness of hell.

Delightful and interesting as it might be to prosecute an inquiry into the precise nature of the atonement, and to define the limitations and restrictions under which substitution is admissible, my limits warn me that such a discussion cannot be undertaken now. It is enough for my present purpose to have indicated the ground upon which, as I conceive, the necessity of the atonement should be made to depend. If I have succeeded in proving that the government of God is not the dictate of policy nor the creature of contingency, but a necessary emanation from the Divine perfections and the relations which He sustains to His creatures; that some rule must, from the nature of the case, be prescribed, and that none can possibly proceed from God but one which is holy and just and good; and that a penal sanction is an essential element of moral law; if I have succeeded in establishing these propositions, it certainly follows, as an inevitable consequence, that God cannot, without denying Himself, any more dispense with the penalty than He can with the precept itself. The unconditional pardon of sin would be morally wrong—in open and flagrant collision with the eternal principles of right. Punitive justice is as truly essential to God as veracity or honour, and He can no more remit the punishment of the guilty without a satisfaction than He can utter a falsehood or break a promise.

Upon the broad basis, therefore, of the inviolable sanctity which attaches to the penalty of the Divine law, I place the necessity of vicarious atonement. It is not merely fit, proper and highly expedient, a stroke of infinite policy, a masterly evolution of Divine tactics; it is absolutely indispensable upon the supposition of mercy. Without it remission could not exist; and as it is the burden of the Gospel, it is therefore the POWER of God unto salvation,—the alternatives, and the only alternatives, being ATONEMENT or ETERNAL DEATH.

It would be easy to show that this is the only hypothesis upon which the scriptural account of a satisfaction to justice can be consistently maintained, and that the majority of those who adopt utilitarian views of government, while they profess to believe in the penal sufferings of our Lord, do in reality make them a substitute for the proper curse of the law. They represent the death of the Redeemer as a grand moral expedient, by which the same impression is produced in regard to the character of God as would have been produced by the everlasting ruin of the guilty. It is something in place of the literal infliction of the penalty of the law, which secures the same ultimate result. Such perversions of the truth will be effectually prevented by just conceptions of the moral government of God, its origin, nature and ends; and such views I have chosen to exhibit rather than combat systems of error in detail.

At the close[1] of my ministerial labours among you as members of this institution, I have brought this subject before you on account of its immense importance in relation to the glory of God, and its vital connection with the dearest interests of our race. The cross of Christ is the centre of the Christian system. From it we are instructed in the character of our Judge, the malignity of sin, our present condition and the prospects which await us beyond the grave. The scheme of redemption is a bright and glorious page in the history of God's administrations—a new book sealed with seven seals, containing lessons of surpassing interest, treating of Jehovah in loftier strains than the seraph's heart had ever reached or the seraph's tongue had ever uttered until the Lion of the Tribe of Judah prevailed to unloose the seals, to reveal the mysteries, and invited the nations to behold their God. His glory is here displayed with a lustre in comparison with which all other manifestations of His name are as the feeble light of the stars. Creation proclaimed His power, Providence His goodness, Conscience His justice, and Hell His vengeance. These were so many stars, differing from each other in glory, in which we might see all that could be known of God; but when Jesus came the Sun of Righteousness arose, darkness was scattered, and the light of God's glory, reflected from the face of His Son, darted its rays through heaven, earth and hell. The Cross became the centre of universal attraction, displayed the perfections of Deity in singular and rare combination, and was the source at once of rapture to angels, of terror to the lost and of hope to men. The death of Christ is without doubt the sublimest event in the annals of time or the records of eternity. And in what a light does it present the malignity of sin! What a commentary upon its intrinsic demerit and turpitude is furnished in the

---

[1] This address was delivered to the class, the members of which were graduated the next day.

groans, agony and anguish of the Son of God! In the Cross it is proclaimed, in living characters, to be the abominable thing which God hates; and if God spared not His own dear Son—holy, harmless and undefiled as He was—when He occupied the legal position of the guilty, we may be as fully assured as if it were written in letters of fire upon the blue vault of heaven that the soul that sinneth it shall die. In the blood of the Lamb, my brethren, and not in the deceitful reasonings of a corrupt heart, learn the estimate to be put upon Sin. There, stripped of her blandishments, unmasked in her treachery, exposed in her seductions, she stands revealed in the hideous deformity of her nature, odious to God and deadly to man. Her steps lead down to death, and her feet take hold on hell.

You are soon, my friends, to enter upon the active duties of life. The responsibilities of manhood are gathering around you, and you will shortly go forth, no longer subject to the authority of tutors and guardians, but your own masters.

Let me impress it upon you that the first, the indispensable element of success in your future career must be sought in the favour of God. If there is a Being who presides over the destinies of men and accomplishes His pleasure among the armies of heaven and the inhabitants of earth; whose favour is life and whose loving-kindness is better than life; whose indignation none can withstand, the fierceness of whose anger none can abide; who compasses us behind and before, and understands all our ways; upon whom we are absolutely dependent for all that we have or are,—it is surely the consummation of folly to look for prosperity in His dominions without His favour. Can you expect enduring happiness when the curse of the Almighty hangs over you, when the awful leprosy of sin is wasting your soul, and the edict has gone forth dooming you to solitude and banishment from God? What prospect is before you when, at every step, you are surrounded by a power which you cannot resist, provoked to vengeance by your negligence and contempt? No doubt, my brethren, your bosoms are bounding with hope, the future seems full of promise, and you are eager to enter upon the scenes of manly life. But be assured that the first care which should demand your attention is the salvation of the soul. What you first need, most pressingly need, is to have your conscience purged from dead works by the blood of Him who, through the Eternal Spirit, offered Himself without spot unto God.

It is no time to settle the subordinate concerns of this life when your souls are in jeopardy every hour—when the wrath of God is revealed from heaven against you, a burning hell is beneath you, and a terrible eternity before you. Be exhorted to seek first the kingdom of God and His righteousness. Secure your immortal interests, and your mortal will not be disregarded. The great subject of solicitude with me is the salvation of your souls. I am fully assured that if you begin your career under the favour of God, His blessing will attend you at every step; and though His way may often be in the whirlwind of adversity or the deep waters of affliction, He will eventually make all things work together for your good. I shall feel that you are committed to the guidance of a Friend who will never leave you nor forsake you, who knows your interests and is able to provide for them. But my feelings will be very different in regard to those who know not God and obey not the Gospel of His Son. To such there is no safety. At home or abroad, awake or asleep, in sickness or in health, poverty or affluence, the curse of God attends you; from His hands there is no escape; and, earnestly as I could wish that all may be well with you, I must constantly feel that nothing is well, that nothing can be well, until you are sprinkled with the blood of atonement. I am afraid to trust you in the world, for the Prince of darkness has a fearful ascendency in it, and may make it the instrument of rendering you still more obdurate in sin. I shall dread to hear of your death, lest your dying hours should fill your friends with gloom, and be too sad an earnest of the awful destiny which follows;

and above all, my feelings are insupportable when I remember that I must meet you at the bar of God and be a swift witness against you.

Suffer, therefore, the word of exhortation while I embrace this last opportunity of urging it upon you with affection, earnestness and solemnity, to seek the Lord while He may be found, to call upon Him while He is near.

The point at which you have arrived is eminently critical. You are now forming your plans for life, and if religion is excluded, it is but too likely that you will never find the convenient season for attending to its claims. If, at this solemn period, when you so much need the blessing of the Almighty—this important juncture of your lives, which is to give shape and character to your subsequent pursuits—you rely upon your own wisdom and trust to your own understandings, there is too much ground to fear that you may be left to yourselves and abandoned to your self-sufficiency and folly. Can there be a more favourable period than the present for attending to the interests of your souls? You are young, and special promises are made to youth. You have reached a critical position. One step now may determine your destiny for ever. How important that you should act wisely and take that step in the fear of God! The cares of life will soon leave little time for the claims of religion; and if you find a strong reluctance to consider them now, that reluctance will increase with the growing power of a worldly spirit and the increasing dominion of inbred depravity. You are now free from those outward annoyances and petty vexations which the business of life always entails upon us, and which just as effectually close the heart against the calls of God as the heavier calamities of our lot. In every respect, then, your present situation is favourable; more so, perhaps, than it will ever be again. Do you mean to let this golden opportunity pass unimproved? Do you mean that gray hairs shall find you veteran sinners against God? Have you any excuse, any plausible pretext, which even your consciences will receive, for refusing at once to attend to the one thing needful? You cannot surely deny that if Christianity be anything, it must be everything—if true at all, it is, as Leslie expresses it, "tremendously true." All other matters dwindle into nothing in comparison with the interests of the soul. What signify the applause of the world, the distinctions of society, the force of genius and the charm of letters, if after all your shortlived honours you are doomed at last to lie down in hell?

Finally, brethren, my ministry now closes with you; the result of my labours and of your attention will not be known till the day of final accounts. Whatever may have been my imperfections—and I feel that they have been both numerous and great—I have always cherished, and shall always continue to cherish, the liveliest interest in your welfare. I have endeavoured to lead you to the fountain of life; I have preached the Gospel with whatever ability God has given me; and if any of you have been brought to serious reflection on the subject of salvation, it is a matter of devout thanksgiving to God. But it oppresses me to think that some of you, at least, will leave these walls as careless as you entered them. If now, at the eleventh hour, I could break your carnal slumber and rouse your attention to the things that belong to your peace, I would gladly employ any lawful expedient to do so. But no voice but the voice of God can reach you. I tremble to see you entering upon life unprepared for its close; but I have faithfully warned you; I call heaven and earth to record against you this day; and if you perish in your sins, your own consciences will tell you that life and death were before you. You have died wilfully. Would that I could utter with as much hope as affection the only word which remains to be pronounced —FAREWELL!

PREFATORY NOTE.

THIS discourse on the Priesthood of Christ was preached as a Commencement Sermon at the South Carolina College on the second day of December, 1849, the text being Hebrews v. 5, 6. It was published in part in the "Southern Presbyterian Review" for April, 1850. It may be considered the complement of the preceding treatise, where was discussed the work of Christ as a legal substitute—the question of the Epistle to the Romans. Herein is discussed the priestly character of Christ—the question of the Epistle to the Hebrews.

THE PRIESTHOOD OF CHRIST.

THE mediation of Christ is represented in the Scriptures as consisting in the discharge of three principal offices—those of a Prophet, a Priest, and a King. That God should instruct and govern us through the agency and instrumentality of another is so perfectly in keeping with the whole analogy of nature that none who pretend to any reverence for the Scriptures, who even admit the historical reality of Jesus, are disposed to deny that He is, in some pre-eminent sense, the moral teacher and moral ruler of mankind. All who acknowledge any revelation acknowledge that through Jesus Christ, God has communicated discoveries of His will which are of the last importance to the improvement and happiness of the race. Too many, indeed, reduce His prophetic functions to the mere publication of truth, and His kingly office to the proclamation of the laws which men are required to obey, thus divesting Him, as a teacher, of the dispensation of the Spirit, and merging His royal prerogative into that of a messenger of the King. But though there has been a disposition to strip these offices of some of the peculiarities which distinguish them as exercised by Christ, and which give them indeed their value and efficacy to us, yet no peculiar presumption has been felt to lie against the general fact that His mediation embraces the elements of instruction and rule. Widely different is the case in regard to His priesthood. This has ever been the stone of stumbling and the rock of offence in the Christian scheme. Every artifice of learning and criticism has been tried to expunge from the Scriptures their plain and obvious teachings upon the subject. The Word of God has been twisted, distorted and mutilated, the simplest rules of grammar set at defiance and the established usages of language disregarded and despised, in order to give some colour of plausibility to the shameless denial of the sacerdotal mediation of the Saviour. What renders this conduct the more remarkable is, that the New Testament gives a prominence to the priesthood which it nowhere concedes to the kingly or prophetic offices of Christ. It was the very end of His incarnation that He might be a merciful and faithful High Priest. There was obviously no necessity for such a miracle as the assumption of human nature by His Divine Person if the only result to be achieved were the discovery of truths inaccessible to the efforts of reason, and the promulgation of laws resting upon the authority of God. Prophets and apostles were abundantly competent to offices of this sort. They could teach, they did teach; the New Testament itself, the very oracles of God, is the labour of their hands, directed by the Spirit of God.

The incongruity is so palpable and monstrous betwixt the pomp of preparation which the common doctrine of the incarnation involves, and the end to be accomplished betwixt the opulence of means and the poverty of result, that those who deny the priesthood do not scruple to deny the Deity of the Son, and, with a painful consistency of error, reduce Him who is over all God blessed for ever to the level of our poor, dependent humanity. The doctrines of a proper Sonship and a proper priesthood are in the Christian economy inseparably linked together, and it is a happy circumstance for the faith of the Church that the enemies of the cross can never hope to prevail without a double work of destruction. Their argument against the priesthood is felt to be incomplete until they have demolished the Deity, and their arguments against the Deity unsatisfactory until they have demolished the priesthood of Christ. They must show that He has never been addressed in the words, in their strict and proper acceptation, Thou art my Son, to-day have I begotten thee, before they can show that it has never been said to Him, Thou art a priest for ever after the order of Melchisedek.

But while the Scriptures insist with peculiar emphasis upon the mediation of Christ, and represent the functions which are discharged in it as essential to salvation, it is not sufficiently considered that these functions themselves are not necessarily sacerdotal—that they might have been discharged by one who was not a priest in the common acceptation of the term. All that seems to be indispensable to salvation is the obedience of a substitute voluntarily assuming our guilt and able to endure the curse of the law. The imputation of an adequate righteousness upon the ground of federal relations is the principle into which the Apostle resolves our justification in the Epistle to the Romans. The government of God demands that sin should be punished and that life should be the reward of perfect obedience; and the salvation of a sinner turns upon the possibility of vicarious righteousness and vicarious punishment. These are the doctrines which Paul enounces and vindicates in that great Epistle which has ever been the bulwark of the evangelical scheme as contradistinguished from the dreams of formalists, Pharisees and mystics. He says nothing there specifically of priesthood. It is Christ a substitute, Christ the federal representative of sinners, Christ obeying and Christ dying in the place of the guilty,—these are the topics of discussion, these are the doctrines which lie at the foundation of our hope, and make the Gospel emphatically tidings of great joy. But these doctrines do not necessarily include priesthood. We can manifestly conceive of a mediation by substitution which shall not at the same time be sacerdotal. The Son of God, for aught that appears, might have become incarnate, assumed our legal responsibilities and brought in an everlasting righteousness; He might have been a sponsor, paying our debt and slain by the sword of Divine justice in our stead; He might have fulfilled all the requisitions of the law or of natural religion, and have pledged the faithfulness and truth of God to our redemption, and yet not have performed any of these duties in the character of a priest. It becomes, therefore, an extremely interesting question why the mediation of Christ has been made to assume the peculiar form of priesthood. If atonement is all that can be proved to be essential to pardon and acceptance, and vicarious obedience and vicarious punishment all that are essential to atonement—if substitution is the fundamental principle of redemption— why is it that the substitute has been ordained a priest, that His death is a sacrifice as well as a satisfaction to justice, and that with the blood of this offering He has passed into the holiest of all to make constant intercessions for His people? If we could have been saved by a substitute who was not a priest, and redeemed by a death which was not a sacrifice, why have a priest and a sacrifice been the chosen means of accomplishing the work? These are not questions of idle curiosity. They have been suggested to my own mind by an attentive study of the Epistles to the Romans and the Hebrews. The first, the Epistle to the Romans, discusses the principles of the Gospel in their general relations to the moral government of God, and demonstrates, as well as asserts upon authority, the absolute necessity of legal substitution in order to life. But if the disclosures of revelation stopped here, we might look upon the death of the Redeemer as the result simply of the operation of justice—a death inflicted by the law, exclusively penal in its nature and relations, exacted of Him in the same sense in which it would otherwise have been exacted of the sinner. We might regard pardon as resulting from faith in that death as a satisfaction to justice, and access to God as immediate and direct in consequence of this historical fact as a past reality. The principles here discussed would resolve the security of our state into the covenant faithfulness of God without the least insight into the manner in which it is actually made available to the saints. All that we could say would be that our debt has been paid, that justice no longer demands our lives, that God has promised in consequence of the Redeemer's death to receive us into favour, and upon the ground of that death we might approach Him ourselves and sue for mercy. This is all that could be certainly collected from the general discussion of this Epistle. But when we turn to the Epistle to the Hebrews we find indeed a substitute, and the substitute demanded by the Epistle to the Romans, but that substitute is embodied in a priest; we find a death, a penal death, a death which is commensurate with the curse of the law, but it is a death which is also a sacrifice—at once the result of the operation of justice and of a free-will offering to God. We find justification and pardon resolved ultimately into the obedience and death of Christ as past historical facts, but immediately due to relations sustained to Him as a living person and Redeemer; and access to God ascribed, not so much to faith in His past achievements as to His present appearance for us in the holiest of all; and the covenant faithfulness of God is seen to be maintained through the agency of Him who ever liveth to make intercessions for us.

The Epistle to the Hebrews may be regarded as a detailed account of the method in which the great law of substitution has been actually applied in the redemption of our race. While that to the Romans shows what must needs be done in order to our salvation, the Epistle to the Hebrews shows how it has been done; and where the arrangements have gone beyond the strict requisitions of necessity, they are demonstrated to be the dictates at once of mercy and wisdom. Priesthood is the perfection of mediation. There is not a single circumstance which distinguishes a priest from a general substitute which is not significant, a proof of goodness, a fresh illustration of the adaptation of redemption to the condition of its objects; not a single circumstance which distinguishes a sacrifice from the ordinary forms of death that does not enhance the preciousness of the Saviour's work. The full effect of this truth is lost upon most Christian minds through inattention to the distinctions in question. They admire the goodness and adore the wisdom of God in providing a substitute for the guilty, able to reconcile the conflicting claims of justice and of grace; but apart from the adaptation of His person to the mighty work they see nothing upon which they are accustomed to dwell as peculiarly indicative of the Divine goodness. They overlook the adaptation of His office; they forget that the manner in which He has accomplished the work is as glorious as the matter—the *how* as sublime as the *what*. The work as done, the person by whom, exhaust their topics of admiration and of praise, and they fail to enter into those other motives of faith, devotion and thanksgiving which are derived from the contemplation of the office in its essential and distinguishing features. They use the terms Priest and High Priest, and have a habitual reference to the appearance of the Saviour in the presence of God; but their High Priest is, after all, but little more than an all-sufficient sponsor, and His intercessions are regarded rather as acts of royalty than sacerdotal pleas. It is amazing how little and seldom we enter into those views of the death of the Redeemer which spring from the consideration of it as a real and proper sacrifice—how little we discriminate betwixt a legal representative and a consecrated Priest, betwixt Christ glorious in His kingdom and equally glorious in the holiest of all, betwixt even His triumphant ascension as a King and His passage as intercessor, not without blood, into the presence of God. As these distinctions are evidently important, and the benefits of that peculiar form of mediation to which the Saviour was appointed are clearly explained by the Apostle, it may be well to show how much we have gained and how pre-eminently God is glorified by this whole arrangement. Let us, then, contemplate Jesus, not simply as the Apostle, but the High Priest of our profession, and let us endeavour to collect from the Scriptures the excellency and glory of this species of mediation.

1. It deserves, first, to be remarked that those conceptions of the origin of salvation which are suggested by substitu-

tion in its nakedest form are rendered clearer and more impressive by the fact that the substitute is also a priest. The appointment of any representative is an act of grace; redemption, no matter how achieved, is the offspring of mercy. The justice which connects punishment with guilt attaches the penalty to the person of the offender; and though it is capable of being satisfied by vicarious sufferings, it is the prerogative of the lawgiver to say whether he will accept a substitute and transfer his vengeance from the original transgressor to an innocent but adequate sponsor. But this grace is more conspicuously displayed in the constitution of a priest than the designation of a simple surety. While, in either case, the whole proceeding is of grace, there are, in the consecration of a priest, a solemnity of purpose and an absolute sovereignty of will which arrest attention and compel the most thoughtless to acknowledge that it is the finger of God. In considering the claims of a surety, all that would seem to be important is his ability to pay the debt he assumes. But in the case of a priest this ability must concur with other qualifications, the anxiety to secure which is an additional proof of the mercy which pities the condition of the lost. It is always an act of sovereign condescension to admit a substitute; but there is nothing inconceivable in the supposition that the proposition to redeem the guilty might proceed from himself and not from God—that he might volunteer his services, and so become the author of the scheme which dispenses salvation to men. But the honour of priesthood no man can take to himself but he that is called of God, as was Aaron. Hence the Apostle insists upon it that Christ glorified not Himself to be made an High Priest, but He that said unto Him, Thou art my Son, to-day have I begotten Thee. A priest is a solemn minister of religion—the channel through which all worship is conducted—the organ of all communications betwixt God and the people. This august agency none can assume without the authority of God. So awful and momentous is this office, which really collects the prayers and praises and thanksgivings of a world into a single person, which centres the hopes of mankind upon the conduct of a single individual throughout all ages,—so tremendous is this responsibility and so sublime this honour, that it would be the climax of presumption on the part of any one to propose that it should be conceded to him. It belongs to God, and to God alone, to designate a priest. The idea of a mediatorial worship conducted by a permanent and glorious minister, and so conducted as to strengthen the ties of personal obligation, is an idea which could only originate in the mind of the Deity; and there were an evident fitness and propriety in the solemnity and grandeur attached to the appointment of Jesus to this office when He was consecrated not without an oath. A scheme which contemplates an arrangement of this sort bears stamped upon it the strongest impress of grace. It sprang from the bosom of God; it was mercy, which conceived the purpose of salvation; mercy, which accepted the substitute; and mercy upon mercy, the exuberance of grace, which made that substitute a priest. This last feature makes it little less than blasphemy to imagine that redemption could have any other source but the bosom of the Almighty. It is a Divine plan.

The acceptance of any substitute, on the part of the Deity, contains an implied pledge that he was adequate to the task. We can scarcely conceive without horror that a Being of infinite benevolence should subject the innocent—however willing he might be to undergo the torture—to unspeakable sufferings, when it was known beforehand that they would be incompetent to redeem the guilty. God, we may rest assured, would never take a surety who was unable to pay. But the guarantee, arising from the Divine character, that an accepted mediation shall be sufficient, is immensely strengthened when the substitute is considered as not only accepted but *proposed* by God, and set apart to his work with a solemnity of installation which would seem to throw the most awful imputation upon the Divine veracity if the sacrifice should fail to be adequate. Can we, for a moment, indulge the suspicion that Jesus shall not infallibly save every sinner who applies to Him, when He has been solemnly appointed to this office by the oath of God? Was that oath an idle flourish, a mere mockery of our woe? or was it not rather a proclamation to all the intelligent universe that the scheme of redemption should be as stable as the eternal throne—the priesthood of Jesus as incapable of disappointing our hopes as God of ceasing to be? This designation of Jesus to the priesthood was the sole ground of security to the ancient saints. The great work was only in prospect— it stood in the counsel of God; and as the Strength of Israel was not a man that He should lie, nor the son of man that He should repent, the patriarchs and prophets looked with steadfast hearts to the great events which are matters of history to us. "And these all, having obtained a good report through faith, received not the promise, God having provided some better thing for us, that they without us should not be made perfect." Such is the strong consolation which the oath of God is suited to impart to the heirs of His grace that if nothing more were known of the economy of redemption than that it depended upon a priesthood appointed by Himself, and consecrated with the solemnity of this awful sanction, this would be sufficient to establish their hearts. They would feel that the scheme could not fail; that the glory of God was so deeply concerned in its success that heaven and earth might sooner pass away than a single sinner fall short of salvation who had fled for refuge to the hope set before him. Such impressiveness could not be imparted to the acceptance of a substitute, or even the selection of a mere representative. The forms of inauguration, the awful rites of consecration, the proofs of love and of confidence implied in the delegation of so imposing a trust,—these must all be wanting, and would strip the transaction of whatever attractions they are fitted to give it upon a sinner's regard. No form of mediation could beforehand so deeply pledge the Deity to its success as that which turns upon an office to which God alone is competent to call. In making it His prerogative to glorify him who shall be clothed with the priesthood, we make it absolutely certain that he who is so honoured shall glorify God in the wisdom of the choice.

As, in every instance of substitution, the free and cordial acquiescence of the substitute is indispensable to the success of the arrangement, it is a favourable circumstance when the form of mediation can be made conspicuously to display it. His consent should not only be presumed, but known. It should be patent and manifest in the whole transaction. There would be an appearance of hardship, if not of injustice, in a proceeding which should doom the innocent to suffer in the place of the guilty without the concurrence of his own will. If arbitrarily done, it would be flagrant and intolerable tyranny; if done from high and solemn considerations of public policy, it would impeach the wisdom of an administration which had been so imperfectly digested as to demand an occasional departure from distributive justice, an occasional disregard of personal worth or delinquency, in order to answer its proper ends. If the scheme of redemption, however, proposed Jesus to His people as only a legal substitute, though His consent might be easily collected from the circumstances of the case, yet it would not be conspicuous from the nature and progress of the work. Still less could it be seen that His consent was the spontaneous movement of His own heart, rather than a pious submission to the will of God, with whom the scheme must originate. But when He is announced as a priest all difficulty vanishes. He must delight in the work; the offering which He brings must be a free-will offering, or it could be no offering at all. If the victim laid upon the altar were not fully and cordially surrendered to God, the external act were hypocrisy and the whole service a mockery. Wherefore, when He cometh into the world, He saith, Sacrifice and offering thou didst not desire; mine ears hast thou opened: burnt-offering and sin-offering hast thou not required. Then said I, Lo I come: in the volume of the book it is written of me, I delight to do Thy will, O my God.

Among the qualifications indispensable to a priest, next to his having somewhat to offer, nothing is more earnestly insisted on by the Apostle than a sympathizing nature. He must feel a real solicitude in the objects of his care. He must be one that can have compassion on the ignorant and on them that are out of the way. He is not to bring his sacrifice from a cold and repulsive sense of duty, nor from abstract regards to the dignity or glory of the deed; but he must be governed by a real *philanthropy*—he must have love and pity in his heart—he must weep for the transgressor while he makes atonement for the guilt. As he is to be a mediator betwixt God and men, he must combine in his person the apparently incompatible elements of zeal for the Divine glory and affection for the souls of men. He must love the Lord his God, and maintain the integrity of His throne, while he commiserates the condition of the lost and would rescue them from their melancholy doom. He must have a brother's heart while he vindicates the decree of eternal justice. It is this zeal for God and man, this admirable blending of piety and philanthropy, which constitutes priesthood necessarily and always a joyful work. This is a qualification which the priest must have—it is of the essence of the office; and if at any period in the progress of his work he should fail to possess or evince it, his acts would cease to be sacerdotal; they would become sacrilegious—the offering of strange fire upon the altar. This consideration puts it beyond the possibility even of suspicion that the substitution of the Saviour was the result of "a momentary enthusiasm, a sudden impulse of heroic feeling, which prompted Him in the ardour of the moment to make a sacrifice of which, on cool deliberation, He repented." The very nature of the priesthood demands that the spirit of sublime devotion to God and heroic self-sacrifice for man, which first secured His consent to the enterprise, should animate Him at every step in His history, and sanctify every function of His office. He is not to be the passive recipient of ill. As a priest He must *act*—there are things to be done even in the endurance of the curse—

and His whole heart must burn with piety and compassion while He bears the sins of the world in His own body on the tree. The lofty and godlike motives which induced the Redeemer, in the counsels of eternity, before the morning stars had yet sung together or the sons of God shouted for joy, to become the Lamb to be slain, must have continued to operate with undiminished intensity, or the prerogatives and glory of His office had been forfeited. The priestly spirit must have continued to dwell and to reign in His heart, or the priestly robes would have been taken from His shoulders. He must have been as free, as cordial, as delighted, when He uttered the cry of lamentation and woe upon the cross, which shook the earth and startled the dead, as when at the glorious suggestion of the scheme He uttered the language, Lo, I come. As the work of a priest, it is stamped upon the whole process of redemption that the substitute gave His consent; that His self-devotion was spontaneous and free—the execution of a settled purpose to which He was impelled by no constraining influence of the Divine will, by no transitory fervours of enthusiasm, no martyr impulse of the moment; that He delighted in the work—it was His meat and drink; He felt it to be an honour and not a hardship, its successful achievement a crown of glory, and not a triumph over cruelty. This single consideration, that it displays so conspicuously the freeness of the Saviour's mediation, is itself a sufficient vindication of the wisdom and fitness of a priesthood. It shows that our felicity has not been purchased at the expense of the rights of another; and though there was an immense cost of suffering and of blood, it was never for a moment begrudged, never for a moment sustained with reluctance. We have no occasion for regrets that the blessings which we enjoy have been put into our hands by cruelty, injustice, or even harshness and severity to others. They are the free gifts of that sublimest of all spirits—the spirit of a priest.

It is obvious from the preceding train of remark that all those views of the origin and success of the scheme of redemption, which the general idea of substitution naturally suggests, are rendered more striking and impressive by the peculiarities of priesthood. If legal substitution involves a dispensation with the primary requisition of the law, attaching punishment always to the person of the offender, which proves that the substitute must be appointed by God—the necessity of this inference is immensely enhanced when that substitute sustains an office which absolutely demands a vocation from above. The proposition to suffer might originate from a competent sponsor; the proposition to be a priest could not be made without blasphemy, and any scheme which comprehends the functions of a real and proper priesthood can spring from no other source but the bosom of God. If the acceptance of a substitute carries a presumption that his proffered mediation must be successful, this presumption is magnified into certainty when the substitute is not only accepted but appointed by God, and invested with an office which requires a formal and solemn inauguration. The presumption in the one case arises from the general principle that whatever means are appointed of God must be efficacious; but the certainty in the latter arises from the awful sanctity of the oath with which the Son was declared to be a priest for ever after the order of Melchisedek.

If the consent of the substitute must, in every instance, be presumed—the righteousness of the procedure depending upon his concurrence—it is obviously important that it should be open and palpable; and this result is effectually attained by an arrangement which could not subsist a moment longer than the consent of the substitute is given. The priestly spirit, which is essential to the priestly office, exacts delight in the work, and all sacerdotal functions would behove to be suspended should the priest fail in the spirit of his vocation. The joy of the Mediator in the work, therefore, and the vindication of God from all suspicion of cruelty, injustice or severity, is complete and triumphant when the Saviour's death is made a sacrifice—a free-will offering to God. But though these considerations are not without their value in illustrating the Divine wisdom and goodness, yet we are far from supposing that they constitute the peculiar advantages of sacerdotal mediation. The pre-eminent importance of the office is rather to be sought in the light which it throws upon redemption as a work achieved, and in the arrangements which it makes for the successful application of its blessings to the heirs of the promise. It is precisely the scheme in which the provisions of the Gospel most conspicuously display the glory of God, and are best adapted to conciliate regard and to inspire confidence and hope. Grace is here seen to be a remedy without the disgust which remedies usually create; it is rendered attractive to all who know their disease and appreciate their danger, and administers strong consolation under circumstances in which no other arrangement could save from the encroachments of despair.

2. When we contemplate the death of Christ as simply the death of a substitute, we see in it nothing more than a full satisfaction to the claims of justice. The sponsor pays the debt, and pays it cheerfully; the legal representative endures the curse which others had incurred, and falls beneath the sword which the guilt of others had drawn from its scabbard. It is a transaction of law and government, the infliction of a judicial sentence. Though it is implied that the substitute approves the equity of the law under which He suffers, and is prepared to vindicate the Divine conduct from the charge of unreasonable rigour,—though the justice of the whole transaction is assumed, yet when it is represented as simply the operation of justice, much of its moral grandeur and impressiveness is lost. We see in the substitute a victim to his own generosity, and considering Him exclusively in this light, there are probably few men who have not had occasion to fortify their minds against a momentary impression of unrelenting severity when regarding those awful attributes of God which make atonement the exclusive channel of mercy to the guilty. We must go beyond the event to its principle

and causes before we can be at ease when we survey the sufferings of Jesus of Nazareth. He is felt to be a passive victim of Divine wrath, He bares His bosom to the stroke, He receives the storm which beats in violence and fury: He simply, in other words, stands and endures, while God, and God in His most terrible forms of manifestation, is the sole agent in the case.

Widely different is the impression which is made when the transaction is contemplated in its true light. There is no room for the remotest suspicion of inexorable rigour when Jesus is seen to be a priest, His death a sacrifice, and the whole transaction an august and glorious act of worship. The position of Jesus is sublime when, standing before the altar, He confesses the guilt of His brethren, adores the justice which dooms them to woe, and almost exacts from God as the condition of His own love that justice should not slacken nor abate. That prayer of confession, that assumption of guilt, that clear acknowledgment of what truth and righteousness demand, make us feel that God *must* strike, that the edict must go forth, Awake, O sword, against my shepherd and the man that is my fellow, saith the Lord of Hosts. Still sublimer is His position when with profound adoration of the Divine character, by His own proper act, His own spontaneous movement, He lays His life upon the altar, virtually saying, Take it, it ought to be taken; let the fire of justice consume it; better, ten thousand times better, that this should be than that the throne of the Eternal should be tarnished by an effeminate pity! We feel that death is not so much a penalty inflicted as an offering accepted. We feel that God is glorious, that the law is glorious in the whole transaction, because Christ glorifies them. He lays down His life of Himself; it is His own choice to die rather than that man should perish or the Divine government be insulted with impunity; and although in accepting the offering Justice inflicted upon Him the full penalty of the law, although the fire which consumed the victim was the curse in its whole extent, yet as it was an act of worship to provide it, and especially as that victim was Himself, every groan and pang, every exclamation of agony, amazement and horror, was a homage to God which, in itself considered, the Priest felt it glorious to render. And if Jesus in all the extremity of His passion proclaimed to the universe what from the nature of priesthood He must have proclaimed, that the whole transaction was a ground on which God was adored by Him, and ought to be adored by all, that His Father was never dearer, never more truly God in His sight, than when He accepted the sacrifice of Himself, the sublimity of the principles involved, and the interest of Jesus in them, are a perfect vindication from every illiberal suspicion. There is something, to our minds, inexpressibly sublime when we contemplate the scheme of redemption as accomplished by an act of worship—when we look upon Jesus not as a passive recipient of woes, the unresisting victim of law, but as a minister of religion, conducting its services in the presence of angels and men, upon an emergency which seemed to cover the earth with darkness. Our world becomes the outer court of the sanctuary, where a sacrifice is to be offered in which the Priest and the Victim are alike the wonder of the universe—in which the worship which is rendered leaves it doubtful whether the Deity is more glorious in His justice or His grace. In this aspect the satisfaction of Jesus is not merely the ground upon which others are at liberty to approach and adore the Divine perfections; it is itself a prayer uttered by the lips of one whose deeds were words—a hymn of praise chanted by Him whose songs were the inspiration of holiness and truth. Every proud imagination is rebuked, every insinuation against the character of God is felt to be a shame to us, every disposition to cavil or condemn is consigned to infamy, when we remember that the whole work of Jesus was a solemn service of religion, as well that by which He descended into the grave as that by which He passed through the heavens into the holiest of all. He was a priest in His death, a priest in

His resurrection, a priest in His ascension. He worshipped God in laying His life upon the altar, He worshipped Him in taking it again, and it was an act of worship by which He entered with His blood into the very presence of the Highest to intercede for the saints. It was religion in Jesus to die, to rise, to reign, as it is religion in us to believe in these great events of His history.

Here, then, is an incalculable advantage of priesthood. While it makes the passion of the Redeemer a full and perfect satisfaction of Divine justice, and so lays an adequate foundation of pardon, it vindicates the Divine glory in every step of the proceeding by making every step an act of adoration and praise. It makes the Saviour adore the Father in His death, makes that very death an offering of praise, redemption itself a mighty prayer, and throws the sanctities and solemnities of worship—and worship on the part of one who knew what was the proper ground of worship—around all the stages in the development of the economy of grace. This seems to us to be the very climax of wisdom. It was glorious to have provided a substitute who should be able to bear our sins in His own body upon the tree, to have devised a scheme by which the conflicting claims of mercy and justice should be adjusted and harmonized—by which God could be just and at the same time the justifier of those who believe in Jesus; but it was the very perfection of wisdom to have executed this scheme so that the intensest sufferings should have produced only a deeper impression of the Divine glory and of the excellence and value of the Divine law. Surely in this arrangement the law is magnified and made honourable.

3. Another circumstance which illustrates the importance of sacerdotal mediation is the provision which it makes for the application of redemption to the heirs of the promise. The discussion has often been agitated, Which precedes, faith or regeneration? On the one hand it has been maintained, and successfully maintained, that faith is a holy exercise, and necessarily supposes a change of heart;

and on the other, with equal truth, that a spiritual nature is the work of the Holy Ghost, and that He is vouchsafed in His saving operations only to those who are entitled to the favour of God. They must be in Christ in order to be recipients of saving grace; they must have received that grace in order to be in Christ. There are but two hypotheses by which this difficulty can be met upon the scheme of simple substitution, and both of them are liable to insuperable objections. The one is the Antinomian theory of eternal justification, which, as it makes acceptance with God compatible with a state of sin, is destructive of the interests of holiness; the other is the theory of a change in the Divine mind in relation to a sinner at a particular period of his history, which change occurs without any particular reason why it should be effected then rather than at any other time. It is supposed that the covenant of redemption included a promise to the Mediator that, at a given time in the history of each, the heirs of the promise should be renewed by the Spirit and enabled to believe on the Saviour. The actual communication of the Spirit is solely in virtue of that promise. Now, if the sinner were not justified in the justification of Christ, if before the critical period arrives he is the object of Divine reprobation, what is to make him less so after it has come? If there was that in his character and relations to God which made it inconsistent with the Divine perfections to impart to him tokens of favour, the original promise has neither changed that character nor those relations, and has consequently not removed the inconsistency. The change towards him in the Divine mind is purely arbitrary. If it should be said that the work of Christ has laid the foundations of that change, the reply is obvious that, at the given time, the sinner's relations to that work are no nearer than they were before; and if that work be the cause of it, the change must have occurred when Christ Himself was justified. These difficulties seem to be insuperable upon the hypothesis of simple substitution. We must fall back upon Antinomian principles, or confess that the conversion of a sinner is utterly inexplicable.

But when we take in the idea of priesthood the whole difficulty vanishes. There is no need for asserting what the Scriptures everywhere deny—an eternal justification, or an actual justification in the resurrection of Christ, or an arbitrary change in the feelings and sentiments of the changeless God. The Spirit in His first operations is imparted, not as a token of God's favour to the sinner, but as a token of His regard to the great High Priest who pleads before the throne. It is not that the sinner is accepted, but that Jesus is accepted. God looks only on the great Intercessor, and gives Him power to give eternal life to all whose names are on His breast-plate; and when, in answer to these Divine intercessions, the Spirit is given to Christ, that Christ may give Him to us—when, in consequence of that gift, He descends not from the Father but from Christ to us, and unites us to Jesus—then, God looks upon us in the Redeemer and justifies us in consequence of that union. Here there is perfect harmony in the whole plan.

4. Another immense advantage of a priesthood is that it quickens and stimulates the devotion of the Church by the assurance it inspires that all true worship, however imperfect or inadequate, shall infallibly be accepted and rewarded. Upon the scheme of simple substitution, the approaches of a sinner to God would be immediate and personal; he would go in his own name, depending for acceptance upon a work which had already been performed; he would plead the promises which were suspended upon it, and cast himself upon the unfailing faithfulness of God. We are far from saying that this would not be a sufficient ground of confidence and hope; but no man that knows the deceitfulness of his heart, the depths of iniquity within him—no man who feels his own vileness and pollution, and appreciates at the same time the transcendent holiness of God—could venture without fear and trembling, however supported by a covenant which guarantees his acceptance, to

come into the presence of Him in whose sight the heavens are not clean and who charges the angels with folly. To talk of confidence and boldness, under such circumstances, would be sheer madness. However we might be authorized to feel it, we could not feel it. The awful holiness of God must be like a consuming fire; an oppressive sense of unworthiness and of immeasurable distance and separation from the high and holy One that inhabiteth eternity must arrest the prayer as it rises in the heart, and check the confidence which atonement as a past historical fact is suited to inspire. We should say with the Israelites that we cannot speak with God. There must be a Mediator of prayer and praise, of all the exercises of religious worship, as well as a Mediator to purchase our pardon. This is accomplished by a priesthood. There is no direct and immediate approach to God. We come before Him only in the name of our Priest, who attracts us by community of nature, and who presents all our worship for us before the eternal throne. Our prayers are not heard and received as *ours*, but as the prayers of Jesus; our praises are not accepted as *ours*, but as the praises of Jesus. The imperfection which attaches to our performances, our pollution and weakness and unbelief, stop with the High Priest; His intercession and atonement cover all defects, and we are faultless and complete in Him. The prayer which reaches the ear of the Almighty is from Him, and not from us, and must be as prevalent as His worth. Here is our confidence, not only that Jesus died, but that Jesus lives—that He is our intercessor in the heavenly sanctuary, and there presents, enforces and sanctifies the religious worship of earth; here is our confidence that in the whole process of salvation God regards the Redeemer and not us, and deals out blessings according to His estimate of Christ; here is our confidence that if any man sin we have an Advocate with the Father, Jesus Christ the righteous. What an encouragement to prayer and praise! And what thanks shall we render unto God for adapting the marvellous scheme of His grace with such consummate wisdom to the wants and weaknesses of men! "Seeing, then, that we have a great High Priest that is passed into the heavens, Jesus, the Son of God, let us hold fast our profession. For we have not an High Priest which cannot be touched with the feeling of our infirmities, but was in all points tempted like as we are, yet without sin. Let us, therefore, come boldly unto the throne of grace, that we may obtain mercy and find grace to help in time of need." "Having, therefore, brethren, boldness to enter into the holiest by the blood of Jesus, by a new and living way which He hath consecrated for us, through the veil—that is to say, His flesh—and having an High Priest over the house of God, let us draw near with a true heart in full assurance of faith." This approach to God through the mediation of a priest is one of the highest privileges of the Gospel, and meets so completely a prime necessity of nature that where it is imperfectly understood we are disposed to make arrangements of our own which shall answer the same end. All corrupt religions have an order of priests. They could maintain no hold upon the people, they could not enlist the sympathies of the heart, without some provision of the sort. It is the glory of the Gospel that it has a Priest who can save to the uttermost all that come unto God through Him—who can sanctify the meanest worshipper and consecrate the humblest offering. None need be afraid or ashamed; it is not they, but He who is accepted in the house of God. It was an ancient reproach of Christianity, both among Jews and Gentiles, that it was a mere spiritual and personal worship, without the intervention of altar, temple or sacrifice. It had indeed no imposing ritual, no pomp of ceremony, no gorgeous solemnities—all was simple and unpretending; its institutions were addressed to intelligence and not to taste, to the heart instead of the fancy. Still, there was a temple in the Christian scheme, more august and glorious than any which could be reared by hands; it had an Altar, a Priest, a Victim and a Sacrifice, which should for ever abolish through their transcendent efficacy all other altars, all other priests, all other victims, however costly or imposing; it possessed in perfection all those advantages of sacerdotal mediation which Judaism and Paganism faintly adumbrated, and instead, like them, of making its priesthood subservient only to a vicarious religion, it secured the real worship of the heart.

5. It deserves, finally, to be added that a mediation of priesthood is the form in which consolation is most effectually administered to the children of men. It is necessary to any substitute that he should be a kinsman of our race, bone of our bone and flesh of our flesh. But besides the possession of our nature free from the stain and impurities of sin, nothing more is required for the purposes of vicarious righteousness and penal expiation than the consent of the substitute to undertake the task. If he *can* die the death to which we are doomed, and is willing to suffer in our stead, he is a competent redeemer. But though this is all which is absolutely essential to a legal substitution, it is not all which the state and condition of men evince to be desirable. We want a redeemer with a brother's heart as well as a brother's nature. Though not indispensable to our safety, it is indispensable to our comfort, that our substitute should be touched with a feeling of our infirmities, that he should be able to bear our sorrows and carry our griefs. Now this exquisite sympathy, which is one of the most powerful incentives to faith and love, is essential to a priest. Every high priest ordained for men must not only be a participant of their nature, but must have compassion on the ignorant and on them that are out of the way. He must enter with sympathetic tenderness into all their temptations and calamities, their fears and apprehensions, their cares and sorrows. He must be prepared to pity and encourage the weak, to comfort the weeper in the house of mourning, to wipe the widow's tears, to hear the orphan's cries, to lie down with the beggar upon his pallet of straw, and to watch with those to whom wearisome nights are

appointed. He must be a friend in all those emergencies in which friendship is our richest boon.

This qualification is found pre-eminently in Jesus. Holy, harmless, undefiled and separate from sinners, He possesses that absolute purity of nature in which the sensibilities have lost none of their delicacy from the petrifying influence of sin. Trained, too, by a protracted discipline in the school of affliction, He knows the temptations of our race—He knows what it is to weep, He knows the burden of a heavy heart. It was, perhaps, one design of the varied scenes of trial through which He passed to give Him that experience of our state which should call into the liveliest exercise the exquisite sympathy of His soul. In generous natures common troubles and afflictions have a tendency to knit them together; it is only where the heart has been seared by sin and immersed in selfishness that it can look with indifference upon struggles of others similar to those through which it has passed. The Apostle assures us that Jesus was tempted in all points as we are, that He might be a merciful and faithful High Priest. And those who have felt His presence in their trials can appreciate the priceless value of His sympathy. He has gone before us through every path of sorrow, and we cannot utter a groan nor heave a sigh which does not go to His heart. His pity for the guilty is as tender as His sympathy with the saints. No language can express the intensity of His compassion for those who in ignorance and folly disregard the day of their merciful visitation, and are heaping up wrath against the day of wrath and revelation of the righteous judgment of God. He has no pleasure in their death: "O Jerusalem, Jerusalem! thou that killest the prophets and stonest them that are sent unto thee, how often would I have gathered thy children together, even as a hen gathereth her chickens under her wings, and ye would not!" "Daughters of Jerusalem, weep not for Me, but weep for yourselves and for your children." The sublimest example of compassion which the world has ever beheld was furnished by the

Saviour in that memorable prayer, in which—when "the clouds of wrath from heaven and from earth, pregnant with materials which nothing but a Divine hand could have collected, were about to discharge themselves on Him in a deluge of agony and blood," when insulted by men, abandoned by His friends, mocked by His enemies, jeered by devils and deserted by God, He was about to expire in solitude and darkness—He could still, for a moment in the plenitude of His pity forgetting these unspeakable calamities, sue for the forgiveness of the remorseless agents of His death. This was compassion like a God. And what an exquisite spectacle of tenderness was that when Jesus, on the cross, just before the consummation of the last event that should fulfil the predictions of ancient prophecy, consigned His mother to the care of the beloved disciple! Surely such an High Priest became us. In our waywardness and folly, in our sins and temptations, in our murmurs and impatience, we should alienate any other friend but Him, that sticketh closer than a brother.

I have now said enough to show the transcendent value of a priesthood, and I trust that I have opened to your minds a field of thought which shall not be wholly unfruitful. Upon occasions of this sort, when there are so many circumstances to impress with solemnity whatever truths may be uttered, and when there is every likelihood that the words spoken may be remembered in after years, I have always been accustomed to insist upon some vital doctrine of the Gospel. It is my earnest desire and prayer that those who hear me may be saved. The solicitude which I always feel for the young men of my charge is collected to its greatest intensity when they are about to be dismissed from my pastoral instruction and care. If it could avail, I could weep tears of blood over those who have never been persuaded to become reconciled to God. I see them going out into a world which is full of dangers: temptations beset them on every side; they have a wily adversary who is plotting for their destruction, a deceitful heart which is readily caught with his guile, and in the midst of gins and traps and snares they are confident of perfect security. A spell is upon them, which, if it be not broken, must undo them. Under these circumstances, when I reflect that they are probably hearing my voice for the last time, I am constrained to cry aloud in one final, desperate effort to dispel the enchantment which, if not dispelled, must seal them up in death. My young friends, I earnestly beseech you to give heed, if you have forgotten all others, to the instruction of this day. Carry with you the lessons it has taught, and before you have yet become immersed in the world reflect upon the obvious inferences which flow from the subject that has just been discussed:

1. Is it so that Jesus is a Priest appointed with the solemnity of an oath? Then have all sinned and come short of the glory of God. There is no need of a mediator to the righteous and unfallen. It is only when guilt has separated betwixt God and men that a daysman is required betwixt them, who can lay his hand upon them both. The incarnation, temptations, trials, sufferings and passion of our Lord are all to be regarded as an awful and solemn proclamation of human guilt.

2. Is Jesus a Priest? Then sin cannot be pardoned without satisfaction and atonement. Is it so that the sacrifice of Christ is an act of worship—that those unspeakable sufferings with which He expiated the curse of the Law were parts of a sublime doxology which, as the minister of religion, He chanted to the King Eternal? Then how clear it is that God is glorious in the punishment of the guilty, and that none can hope to escape!

3. Is Jesus a Priest—now a Priest in the holiest of all? Then with what confidence and boldness, notwithstanding our guilt and pollution, may we come to the throne of grace! Why should we perish when the mercy-seat is before us, and a reconciled God accessible to all? And can we imagine that if with such advantages, with such a redundancy of grace as God has provided for us, we are finally lost, we

shall perish with any common overthrow? Abused mercy will kindle the fires of justice. These solemn truths, which have often been urged upon you before, I would now impress again with all the earnestness of which I am capable. These things are your life. Young, buoyant, you may not feel the importance of religion now. But the scene will change. The days of darkness must come. Calamities may overtake you in which you will need the support of a friend with a stronger arm than any that can be found among the sons of men. The hour of death must come, and after death the judgment. The world now smiles before you, its prospects enchant, its honours charm you. But the fashion of this world passeth away. Religion is the principal thing. Let it then be your first care to have Christ as your patron and friend. There is none other name under heaven given among men whereby you can be saved. The alternative is faith in this Divine Redeemer, or Eternal Death. Can you hesitate which to adopt? Can you endure the thought of eternal banishment from God? Who can dwell with devouring fire? who can abide in everlasting burning? Make Jesus your friend—confide in Him as your Saviour, and you conquer the world, trample over death and take hold on eternal life.

This is now my prayer for you, and shall ever be my prayer for you, that you may know Jesus in the sweetness of His grace and the power of His resurrection. Then, though separated here and scattered to distant fields, we shall be united again where parting shall be no more. If I could be sure that you would all meet me at God's right hand, I could now bid you farewell without a tear and with a cordial God-speed to your various pursuits in life. But the thought is agony that any here may perish, and my heart sinks within me as I am compelled to send into the world so many that I love, so many that Jesus as a man would love, who yet love not Him, and care little for His sacrifice or prayers. May God give you all the spirit of grace and wisdom in the knowledge of Him! FAREWELL.

PREFATORY NOTE.

WHAT follows on the subject of our Lord's temptation was the substance of a discourse delivered May 21, 1854, in the chapel of the South Carolina College, and on the following Sunday in Glebe Street Church, Charleston. It was based upon the records of the transaction in the three Gospels. One who heard it has testified to its marvellous power and force as delivered, but it has never before appeared in print.

CHRIST TEMPTED AS THE SECOND ADAM.

THAT the temptation in the wilderness is a most important portion of our Saviour's history may be fairly presumed from the prominence given to it in the evangelic record. It is minutely detailed by Matthew and Luke, and noticed in general terms in the compendious Gospel of Mark. No part of the New Testament has been more perplexing to the pride of human reason. To say nothing of those who have turned the whole account into ridicule and made it a pretext for rejecting the authenticity of the narrative, many have adopted explanations which, though originating in the professed purpose of obviating difficulties, have terminated in others greater than those that were attempted to be removed. Among that class of writers tinged with Rationalism the impression is universal that the facts are not to be literally taken as they stand in the record. It is assumed that such a personal conflict of Christ and Satan, under the precise circumstances detailed by the Evangelists, is altogether incredible. Especially the transportation to the temple and to the mountain, the momentary exhibition of all the kingdoms of the world and their glory, the shocking proposal to worship the Devil,—these are said to be so intrinsically improbable as facts that, to save the credit of the Evangelists, we must regard them as the drapery in which they have chosen to invest a spiritual conflict in the soul of Jesus. They were suggestions made to His imagination—visions of His own mind. Some have gone so far as to make them the products of His own thoughts.

In order to add to the incredibility of the narrative, circumstances have been forced into it which do not properly belong to it, such as that Satan transported Jesus through the air, so as to put Him at one time on the pinnacle of the temple, and at another on the summit of a mountain. There is not a word of this in the Gospels. Their language implies no more than that Christ went to these places and that Satan accompanied Him; and the inference is that as He was led up of the Spirit into the wilderness, so it was under a Divine impulse that He submitted to the continuance of the temptation in these places. There is no more intimation of a miraculous conduct to the temple or the mountain than to the first scene of the conflict—least of all is it intimated that a real miracle was wrought by the Devil.

But the ground upon which the narrative is set aside, supposing the facts to be as just represented, is altogether fallacious. It is assumed that intrinsic probability is the measure of the credibility of testimony—that we believe a witness, not for himself, but on account of the nature of his testimony. On the contrary, testimony is a positive source of knowledge, to be credited on its own account, and to be judged of by its own laws. There is but a single case in which it can be set aside by intrinsic improbability, and that is when the fact alleged is of such a nature that it could not be cognized by any intelligence—in other words, when it involves a contradiction, a contradiction to itself or to some known truth. It then becomes an absolute impossibility; and as testimony, and indeed all evidence, is only within the limits of the possible, there can be no real testimony in any such cases. What pretends to be so must be sheer lying or gross delusion. But as there is nothing in this narrative contradictory to itself or to any known truth, there is nothing which puts it beyond the range of testimony. The facts are possible, and therefore can be rendered credible.

Is it objected that they are unlike our ordinary experience? In the first place, it may be answered, that analogy itself is the creature of testimony, and in the second, that diversity of existences is as much characteristic of nature as uniformity of law. The same laws indeed may pervade, the same great principles be involved in a multitude of facts which have not a single phenomenal point of resemblance. Look at the variety of beings among animals, unlike in everything but the laws of organic life. Look at the varieties of inorganic matter, unlike in everything but the great laws of attraction or repulsion. Just so the facts before us may be new—wholly diverse as phenomena from anything that we have ever witnessed—and yet they may turn upon moral principles as broad as the universe. It is not reason, therefore, but arrogance, that sets them aside in their literal significancy.

Taking them, then, precisely as they are recorded, let us endeavour to study their import:

1. Christ is here to be considered in His public character as the representative of men and of unfallen angels. His mission upon earth was to redeem the seed of Abraham and confirm the angels that had kept their first estate. His work was much more extensive than that of Adam. The benefits of Adam's obedience we have no reason to believe would have transcended his own race; those of Christ's were to extend to principalities and powers, to angels and archangels, cherubim and seraphim. The great problem was to be solved whether, on the principle of probationary government, an end could be put to sin.

2. The trial must be more severe and protracted than that to which Adam was subjected, for two reasons: (1.) The magnitude of the benefits to accrue from its success; and (2.) As a vindication of the principle on which man had fallen. It must be shown that, in still more unfavourable circumstances than those in which Adam was placed, human nature is capable of maintaining its integrity. 3. In this aspect, as a vindication of the Covenant of Works, it behoved to be public, and to be conducted upon the same principles with the trial in the garden of Eden. It was public, it

was notorious to angels, notorious to devils, and has been made notorious to men. It did turn upon the same principles with the Adamic trial, which was essentially the test of obedience through impulses intrinsically lawful.

From these considerations it must have been a real trial, a severe trial, and one in which success was glorious. The destinies of the universe actually turned upon it. The bitterness and intensity of it may be seen from comparing it with the trial of Adam:

1. The place. Adam's was in the garden of Eden—this in the wilderness. Adam's, with a companion to relieve his solitude—Christ alone. Adam's, with the beasts tamed and in harmonious subjection to his authority—Christ among the beasts, wild and savage. Adam's, in the midst of plenty and abundance—Christ struggling with hunger. How differently were the two placed! How favourable the circumstances in one case! how unfavourable in the other!

2. The extent of the trial—that is, the points at which both might be assailed. The test to Adam was condensed into a simple precept involving comparatively no self-denial. He could not fall as long as he abstained from the one tree of the garden. Christ was open to assaults upon all points. Every appetite, every impulse, every active principle of human nature might be plied with arguments, and success at any point would have been ruinous. There was but one sin against which Adam in the first instance was not absolutely guarded. Christ must rely upon His integrity to preserve Him from all. Behold, therefore, the severity of the conflict by which men have been redeemed and angels confirmed!

3. The thing to be tested in both trials was allegiance to God, and the mode of attack is adapted to the different circumstances of the parties. Adam was only a man, and the insinuation to him was that he was a god in capacity, and had only to put the thing to the proof. Christ was the Son of God, and the insinuation to Him was that He was only a man, and He was challenged to put to the proof His claims to being considered as anything more.

This, then, is the light in which the whole case is to be regarded—as the second probation of the world. Christ is the second Adam—the head of a family consisting alike of angels and of men. His success proves—

1. That the race had not been hardly dealt with in Adam —that they might have stood, that they might easily have stood. The argument is from the greater to the less.

2. It illustrates the sublimity of Christ's virtue. Here was a human being who actually did pass through the world from the cradle to the grave without sin. If He had been placed in only ordinary circumstances, this is a truly astonishing phenomenon. The most humble and retired man is seduced on all hands in a world like this, where sin has reigned for thousands of years. But the case of Jesus is remarkable in that He was exposed to special and extraordinary trials. He was providentially dealt with as if He had been a sinner. The world and the Devil were let loose upon Him with aggravated intensity. The severity of the conflict was condensed into two periods—one at the commencement and the other at the close of His career—and yet He held fast His integrity. This is godlike virtue. Well did Paul say, If any man love not the Lord Jesus, let him be *Anathema Maranatha!*

3. Individual life is an analogue of the dispensation which rules the history of the race. There are crises in the history of each of us—points at which a determinate direction is given to the character, whether intellectual or moral. The will stands face to face with some great question of duty; we debate it; we meditate; there is an earnest and bitter conflict—an agony; the issue gives a tremendous impulse one way or the other! This is pre-eminently the case with religion. The law stands face to face with us; the Spirit stimulates conscience; we struggle; we resist; we evade; matters are finally brought to a *crisis*—we must decide, and often that decision is final! Oh, the importance of having every decision right! Every act propagates itself, but an act after a conflict multiplies by scores—its like spring up

then like dragon's teeth. Satan knew that hereafter, in all ordinary circumstances, Christ was invulnerable. The first great crisis was past, and he never returned to Him until he was placed in a condition to constitute another crisis, when he was called to confront the Cross and Hell.

PREFATORY NOTE.

THE discourse which follows was preached as a sermon by its author at least four times—first, in the church at Columbia, August 30, 1840; then in the chapel of the college, March 21, 1841; next, at the opening of the Synod of South Carolina in Columbia, October 14, 1847; and again in the chapel, October 31, 1852. The preacher took his text from 1 Corinthians i. 22–24. It now appears in type for the first time.

THE GOSPEL, GOD'S POWER AND WISDOM.

THE Apostle Paul gives to us, in the first chapter of his first Epistle to the Church of Corinth, a graphic picture of a common spirit of infidelity as it was differently modified by peculiar circumstances in the history and character of the Jews and Greeks. The former, having been early selected as the peculiar people of God, had been signally indulged with miraculous exhibitions of His power in delivering them from the hands of their enemies and in confirming the messages of their prophets. They had been so long trained to signs and wonders and mighty works, as the pledges of a Divine commission, that they could hardly be expected to listen to the voice of any teacher who could not produce these credentials from heaven. And yet, by a singular infatuation of mind and heart, they gave a cordial reception to the traditions of the elders, which were sealed by no impress of Divine power, and cheerfully received those who came in their own name, whose wonders were only lying delusions; while they rejected Jesus, a man approved of God among them by miracles so stupendous as to challenge the reluctant confession that it was never so seen in Israel. They were sealed up in invincible prejudice against all the proofs of a Divine commission which the Saviour presented in fulfilling the predictions of ancient prophets, in healing the sick, in raising the dead and controlling the elements by a single word. It seems that his countrymen had somehow or other conceived the preposterous notion that their long-expected Messiah was to come in the character and with all the pomp and pageantry of an earthly prince; that His advent was to be heralded by some portentous sign in the heavens, which would prove a signal token of Divine blessing to themselves and of fearful vengeance on their enemies; that He would at once restore the kingdom to Israel by taking possession of the ancient throne of David and bringing their haughty and imperial masters under tribute to Himself; and hence we find that the most astonishing miracles of Christ could never divert their attention from an anxious seeking of the Sign from heaven. Having defined for themselves the sort of evidence with which they expected their Messiah to attest His authority, they obstinately perverted or closed their eyes against every other proof, determined not to believe until the Sign from heaven should be revealed; and because the Saviour repeatedly declared that no sign should be given but the sign of Jonas the prophet, they were offended at Him—they stumbled at that stumbling-stone.

The disgust which His first appearance among them in humility and poverty had produced was firmly and immovably settled by the ignominious circumstances of His death. They could never dream of owning Him as their Lord who had been nailed to a cross; and all the arguments which inspired apostles could produce from their own Scriptures, or the acknowledged miracles of Jesus, they considered as amply refuted by the simple circumstance that hanging on a tree was an unquestionable token of the Divine malediction. That Jesus died under a curse was a plain proof to their minds that He could not be the anointed of God—the favourite of heaven and the Saviour of His people Israel. In the life and death of the Redeemer they found anything but that Sign from heaven by which He should be proclaimed as the Son of David, and introduced among his countrymen with the dignity and grandeur which befitted the station of a great monarch. Such were the grounds of Jewish infidelity.

The Greeks, on the other hand, sought after wisdom. Naturally curious and speculative, they were assiduously engaged in philosophical disquisitions about the First good, First perfect and First fair. Divided off into different sects each headed by some illustrious master, they spent their time in discussions which, however they sharpened their wits, left their hearts barren of improvement, and eventually brought on a general skepticism in regard to all truth. There were the Stoics, the Epicureans, the Sophists and Rhetoricians, all representatives of different principles and different interests, whose very existence depended upon their contests with one another, and whose highest glory consisted in technical niceties and subtle disputation, which they vainly enough denominated *wisdom*. The forms of philosophy were preserved among the Greeks long after its spirit had fled. In the days of Paul a spirit of candid inquiry after truth, which to some extent was possessed by Plato, Socrates and Aristotle, had given way to the war of dialectics and the strife of sects: the highest boast of intellect was to involve the plainest truths in doubt, and to frame syllogisms against what all the world had believed without the aid of argument. The natural curiosity of the Greek prompted him to pry into everything, and his natural pride to dispute everything rather than acknowledge his own ignorance. It is a just picture of Greek society generally which Luke gives us of that at Athens: " For all the Athenians and strangers which were there spent their time in nothing else but either to tell or to hear some new thing;" they always had some new question to discuss, some old argument to refute, or some new doubt to defend; they were ever learning, and never able nor even desirous to arrive at the knowledge of the truth.

When Paul wrote the Epistle to the Church at Corinth, that city was the metropolis of the province of Achaia, the seat of its learning, elegance and arts, the rival of Athens in its schools of philosophy and rhetoric, and the acknowledged mistress of Greece, and perhaps of the world, in sensuality and voluptuousness. The Corinthians seem to have blended in their character the active curiosity of the Greeks with the effeminate luxury of the Asiatics—to have been a compound of whatever could give acuteness to thought and unbridled licentiousness to lust, and so to have combined an uncommon degree of intellectual vigour with an equal corruption of manners. We can form some conception of the state of society among them from the fact which Strabo mentions, that the temple of Venus at Corinth contained more than a thousand harlots whose devotion was prostitution and whose religion was their shame. The destruction of the city did not eradicate the evil. The same excesses prevailed after it was rebuilt that had disgraced it before; and as it became a second time the eye and the glory of Greece in magnificence and elegance, commerce and the arts, it became also the mother of harlots and the mistress of abominations. That the inhabitants of such a city, busily intent upon the vain pursuits and the keen rencounters of intellectual dynamics, and slavishly devoted to the most disgusting licentiousness of personal habits, should have rejected the Gospel of Jesus is not to be thought strange; and it was still less strange that they should denounce it as foolishness when we remember what they were accustomed to regard as wisdom. Conceiving of nothing higher in the scale of intellectual distinction than to be the founder of some new sect in philosophy, they probably looked upon Jesus as the setter-forth of strange doctrines upon their favourite and darling subjects of speculation, and Paul as an able champion of his peculiar opinions, and hence may have felt a strong curiosity to hear what he had to say in defence of the doctrines of his Master. As in Athens, so probably at Corinth, he was encountered on the one hand by the "budge doctors of the Stoic fur," armed at all points to maintain the sullen dogmas of their school, and on the other by the sleek and voluptuous disciples of Epicurus, acknowledging no religion but pleasure, no law but lust, while the prim and starched Rhetoricians stood ready to try every sentence which he uttered by the technical niceties of trope and figure. We can well conceive that as he rose to announce his message, they were all eye, all ear—curiosity stood on tiptoe; and as he proceeded to reveal the unknown God, and to summon their consciences to the tribunal of eternal justice, and to unravel the sublime mysteries of redemption, they probably looked in amazement upon his glowing fervour and holy enthusiasm, utterly at a loss how to account for them except as the ravings of the mystical Apollo. But when he came to the doctrine of a future resurrection, it was beyond all endurance: the Stoic could not abide it, and the Epicurean abhorred it for its consequences; and perhaps in charity they may have come to the conclusion of most noble Festus, that Paul was beside himself, though they were not likely to attribute his madness to an excess of learning. Certain it was, that the instructions of the Apostle had none of the characteristics of what they called wisdom. Instead of proposing a system of philosophy as a matter of subtle and doubtful disputation, to be discussed and treated upon the same principles with the systems of the Porch, Lyceum and Academy, he announced a series of the most momentous truths, and enforced their reception as a matter of imperative duty upon the solemn authority of God. He stood forth, not as the advocate of a sect, but the messenger of Heaven; and he proclaimed truths in the name of the Lord God which were not to furnish amusement for the intellect, but to take possession of the man and bring every high thought and lofty imagination in captivity to the obedience of his Master. They saw at a glance that the system of Paul demolished the wisdom of man; that it was peculiar and exclusive; and that, as it was intimately connected with the life and history of a Jew who had notoriously been put to death as a malefactor—as it held forth this victim of a nation's vengeance to be the only Saviour of lost sinners—they could find no milder form of expressing their contempt for it than by denouncing it as *foolishness*.

To those unacquainted with the Jewish Scriptures, and familiar only with the humble circumstances of the Saviour's life and its shameful and ignominious close, the first proclamation of the Gospel must have appeared prodigiously preposterous. What would be the natural thought of the human mind? Am I to believe that Jesus is able to save to the uttermost all who come unto God through Him who could not deliver Himself from violence and shame? Am I to regard Him as the ambassador of God whose birth-place was a stable, whose cradle was a manger, and who wandered through the world a homeless and outcast stranger? Must I worship Him as King of kings and Lord of lords who paid tribute to Cæsar, stood as a criminal before the bar of man and died the death of the lowest order of malefactors? These were strange enigmas; and the least to be expected from a blind and unbelieving world was that they should have been ridiculed as *foolishness*. The grand difficulty of the Gospel was Christ crucified—the humiliation, reproach and death of Jesus. Jew and Gentile stumbled here. The Jews required a sign, and the Greeks sought after wisdom, yet the Gospel gave the Jew no such sign as he demanded, and the Greek no such wisdom as he sought for. It simply held forth Christ crucified, and this to the Jews was a stumbling-block and to the Greeks foolishness. Still, the Apostle persisted in preaching it, because to those who were called or supernaturally enlightened by the Spirit of God, whether Jews or Greeks, it was found to be the power of God and the wisdom of God. It displayed, in other words, an interposition of Divine power more signal and glorious than could have been afforded by the most portentous signs from heaven, and revealed an arrangement of Divine wisdom compared with which the dialectics of the schools were vain deceits and empty babblings. Christ crucified is a compendious phrase for the whole scheme of redemption; and Paul's language conveys the idea that such power and such wisdom are nowhere to be found as are developed in the economy of grace. Let us consider then, in the first place, the Divine power, and in the next the Divine wisdom, as these attributes are illustrated in the plan of redemption:

I. There are three forms in which the power of God is displayed in the salvation of men, differing from each other in excellence, yet equally essential to the success of the enterprise.

1. The first is in the exercise of naked strength, or of direct and immediate causation, by which physical effects are produced which did not exist before. As this seems to be the simplest idea of power, so it is the form under which it is most commonly and naturally contemplated. If we were required to produce a proof of the Divine omnipotence, we should spontaneously turn to the works of creation, and particularly to those enormous masses of matter which, according to the Apostle, declare the invisible things of their Maker, even His eternal power and Godhead. The results here are striking and obvious, and arrest the attention of the most stupid understanding; but in the mere exercise of force of this sort, though there is much to command admiration and inspire dread, there is nothing in itself really venerable —there is nothing which declares the moral character of its possessor and lays a foundation for hope or trust. This kind of power, which may be styled *the omnipotence of causation*, though it is called into requisition in the business of redemption, is perhaps not more conspicuously displayed than in the works of creation. To it we ascribe the incarnation of the Son, for it was certainly an act of power to create the human nature of Jesus and to bring it into intimate and indissoluble union with His Divine personality. This cementing of heaven and earth, Deity and humanity, weakness and omnipotence, time and eternity, dependence and sovereignty, is surely an exercise of strength as prodigious and amazing as calling the worlds into being and upholding them in their courses. The miracles of Jesus, also, which were wrought in attestation of His Divine commission, must be referred to the same kind of power, together with His own resurrection from the dead, and that of all His people which is yet to take place. In the production of these results there is involved the exercise of naked force, of pure, irresistible might, or whatever is contained in the true conception of a cause. But as this is not the power which the

Apostle particularly celebrates, we pass on to notice a nobler form in which the strength of the Almighty is brought to bear upon the salvation of men; and that is—

2. In the secret and silent influence which He exerts upon their minds. As mind, which is essentially active, is the immediate and the only seat of power, the control of it must necessarily demand a higher order of energy than the shaping, wielding and arranging of matter which is purely passive, and therefore contains no principle of opposition to any external influence exerted upon it. Hence the creation of the universe does not evince a power so glorious as the successful government of a single province of intelligent creatures. To call a world into being is certainly a great work, but to turn the heart of a king as the rivers of water are turned is a greater. David tells us that "God by His strength setteth fast the mountains, being girded with power, and stilleth the noise of the seas, the noise of their waves, and the tumult of the people," evidently implying, from the form of the expression, that it was a more stupendous exhibition of power to still the tumult of the people than to settle the mountains and control the sea. Even among men the power over mind is regarded as a much more enviable distinction than the power over external nature, and hence the orator and poet, who wield successfully the elements of persuasion and of pleasure, have always received a large share of homage and applause even from the rude and unpolished. We are not to look, then, for the highest and most glorious displays of Divine power in what is obvious and sensible—in the whirlwind and the storm, the starry heavens or the expanded firmament—but in the *minds* which He has formed with active principles, rendering them capable of obedience or rebellion, of happiness or woe. To keep busy, inquisitive and thinking spirits within the bounds which His will has prescribed, though not so imposing and striking, is a much more arduous work than to keep the sun in his place and the planets in their orbits. Yet such an influence over minds is put forth by God, the Holy Spirit, in His depart-

ment of the work of redemption. The power which He exerts in the regeneration and sanctification of the sinner consists partly in a direct action upon the faculties of the soul and partly in what has been technically styled moral suasion. In other words, He first, by a direct and immediate exercise of power, puts the soul in a condition to receive the truth, and then by the truth effectually persuades. These two operations are always associated in His saving work. He first enables and then persuades; and at every step in the subsequent progress of the Divine life He must sustain and invigorate the holy principles which He at first implanted, or the work of sanctification would come to a stand. This *direct action* upon the soul is peculiar to God alone; it is His royal prerogative, and we find nothing in the influence which men or devils can exert upon each other at all analogous to it or that can even remotely illustrate it. God compares it to the power employed in the first creation: those who are born again or effectually called are said to be new creatures in Christ Jesus, the workmanship of God. They are said to be the subjects of a power as great as that which raised Jesus from the dead, to be quickened into life by the Spirit of the Lord. What the nature of this power is, or how it is exerted, it is impossible for man to comprehend. The wind bloweth where it listeth; thou hearest the sound thereof, but canst not tell whence it cometh nor whither it goeth: so is every one that is born of the Spirit. As in the original creation the Spirit brooded over the formless mass and brought beauty and order out of chaos and confusion, so in the new creation He broods over the benighted mind and distracted affections, and brings light out of darkness, holiness from sin. He slays the old man, and raises a new man like the fabled phœnix from the ashes, formed in knowledge, righteousness and true holiness after the image of Him that created him. It is a great work to transform the children of the Devil—for such we all are by nature—into the children of God, and to plant the spirit of heaven where the spirit of hell had reigned. It is the Lord's doing, and marvellous in our eyes.

But there is among men, in the achievements of the orator, something analogous to the power of moral suasion. It consists simply in suggesting such truths and motives to the mind as are calculated to influence its determinations. It just brings the truth in contact with the soul, and its work is done. It is obvious that moral suasion is impossible unless there be a congruity between the state of the mind and the truths which are brought to bear upon it. The mind must be able to apprehend them, the motives must be such as are adapted to the real state of the heart, otherwise you might as well talk of the power of truth over beasts and rocks. Truth has no influence except as it falls in with the current of the soul; and hence moral suasion necessarily supposes that men are already renewed—that their minds and hearts are in unison with the truth, capable of apprehending its power and feeling its force; and hence God employs it as a means in the guidance and government of His people. To suppose that spiritual truth can make a spiritual man is just as absurd as to suppose that scientific truth can create a natural understanding. The understanding must first exist, and then the truth is received, and so the spiritual man must first exist, and then the truth may have its influence upon him. When the direct action of the Spirit and moral suasion are brought together, then you have a correct idea of God's power in the application of redemption or effectual calling.

3. The third form in which the power of God is displayed in redemption is under the character of a just and righteous Governor; and here it assumes its most glorious and august form. In His moral government God reveals Himself as the patron of holiness and the avenger of sin; it is a government of law adapted to the capacity of moral agents and supported by adequate sanctions. It is here, and here only, that the moral character of God is made known to His creatures. The power which is employed to sustain the

interests of righteousness and to uphold the eternal principles of justice and truth is sublime and venerable. As the natural government of God consists in maintaining the established order of nature or those physical laws, such as attraction and repulsion, in conformity with which all physical changes take place, so His moral government consists in administering the affairs of moral agents, dispensing to them happiness or misery according to the eternal principles of rectitude which necessarily grow out of the Divine character. The justice and holiness of the Divine nature are the rule of the Divine will, and without denying Himself, God cannot, as Judge of all the earth, do otherwise than right. But it may be asked how God as a righteous Governor has displayed His moral power any more strikingly in the redemption of men than it was displayed in the happiness of angels and the destruction of devils, or than it would have been displayed by the perdition of our race. There is a peculiarity in His power in this case, because there were peculiar difficulties to be overcome. The entertaining of a purpose of mercy created a crisis in the Divine government; it seemed to unhinge all the principles upon which that had previously been conducted. The grand problem to be solved was, How shall God spare the sinner without letting down the majesty of the law—without ceasing to be the patron of righteousness and the avenger of guilt? There appeared to be a moral impossibility in the salvation of the sinner, because the principles of eternal justice demanded his condemnation. It was in reconciling the conflicting elements of mercy and justice, benevolence and truth, and in building up a stupendous fabric of grace without compromising a solitary principle of equity, that the power of God was illustriously displayed. And as the resurrection of Jesus was the consummation of the plan by which He proposed to magnify the law without destroying the transgressor, the Scriptures speak with pointed emphasis of the exceeding energy of God's mighty power which it required to raise Jesus from the dead. The difficulties in His resurrection were not physical, but moral: He was the representative of sinners, and could only be raised as the first-fruits of His people after a full satisfaction rendered to justice and an ample reparation to the Divine law. The power of God, however, in redemption can only be known from the plan which He devised, and hence—

II. We come now in the next place to consider the wisdom of God as displayed in the work of redemption. Wisdom consists in the accomplishment of noble ends by excellent means. It is not enough that there be skill in the adaptation of the means; the end which is proposed to be compassed must be worthy of the mind which designs it. But where the end is truly valuable, and a just correspondence is borne to it by the means employed to secure it, *there* true wisdom is found. To bring the wisdom of God in the economy of grace to the standard of these principles, it will be necessary to consider the end which God proposed to Himself, the means by which He has accomplished it, and their mutual correspondence or adaptedness to each other.

1. The chief and highest end of redemption, as of all the other works of the Almighty, is the manifestation of His own glory. No less an object would be worthy of the attention of the Divine Mind. Whatever excellence the creatures possess is derived from the bounty of their Creator, and bears a slighter proportion to His infinite and everlasting perfections than a drop of water to the boundless stores of ocean. Independent and self-sufficient, He must work all things according to the counsel of a will which is determined by nothing but the eternal and essential principles of His own nature. He cannot neglect the infinite excellences of His own character to take His plans or to borrow His motives of action from the fleeting, perishing, and, compared with His own, the vain perfections of the creature. In creation, providence and the moral government of the world, God proposes no less an end than the development to the mind of His intelligent creatures of His own glorious excellence. His works are so many mirrors in which He reflects so much of His own image as they are able to behold. There they

may read what He is by contemplating what He does. They cannot approach His awful throne; the light would be intolerable to created eyes; but they can behold Him veiled and shadowed in His works. They cannot fathom His glorious essence, but they can learn His character from what He hath wrought before them and around them. It is this manifestation of His character and perfections, which in themselves are infinitely glorious, that the Scriptures mean when they speak of God's working all things with a reference to His glory. His real glory is to be what He is, and as His works declare what He is, so they reveal His glory to those who are wise and attentively observe them. The heavens declare God's glory, and the firmament showeth His handiwork, because the invisible things of Him from the creation of the world are clearly seen, being understood by the things that are made, even His eternal power and Godhead. But Creation and Providence reveal only the back parts of the glory of the Lord; the brightest beams of His glory, His face or countenance, can be seen only in the person of His Son. The mystery of redemption exhibits His character in a new and marvellous light. It is a new and brilliant page in the history of God's administrations—a new book sealed with seven seals, containing lessons of surpassing interest, treating of God in loftier strains than the seraph's heart had ever reached, or the seraph's tongue had ever uttered, until the Lion of the tribe of Judah prevailed to unloose the seals and to open the book, and called upon the nations to come and know their God. The glory of Jehovah, as it was manifested to the world previously to the revelation of His scheme of grace, is as far eclipsed by the plan of salvation as the light of the stars, beautiful and lovely as they are, is eclipsed by the blaze of the rising sun. Creation and Providence proclaimed God's power and goodness; Conscience proclaimed His righteousness, and Hell proclaimed His vengeance. These were so many stars, differing from each other in glory, in which we could see all that could be known of God, but they were only stars; the light was feeble! But when Jesus came the Sun of righteousness arose, darkness fled away and the light of God's glory, reflected from the face of Jesus Christ, scattered its rays through heaven, earth and hell, sending a deeper thrill of joy through the breasts of angels, opening a prospect of hope to perishing men, and wringing a heavier wail of anguish from the bosoms of the damned. In contemplating the stupendous scheme of grace—

> " Our souls are lost in reverent awe,
> We love and we adore;
> The first archangel never saw
> So much of God before."

In order to understand fully how the perfections of God are so illustriously displayed in this great work, we must consider its *direct* and *immediate* end, which is the Salvation of sinners. Christ is the power of God and the wisdom of God *unto salvation.* And let it not be thought that the salvation of the lost as a subordinate end is unworthy of the great and ever-blessed God. On the contrary, when it is made to furnish a suitable occasion for the exhibition of the most exalted excellences of character, it becomes as worthy of the Divine regard as any other matter in His moral government of His creatures. It is not for the sake of the guilty, but for His own Name's sake that He has mercy upon them. There are three considerations which illustrate the Divine wisdom in this matter, and vindicate the character of God from all suspicions of stooping beneath the glory of His throne:

(1.) The very existence of such an attribute as mercy or grace could not have been known without the development of some such scheme as that of our salvation. To His holy and unfallen creatures God was known to be benevolent from the constant communications of His goodness, but it is one thing to bestow favours upon the upright, and quite another to bless the unthankful and disobedient. It is true that the holiest deserve nothing on the score of merit from the hands of their Creator, but although they have no necessary claims to His favour, they have never provoked His anger. The guilty on the other hand not only deserve no good, but are justly exposed to the inflictions of vengeance. They have sinned, and God, as a righteous Governor, cannot overlook their transgressions without letting down the majesty of His own law and revoking those awful sanctions which support the purity of His throne and proclaim the hatefulness of sin. The principle of justice, which consists in rendering to every man his due, and of course to the sinner the wages of sin, which is death, is an essential attribute of God. The punishment which is threatened in the law is not an arbitrary sanction of the precept. When we behold a deed of perfidy and baseness there is an instinctive feeling that the transgressor should undergo a certain degree of pain; and this feeling arises apart from all considerations of personal resentment or political expediency. We feel that it is right, it is due to his deed, that he should suffer. Should you see a son who had been affectionately nursed by a tender mother, in order to free himself from the responsibility of soothing her declining age plunge a dagger into that mother's heart, you would not only be chilled with horror at the crime, but you would at once feel that no amount of pain would be disproportionate to the magnitude of his offence. The reflection would probably never enter your mind that if such cases were permitted to pass with impunity the consequences would be disastrous to society; but your instinctive sentiments, the moral emotions of your heart, having linked together crime and pain, the transgressor and punishment, would doom the ingrate to a dreadful end. In these instinctive feelings you may recognize the true idea of justice—a quality which, as it exists perfectly in the mind of God, must always be the avenger of His law. As sin is an infinite evil, the sanction of the law, on the principles of justice, must contain an infinite curse. God must denounce this curse upon the disobedient—the sanction must be enforced; or God must deny Himself, cease to be what He is necessarily, and vacate His throne, leaving His universe to the darkness and horror of anarchy and misrule. If the punishment of the guilty were a mere matter of expediency, mercy might be exercised freely where prudence did not forbid it; but as it is a matter of right, of eternal, unchanging, essential rectitude, there would seem to be no place in the moral government of God for such an element as pardon, and consequently no such attribute in the Divine character as mercy to the guilty. But such a quality is necessarily involved in the scheme of salvation. Had there not existed in the Divine mind a previous willingness to receive the disobedient into favour, justice would have had its course and the sanctions of the law have been enforced. If there be salvation, it must be from grace; there is no other principle from which it could proceed; and hence the salvation of sinners has been made to develop in the government of God an attribute of His nature which our limited capacities would have pronounced it to be impossible that He should possess —an attribute so glorious that God rejoices in it, and regards with peculiar complacency all who hope and delight in it. If the salvation of men in no other sense glorified God than as it evinced that He is merciful and gracious, it would have been worthy of His majesty to save them. Shall He create worlds upon worlds to display His power and make known the manifold riches of His goodness, and shall Mercy, which rejoices over judgment, be for ever eclipsed by the clouds of justice? If it is not beneath God to create a world to reveal His might, it is as little beneath Him to redeem the guilty to display His grace. If, when we look to the starry heavens and contemplate the countless worlds of stupendous magnitude moving in harmony and grandeur through the fields of space, we adore His power and acknowledge the scene to be worthy of God, why should we turn away from that grander scene beyond these lower skies, where, instead of masses of matter, the monuments of power, we behold immortal spirits, the monuments of grace—where, instead of worlds moving in harmony around other worlds, we behold enraptured minds moving in glory and blessedness about the throne of God? Just as far as mind surpasses matter, and activity inertness, so far is grace more glorious than nature; and just as far as heaven surpasses all the other works of God, so far does mercy rejoice over all other qualities of His being. And yet this perfection supposes guilt and misery, and God could not reveal it without stooping to the lost. Hence, there is wisdom in the very purpose of salvation; the end from its relations to God is a noble one, well worthy of His signal interference.

(2.) This will farther appear from considering that the scheme of redemption not only proves the existence of grace, but solves the mysterious problem of its compatibility with the exercise of justice. It explains the otherwise inexplicable enigma that God can be just, and at the same time the justifier of those who have transgressed His law. When we consider the relations which fallen man bore to his Creator and offended Lord, we shall see at once that his salvation involved a difficulty which created minds were unable to explain, and which, it would seem, tasked the resources of infinite wisdom to remove. There was a question to be answered which, as it silenced all orders of intelligent creatures, it was becoming in God to step forward and resolve. Justice demanded that the rebel should die, truth required that God's threatening should be executed, and holiness sustained the cause of justice and of truth, since God is of purer eyes than to behold iniquity. How, then, shall the captive be delivered and the prey be taken from the mighty? Mercy says, Spare! but all the other attributes of Jehovah seem to conspire against the purpose of His grace and protest against the salvation of the guilty. "The sublimest spirits in heaven," says the charming Bates, "were at a loss how to unravel the difficulty and to find out the miraculous way to reconcile infinite mercy with inflexible justice—how to satisfy the demands of the one and the requests of the other. God was to overcome Himself before He restored man. In this exigence His mercy excited His wisdom to interpose as an arbiter, which, in the treasure of its incomprehensible light, found out an admirable expedient to save man without prejudice to His other perfections." And in the plan which was actually devised, as the same writer subsequently remarks, there is "a sweet concurrence of all the attributes. Mercy and truth are met together, righteousness and peace kiss each other. Who can count up this heap of wonders? Who can unfold all the treasures of this mysterious love? The tongue of an angel cannot explicate it according to its dignity; it is the fairest copy of the Divine wisdom, the consummation of all God's counsels, wherein all the attributes are displayed in their brightest lustre; it is here the manifold wisdom of God appears. The angels of light bend themselves with extraordinary application of mind and ardent affections to study the rich and unsearchable variety that is in it. Only the same understanding comprehends it which contrived it. But as one that views the ocean, though he cannot see its bounds or bottom, yet sees so much as to know that that vast collection of waters is far greater than what is within the compass of his short sight, so, though we cannot understand all the depths of that immense wisdom which ordered the way of our salvation, yet we may discover so much as to know with the Apostle that it surpasses knowledge." And how exalted must that end be which in the process and mode of its accomplishment reveals the character of God, not in detached and isolated features, but brings all His attributes together in harmonious accord, and presents the Divine perfections as a beautiful, glorious and consistent whole; and such an end is the salvation of man by Christ crucified!

(3.) And what still more enhances the Divine wisdom in this whole matter is that all this harvest of glory has been reaped from a most unpromising soil. Sin, which in itself is essentially odious to God and at war with all the principles of His nature, has been made by His infinite wisdom to furnish an occasion for the manifestation of His moral excellences more striking and glorious than could have taken place without it. In this is the triumph of His wisdom, that He has extracted praise from the provinces of rebellion, and made His holiness peculiarly illustrious in the midst of sin. He has gone into the very chambers of death, and waked up the energies of life among those whom He represents as emphatically dead. The weapons of the Devil have been turned upon himself—his guile and malice, in introducing sin into our world and so bringing it under the frown of its Maker, have been most signally defeated. Instead of the widespread ruin from the blasting curse of the Almighty which he no doubt anticipated would make this earth the very door of hell, behold, the fallen creature is exalted to a glory and enriched with a blessedness far beyond what would or could have been enjoyed if Adam had maintained his integrity! He is not only enriched with eternal life, but his nature has been brought into mysterious union with that of his Creator, and exalted to the throne of God and made the judge of angels themselves. Sin, instead of banishing man for ever from his God, has cemented a union so close and indissoluble as to make it impossible that the believing soul should ever again be separated from the Fountain of all holiness and good. "It is a mystery in nature," says the same author from whom we have quoted already, "that the corruption of one thing is the generation of another; it is more mysterious in grace that the fall of man should occasion his more noble restitution. Innocence was not his last end; his supreme felicity transcends the first. The holiness of Adam was perfect, but mutable; but holiness in the redeemed, though in a less degree, shall be victorious over all temptations, for they are joined to the heavenly Adam in a strict and inviolable union. And those graces are acted by them for the exercise of which there were no objects and occasions in innocence, as compassion to the miserable, forgiveness of injuries, fortitude and patience; all which, as they are a most lively resemblance of the Divine perfections, so an excellent ornament to the soul and infinitely endear it to God;" and the glory of our renewed state exceeds our primitive felicity from the mysterious relation which we bear to the Son of God. Such are the magnificent blessings which by heavenly wisdom are extracted from sin, which naturally has a tendency to produce nothing but a curse. Surely our fallen world was a fit theatre for the gracious interposition of God when His unsearchable counsel, contrary to the very nature of things, and contrary apparently to all the principles of His government, could elicit light from darkness, a blessing from the curse, life from death, and holiness from sin. Grace has proved to the ruined family of Adam a heavenly elixir, transmuting all its coarse materials into the pure gold of the sanctuary.

2. Having now evinced the wisdom of God in the end proposed in the redemption of sinners, let us next consider the fitness and excellence of the means by which it is accomplished. It must strike us as at least becoming, if not absolutely necessary, that the arrangements of our salvation should have been made upon the same principle by which death and all our woe were originally introduced. God has never dealt with men personally and individually as in all probability He dealt with angels; but as He has established a sort of unity in the race by the peculiar mode of its propagation, having made all nations of one blood, so He has, in both of the covenants which the Bible makes known, dealt with men collectively through a common representative. The Covenant of Works was entered into with Adam as the federal head of his race, and the Covenant of Grace was entered into with Christ as the federal head of His seed. Sin and misery flowed in upon our world through the channel of imputation, and life and joy and blessedness are dispensed upon precisely the same principle. If God had communicated the blessings of the second covenant upon a different principle from the one which He established as the basis of all His transactions with our race in the first covenant, it would have argued a change of the Divine mind; it would have broken up that variety which obtains in the moral government of His creatures, and it would have been a virtual im-

putation upon His wisdom in originally adopting a principle which He was subsequently unable to carry out. God therefore has manifested His wisdom in building the fabric of mercy upon the very same foundation on which the hopes of the race were originally placed and destroyed. He has thus shown it to be a principle which does not contain the elements of failure within itself. He has shown that it is fully adequate to all the various exigencies of His government over man, and thus thrown upon man himself the guilt and responsibility of his fall. The very rock on which he stumbled is that on which he must stand for ever—the principle which ruined him is the principle which must save him. God will not change the radical principles of the government—the established constitution, if I may so speak—of this province of His moral empire. Those who quarrel with the doctrine of imputation do not seem to be aware that they are rebelling against a cardinal law, and perhaps the distinguishing law, of God's dealings with the family of man; and they might just as reasonably insist upon each man's being created at once perfect and full grown, complete in all the faculties of soul and body, without the tedious process which now obtains, as to contend that each of the race should be upon trial for himself. In other words, they might just as reasonably arraign infinite wisdom for not making us angels as for not treating with us in the matter of salvation as He treated with them. Those spirits of light, having been brought into being without dependence upon each other, were placed each for himself upon independent, personal probation, and each stood or fell by his own personal obedience; but we, having been brought into the world by a necessary connection with each other, were put upon trial in the first of our species, who just as effectually evinced what human nature would do as though that nature had been tested in all its possessors. The fundamental law, then, upon which the moral interests of humanity were suspended, or the distinctive feature of the Divine administration in regard to man, is the principle of federal representation, and, by necessary consequence, of direct and immediate imputation. To inquire therefore into the suitableness or excellency of the means by which redemption is accomplished, is just to inquire into the suitableness and excellency of the Federal Head whom God has appointed for the Church; and this is none other than the second Adam, the Lord from heaven.

The wisdom of God was remarkably displayed in the extraordinary constitution of the Saviour's person. Had Jesus been God alone, He could not have been the representative of man; He could have been only the just Judge and the righteous Governor, upholding the insulted majesty of His law and visiting its vengeance upon the heads of transgressors. Had He been man alone, He would have been utterly incompetent to sustain the load of human guilt and to make satisfaction for the sins of His people; but by combining the two natures in one mysterious personality, He is qualified by His participation of our flesh to be our representative and head, and abundantly able to do the office of a kinsman. The law required obedience from *man*, and denounced the curse of rebellion upon *man;* the law will accept no other obedience but the obedience of humanity, and no other suffering but the suffering of humanity. Could an angel have interposed in our behalf, the law would have turned aside from His proffered substitution, because it was man's blood which alone could satisfy its curse. It would accept no mediator but one who claimed a fellowship with our race, was bone of our bone, flesh of our flesh, and blood of our blood. The Saviour of sinners, whoever he be, must be able also to sustain the infinite weight of Divine wrath without being crushed by the burden; must be able to receive the sword of justice into his own bosom, and yet rise undestroyed from the stroke; must be able to stand between the sinner and an angry God, and maintain his position unshaken and firm until all the clouds of infinite vengeance have burst and wasted their fury on his head and left the sinner unscathed by the storm. He must be able to bring in a righteousness which meets the highest demands of law and affords a title to the kingdom of glory. He must be able to storm the citadel of hell, and by the arm of power to spoil the hosts of darkness and deliver the captives from the hands of the destroyer. He must be able to reunite the soul to God and engrave the Divine image again upon it, and establish it in righteousness and holiness for ever. He must be able to raise the body from the tomb and fit it in glory and spiritual excellence for the immediate presence of Jehovah. All this he must be able to do, and yet be a *man*, or the work of redemption must come to an eternal stand. And where shall such a man be found? All the descendants of Adam, as they successively rise into being, pass under the curse, and so none can by any means redeem his brother or give to God a ransom for his soul; or could one, by extraordinary interposition, be born holy and undefiled, his limited capacities would be crushed under the weight of infinite guilt. He must possess in his own person the incommunicable perfections of God in order to make an infinite atonement, to destroy the works of the Devil, to bring in an everlasting righteousness, to create the heart anew in knowledge, righteousness and holiness, to pluck the sting from death and to open the kingdom of heaven to those who by nature were children of wrath. God and Man he must be to meet the exigencies of our case. One person of the adorable Trinity must become incarnate, and wisdom pitched upon the Second as the most suitable and proper. It was not fit that the Father, who is of none, neither begotten, should be placed in an attitude of subjection to His own Eternal Son, who by an ineffable and eternal generation received the essence of Divinity from the Father. It was not fit that the Holy Ghost, who eternally proceeded from the Father and the Son, should be placed in an attitude of authority over the Son, as would have been the case had He become incarnate and had the Son fulfilled His functions in the plan of salvation; so that none could so appropriately assume our nature as the Second person in the blessed Godhead. But supposing this matter determined, how shall He assume the nature of man without the stain of original sin? Divine wisdom met this difficulty by making Him emphatically the Seed of the Woman, by suspending the usual law of propagation and miraculously communicating our blood and nature through the medium of a virgin, so as to avoid the bond of federal union with Adam and thus evade the curse of the covenant. Being thus marvellously qualified by the peculiar constitution of His person to discharge the functions of Redeemer, Jesus, in human nature and as the Divinely-appointed representative of His people, did all that they were required to do, suffered all that they were required to suffer, and so gave them a title to everlasting life. The salvation of sinners was secured by such a Mediator without compromising a solitary principle of the Divine government. The law maintained its authority, and was more magnified and honoured by the obedience of the Son of God than it could have been by the obedience of all men. Justice received its due, and became more august and venerable when pouring its vials of vengeance upon the head of Jesus than if a fallen world had sunk beneath its curse. Truth was preserved inviolate, for human nature died the death and the Seed of the Woman descended into hell. Holiness remained unsullied, for the groans and agonies of the cross proclaimed God's abhorrence of sin in louder accents and deeper tones of emphasis than the wails of the damned in the gloomy prison of despair. And Mercy, charming Mercy, became the brightest star in the constellation of heavenly excellences, shining the more gloriously in the rigorous maintenance of justice, holiness and truth. Surely there is wisdom in the cross of Christ when the highest glory of God and the eternal salvation of men alike proceed from it, and well might the angels introduce the birth of Jesus with songs of joy and anthems of praise!

Neither Jew nor Greek could understand how He who died as a condemned malefactor should yet be the righteousness of God for the acceptance of men—how He who descended to the grave should bring life and immortality to light from the darkness of the tomb. They could not comprehend how "life should spring from death, glory from ignominy, and blessedness from a curse;" but the mystery is cleared up when we remember who it was that died, and what relations He sustained when He hung upon the cross; and so, instead of stumbling at this stumbling-stone, or denouncing it as foolishness, we contemplate in Christ crucified the stupendous expedient of infinite wisdom for saving those who are called. We feel it to be a sublime doctrine, so utterly surpassing the invention of man or the counsel of angels as to bear visibly stamped upon it the impress of Heaven. We feel the blood of Jesus to be so transcendently glorious "that the justice of God, not to be propitiated by any other means, pursues the transgréssor on earth and in hell, and that nothing in the universe can arrest it in its awful career until it stops in reverence at the cross of Christ." We there behold Deity incarnate, the Lord of glory sinking under a weight of suffering, and the Sun of righteousness sustaining an awful eclipse. Let us turn aside and behold this great sight, and as we survey it in all its astonishing relations let us confess it to be the wisdom of God in a mystery.

3. The wisdom of God is further displayed in the scheme of redemption by applying its blessings in such a way as that His grace, which is in truth the fountain of salvation, shall be prominently acknowledged. The medium through which we receive the benefits of Christ's mediation is faith, which consists in an entire renunciation of our own strength, righteousness and achievements, and in a simple dependence upon the kindness and favour of the Redeemer. We are to lean upon Him for the righteousness which alone can render us acceptable to God, for the knowledge which alone can make us truly wise, and for those communications of life and strength which alone can secure our personal holiness. In the Gospel the righteousness of God is revealed from faith to faith, that all boasting may be excluded, and that he that glorieth may glory only in the Lord. All

schemes of salvation which have been devised by man, and all corruptions of the Gospel which have been popular, have proceeded upon a mixture of Divine grace and human obedience, representing God as propitious to man only when man has complied with certain specified conditions, thus sharing the glory of salvation between the creature and Creator. But the gospel of Jesus humbles all flesh in the dust, and holds forth Christ as our wisdom and righteousness and sanctification and redemption. Even faith does not secure the blessing as an act of obedience or principle or duty; it is no part of the righteousness by which we are justified. It is simply an instrument by which we appropriate the obedience of Christ, and through which it is imputed to us. Just as ordinary generation and a natural birth is the channel through which we become really connected with our first head, Adam, and receive the curse of his broken covenant, so spiritual generation and the new birth which implants or originates the principle of faith is the channel through which we become connected with the second Adam and are constituted heirs of his spiritual blessings. As the curse of Adam falls upon his race only when they have a real existence, so the blessing of Christ is bestowed upon his seed only as they are born into his spiritual kingdom. Faith, then, is no more the ground of justification and salvation than natural birth is the ground of condemnation, though it is true that none are justified but believers, as none are condemned but the posterity of the first man. Faith unites us with Christ, and all the blessings of the covenant are consequent upon this union. Christ is the salvation of God, and faith lays hold of Him under that character, and in the very act renounces itself as a procuring cause of favour. And if indeed our hopes are made to depend upon the doings and sufferings of a mediator and representative, it is surely befitting that we should be brought distinctly to acknowledge it, so as to assume our own position in the dust and to put the crown of glory on the head which deserves to wear it. If our salvation from first to last is a matter of pure grace, it is certainly becoming that this fact should be prominently pressed upon the sinner as he receives its blessings. If self-denial is the first great law of our religion and the confession of Christ its most imperative duty, it is peculiarly fit that the whole plan of salvation should be so conducted as to keep these principles constantly before the eyes of the redeemed. This is accomplished by the mystery of faith. God is exalted, the flesh is abased, and Christ is the all in all. The law of representation is preserved in its integrity, and imputation direct and immediate is the foundation of our hope. A beautiful consistency is maintained in the whole plan of the Gospel. The spiritual temple goes up without the sound of an axe or hammer, and as the headstone thereof shall be brought forth there shall be shoutings of Grace, Grace unto it! It is the Lord's doing and marvellous in our eyes. He laid the foundation of this fabric in setting forth Christ as a federal Head, and He piles stone upon stone as He calls His seed into spiritual being and cements them by His Spirit to the great foundation. The simplicity of faith never appears more lovely than when contrasted with the bungling devices of men. Their legal schemes, like the black ground of a picture, heighten its brighter colours and proclaim it to be from God and themselves from man;—just as the glory of the sun declares its original more strikingly when contrasted with a farthing rushlight.

Just examine the Arminian scheme, which is probably the most imposing of all the devices of man, and you will see what fearful confusion it introduces among the principles of the Gospel. It maintains that the death of Christ only bore such a relation to the race as to put each man on a new and modified probation, with the terms of which he is enabled to comply. Accordingly, each man is on personal and independent trial for himself. Then God has *changed* the fundamental principles of His previous government of man. He has revoked the law of federal representation under which we were unquestionably placed at first, and the stupendous sacrifice of Christ was only a grand expedient to enable Deity to change His mind and institute a new order of government, as the old had proved a failure! Ah! how true it is that the wisdom of man is foolishness with God! He is the everlasting Jehovah, and changes not. The basis of His government on earth is still Representation, the great law of His kingdom is still Imputation; and these laws deal out a blessing or a curse according as we are found in the first or second Adam, natural birth connecting us with the first, and spiritual birth or faith with the second. Here is wisdom, the wisdom of God, though it may be denounced as foolishness by man.

4. Finally, the wisdom of God appears in the plan of salvation by so arranging its provisions as to allure human confidence at every step and to secure the interests of personal holiness. What can more strongly draw us to Christ than His mysterious participation of our nature? We look upon Him as an elder brother sympathizing with us in all our sorrows, knowing the force of all our temptations, and pitying our weakness in all our fears. We can go to Him as to a friend, and unbosom our cares and seek His assistance and direction. Again, when we look beyond His flesh and behold Him clothed with all the perfections of the Godhead, we feel that He deserves our confidence—that He is indeed a shelter from the storm, the shadow of a great rock in a weary land. What a wonderful Saviour! When we rise yet higher and ask whence arose this mysterious incarnation, we are conducted to the counsels of the Eternal Mind, and find that the wonderful scheme of saving the guilty originated in the bosom of infinite Love. We contemplate a grace so astonishing and stupendous as apparently to rise above the ineffable regard of the eternal Father to His beloved Son—a love to sinners so mighty and overwhelming as to drown the attachment of the Son to His own glory and even His life; and we feel that the God who has

loved us with such a love is worthy of our hearts and should be trusted for all things.

And just in proportion as we are drawn to Christ we are drawn from sin. In His cross we see God's abhorrence of it more strikingly displayed than in the torments of the lost; and as we become animated by the Spirit of the Saviour, and enter into the true meaning and intent of His sacrifice, we die to the flesh, we renounce the world, we overcome the Devil and live for God, for heaven, for immortality. We have a secret fellowship with Christ in His sufferings and death, and as He arose from the grave by the glory of the Father, even so we also walk in newness of life.

Such in a brief view is the wisdom of God in the work of man's redemption through Christ crucified—His wisdom in the end, His wisdom in the means, in the application and practical results of the scheme of grace. Let the Jews require a sign and the Greeks seek after wisdom, but let it be the immovable purpose of our minds that we will know nothing but Christ crucified, being fully assured that Christ is the power of God and the wisdom of God. What think ye of Christ? is and ever has been the distinguishing test of character among men; and while some call Him a Prophet, others an Impostor, and others One of the People, none are safe but those who can say with Peter, Thou art the Son of the living God, and hast the words of eternal life!

To those who have been enlightened by Divine grace to behold and understand the glory of the cross, may be presented a few motives for overflowing gratitude. They have been introduced into a new world; they have been endowed with a knowledge which the most laborious efforts of the natural understanding could never reach; they have been taught mysteries beyond the reach of reason or of sense, which eye hath not seen nor ear heard, neither hath it entered into the heart of man to conceive, but God hath revealed them unto us by His Spirit. The world of grace is a supernatural world; and as sense is the medium of our correspondence with matter, and reason with speculative truth, so faith is the medium of correspondence with the unseen mysteries of grace. And the knowledge of the truths connected with redemption is more glorious in its objects, more certain in its evidence and more valuable in its influence than the discoveries of sense or the demonstrations of science. It is more noble in its objects, for what can be a sublimer subject of contemplation than the being, character and perfections of the Eternal God? The ancients pronounced Theology to be the first philosophy, but how dim and indistinct are the clearest intimations which Nature can afford us of the infinite God! It may present Him as a being of uncontrollable power, the cause of all other beings besides—it may give us some intimations that He is pure spirit, and present some shadowy evidences of His goodness and holiness; but in regard to the sublime mystery of the Trinity, Nature is dumb. In regard to the still sublimer mystery of the incarnation of the Eternal Son and the way of salvation through His blood, she is compelled to preserve the silence of the tomb. Take away the light of redemption and leave us only to the guidance of reason, and how dark and dreary become the prospects of man! Unacquainted with the Being who made him; unacquainted with his own everlasting destiny; strangely distracted between the ills of life and the fears of death; trembling, he hardly knows why, with involuntary dread at the prospect of being summoned to the mysterious tribunal of an unseen power; he passes on through life in darkness and apprehension, meets death in horror and despair, and lies down in the grave without the hope of rest even there to his soul. Man to the heathen world is a profound mystery only because they know not God. And we can never be sufficiently thankful for that grace which has brought life and immortality to light, which has revealed God as a merciful Father, has plucked the sting from death and shed a lustre upon the darkness of the tomb. Surely God, heaven and eternity are the most noble themes which can occupy our thoughts. These are the themes which the Gospel discusses. The subjects which it brings before us are those which occupied the Eternal Mind before time was born or providence in motion. They are those which angels study with profoundest reverence, those which were discussed upon the Mount of Vision, and which will be the perpetual song of heaven as long as heaven or God shall endure. They are not the temporary subjects which embrace the fleeting interests of time and sense; the impress of eternity is on them, the glory of God is involved in them, and the interests of immortality depend on them. Here is knowledge—the knowledge of God, the knowledge of ourselves, the knowledge which shall never vanish with tongues nor cease with prophecy. Ah! how frivolous are all the discussions of Greek philosophy or human science compared with the mystery of God manifest in the flesh!—the veriest babe in the kingdom of heaven far outstrips all the attainments of the Porch, Lyceum or Academy. Those schools have passed away, and the glory of their masters is known only as a matter of history; but Christ crucified is still the magnet of souls, the hope of earth and the wonder of heaven. "Blessed are the eyes which see the things which we see; for I tell you that many prophets and kings have desired to see those things which we see, and have not seen them, and to hear those things which we hear, and have not heard them."

These things are confirmed to us by the most indisputable evidence. They do not depend upon the deductions of our own reason, but God has revealed them to us by His Spirit. We see them in the supernatural light of faith, which is to the spiritual what sense is to the natural, and reason to the intellectual world; and as it rests upon the testimony of God, we have no more right to question the truth of its disclosures than we have to disbelieve the information of our eyes or ears. Faith is a spiritual eye by which we converse with distant and supernatural realities—the organ through which God corresponds with the soul, and true faith, consequently, can never be mistaken so long as God continues a faithful and true witness. But as this knowledge is most certain in its principles, so it is also eminently happy in its influence. It does not terminate in barren speculation. When we behold the light of the glory of God in the face of Jesus Christ, we are transformed into the same image from glory to glory even as by the Spirit of the Lord. It is a light which cannot dwell with the darkness of sin; wherever it appears the shadows of death flee away, and holiness, peace and comfort take possession of the soul. Such is the knowledge of Christ crucified. Let us rejoice if this Saviour, this wisdom of God in a mystery, has been revealed to our hearts. We have found a treasure compared with which the riches of all other knowledge are emptiness and beggary. And let us be sure that we exhibit its transforming influence by a holy walk and a heavenly conversation. If Christ crucified has been revealed to us, He has been formed within us, and the life which we now live in the flesh we will live by faith upon the Son of God who loved us and gave Himself for us.

But there are those to whom the preaching of the Cross is foolishness. Should it not alarm them that where God and angels and just men made perfect see so much to admire and rejoice in, they should see nothing to arrest their attention or enlist their regards? Is it not a proof that there is some terrible disorder in the souls of such, that they can turn away from God incarnate to pursue the trifles of time and sense? The burning bush was a great curiosity to Moses, and he turned aside to contemplate the wonderful phenomenon; but here is a stranger wonder. It was a wonder even in heaven that God should be found in mortal flesh and bow His head and die. Here was a scene so portentous and wonderful that angels beheld it with amazement, hell with terror, and even inanimate Nature was moved at the spectacle. That was no common event that shook the earth with convulsions, clothed the sun in sackcloth, and called up the dead themselves from the slumbers of the tomb. It was an hour of dreadful darkness—Nature in mourning for the expiring Son of God! but in that moment of darkness the foundations of a new kingdom were laid, eclipsing by its splendour all the glories of Creation and Providence. The stone was cut out of the mountain without hands, which was not only to fill the earth, but the invisible realms of God's extended dominions. A new throne was erected so transcendently glorious that all other thrones must be prostrated before it, and all power in heaven and earth lodged with Him that sat on it. The day which from the beginning had been set apart to commemorate God's goodness in creation was set aside, and that became the day of days which saw the incarnate God rise from the tomb in triumph over death and hell and sin. Oh how blind are those who see no glories in the cross of Christ, who can make light of what Heaven esteemed so highly, and rejoice more in farms, merchandise and pleasure than the unsearchable treasures of grace! Alas for impenitent men! They walk in darkness! The light which they have, conversant only about sense, is "like the funeral lamps which by the ancients were put into sepulchres to guard the ashes of their dead friends, which shine so long as they are kept close, a thick, moist vapour feeding them and repairing what was consumed; but in opening the sepulchres and exposing them to the free air, they presently faint and expire." So, whenever the minds of unbelievers are turned from the sensible to the supernatural and spiritual, their light goes out in darkness. Like the owls and bats, they riot in darkness and love the midnight gloom, but when the sun arises they find nothing congenial in his beams, and endeavour to screen their eyes from the glory of his light. Ah! if our Gospel be hid, it is hid to them that are lost. If the preaching of the Cross be foolishness, it is foolishness to them that perish. Let the children of the night awake and leave this little scene of sense with its trifling gewgaws, and turn their eyes to the sublimer glories of that kingdom which shall never be moved. Let them come to the cross of Jesus and there learn things unutterable which God hath prepared for them that love Him. The light of the Gospel now shines about us. Let us improve the day of our merciful visitation lest

God in righteous vengeance should leave us to our spiritual darkness, which would be the certain presage of the black night of everlasting despair. The golden opportunities which we now possess if once lost are lost for ever: neither gold, nor tears, nor blood will prevail to buy them back, and we shall be compelled to lie down in sorrow with the doleful lamentation, "The harvest is past, the summer is ended, and we are not saved."

PREFATORY NOTE.

THIS Discourse on the Personality of the Holy Spirit was delivered, so far as appears, only twice—the first time, in the College Chapel, December, 1843; and the second time, at Charleston, in April, 1845. It has never before been published. The text was taken from Acts xix. 2.

THE PERSONALITY OF THE HOLY GHOST.

THAT the standard of popular belief in regard to the nature, office and operations of the Spirit falls far below the requisitions of the Scriptures is too painfully evident to be denied. The spirit of Festus, which brands with enthusiasm every pretension to supernatural assistance, not only lingers in the world, but has found its way into the sacred enclosures of the Church. Such is the deplorable skepticism which prevails, especially among those who claim to be of the better sort, upon the whole subject of Divine influences, that many are afraid to expect them, others despise them, and multitudes, like the disciples of the Baptist at Ephesus, have not so much as heard that there is a Holy Ghost. He who refers his conversion to the special agency of God, and exhibits a becoming fervour of gratitude for the grace which he has felt—he who professes to believe by a Divine power, to see the truth in a Divine light, and to relish its beauty with a Divine affection,—will be mocked as an enthusiast and denounced as a visionary. The language of spiritual religion is regarded in any other light than as the words of truth and soberness. Convictions of sin are represented as the infirmities of a melancholy temperament, the joys of faith are derided as expressions of physical excitement, and the confidence of hope is insulted as the dictate of spiritual pride. Now, if it should be found that those who are despised as rabid fanatics are really the children of God, and that what are regarded as their dreams of folly are really the suggestions of the Holy Ghost, the fastidious skeptics who denounce them would be involved in as awful a sin as the haughty

Pharisees who ascribed our Saviour's miracles to the finger of Beelzebub. If there be any one doctrine that may preeminently be styled the doctrine of the New Dispensation, it is that concerning the *Spirit*. The parting benediction of our Saviour was the promise, soon to be executed, that He would give to His disciples another Comforter, who should abide with them for ever, and who, by His rich consolations and copious instructions, would more than supply the place of their absent Redeemer. "It is expedient for you," says He in the last interview which He held with His friends before the fatal tragedy of Calvary—"it is expedient for you that I go away, for if I go not away the Comforter will not come unto you; but if I depart, I will send Him unto you. And when He is come, He will reprove the world of sin, of righteousness and of judgment."

The times of the Gospel, in contradistinction from the period of the Law, are pronounced by the Apostle to be not only the ministration of the Spirit, but to be, on that account, transcendently glorious. "But if the ministration of death," says he, in evident allusion to the awful scenes which attended the giving of the Decalogue—"if the ministration of death written and engraven in stones was glorious, so that the children of Israel could not steadfastly behold the face of Moses for the glory of his countenance, which glory was to be done away, how shall not the ministration of the Spirit be rather glorious? For if the ministration of condemnation be glory, much more doth the ministration of righteousness exceed in glory. For even that which was made glorious had no glory in this respect by reason of the glory that excelleth. For if that which is done away was glorious, much more that which remaineth is glorious." In every circumstance of external splendour, in all that was adapted to please the eye or fascinate the ear—pomp of ritual, imposing decorations and majesty of forms—the Levitical economy was certainly unrivalled either by the "gorgeous solemnities of Paganism" or the simple institutions of the Gospel. Despising, as it does, the tinsel of ceremony, the mystery of symbols, the ornaments of art and the aids of eloquence, in what does the glory of the Christian dispensation consist? How does it transcend a ministration in which the name and authority of God were displayed amid the sound of a trumpet and the voice of words, amid fire and thunder, blackness, darkness, tempest and smoke? How does it surpass an economy adorned by visible symbols of the Deity, a cloud by day and a column of fire by night, the mercy-seat and cherubim, the altars and laver, the Urim and Thummim, and the special ministration of prophets? Our Saviour Himself answers the question, and the instructions of His Apostle fully conform thereto; it was the simplicity of truth and the power of the Spirit. These constitute the glory of these latter days. The magnificent truths of revelation are no longer shrouded in types and shadows, wrapped in mystery and contemplated only through a glass darkly, but God has revealed them unto us by His Spirit. He who commanded the light to shine out of darkness has shined into our hearts, and revealed the light of the knowledge of the glory of God in the face of Jesus Christ. His throne of grace is no longer concealed under the elements of earth, to be approached only with bleeding victims or smoking incense or eucharistic offerings, but it stands revealed in the light of day, accessible to all who are willing to approach in that living way which has been consecrated for us through the blood of the Lamb. It is evident, from repeated attestations of the Scriptures, that the whole power of the Gospel lies in the *demonstration of the Spirit*. The simplicity of its truths, the solemnity of its sanctions and the overwhelming grandeur of the prospects which it opens are all ineffectual in reclaiming men from the sins, follies and vanities of time, so long as the Eternal Spirit " holdeth back the face of His throne and spreadeth His cloud upon it." "Who then is Paul, and who is Apollos, but ministers by whom ye believed, even as the *Lord gave* to every man?" He that planteth is nothing, he that watereth is nothing; it is God alone who can give the increase.

The distinguishing badge of the faithful followers of Christ, that by which they are known in heaven and recognized on earth as the sons of God and the heirs of everlasting life, is the possession of the Spirit. This is the stamp which is put upon the forehead—the evidence at once of their glorious adoption and of their consequent exemption from the penal visitations of wrath. When the Lord arises in the majesty of justice and makes terrific inquisition for blood, those who bear this mystical mark shall find protection in the secret of His tabernacle and be kept in His pavilion until the calamities are past. All their hopes, all their accomplishments, their graces and their joys, their beauty and their strength, spring from their mysterious possession of the Spirit. Without Him they are poor and wretched, blind and naked, and destitute of all things. He is to them as refreshing showers to the thirsty earth. It is He who gives them beauty for ashes, the oil of joy for mourning, and the garment of praise for the spirit of heaviness. Is Christ, in the eyes of His redeemed, the chief among ten thousand and altogether lovely? The same Spirit which framed His body in the virgin's womb has formed Him in them the Hope of glory, and joined them together in indissoluble bonds. Do they rejoice in the prospect of future felicity, and sigh for that inheritance which is incorruptible, undefiled and fadeth not away? It is the Spirit of God that gives them an earnest, a refreshing foretaste, of that eternal weight of glory reserved for them at their Father's right hand. Do they, like Jacob, wrestle with God and cling to His promises with importunate faith? It is the Spirit that maketh intercessions for them with groanings that cannot be uttered. The Spirit first found them in their guilt and wretchedness, and reduced to order the chaos of their souls. He led them to the light of Christ. He it is who continually feeds them with the true manna which came down from heaven. He purifies their hearts, watches their sleeping dust in the grave, raises their bodies on the great day, and for ever abides in them as His consecrated temples, His chosen and beloved habitations. To teach, to guide, to sanctify, to comfort—these are the healthful and saving offices which the Holy Ghost accomplishes in the hearts of all who believe; and if we know not Him, if we are strangers to His grace and unacquainted with His power, we are involved in fearful darkness in relation to our highest and noblest interests. No man can call Jesus Lord, but by the Holy Ghost.

As the Spirit discharges such important functions in the economy of grace, it is intuitively obvious that our views of redemption must be essentially modified by the conceptions which we form of the nature and operations of the Holy Ghost. If we detract from the glory of His work, we shall proportionably detract from the fullness of salvation. Most of the errors which have infested the peace and corrupted the purity of the Christian Church have arisen, in the first place, from mistaken apprehensions of those special points in the scheme of salvation in which it comes directly in contact with the hearts of men. Pelagianism is clearly a sin against the Spirit. In the same proportion in which it magnifies the powers of man, it debases the riches of Divine grace. Socinianism springs as much from defective views of the moral government of God and the consequent meanness, sinfulness and wretchedness of man, as from those perverse speculations which the Apostle denounces as philosophy and vain deceit. To have correct apprehensions of the Divine law, the beauty of holiness and the immutability of moral distinctions—to admit the moral necessity of visiting disobedience with tokens of displeasure—to admit, at the same time, the extent of human guilt and the depth and malignity of human depravity and sin—is to admit a series of propositions which necessarily involve the Divinity of Christ, or deny the possibility that God can be just and yet receive into favour the fallen sons of men. Let the Holy Spirit reveal the Law to the understanding and the conscience in its purity, strictness and extent; let the inflexible integrity of Jehovah be distinctly apprehended and the measure of our iniquities clearly displayed to our view, and no power of sophistry, no magic of eloquence, no artful delusions of the Devil, shall be able to convince us that any other Saviour can be suited to our need but one who can thunder with a voice like God, who can bear the keys of heaven and hell, who can shut and none can open, and can open and none can shut. All forms of heresy, skepticism and will-worship, the dreams of the formalist, the pride of the Pelagian and the presumption of the Socinian, will assuredly be dispelled by the mysterious operations of that Spirit whose office it is to take of the things of Christ and show them unto men. To be right, consequently, in the doctrine of the Spirit is to be right upon every other point; to be wrong here is to walk in darkness, or, what is worse, to walk in the light of our own eyes and after the imaginations of our own hearts. Let us have the Spirit, and He will assuredly conduct us to Christ, and Christ will conduct us to God. Let us be devoid of the Spirit, and however seemly our conduct or orthodox our creed, we are children of hell, bearing the image of the wicked one, enemies of God and destroyers of ourselves. It is, in the emphatic language of inspiration, to be earthly, sensual, devilish.

The doctrine of the Trinity is so evidently involved in the scheme of redemption that it is morally impossible to deny the one without denying the other. The most satisfactory proof of the essential unity and personal distinctions of the Father, the Son and the Holy Ghost is to be found in the offices which each discharges in the economy of grace. If not a single passage existed in the Scriptures directly establishing this mysterious truth of revelation, it might be collected as a necessary inference from the moral appearances which we are called to contemplate in the plan of salvation. The same principle of ratiocination by which we establish the Being of God from the operation of His hands, the natural disposition to ascend from effects to the causes which produce them—to follow a stream until we reach the fountain by which it is supplied—will also lead us from the phenomena of grace to acknowledge three agents of unlimited perfections, essentially the *same* and yet *distinct*. As the heavens declare the glory of God, and the firmament showeth His handiwork, as the invisible things of Him are clearly seen, being understood by the things that are made, so the purpose, execution and accomplishment of that wonderful method by which the guilty are accepted, the dead are quickened and the ruined saved, reveal, clearly as any effect can disclose its cause, the separate, distinct and harmonious operations of the Triune God.

The evidence, perhaps, upon which the large majority of Christians receive this article of faith is the spiritual experience of their own hearts. They have not studied isolated texts nor collected together the names, titles and achievements which are promiscuously ascribed to each of the Persons of the Godhead; but they have been conscious of their own moral necessities—they have admired the beauty and rejoiced in the fitness of those exquisite arrangements by which their need has been relieved. They know, because they have felt, the love of the Father, the grace of the Son, and the communion of the Holy Spirit. Their minds are established in the truth, because they distinctly perceive that however unsearchable and mysterious the doctrine of the Trinity may be, it is a doctrine which is *obliged* to be true. The phenomena of grace demand it. They can no more permit themselves to doubt it than call into question the reality of their daily food, or deny the separate existence of external objects as the causes of the constant changes which they experience in the history of their own minds. Ingenuity may torture, and, under the pretext of profound interpretation, explain away detached and isolated texts; the dexterity of criticism may perplex with unreasonable doubts or confound with learned plausibilities the minds of the simple and illiterate; and the subtlety of logical skill may raise such a cloud of dust that language shall appear like a riddle and truth be lost in the distinctions of sophistry; but the argument from *experience*, from the indisputable wants of our own nature and the provisions which alone can be adequate to meet them, is clear as consciousness, palpable as sense and irresistible as light. The speculations of philosophy may find insurmountable difficulties in this and every other mystery of the Gospel, for who by searching can find out God? But the measures of antecedent probability are not the standard by which we should judge either of the facts of nature or the more wonderful provisions of grace. The essence and personality of God can never be degraded to the limited capacities of man. To divest the Trinity of the awful mystery which enshrouds it, to remove the veil which conceals from mortal eyes the august and glorious Being whose majesty is as terrible as His mystery is profound, would be to depress the inconceivable sublimity and contract the illimitable grandeur of His nature. We are permitted to know of God only what can be gathered from the faint adumbrations of His character in the diversified departments of creation, or what has been displayed with greater brilliancy in the stupendous economy of grace. Redemption, as a grand whole, a magnificent moral phenomenon, a sublime evolution in the righteous government of God, reveals the perfections of its Author with a degree of splendour which completely eclipses the brightest discoveries of nature. While the Jews look for a sign and the Greeks seek after wisdom, "we," says the Apostle, "preach Christ crucified, to the Jews a stumbling-block and to the Greeks foolishness, but to them which are called, Christ the power of God and the wisdom of God." We, in other words, develop the overwhelming scheme of redemption, which, however neglected, insulted or despised by the miserable votaries of sense, displays to the illuminated eye of faith, in the depths of its wisdom, the resources of its power and the exhaustless riches of its grace, the glory of God in a light which the most portentous signs from heaven or the deepest investigations of learning and philosophy can never be adequate to compass. As the stars hide their diminished heads when the sun emerges from his chamber to run his career in the heavens, so all the discoveries of God which nature and Providence are competent to make fade into comparative insignificance before the transcendent disclosures of redemption. That scheme stands like a temple of majestic proportions, and bears visibly engraved upon its portals, not only the name of God, like the ancient temple of Isis, but also the sublimer mystery of His personal distinctions. In walking about Zion, telling her towers and marking well her bulwarks, we perceive the hand of the Father, the hand of the Son and the hand of the Holy Ghost. There are palaces adorned for the great King which we are exhorted to consider, for there the Trinity reigns, there God displays His mysterious personality, and the whole house is filled with His glory.

It is a melancholy fact, however, even among those who admit, in general terms, the doctrine of the Trinity, that in consequence of their low views of the operations of grace, the distinct personality of the Spirit is practically denied.

That experience which does not recognize the *supernatural* character of the work which we attribute to the Spirit, as well as the necessity that it should have been accomplished by an intelligent, voluntary agent, falls below the measure of the Scriptures. We may in words profess to receive the operations of the Spirit, but it is only an empty declaration if we do not feel that influences have been exerted on us— our own hearts, understandings and consciences—that could not possibly have been effected without the agency of a glorious and extraordinary Person. We must have experimental evidence, the witness within ourselves, that the Author of our faith, our hopes and our joys is a living Person, abundant in goodness, rich in grace and unlimited in knowledge. Such are the relations of the Spirit to the understandings and consciences of men in applying the great salvation of the Gospel that it seems to be impossible that His office should ever be discharged in the mind of a sinner without producing a consciousness of the extraordinary change which has been effected, and a consequent impression of the distinct personality of the agent by whom it was wrought. Wherever He dwells there must be displays of His glory and power. No heart can become His abiding habitation without adoring His goodness and responding to His love. We should question, without hesitation, the piety of any man who should refuse to admit the personality of the Father or the distinct subsistence of the Son. There are peculiar offices accomplished by each, peculiar relations in which they stand to us, and consequently peculiar affections which are due to each that cannot possibly be conceived upon any hypothesis that blends the Father and the Son into one personal subsistence. The idea of mediation becomes absurd, the whole doctrine of atonement dwindles down into unmeaning jargon, if the Son be not a separate agent from the Father. That religion which consists in the worship of the Father through the Son—in access to God through the atoning blood of His own beloved Son—becomes an enigma, a riddle, an inexplicable mystery, if Father and Son are only different names for precisely the same Almighty Being. If, then, we should brand as a dark and dangerous delusion any scheme of securing salvation which did not proceed upon distinct offices, and consequently the acknowledgment of a distinct personality in the first two persons of the adorable Trinity, how can it be safe to admit a doctrine of Divine influences which does not leave upon the mind clear and manifest impressions of the personality of the Holy Ghost? Is the glory of the Third Person less to be promoted than that of the First and Second? Must He not have the honour of His own work? And is it possible that men can ascribe to Him the glory due unto His name unless they are conscious of His hand in the work which He is said to perform—unless they know that it is His influences which their hearts have felt in submitting to the righteousness of God, and receiving that record which He hath given of His Son? It is intuitively obvious that as the very essence of religious worship consists in the inward affections of confidence, love, joy and hope directed to the persons of the glorious Godhead, the Holy Spirit, wherever He leaves the impressions of His grace and reveals the knowledge of the Father and the Son, must at the same time record His own name. How, otherwise, could He be the object of adoration, gratitude and praise? Can there be communion with a Being of whose personal and separate subsistence there is not a distinct apprehension?

It requires but little sagacity to perceive that the personality of the Spirit is consistent with no views of His influences that fail to present the supernatural character of faith. The theory of the formalist admits, in general terms, that no man is able to call Jesus Lord, but by the Holy Ghost; but it so connects the operations of the Spirit and the efficacy of grace with instruments and means as to make the result as much a matter of natural consequence as the success of the husbandman, merchant or mechanic. It is possible to acknowledge that Paul may plant and Apollos water, but that all will be in vain unless God give the increase, and yet to suppose, at the same time, that the blessing of the Almighty is so inseparably conjoined with industry, zeal and diligence in the use of proper appliances as that success shall attend our efforts in religion with the same unvarying uniformity with which the phenomena of nature result from its established laws. We may make a *course of grace* in which one spiritual event shall succeed another with the same regularity and order as the changes around us observe in the constitution and appointments of nature. What, in fact, is usually denominated the *course of nature* is nothing but the uniform succession of events—the same antecedents being invariably connected with the same consequents. The laws of nature are only compendious expressions for uniformity and order in the phenomena around us, and what I understand by *natural consequence* is the conjunction which we learn from experience between a physical cause and its effect, from which we can confidently predict that the effect will invariably follow the cause, or that the cause will invariably precede the effect. All the results of mechanism take place, obviously, in the way of natural consequence. The material elements which compose the machine are so combined and arranged, antecedents are so determined and adjusted, that the invariable consequents must be the ends which we propose to accomplish. We simply avail ourselves, in other words, by mechanical arrangements of the known operations of natural laws to compass the objects which we have in view. The telescope, for instance, is simply particles of matter of such properties and so arranged as to be suited precisely to the refraction of light, so that through the operation of that law it can approximate what is remote and increase its apparent magnitude. That, therefore, is *natural* which uniformly happens under the same conditions—which takes place in conformity with fixed and invariable laws, and in regard to which the experience of the past is a certain index of the future. If, now, there be an order established in the system of grace in obedience to which faith is produced as a natural consequence, the personality of the Spirit is just as completely excluded as in the results of machinery or the common phenomena of nature. It is true that just conceptions of cause and effect must ultimately lead us to the Supreme Mind as the only source of efficiency and power. The works of nature in all the departments of matter and mind, the changes and vicissitudes which are constantly occurring within us and around us—whatsoever is, has been or will be—are only a chain of effects connected together in the order of time, of which no satisfactory account can be given until we ascend to the Will of the Almighty. There is the seat of power; the laws of nature possess no efficiency in themselves: they are simply uniform effects which the agency of God calls into being. The results of machinery, therefore, are as truly produced by the power of God as the creation of the world, the establishment of its order and the government of its affairs. No canvas can swell in the breeze, no water-wheel can be turned by a stream, the sun must fail to rise, seed-time and harvest must disappear from the earth, the variety of the seasons and the succession of plants and animals must all be arrested, unless there be an actual concurrence of God in every event that occurs within the limits of His empire. Without His will not a sparrow falls nor a flower blooms; so that in a sense widely removed from that refined and specious Atheism which identifies God with the operations of His hands, the sublime inscription upon the temple of Isis, the fabled mother of nature—" I am whatsoever is, whatsoever has been and whatsoever shall be"—may be applied to the real Father of the universe in full consistency with truth. Divine influences, accordingly, must be acknowledged in purely mechanical operations. Those effects which are produced in regular and established order are just as truly the works of the Almighty as signs, wonders and miraculous achievements. But when events occur in accordance with a fixed constitution, the very regularity of the series excludes from our view the immediate agency of God. Our attention is confined to the phenomena themselves; the constitution of our nature leads us to expect that the future will resemble the past; and the fact that this inborn instinct is gratified in the actual appearances around us represses curiosity, or stimulates our efforts only in arranging and collecting the results of past observation to serve as a guide in making calculations for the future and subduing nature to our purposes of interest and convenience. Hence it is that miracles which interrupt the order of natural sequences and consequently disappoint our natural expectations are such signal proofs of the presence of God. The birth of man is an event which requires no less an exertion of Divine power than his resurrection from the dead; and yet a thousand births may take place about us without exciting one thought of God, while no one could raise the dead before us without creating the impression that he was a special messenger of God. Whatever coincides with an established order is regarded as a matter of course. It is something that we expect. Our natural instinct has the same effect in regard to such phenomena as familiarity, and it requires a deep infusion of the spirit of religion as well as the spirit of philosophy to see God in the lilies of the field, the fowls of the air, the succession of the seasons and the ordinary occurrences of life.

It is evident, then, that the only way in which the personality of the Spirit can be immediately and directly recognized in the production of faith is to make it a supernatural endowment. To establish an *order* in conformity with which the grace of God is imparted to the soul is to treat the operations of the Spirit as purely mechanical. Upon this theory Divine influences are no more conspicuous in the new birth, the illumination of the mind and the sanctification of the heart, than in our natural generation, the growth of our bodies, the development of our faculties and the daily business of life. It is not enough to say in general terms that the Spirit is the author of faith—there must be something in the mode of its production that shall infallibly impress upon the mind the intuitive conviction that a voluntary agent is the cause of the phenomenon.

Hence the operations of the Spirit, in communicating spiritual life, must be analogous to those exercises of power by which miracles are wrought, and not to that method of operation which sustains the fabric of nature. Any system of religion, therefore, which teaches us to look for the blessing of God only in the way of natural consequence; which regards it as a thing of course when the proper instruments have been put in requisition; whatever else it may be called, has no pretensions to be treated as spiritual and Divine. If it acknowledges the Spirit at all, it is in such a sort as to involve a practical denial of His free, sovereign and personal agency. His will—and the essence of personality is supposed by many to consist in will—His will is not made the standard of gracious expectation, but our own industry and diligence in bending to our purposes the institutions and appointments of the Gospel. What are usually denominated the means of grace are presented in this theory in the aspect of laws, and the Spirit accordingly is nothing more than the invisible means—the Divine influence or the concealed determination of the Divine will—which connects the spiritual cause with its effect, the antecedent with its consequent, a proper application of means with the regeneration of the heart. The conversion of the soul is a process of spiritual mechanism brought about upon precisely the same principles of natural sequence as the construction of a telescope, the arrangement of a watch or the erection of a loom. The inevitable consequence is that conversion is just as much an achievement of our own as any of the natural operations which we daily perform.

It is intuitively evident, however, that the tendency of a fixed constitution to veil the personality of God can only be developed where the laws which regulate the succession of events are capable of being known and ascertained by us. The difficulty does not lie in the fact that order is observed, but in the fact that the order is *known*. In such cases the antecedents themselves, apart from all reference to God, are regarded as the *real* causes of the effects which ensue, and the Hand accordingly which governs and directs all the movements of nature is concealed from our view. Hence, God manifests His wisdom as well as His glory in so conducting the dispensations of His providence as that many of its most remarkable events shall appear to be fortuitous. The birth of individuals, the period of their death, that tide in their affairs which determines their destiny, though unquestionably parts of a scheme as uniform and regular as that course of nature which we are capable of tracing, are yet concealed in all but their proximate causes; and no satisfactory reason can be assigned why Hannibal was not a citizen of Rome and Alexander a hero of the nineteenth century. This large infusion of " chance" in the moral administration of the world is suited to operate as a check upon the obvious tendency to Atheism which a known constitution is fitted to produce. The mind is called off from the mere contemplation of physical causes to that sovereign Will which orders all things in heaven above and in the earth beneath. Fortuitous events are so many monuments of the Divine personality, so many memorials of God in the midst of a scene in which we are too prone to forget

Him. We may lament the proclivity of our minds to overlook the Author of Nature where we are capable of tracing the succession of its phenomena—we may denounce it as a signal proof of the depravity of our hearts and the perverseness of our will—but the fact is unquestionable. And hence the supremacy of the Spirit and the absolute sovereignty of His will must cease to be necessary elements of religious experience upon any hypothesis of grace which does not recognize a direct, immediate, intuitive perception of Divine operations. To establish a *course of grace* at all analogous to that we are accustomed to denominate *the constitution of nature* is to divert our attention from the agency and efficiency of the Holy Ghost, and to fix our hopes upon that series of subordinate antecedents which are supposed to be invariably attended with the results which we are anxious to secure. If reading, meditation and prayer, together with a diligent attention to all the other appointments of the Gospel, be recommended as standing in the same relation to faith in which industry, economy and prudence stand to success in the ordinary business of life, there is unquestionably in the nature of religious experience no more recognition of the hand and sovereignty of God than in the usual transactions of the world. A man, in other words, in consistency with this hypothesis, may be truly converted and yet be totally unmindful of any peculiar grace, power or mercy on the part of the Almighty. His hopes and expectations are all placed upon the means which He employs; and the ground of his confidence is the conviction, whether true or false, that these means are certainly connected with the ends which He proposes to secure. The planter who deposits his seed in the ground founds his expectations of a crop not upon the interpositions of God, but upon the fertility of the soil and the skill of his culture. The mechanic who erects a loom arranges all his materials with reference to the laws of motion, and never once thinks of the agency of the Supreme Being. He adjusts his antecedents, and takes it for granted that the usual consequents must follow.

Now, if the means of grace are really and truly *laws* of grace, there may be just as much practical atheism among the redeemed as among successful planters and mechanics. Accordingly, we find, in fact, that those who take low views of gracious operations are accustomed to maintain that we are not directly conscious of the possession of the Spirit. It is a fact which they suppose that we gather in the same way of philosophical analysis or necessary inference by which we recognize the power of God in the succession of the seasons or any of the beautiful arrangements of Providence. We compare, according to their statement of the matter, what we have felt and experienced with the declarations of the Word, and if we find that the spiritual phenomena of which we have been conscious are such as are there attributed to the agency of the Spirit, we are authorized to believe that we are taught of God, although our impressions themselves in their own nature would never have led us to look for an extraordinary or supernatural cause. Our experience itself would not have awakened the suspicion of Divine influence if we had not been previously informed by the Scriptures that all religious affections proceed from God; we are so clearly capable of tracing the process by which our impressions have been produced in the secret, silent and imperceptible influence of reading, meditation and prayer that we should never have dreamed that any external cause was at work if we had no other evidence of the fact than the consciousness of what has been passing within. The Bible, such persons will inform you, is written in the language of men, it is adapted to mortal comprehension, and they can perceive no substantial reason, either in the blindness of man or the mystery of the subject, why the coherence and connection of its parts, the meaning and dependence of its various propositions, may not be mastered by the same sort of diligence by which we master the visions of poetry or the speculations of philosophy. The Divine authority of the Scriptures rests, they will tell you, upon historical and internal evidences which are capable of being understood and appreciated by all who are able to reason; and when the disclosures of revelation are once received as *truth*, there is nothing more strange and wonderful in the effects which they produce than in the operations of any other truth. Such is the power of its motives, the solemnity of its sanctions and the fervour of its appeals that it is invariably followed in all who attend to it by results similar to those achieved by the orator or poet. Hence, we are conscious of no more *grace* in receiving the instructions of the Bible than in understanding the writings of Cicero or Plato.

Now, if the scheme of redemption has been so arranged as to produce in the experience of the faithful a full conviction of the personality of God, this hypothesis of grace, however ingenious or plausible, must be false. So far as the Holy Ghost is concerned, the economy of salvation according to this view is as dumb as nature, and every believer might justly exclaim, in the language of the Ephesian disciples of the Baptist, "We have not so much as heard whether there be a Holy Ghost." That stupendous change which the Scriptures everywhere illustrate by the analogies of creation and resurrection from the dead is reduced to a natural process. Conversion is brought within the competency of man. He can regenerate his heart by employing the proper means just as really and truly as he can raise enormous weights far transcending his physical abilities by pulleys and steam. There are laws by which he can avail himself of the power of God in the department of grace as well as in the department of nature—a moral machinery as potent in spiritual results as natural machinery in material effects. The solemn assertion of the Apostle, "It is not of him that willeth nor of him that runneth, but of God that showeth mercy," becomes palpably false, and the true statement is that, Whoever will employ the antecedents which are placed before him in the means of grace will assuredly find that faith, holiness and love will follow as the natural and uniform effects.

There cannot be a more overwhelming condemnation of

these mechanical operations of the Spirit than is furnished by Paul in the memorable text: "The Spirit itself beareth witness with our spirits that we are the children of God." How can there be a testimony of the Spirit separate and distinct from the testimony of our own hearts if, after all, we know the presence of the Spirit only from the effects which He impresses upon us? How can a witness assure us of a fact when we do not *know* that the witness is speaking? If Paul does not proceed on the assumption that we are conscious of the *personal* presence of the Holy Ghost, language may cease to be employed as a vehicle of thought. The complete reversion of this text by those who deny supernatural influences is a humiliating instance of the stubborn reluctance of man to prostrate his pride of understanding before the authority of God. The Spirit, according to the Apostle, bears witness to us that we are the children of God. That we are the children of God, according to the common exposition, is the only proof which we can have that we really possess the Spirit. So that we make Paul's proof our question, and his question our proof.

To the train of argument which I have attempted to develop it may be, and perhaps plausibly, objected that because the means of grace are denied to possess the efficacy of laws, therefore they are rendered useless and nugatory. Such miserable skeptics might be asked what idea our Saviour probably intended to convey when He assured His disciples that the first should be the last and the last first. Can there be uniformity in a kingdom where the laws of its proceedings are frequently reversed?

To say nothing of the repeated instances in which the blessings of the Gospel were evidently dispensed without the least reference to personal qualifications or previous preparation—a fact inconsistent with the theory of an uniform method, and consequently of *laws* in the kingdom of grace—the means of grace have a clear and definite use which would be entirely defeated by making them equivalent to laws. Their end is not to impart grace, but to remind us of our dependence upon the Spirit. They are not channels through which the waters of salvation are conducted to our hearts; they are rather the chambers or palaces in which we meet with the King Himself, and transact our affairs in His immediate presence. Reading, for example, has no necessary tendency to ingenerate Divine and supernatural faith. On the contrary, it shows the darkness of the mind and the hardness of the heart, just as a picture spread out before a blind man forcibly reminds him of his defect of vision. A sense of need is consequently awakened, which directs attention to a *living agent* by whose benevolence and power our wants may be relieved. Prayer is only an outward expression of that conviction of indigence and weakness which leads us off from the resources of the creature to the will of the Almighty. Hence, any proper view of the means of grace prevents us from attributing the least degree of efficacy to them. They do their office when they have convinced us that there is no help in man, and prostrate our hearts before the throne of God in entire dependence upon the will and grace of His Holy Spirit.

Now, if the ultimate end of these Divine institutions be to produce a conviction of need, so far is their use from being inconsistent with the personality of the Spirit, that they confirm and establish it. He who has tried them finds them to be empty and dead, incapable of supplying his wants, and consequently worthless as his ultimate dependences. He must, of course, look beyond them, and whatever comfort he receives must be attributed to the agency or influence of an external cause. They conduct him directly to the Spirit. To that august and glorious agent he presents himself burdened with the load of his sins and overpowered with a sense of his blindness, and he feels that nothing can relieve him but the grace, power and will of the Holy Ghost. They teach him his need of *personal* interference, and through them that condition of the soul is produced in which a manifestation of the loving-kindness of the Lord shall be acknowledged as a direct and immediate interposition of God. Hence, to depend upon the means of grace, which we would be authorized to do if they were *laws*, is completely to destroy their legitimate tendency and render them worse than useless. They should only be employed as the way to the Spirit, as the galleries in which His glory will be manifested, as the instruments by which we are reminded that our help is in God. When properly employed they are most forgotten when most earnestly used; the eye is fixed exclusively on the Spirit.

Our vindication of supernatural grace will perhaps be complete if it can be shown that in avoiding the extreme of a dead and spiritless formality we are not necessarily exposed to the extravagant follies of a rabid enthusiasm. The fact, however, that this accusation is so repeatedly urged against those who maintain the personality of the Spirit as an essential element of Christian experience is a strong presumption that their doctrine is substantially the same as that of the illustrious Apostle of the Gentiles. When Paul related the astonishing history of his conversion before the Roman judges, Festus said with a loud voice, " Paul, thou art beside thyself; much learning doth make thee mad." The governor did not mean to charge the Apostle with actual insanity, or that melancholy derangement of the mind in which all its powers are confounded and the distinctions of truth and falsehood, of right and wrong, are neither felt nor perceived. He rather looked upon his prisoner as deluded, as a dupe to his own imagination, mistaking the visions of fancy for the realities of fact. There is nothing strange in attributing such madness to excessive learning. The profound and solitary studies of Democritus exposed him to a similar imputation among his stupid countrymen of Abdera, from which, as the story goes, he was eloquently defended by his friend, Hippocrates. As Festus could not bring himself to believe the marvellous narrative which the Apostle had just given of his sudden conversion to the Christian faith by the immediate agency of God, and as the evident sincerity of Paul's convictions, the depth of his feelings, the fervour of his manner, his disinterested labours and extraordinary sufferings in behalf of Christianity evinced an honesty of heart and simplicity of purpose wholly incompatible with the supposition of imposture, no alternative was left but to treat the whole matter as a strong delusion. Paul was accordingly dismissed as a visionary, though in the great day it will be found, to the consternation and dismay of all Pharisees, formalists and hypocrites, that such enthusiasm was the real production of the Spirit, the words of truth and soberness.

The charge of enthusiasm which we find upon the lips of Festus, and which has since been repeated by a thousand tongues, is, from the vagueness and ambiguity of the term, admirably adapted to the purposes of scandal. In ancient times the word seems to have been used in three different applications. It was first employed to denote that ecstasy of the Sibyls, Priests, and Prophets, in which the powers of the mind and the organs of the body were under the complete control of the inspiring god. This sort of enthusiasm is what Cicero calls *divination*. It was next applied to those strong and vehement conceptions of an excited imagination in which the balance of the soul was disturbed and the distinctions of vision and reality destroyed. This species of enthusiasm was, among the people, as also among some of the philosophers, ascribed to the agency of the gods, and hence it received the same general name with prophetic inspiration. The third sense in which we find the term employed by the ancient writers is in reference to the extraordinary achievements of genius and learning. As those effects of the orator, the poet, and the philosopher which were distinguished by unusual ability and fervour were ascribed to supernatural assistance, they were likewise embraced under the general head of enthusiasm. Hence, it would appear that *enthusiasm*, or *madness*, among the ancients was a term invented to denote the cause of a large class of phenomena, which, as they could not be explained upon the established principles of mind and matter, were referred to Divine interposition. The inspiration of the Sibyl, the dreams of the visionary, and the sublime effusions of the poet or the orator had nothing in common but the extraordinary impulses with which they were attended, and they received a common appellation only in consequence of the vulgar apprehension that they all proceeded from the gods.

As employed in modern times to cast reproach upon the gracious operations of the Spirit, the term may imply either diabolical possession or fanatical delusion. The fundamental idea conveyed is that all pretensions to supernatural assistance are extravagant and wicked, proceeding either from the craft of an impostor, the excitement of the passions or the artful suggestions of the tempter. The leading assumption, upon which alone any plausibility can be given to the charge, is that the Divine illumination, which is made essential to the reality of faith, is philosophically absurd. It is supposed to be impossible that we can be conscious of the immediate agency of God. To say nothing of the numerous and pointed declarations of the Scriptures which directly teach that faith is an extraordinary gift of the Spirit, the fact that Prophets and Apostles must have known that their minds were possessed of the Holy Ghost is conclusive proof that there may be manifestations of the Spirit which are accompanied with intuitive convictions of His presence. We have no reason to believe that the holy men of old, who spake as they were moved by the Holy Ghost, were left to deduce their own inspiration from the miracles which they found themselves capable of working. It is not for us to say in what way the prophetic impulse indicated its Author. It is certain, however, that there must have been such impressions of the Divine goodness, glory, knowledge and power made upon their minds as rendered it impossible to doubt, antecedently to any external signs of their supernatural commission, that the Lord was with them. In some way they felt His presence and knew Him to be there as certainly as any natural phenomenon is ascertained by the senses. To say that God cannot communicate an intuitive conviction of His presence to the mind is not only to deny that Prophets and Apostles were directly conscious of their own inspiration, but boldly and presumptuously to limit the Holy One of Israel. No good reason can be given why an immediate revelation of Himself is not as possible and easy as an indirect manifestation of His glory through the wonderful works which He has made. The fact, therefore, that the doctrine of supernatural illumination involves an immediate conviction of the presence of the Spirit is no necessary presumption against its truth.

I do not mean to insinuate, however, that the Divine illumination which is the only cause of supernatural faith is, by any means, identical with prophetic inspiration. There is certainly a vast difference betwixt imparting original revelations, and enabling the understanding to perceive the impressions of Divine glory in a revelation already communicated. But He who, in the one case, can manifest His presence so as to silence doubt and generate conviction, can also do it in the other.

That to make faith depend upon Divine and supernatural illumination is virtually to make it a new endowment of the soul is no valid objection to the truth of the doctrine. There are unquestionably original powers by which, in reference to every department of knowledge, we are enabled to distinguish the fictitious from the real, the true from the false. In a sound condition of the senses, phantasms are never confounded with material impressions; we readily discriminate betwixt existing objects and the creatures of fancy. So also in matters of science we rise by degrees from intuitive perceptions to legitimate deductions, keeping a steady hold of truth by means of judgment and reasoning. What sense is to matter, what intuition and reasoning are to science, faith is to supernatural revelation. It is a gracious faculty by which we recognize spiritual truth, trace the impressions of Divinity upon the disclosures of the Gospel and behold the glory of God in the face of Jesus Christ. As the measure of faith is the testimony of God, it may be defined as a supernatural perception of the reality and glory of that testimony. Our Saviour, accordingly, teaches that in the spiritual apprehension of the Gospel the flesh, or the natural understanding, profiteth nothing. There must be an evidence, or, as the Apostle styles it, a powerful demonstration of the Spirit, which genius, industry and learning are utterly inadequate to compass, and which produces conviction by its own irresistible light. If the Scriptures are indeed the Word of God, the traces of His character must be indelibly stamped upon them, their doctrines must reflect His glory, and the whole scheme which they are intended to develop must bear His name visibly engraved upon it. Now the Spirit, in the production of supernatural faith, shines into the heart and reveals a light by which we are enabled to perceive the Divinity and feel the efficacy of the mysterious truths of the Gospel. Hence, from the very nature of the case, faith must become an extraordinary gift—a new faculty of the soul directly conversant with spiritual truth, distinguishing the true from the false, answering to perception in matters of sense, to intuition in matters of reasoning, and to demonstration in matters of science. It is the eye of the spiritual man by which he beholds the things of God, and as sense and intuition carry their own evidence along with them, so faith is justified by its own light.

To maintain such an intuitive perception of the reality and excellence of spiritual truth is generally supposed to be fatal to the interests of sobriety and order by opening a wide door for extravagant delusions and fanatical excesses. Every dreamer, it is said, may receive the ravings of a frantic imagination as the genuine impulses of the Spirit of God. This is nothing more than to say that Faith, like every other faculty of our nature, is capable of being abused; and as in every other case the existence of counterfeits is generally regarded as a presumption that an original exists of which the counterfeit is only an imitation—as hypocrisy itself, in conformity with the famous aphorism, is an indirect acknowledgment of the reality and excellence of virtue—so the delusions of fancy could never be mistaken for the inspiration of the Spirit if there were no reasons to believe in the truth and genuineness of Divine and supernatural impressions. Still, the argument from abuse is never legitimate. The perceptions of the senses are sometimes delusive. In a diseased condition of the eye colours are often confounded, and to the muscles of the senseless paralytic the impression of resistance is impossible. The maniac reasons coherently and closely from arbitrary premises, mistaking the strong appearances of delirium for the indisputable truths of intuition. Shall we, therefore, from the known and acknowledged abuse of the fundamental principles of knowledge, be led to deny the reality of sensation or the certainty of intuitive convictions? If the abuses of Religion are greater, more numerous and terrible than the abuses of any other subject, the only proper conclusion should be that religion itself is of infinitely greater importance than all other subjects combined. The evils of abuse are always proportioned to the intrinsic excellence of that which is perverted. That ocean which purifies the atmosphere, moderates temperature and binds the nations together in the enduring ties of brotherhood and interest, diverted from its bed would be the most appalling scourge with which the earth could be visited. The greatest temporal blessing which any nation is capable of enjoying is a wise, equitable, free and magnanimous government; the most awful calamity with which any country can be cursed is tyranny. Fanaticism may well be called Legion, for its horrors are unspeakable and its dangers inconceivable both in time and eternity; but it derives its malignity from the perversion and abuse of the sublimest truths and most elevating doctrines which can possibly be addressed to the human understanding. It poisons the waters of life at the fountain, converts them into elements of death and spreads devastation and terror in the whole extent of its progress. The Devil will sometimes transform himself into an angel of light, so that the corruptions and excesses both of superstition and enthusiasm seem to be inseparable, without the special interference of God, from our fallen condition. The great deceiver will endeavour to mimic the real operations of the Spirit; he will endeavour to substitute the glare of hell for the illumination of grace, and the revelry of intoxicated feeling for that joy in the Holy Ghost which is the special prerogative of the saints. He will deceive multitudes with the furious dreams of fanaticism, and yet the foundation of God standeth sure. The seal of the Spirit is no vain delusion, though thousands may bear a stamp which is only a counterfeit—a wicked and diabolical imitation of the impression of the Holy One. Let every man look well to his own heart.

I have thus presented a subject which it is useless to declare lies at the foundation of our highest interests. If we have correct apprehensions of the personality of the Spirit as an essential element of religious experience, we shall be guarded at once from the evils of formality and the extravagant excesses of fanaticism. We shall be led to regard Christianity as a Divine life in the soul—as consisting not in forms, rites and ceremonies, but in the communion of the Spirit, the love of the Father and the grace of the Son; and we shall perceive that the worship of the glorious Trinity is the sum and substance of spiritual religion. The great doctrine of supernatural grace is the great opprobrium of the Gospel. Multitudes who have the form of godliness without its power, who are sleeping in carnal security though their consciences have never been purged from the sad defilements of sin, will represent all anxiety about the condition of the soul as the result of melancholy or the incipient stages of insanity. From such we must turn away in pity and in fear—in pity, because, if there be truth in the Bible, they are in the gall of bitterness and the bonds of iniquity; in fear, because contact with them is the torpedo-touch of death. Others, who are full of life and zeal and boisterous pretensions, will talk largely about the supernatural influences of the Spirit and the cheering operations of grace, but if their characters be tested by the infallible standard of the Word, there will be detected the elements of pride, vain-glory and selfishness under the specious mask of religious devotion. Their zeal is without knowledge, their fervour without piety, and their comforts without faith. They are like waves of the sea or clouds of the air, wells without water, shooting-stars to whom is reserved the blackness of darkness for ever. There are many false Christs abroad in the world. The forms of deception are so numerous, and its consequences so unspeakably disastrous, that we need a Teacher who alone can guide us through the labyrinths of error, reveal to our hearts the economy of grace, unite us effectually to the Son of God, and make us partakers of everlasting life. The Eternal Spirit is the true Minister of the Tabernacle which the Lord pitched, and not man. Under His Divine guidance and direction we may pass through the world in safety and peace; its elements of disorder shall be rendered subservient to our good, and even afflictions and calamities made to work out a far more exceeding and eternal weight of glory. If He dwell in our hearts and control and regulate our lives, our peace shall flow as a river, and our hope shall be as an anchor to the soul both sure and steadfast. It is His presence that renders the Church fair as the sun, clear as the moon and terrible as an army with banners, and to every true believer He will infallibly be found a cloud by day and a pillar of fire by night.

Soon every other distinction will fade away but that which is created by the possession of the Spirit. In the great day which awaits us all, when God shall arise to shake terribly the earth, and the destinies of all the race shall be sealed for ever, our right to life will depend exclusively on the witness of the Holy Ghost. None can sustain their title as sons but those whom He has sealed unto the day of redemption. To appear without His signet on our foreheads and His impress upon our hearts is to awake to the resurrection of damnation, to be doomed to shame and everlasting contempt. It will not be a question whether we have been great or mean, honoured or despised, rich or poor. All the trappings of earth must be laid aside at death, but it will be a question, and a question of overwhelming importance, whether or not we have possessed the Spirit. The complexion of eternity must depend upon the answer to this awful question. If we have been among those miserable skeptics who have not so much as heard that there be a Holy Ghost, if we have despised religion under the name of fanaticism, and laughed at grace as the effervescence of enthusiasm, unlimited duration will be the period assigned us to lament our folly and bewail the consequences of our terrible delusion. If we have preferred the light of our own eyes to the light of the Spirit, and the imagination of our own hearts to His heavenly guidance, we shall be left at last to stumble irretrievably upon the dark mountains of despair, to eat the fruit of our own ways and be filled with our own devices. Without the Spirit of the living God we are dead, irrecoverably dead—dead for time and dead for eternity.

In addition to these considerations, which ought to be sufficient to impress upon us the transcendent importance of seeking the grace of the Holy Ghost, the tremendous sanctions with which His majesty and glory are sustained deserve to be seriously pondered. If we blaspheme the name of the Father, there is a place left for repentance and salvation—we may be forgiven. If we blaspheme the name of the Son, that also may be forgotten and blotted out for ever. But if we blaspheme the name of the Holy Ghost, we shall never be forgiven, either in this world or that which is to come. There is no place left for repentance, though, like Esau, we seek it bitterly and with tears. This tremendous sanction is like a wall of fire thrown around the Spirit to protect Him from insult and to attest the grandeur of His nature. Coming directly in contact as He does with the darkness, corruption, impurity and defilement of the hearts of men, His authority is maintained and His honour vindicated by the unspeakable malediction with which they are visited who despise His majesty. Because there is wrath let us beware. Let us not venture to sport upon the edge of a precipice so inconceivably dangerous. What the blasphemy against the Holy Ghost is, we are perhaps unable to determine, and in this acknowledged ignorance of its nature we may commit it while we are amusing our hearts with the siren song of prosperity and whispering all is well. The day of our merciful visitation may pass away, and the things that belong to our peace be for ever hid from our eyes, while we have been conscious of no greater sin than just the grieving by neglect and delay of the Holy Spirit of God. There is a point at which mercy shall kindle into vengeance, at which the insulted Spirit shall take his everlasting departure, and leave those who would not believe under the terrible calamity of judicial blindness. Let us, then, see that we grieve not the Holy Spirit of God. The salvation of the soul is invested with too much solemnity, eternity is too vast an interest, to be treated with levity and postponed for our convenience. The dictate of reason and prudence, as well as the command of God, is to seek first the one thing needful; let that be secured before we distract our minds with the vain anxieties of the heathen about what we shall eat, or what we shall drink, or wherewithal we shall be clothed. Let not the summer pass away nor the harvest disappear until we can say that our souls are saved.

If we could be brought to apprehend our real condition as condemned malefactors, if we knew our guilt, our misery, our weakness, if we felt the magnitude of the interests at stake, we should cease not day or night to cry mightily to God that He would bow the heavens and come down, and make our hearts His chosen habitations through the Spirit. We should prize the Holy Ghost as our hope, since He alone can sprinkle the blood of atonement on our consciences, repair the ruins of our moral constitutions, prepare us for death, for judgment, for eternity. Christ must for ever remain to us a stone of stumbling and a rock of offence, unless the Spirit reveal His glory as of the only-begotten of the Father, full of grace and truth. God must for ever continue a consuming fire unless the Spirit purify our hearts by faith and fit us for communion with the Father of lights. Heaven must ever remain inaccessible to our efforts unless the Spirit seal us as the sons of God and the heirs of immortality. So deep is my conviction of the importance of the Spirit that I know not where to find the language that is suited to express the transcendent value of His grace. Eternity alone can reveal how much they lose who know nothing of His love, His consolations and His joys. It was the Spirit who garnished the heavens and the earth; traces of His glory are found in all the visible creation; the only spot where His light does not shine is among the spirits of the lost. Hell, and hell alone, is adorned with no memorial of His grace, and to hell all must be finally consigned who have not His witness within them.

PREFATORY NOTE.

THIS short, but sweet and touching, exhibition of what the salvation of the Gospel is, would appear from the handwriting to have been amongst its author's earlier productions. It was written in the form of a sermon on John iii. 17, but there is no record on the manuscript of its ever having been preached, and it certainly was never before put into type.

THE NATURE OF SALVATION.

WE read in the third chapter of John that God sent not His Son into the world to condemn the world, but that the world through Him might be saved. Now, while in accordance with these words it is universally admitted by all who acknowledge the Divine authority of the Scriptures that Jesus Christ is the Saviour of His people, various opinions are supported in regard to the nature of His salvation and the means by which it is effected. In cases of signal deliverance or eminent success the Greeks and Romans erected temples and dedicated altars to the false objects of their worship under the title of *saviours*, and even princes and heroes, for daring achievements in the hour of conflict, received the same mark of honour and respect from the grateful adulation of the people. Inspiration itself applies the term to Othniel and Ehud, evidently showing that the mere word does not necessarily imply attributes and powers inconsistent with the nature of man. We learn from Plato that the Greeks, at their banquets, uniformly made a libation to Jupiter from the third goblet, under the title of *saviour*, as the giver of prosperity. In Scripture phraseology, the word *salvation* is applied to any deliverance from evil, whether moral or physical. It was common with Christ to say to the invalid, "Thy faith hath saved thee," meaning only, Thy faith hath *healed* thee. The word is so broad and extensive in its import that the mere phraseology of the passage from John, separate and apart from other declarations of Scripture, does not prove that Jesus is at all distinguished from Moses or from Joshua, from Othniel or Ehud. To be sure, He is represented as offering salvation to the world, while *their* operations are confined to the children of Israel. But if this passage in John stood isolated and alone, or were the only passage of the Bible which attributes salvation to Jesus, we would not be bound to conclude that He was anything more than a distinguished teacher or illustrious prophet. *To save the world* may mean only to dispel the ignorance which prevails among men and to diffuse the light of knowledge and of truth. The Apostles are frequently styled the *saviours* of those who were converted by their preaching, because they delivered them from the dangerous influence of idolatrous error by spreading the knowledge of the true religion. If Jesus had done nothing more than reform the abuses and correct the errors of society; if He had only promulgated a system of moral and religious truth, fixing accurately the nature of right and the extent of human duty; if He had only added fresh and stronger sanctions to the eternal principles of rectitude and virtue; if He had done nothing more than teach, reform and elevate our race,—He would have done enough for the world to elicit its gratitude and gain the honourable title of its *Saviour*. Valuable, however, as the moral teachings of Jesus unquestionably are, His salvation includes something higher and more difficult. Pythagoras, Socrates and Plato were eminent philosophers, and did much towards reforming abuses and correcting errors amongst their countrymen, and yet we should hardly think of comparing the Messiah with a Grecian sage or a Roman seer. Solomon uttered dark sayings of old, and was a teacher of wisdom to his subjects, but a greater than Solomon is here. In what, then, does the salvation of Jesus consist, or in what peculiar and emphatic sense is He denominated the *Saviour of His people?*

The passages which stand in immediate conjunction with the words quoted above from John distinctly declare that the great object of the mission of Christ was to deliver His followers from the ruin and misery of sin, and to give them the blessings of eternal life. "As Moses lifted up the serpent in the wilderness, even so must the Son of man be lifted up, that whosoever believeth on Him might not perish, but have everlasting life." "For God so loved the world that He gave His only begotten Son, that whosoever believeth in Him should not perish, but have everlasting life." Here the salvation ascribed to Christ evidently has a primary reference to the beatitude of heaven and the ruinous punishment of sin. He is styled a *Saviour* because He delivers His people from eternal death and gives them eternal life. If we bear in mind that happiness is not an independent, isolated object of existence, but merely the natural consequence and uniform concomitant of holiness, we shall see at once that the salvation of Jesus necessarily includes ample and adequate means of destroying the depravity of the heart and of rendering His followers holy. Happiness and virtue have been linked together by the eternal fiat of Jehovah, and no human ingenuity can tear them asunder. Without holiness it is impossible to see the Lord—that is, to be completely and eminently happy. Jesus cannot—such is the moral government of God—Jesus cannot be a Saviour without delivering His people from their sins. It is a profound remark of a writer in other respects dangerous and heretical that a "man is saved only so far as he is holy." Jesus received His name by the express and solemn appointment of God, because He should save His people from their sins. In view of the intimate connection which obtains between vice and misery, virtue and happiness, and in view of the passages which ascribe salvation to Christ because He delivers us from a state of misery into a state of happiness, and of those which ascribe salvation to Him because He delivers us from sin and corruption, we should say that the true scriptural idea of salvation can only be found in combining the two. Jesus would then be called a Saviour, because He frees His followers from sin, and consequently from misery—because He makes them holy, and consequently happy. If we have correct notions of the government of God, we shall see that these ideas are substantially the same. To be freed from sin and misery is to be made holy, and to be made holy is to be made happy. Holiness, therefore, itself, in its cause and results, covers the whole ground of salvation. We can indeed conceive of a state of things in which holiness should be essentially different from happiness, but this is not the state of things which actually obtains under the providence of God. The formation of a holy character, therefore, is the great point to which Jesus as a Saviour must direct His efforts. His salvation is incomplete—nay, it is a total failure—unless this great point is effectually secured, and when it shall have been completely gained, happiness and eternal life necessarily follow.

According to the Scripture account of the matter, we are all clean gone from original righteousness—totally averse from all good and pertinaciously inclined to all evil. We are said to be conceived in sin and shapen in iniquity, and it is a well-known fact that our first exhibitions of moral agency, how guarded soever our educations may have been, manifest a fearful disregard to the laws of God, to holiness and to truth. It was the curse of our great progenitor to transmit to his posterity the corruption which he brought upon himself. In the wild infatuation of his heart he sought out the strange invention of moral deformity and death, and his whole issue to the latest generation became involved in his ruin. The recorded experience of the world proves beyond all doubt that man is naturally depraved—completely, totally, utterly depraved. When I say that men are totally depraved, I do not mean that they are incapable of performing any acts which, in themselves considered, are conformable with the law of God. The reciprocal duties of humanity may be faithfully discharged by a man who, in the view of God, is regarded as dead in trespasses and sins. Depravity consists in a total defection from the authority of God—in an alienation of the heart from its Maker. With fidelity and zeal we may perform the duties which devolve upon us in all the important relations of life. We can pity the unfortunate and relieve the distressed; submit with quietness to the laws of the country; sustain the offices of a father, a husband, a brother and a friend; and yet be wanting in the only principle of living obedience and genuine virtue which the Scriptures recognize. The heart is yet at enmity with God, and until this enmity is slain our very best actions are only splendid sins. Morality is important to society, but the morality which proceeds from any other principle than a principle of love to God is like a statue, beautiful, elegant and well-proportioned, but, alas! wanting in life. The carnal heart is enmity with God, and this is the secret, the great secret, of human depravity; into this principle it can all be resolved, and is resolved by the sacred writers. The rebel and revolted spirit must be brought back to its allegiance to God before it can perform an act of genuine obedience or of genuine holiness. How, then, can this be done? This was the great problem which infinite wisdom had to solve in planning the salvation of the world. This was the great riddle which puzzled the universe—the mystery into which the angels desired to look. Man could not be reclaimed to his allegiance by the thunders of the law which he had violated; these would only drive him to a stouter resistance. His affections could not be recalled by the frowning aspect of a menacing Deity; this would excite a deadlier hate. How, then, can he be reclaimed? The answer is, By removing the procuring cause of his enmity to God, for when the cause is removed the effect, as a matter of course, ceases to exist.

Now, what mainly produces the enmity of the carnal heart against God is a consciousness of sin and a dread of its awful consequences. It is a radical doctrine of all religion that no sin is unconditionally pardonable, and the feeling is deeply rooted in the human heart that some satisfaction must be rendered to the Divine law before the sinner can gain the approbation of his God. Hence, all superstitions have instituted rites and ceremonies, penances and sufferings, in order to appease the anger of Heaven. The connection between guilt and punishment has been written by the finger of Omnipotence on the human heart, and in the darkest midnight of the mind we find the idolatrous heathen and the wandering savage responding to the sentiment of the Apostle, that without the shedding of blood there is no remission. Repentance was felt to be inadequate, for it could only act on the future without touching the past. The law had been broken in days gone by, and the future could only discharge its own incumbent obligations. Resort was consequently had to the blood of bulls and goats, and even the body was lacerated and torn to purge the sin of the soul. But these penances gave only a temporary quiet without affording permanent security. Men still felt that they were debtors to the law and justly exposed to punishment. The fear of punishment clung to them, an intolerable burden; they feared the might of God's right hand. A thought of God was a thought of terror, and the grave was black as midnight. This dread of God's justice, arising from a sense of guilt, is the great ground of the sinner's hatred to God, and can only be removed by appeasing that justice and assuring the sinner that he can be pardoned. In other words, some plan must be devised to assure the sinner that he can be regarded as just—as a being who has never offended in the sight of God—and the integrity, at the same time, of the Divine attributes be preserved unimpaired. Every scheme of salvation which fails to comprehend this important principle can afford no permanent or solid security to the hopes of the guilty. The sinner must be certainly assured that he can stand on the same footing with a man who had never sinned, without detracting from the honour of God, before he can be brought to view his Maker with affection or to dismiss his sentiments of dread. It is all idle to talk of his loving God while the weight of unpardoned guilt hangs over him. The terrors of the Lord encompass him about, and the horrors of the grave seize hold upon him. In the nature of things, a vindictive deity cannot be the subject of delight to the fallen object of His vengeance. Terror and dread are not the native elements of love. We may quail beneath the fiery justice and uplifted arm of a menacing Deity; we may tremble and shake at the awful exhibitions of an angry God, when the heavens grow black with His wrath and the firmament smokes with His hot displeasure. Aye! He may alarm and appal us by exposing to view the revolting scenes of the lower pit, where the worm dieth not and the fire is not quenched, but where there is wailing and woe and black despair for ever and ever. But exhibitions like these will only steel our hearts to deeper defiance and sterner hate. They cannot unbar the doors of our love. They may make us muster the energies of dark despair and clench our fists and nerve our souls to battle with Omnipotence. Love can only be gained by love, and God must show to the sinner a smiling face and an approving eye before He can win the sinner's affections. The sinner must know that his guilt is gone, that God has forgotten it and is disposed to treat him as a just man, as a being who had never sinned.

Now the principle of imputation, the very keystone which supports the arch of the Christian system, is admirably suited to dispel the fears and quiet the apprehensions of conscious guilt. The iniquities of the sinner are taken from his own shoulders, and all their burden is imposed upon Christ. The penalties of the law are met and satisfied by His vicarious sufferings, and His perfect obedience to the law of God being imputed to the sinner as his own obedience, the sinner comes to be regarded in the eye of God as a just man, as a being who had never offended. The law has no further claims upon him; he is restored in the view of Heaven to the same situation of sinless purity which belonged to Adam before his fall. He is as though he had never transgressed. All this results from the great principle of imputation—a radical principle of the Gospel clearly set forth in the writings of the Apostles and that old Evangelist, Isaiah; nay, it is deeply grounded in the moral government of God, and he that denies its existence will find many anomalies which he cannot unriddle and many appearances which he cannot explain. Those who deny that the sufferings of Christ were truly and properly vicarious are reduced to the awkward dilemma of denying entirely all moral distinctions or of denying that Jesus is a Saviour. If they hold to moral distinctions, they must likewise hold to a moral government. Now, a moral government is a government of law, and every law implies a sanction, a reward for obedience and a punishment for disobedience. When God promulgates a law, He does it with a view of having it observed, and the object of the sanction is to supply a strong and adequate motive for the observance of the law. Now, the force of the sanction depends essentially on the certainty of its execution. Unless the sanction be uniformly enforced the law is a dead letter. Those who deny that the sufferings of Christ were truly and properly vicarious, and at the same time contend that Jesus is a Saviour, actually maintain that the sanctions of the law have been left unexecuted, and that the law consequently is a dead letter; in other words, that there is no distinction between vice and virtue, a duty and a crime. They charge God with the ridiculous farce of promulgating a law with awful solemnity which He never meant to enforce, and with the downright duplicity of uttering threats which He never designed to execute. A law without a sanction is no law, and a sanction unexecuted is no sanction. Its efficacy depends altogether on the absolute certainty of its being enforced. Let the law be once violated with impunity, and there is an end at once of all obedience and authority. On the other hand, those who hold to moral distinctions and deny the atonement leave man exposed to the penalty of eternal death, quailing beneath the justice of God, a child of wrath and an heir of woe. They leave man just where they found him, oppressed with guilt and hating God on account of the terrors which surround His throne. We conclude, then, that the sufferings of Christ were truly and properly vicarious, that He died the just for the unjust, and that on Him was laid the iniquity of us all. This is the only view of the subject which can give quiet to the troubled spirit and relieve the apprehensions of the guilty mind. Let the sinner believe firmly in the atonement of Jesus, and he can look to heaven without horror or dismay, for he sees there an approving Father and a smiling God. No sins oppress his soul, for he wears the robe of Christ's obedience and stands out in the light of day a just man. The great cause of his hatred to God is removed, the doors of his love are effectually unbarred, and what the Law with all its threats and penalties and terrors could not do, is gloriously accomplished by the Cross of Christ. His spirit of stern rebellion and stubborn defiance is effectually subdued when he sees his God bending from the Mount of Crucifixion with outstretched arms and a smiling face, imploring the children of men to come and be saved. He may stand out against all the threats and terrors of an incensed and vindictive Deity, he may defy his Maker when He frowns in wrath or uplifts the sword of eternal vengeance, but he cannot resist that supreme love, that wonderful love of God which spared not His own Son, but delivered Him up for His enemies. The sinner may hate an angry God, but he cannot but love a reconciled Father. Here is the magic of the Cross; it presents a scene of love such as the world had never seen before and will never see again. When the world was lost, ruined and undone, when all hope had fled from earth, and apparently fled for ever, Jehovah bows the heavens and comes down, and, travelling in the majesty of His strength, works out a redemption for His imprisoned subjects which astonished the angels and made the universe stand aghast. Here was love, unspeakable love, "When God the mighty Maker died for man the creature's sin." And when this amazing love is fully apprehended and distinctly realized, the stoutest heart of the proudest sinner will yield to its mighty influence. Love is the talisman by which God subdues the sinner's heart and gains his supreme affection. Let him firmly believe and strongly realize that Jesus was indeed the Lamb of God, slain for the sins of the world, and that it was Love, almighty Love, which occasioned the awful sacrifice, and he will bow his soul in the depths of humility and give his heart to God. So the Gospel accomplishes what the law could not do; it infuses into the sinner's mind a principle of holiness and living obedience; it gives him what nothing else could give him, a love of God, and under the sacred influence of the Holy Ghost fits him to enjoy the blessedness of heaven. Thus is Christ the Saviour of His people.

The cross of Christ portrays at the same time in living characters the awful turpitude of guilt. We cannot regard sin, that abominable thing which God hates, as a matter of little moment when we call to mind the intense agony and withering suffering which the Son of God underwent in order to remove its curse. Chained as we are to this little corner of the universe, we can neither see clearly nor estimate exactly the dreadful breach which it makes in the government of God. But we are satisfied that God would have spared His Son if He could have done it consistently with His honour. We know that it was not a light affair which robed the sun in the darkness of midnight and awoke the dead from the slumber of ages. God does not exhibit His power from the mere vanity of show. There was a cause, a real, substantial, adequate cause, of these mighty changes in the course of nature. The Son of God in bleeding agony is enduring the hot displeasure of His Father against the ungodly, the vials of Divine wrath are poured upon Him, and He bows His soul in meek resignation to meet the punishment which the sins of His people had incurred. The sufferings of Christ are a living comment on the awful turpitude and dreadful consequences of guilt; and he that brings home to his own bosom the terrible tragedy that was acted on Calvary, while he feels his heart melt within him at the amazing love of God to His fallen creatures, will hate sin with a perfect hatred. Two points are gained at once—the love of God and the hatred of sin.

PREFATORY NOTE.

THE article upon Antinomianism is the Appendix added by Dr. Thornwell to Traill's Vindication, which he published, as before mentioned, amongst other Doctrinal Tracts, at Columbia in 1840.

ANTINOMIANISM.

THE term *Antinomianism* is employed to denote a system of doctrine which naturally leads to licentiousness of life. Those who deny that the law of God is the measure of duty, or that personal holiness should be sought by Christians, are those alone who can properly be charged with Antinomian principles. The Scriptures are so pointed and explicit in pressing upon believers that "denying ungodliness and worldly lusts they should live soberly, righteously and godly in this present world," that it becomes a matter of no little interest, even to the speculative inquirer, to account for the origin of Antinomianism. We must not confound the origin of the *word* with the origin of the *thing*. The latter existed long before a single term expressive of its true character was applied to it. The word was coined in the sixteenth century to denote the peculiar opinions of John Agricola and his followers in regard to the Law. Agricola was a native of Aisleben, and, until he began to propagate his extravagant opinions in the year 1538, a friend and abettor of Luther. The *thing* existed as far back certainly as the days of Paul and James. That the preaching of the "Word of the truth of the Gospel" should have been attended with Antinomian consequences upon any mind, however illiterate, can be accounted for only by the singular tendency of man to oscillate, in his opinions and practices, from one extreme to another. When, after a dreary night of Arminian darkness and of legal bondage, the doctrines of grace are proclaimed with clearness and power, there are always found men who, unable to endure the light which reveals the folly of their slavish toils and unchristian schemes, pervert the Gospel and turn the grace of God into lasciviousness. If the Pharisees and doctors of the law had not galled and broken the necks of the people by the yoke of servitude which they imposed upon them, Paul perhaps would never have been slanderously reported as teaching men to do ill that good might come, neither would any have been tempted to boast of a faith which produced no fruit. Christians in his day, no doubt, indirectly and incidentally afforded plausible pretexts to the carnal and profane. Those who had been required to go through the laborious drudgery of establishing their own righteousness—a toil not unlike that imposed upon the Hebrews by the Egyptian taskmasters—who were at all enlightened to perceive the defects and wickedness of their best performances, could not but hail with joy the proclamation of a perfect righteousness which was the " end of the law to every one that believed." And in their anxiety to free others from the same gross and slavish delusions under which they had laboured themselves, it is not strange, it is natural, that in some instances a phraseology more remarkable for point than accuracy should have been adopted for the purpose of effect. They saw the reigning power of legalism, they had felt its bitterness and knew its curse, and consequently spoke with the energy and pathos of men in earnest when endeavouring to arrest the pharisaical bias of the carnal heart. The dreams of the sleeper may be changed while his slumbers are unbroken. Many, no doubt, received opinions in the head which found no entrance in the heart, and confounding the important distinction between justification and sanctification, and wilfully misled by the incautious statements of true disciples, pretended to receive Christ; but it was a divided Christ, so that they might freely indulge the lascivious propensities of the carnal mind. These are the men whom Jude and

Peter denounce, and whose monstrous opinions James refutes.

Three circumstances, therefore, conspired to produce the Antinomianism of the apostolic age: 1. The previous prevalence of legal opinions; and, 2, the reception of the true doctrine of justification as a matter of the head without the concurrence of the heart, and consequently separated from the Gospel doctrine of sanctification. The mutual action and reaction of two such circumstances gave a violent impetus to these extravagant opinions. The natural vibration of the mind is from the extreme of legalism to that of licentiousness, and nothing but the grace of God can fix it in the proper medium of Divine truth. The Gospel, like its blessed Master, is always crucified between two thieves—legalists of all sorts on the one hand and Antinomians on the other; the former robbing the Saviour of the glory of his work *for* us, and the other robbing him of the glory of his work *within* us. 3. Another circumstance which should be specially noted as contributing to a spirit of blasphemy among the ungodly was, that the Gospel laid its axe at the root of human pride. It excluded all boasting on the part of man. In the plenitude of his pride he had indulged the golden dream of buying the favour of his God by his vain oblations, his empty sacrifices and his heartless formality of worship; and when assured that even his righteousnesses, were as filthy rags, when reminded of his native depravity and helplessness, like the encaged but untamed tiger he gnashed his teeth in rage, and vented his blasphemy against God by abusing, perverting and corrupting the glorious Gospel of grace. Such was the spring of Antinomianism in daring blasphemers. To men inflated with conceptions of their own sufficiency and intrinsic goodness, the Gospel, when unaccompanied by saving grace, will produce one of two effects—either contempt for its doctrines or unblushing licentiousness. In the one case its principles are utterly rejected; in the other, they madden and destroy. Both effects flow from the same principles of pride. They are only different streams from the same fountain.

The Antinomianism which sprang up in the time of Luther (if indeed it can be called Antinomianism) seems to have been nothing more than a very violent revulsion in weak minds to the opposite extreme from the papal doctrine concerning good works. Whatever may have been the errors of Agricola and his followers, Popery should be regarded as their legitimate father. As long as men act upon the principle of *contraria contrariis curantur*, legalism, when the Gospel once comes to be proclaimed, will infallibly be followed among unrenewed men by abuses of some sort. The effect will be different according to the aspect in which the Gospel is most strongly contemplated. If it is seen as coming directly in collision with our pride and natural self-sufficiency, the result will be infatuated blindness to its truth or an open profligacy of life. If it is viewed as a system of grace providing a full and free salvation without the works of the law, as a free gift of God, the result will be a greedy appropriation of the blessing, without receiving Him by whom alone it is bestowed. The idea uppermost in the mind is the absolute *freeness* of Divine grace; and hence that spiritual training by which we are rendered meet for the inheritance of the saints in light is totally disregarded or presumptuously denied, as if an unholy heart could hold everlasting communion with a holy God.

Whatever form, however, Antinomianism may assume, it springs from legalism. None rush into the one extreme but those who have been in the other. If Dr. Crisp was really, as he has usually been regarded, the founder of English Antinomianism, let it be remembered that he was notoriously, at one time, "a low Arminian, who held the merit of good works, and looked for salvation more from his own doings than from the work and grace of a Redeemer." The Antinomianism of Dr. Crisp consisted more, however, in loose and unguarded expressions than in real licentiousness of principles. He was an humble and a godly man. The testimony to his excellence and worth, signed by a divine whom none can charge with the least tincture of libertinism—Rev. John Howe—deserves to be seriously pondered by those who can find no epithets too scurrilous to apply to Dr. Crisp. It may be found prefixed to Flavel's "Blow at the Root." From the statement there given, Dr. Crisp's Antinomianism seems to have been very questionable. His works, published after his death, which took place in 1643, nearly about the time of Traill's birth, gave rise to what has been called the Antinomian controversy in England.

The "middle way" to which Traill alludes is probably the scheme of doctrine borrowed substantially from Vossius and Grotius, and maintained by Richard Baxter among the Dissenters, and Bishop Bull among the Churchmen, who took an active and even a violent part in this controversy against those whom they denounced as Antinomians. Their views, though the one professed to receive the Westminster Confession of Faith and the other the Articles of the Church of England, were substantially Arminian. They maintained that the death of Christ purchased for us a new and an easier law, which they called the law of grace or Gospel covenant, by obedience to which we were justified. This obedience they denominated *evangelical righteousness*, and contended that it is the matter of our actual justification before God. The new law of grace prescribed repentance, faith and sincere obedience as the conditions of our acceptance and salvation. Whatever opposed this scheme, which is essentially legal and eminently dangerous, was denounced as Antinomian. Hence, it is no marvel that Baxter should have abused Owen, who triumphantly exposed his futile aphorisms on justification, and maintained the true Gospel doctrine which Traill so ably defends in his Vindication.

According to Arminians generally, Antinomianism and the system of grace, which is usually called Calvinism, are synonymous terms. Because the Gospel excludes our own works from forming any part of the matter of our justification, they most preposterously conclude that it excludes all personal holiness; because it does not confound justification and sanctification, they take it for granted that it denies the latter entirely. The following beautiful passage from Traill's "Sermons on the Lord's Prayer" may be commended to their special notice:

"Christ represents His Church unto God for their sanctification. Election in Christ is an eternal purpose in God's heart and counsel about His people. Redemption by Christ is a Divine bargain for them and their salvation betwixt the Father and the Son. Justification is a gracious sentence of God in Christ on them that are represented by Him for acceptance. By this act and sentence the state of their persons is favourably changed. But sanctification is a Divine work in them that changeth their heart and nature. The Spirit of sanctification is a precious gift of Divine love, and is only given to them that are in Christ and because they are in Him. Gal. iv. 6: 'And because ye are sons, God hath sent forth the Spirit of His Son into your hearts, crying, Abba, Father.' All the anointings of the Holy Ghost that believers receive are but some drops that fall down from the head of our High Priest 'unto the skirts of His garments.' (Ps. cxxxiii. 2.) 'He received the Spirit without measure' (John iii. 34), that to His people, even 'to every one of them, grace may be given according to the measure of the gift of Christ' (Eph. iv. 7); not according to the measure that Christ got, but the measure that Christ giveth. And all of them received it. Rom. viii. 9: 'If any man have not the Spirit of Christ he is none of His.' Let him not 'name the name of Christ' (as his Lord and Master) 'that departeth not from iniquity.' (2 Tim. ii. 19.) All whose iniquities Christ did bear for their expiation, in due time Christ 'blesseth them in turning every one of them away from their iniquities.' (Acts iii. 26.) This blessing of sanctification is of pure grace, for as there is nothing of worth in a man, or regarded by God in justifying, so there is nothing of goodness or of fit matter for God to work upon in His sanctifying. God's word is as clear about this as about the other. The account that we have so largely of the natural state of all men without Christ is sufficient to show the absolute necessity all stand in of God's grace to save them, and to declare both the freedom and power of that grace in all its applications to men. Grace is the spring of salvation and of all its parts; Christ is the root of all; and eternal life and glory is the ripe fruit of all that grace of God that 'reigns through righteousness unto eternal life by Jesus Christ our Lord.' (Rom. v. 21.) See but these texts and read them, and conclude this truth: 1 Cor. vi. 11; Eph. ii. 1-7; and Tit. iii. 3-7. In all which places justification and sanctification are joined (as they are certainly and constantly in all that partake of them), unworthiness in the receivers overcome and passed over by the grace of the Giver, and the interest of Jesus Christ, in God's giving and in His people's receiving of both these blessings, is plainly told us."

Holiness so far from being the cause of salvation is a part of it: "He shall be called Jesus because He shall save His people from their sins." Sin is that body of death from which we are delivered by the effectual operations of the Spirit of Christ. Hence, it is perfectly ridiculous to represent works as conditions of salvation, since the ability and disposition to perform good works are blessings which we receive from our Saviour in fulfillment of his office as Redeemer. Holiness is a benefit received, and not a price paid; it is our meetness for heaven, not our title to it. "Gospel justification," says the Rev. Robert Bragge, "is a change of state and condition in the eye of the law and the lawgiver, whereas Gospel sanctification is a blessed conformity of heart and life to the law or will of the lawgiver. The first is a relative change from being guilty to be righteous; the other is a real change from being filthy to be holy. By the one we are made near to God, by the other we are made like Him. By being justified, of aliens we are made children; by being sanctified, the enmity of the heart is slain, and the sinner made not only a faithful, loyal subject, but a loving, dutiful child. This may be set in the clearest light by the following simile: Our children, the day they are born, are as much our children as they are ever after, but they are many years growing up into a state of manhood; their likeness to us as it respects the mind as well as the body is daily increasing. Thus a king's firstborn son is heir-apparent to the crown while lying in the cradle; after-growth adds nothing to his title, but it does to his fitness to govern, and succeed his father. Our right to heaven comes not in at the door of our sanctification, but at that of our justification; but our meetness for heaven does. By Christ's righteousness, it being upon us, we have a right to the inheritance, and by Christ's image, it being drawn upon us, we have our meetness."

Those who are anxious to see an elaborate and very able effort to reconcile the doctrine of justification by works with the grace of God as revealed in the Gospel will find ample satisfaction in the "Harmonia Apostolica" of Bishop Bull. If my limits allowed, I would present an abstract of the work for the purpose of exposing the radical error which pervades the whole system. The Bishop inveighs severely against Pelagianism and those works which are done by the power of nature without the grace of Christ, and denies that even our evangelical obedience possesses any merit in itself; all its value is derived from the merit of Christ. Christ merited, not that we might merit by our works but that we might obtain. We have no strength in ourselves to do good works. This we derive from grace, but the efficacy of grace depends entirely upon our own wills. Now the reigning error of Arminianism, Pelagianism and this Neonomianism—for they are all substantially the same, they rest upon identically the same principle—is an utter disregard of the true Scripture doctrine of grace, and a fatal misapprehension of the present condition of man in the sight of God. The friends of these systems will all admit that a man is justified by grace, but when they undertake to explain their meaning, " grace is no more grace."

The source of the error in many minds is the unfounded

notion that grace is whatever is opposed to merit. They judge of the former by comparing it with the latter, and hence they suppose that they are contending for salvation by grace when they are only denying salvation by merit. According to the conceptions which we usually frame of merit in our intercourse with one another, it is impossible that man can deserve anything at the hands of his Maker. Wrapped in the blessedness and immensity of His own nature, the Eternal Jehovah stands in no need of any services from us, and our constant dependence upon His benevolence and bounty for all the blessings which we enjoy renders our holiest obedience nothing more than a suitable expression of gratitude. We only give Him of His own. The purest angels that surround His throne strictly and properly speaking deserve nothing at His hands; their joy and blessedness are nothing but the results of unrestrained loving-kindness on His part. To suppose that man can merit any of the blessings of God is just to suppose that the obedience of man is a full equivalent for the favour of his Creator—that it constitutes a value received, an actual benefit, which God is under a moral obligation to acknowledge. If grace, then, is only that which is opposed to merit, such a thing as salvation by grace in distinction from any other scheme is utterly impossible. The necessary relations subsisting between the creature and the Creator preclude for ever, even from the holiest, the most remote approximations to merit. Hence, every scheme of justification would stand upon the same footing on the score of *grace*, and one could no more be said to be of grace than another. If Adam had kept his first estate, and secured the fulfillment of the promise to him and his posterity, he would have been just as far from *meriting* eternal life as the sinner redeemed by Christ, and consequently, according to this absurd conception of the matter, would have been just as much saved by grace. We are not, then, to look into the antithesis of *merit* for just conceptions of grace. The Scriptures nowhere speak of the merit of the creature. This idea, unknown to the holy and the good, is to be found only in the hearts of the ruined and the lost. Its only lodgment is in that cage of unclean birds, the unsanctified heart of man. Strange that the wretch who is so far from God, who is dead in trespasses and sins, should enhance his guilt by inflated conceptions of worth! "Surely men of low degree are vanity, and men of high degree are a lie." To what, then, do the Scripture oppose grace? To works, to works of law. Grace is the opposite of *legal obedience*. Justification by grace is justification without the deeds of the law. Salvation by grace is salvation which is not of works. "Being justified freely by grace" is used as synonymous with "being justified by faith without the deeds of the law." (Rom. iii. 24, 28.) Grace and works are clearly opposed in Rom. xi. 6: "And if by grace, then is it no more of works; otherwise grace is no more grace. But if it be of works, then is it no more grace; otherwise work is no more work." Also in Eph. ii. 8, 9: "For by grace are ye saved through faith, and that not of yourselves, it is the gift of God: not of works, lest any man should boast." The nature of a legal dispensation, or a state of proper probation, is that it is one in which God promises eternal life upon condition of obedience to be rendered to a specified law. The very essence of such a state consists in the prescription of conditions. To prescribe the condition is purely an act of sovereignty and grace; to bestow the blessing when the condition has been fulfilled is an act of faithfulness arising only from the obligation which God by His promise has imposed upon Himself. In this way, and in this way only, a Divine blessing may become a matter not of merit, but of debt. Rom. iv. 4: "Now, to him that worketh is the reward not reckoned of grace, but of debt." It is due to the obedient by the Divine promise.

Any plan of salvation, therefore, which lays down anything to be *done by man*, no matter *what* and no matter *how*, whether with or without the assistance of Divine grace as a condition of the Divine favour, is a *legal* plan, and rests upon the same fundamental principle, and is precisely of the same essential nature with the scheme on which the hopes of the race were suspended before the Fall. By a *condition* is meant that for sake of which the blessing is bestowed, that to which it is promised, and without which it would not be bestowed. It is not a value received for the blessing, or a strict and literal equivalent; the blessing becomes due to it only by the grace and sovereign appointment of God. The term *condition* is sometimes employed to express that which is prior in the order of nature or of time. In this sense it is what Boston calls a *condition of connection;* it denotes that one of them must take place before another in consequence of their connection in the scheme of grace. Thus, in this sense, faith is a condition of justification; not that it is a something to be done, for the sake of which we are justified, but we must be united to Christ before we can become partakers of his everlasting righteousness. Holiness is a condition of seeing God; it is necessary to the full enjoyment of the beatific vision. The successive rounds in the ladder must be passed before we can reach the top. When used in this sense, the word *condition* conveys no dangerous idea, but as an ambiguous word liable to be abused it should be laid aside by all sound ministers of the Gospel.

If, then, God has made our salvation dependent upon anything to be performed by us, it is not a matter of grace, but of works. The notion that legalism is avoided by ascribing our power to comply with the conditions to the grace of God is a mere evasion of the difficulty. A legal dispensation necessarily supposes power in its subjects to comply with its requirements. We would instinctively revolt at the tyranny involved in the supposition that Adam was destitute of the power necessary to fulfil the condition of the Covenant of Works. It is hardly conceivable that God would make a covenant with man, and solemnly ratify it, without giving man the power to obey its requirements. It signifies little whether this power come from nature or from grace (in either case it is from God); man must have it before he can be the subject or the party of a legal covenant. Neither is the principle affected by the thing required to be done; whether it be obedience to the whole moral law, or only sincere obedience, or only faith, repentance and perseverance which are required, something is *to be done*—a condition is prescribed—and God's favour ultimately turns upon man's will. The principle of works is as fully recognized in a mild law as in a strict one. He as truly *buys* who pays only a *farthing* as he who pays a *thousand pounds*. If these principles are correct, the Arminianism of Bishop Bull and Baxter, and all who coincide with them, is common ground with barefaced Pelagianism. There is no medium in principle between Pelagianism and Calvinism. Man is either not under a legal dispensation at all, or there is no such thing as salvation by grace. Man is saved either by works or not by works. There is no halfway ground, and all the efforts to find one have proved unsuccessful. Calvinists maintain that man is not in a state of legal probation—that he is condemned already; destitute of life and power, and therefore incapable of being the party to a legal covenant, and that God has never qualified him by grace to become so. He is under the curse of such a covenant, and therefore cannot hope for its blessing. He is delivered from the guilt and dominion of sin by the power and grace of a Redeemer. Being destitute of all things in himself, he is justified by the righteousness of another and sanctified by the Spirit of another. Salvation, as a harmonious whole embracing pardon, acceptance, adoption, peace, holiness and everlasting joy, is the free gift of God through Jesus Christ our Lord. This is our testimony. In the faith of these principles we would live and die, and consequently we would glory in nothing but the cross of our Lord Jesus Christ. He is all our "salvation and all our desire."

PREFATORY NOTE.

THE article on CHRISTIAN EFFORT was written as a sermon on Philippians i. 27: "Only let your conversation be as it becometh the Gospel of Christ, that whether I come and see you, or else be absent, I may hear of your affairs that ye stand fast in one spirit, with one mind, striving together for the faith of the Gospel." But there is no record of its having ever been preached. The handwriting makes manifest that it was one of the author's earlier productions. It is placed here as properly following and applying the principles of the Doctrines of Grace set forth in the previous portions of this volume.

CHRISTIAN EFFORT.

THE life of the Christian is not a life of inactivity and ease. He becomes the servant of God by receiving the Lord Jesus Christ, and is sent into his Master's vineyard for the purpose of working for his Master's glory. The Apostle, in Philippians i. 27, gives us a brief but comprehensive description of the work which the Christian is required to do and the manner in which it should be done.

I. The followers of Christ must "strive together for the faith of the Gospel." This is their business—their duty—their Master's work which they must perform. The faith of the Gospel may mean only that particular feature of the Gospel which relates to justification, or all the doctrines and precepts of the Gospel taken together as a whole. It is a matter of very little consequence which interpretation we adopt, as they both come to the same thing at last. There can be no cordial acceptance of Christ for righteousness without a cordial acceptance of Him for sanctification. He cannot be divided. No man can receive Him as a priest who does not at the same time receive Him as a king. The general idea of the Apostle, therefore, is that Christians should strive together for the purpose of promoting the success of the Gospel in themselves and others. Here, then, are two important objects held up before the Christian, demanding his efforts, and these are, The sanctification of believers and The conversion of sinners. The Gospel is not the power of God to salvation until it is cordially received and cheerfully obeyed, and it is the business of the Christian to strive that it may have free course in his own heart, the hearts of his fellow-disciples and the world lying in wickedness.

1. His own heart is the first theatre of his efforts. If he be really the servant of Christ, it must be his supreme desire to glorify his Father in heaven by a well-ordered life and godly conversation. He cannot be content with a bare hope that he has passed from darkness to light, but he strives and prays and labours that the body of sin may be mortified in him, and that he may day by day become more conformed to the image of Christ. His regard is fixed on holiness, his hatred is directed against sin, and he can neither be content nor at rest until he is freed from every vestige of corruption and indwelling sin, which will only be when he awakes from the sleep of death in his Redeemer's likeness. "I shall be satisfied," says David, "when I awake in Thy likeness." Sanctification, progressive growth in grace, and the having his light shine brighter and brighter until the perfect day he knows is his privilege, secured to him in the Covenant of Grace, and he shows by his efforts and evinces by his life that he feels it to be a sweet, delightful, precious privilege. Such are the Christian's views of his own heart, such his regard for the glory of God and the beauty of holiness, that he cannot intermit or relax his efforts so long as the deceitfulness of the one distresses or the loveliness of the other allures him. Now this holiness of heart can be obtained only through the faith of the Gospel. Christ by His Spirit sanctifies the soul, and the Christian must be found resting upon Christ and looking to Christ for every blessing of the Covenant of Grace. "Without Me ye can do nothing;" and hence the faith of the Gospel is peculiarly dear to him who hungers and thirsts for holiness of heart. There alone we see our strength—that strength of Christ which is imparted to us through the medium of faith.

2. The edification of the body of Christ is another field of important effort presented to the Christian. The believer is not to be viewed merely as a solitary individual; he is a member of a great and glorious community, and his efforts

must be aimed at the welfare of that whole community on earth as well as of himself. He must look not on his own things alone, but on those of others. The good of the visible Church would be much more extensively promoted if each individual member could be brought to feel more deeply his own personal responsibility to labour for its welfare. The Church is the light of the world, and upon the conduct of every professing Christian much depends in regard to the brilliancy or dimness with which that light shall shine. There should be no spots in this moral sun. Now, if each Christian should keep the good and holiness of his own brethren in the Lord prominently in view as an object of his efforts, there would and could not be dissensions and animosities, coldness and lukewarmness in the Church. There would be a delightful scene of perpetual revival. It ought, then, to be an object of anxious effort with every follower of Christ that all his brethren might daily grow in grace and in the knowledge of the Lord and Saviour Jesus Christ. And for this end there ought to be a mutual striving together for the faith of the Gospel. The sanctification of every believer is accomplished by the same glorious Agent, and His influences are received by all through the same medium.

3. The conversion of sinners is another object of effort which the sincere Christian should never forget. The world is lying in wickedness, under the wrath and curse of God's violated law. The impenitent are daily and hourly in danger of experiencing the realities of an undone eternity. They are already under the condemnation of a holy law, and the short season of their reprieve is the only period which they have of obtaining pardon and securing eternal life. The only possible mode of salvation is through the faith of the Gospel. "There is no other name given under heaven or amongst men whereby we must be saved" but the name of Jesus. "He that believeth and is baptized shall be saved, but he that believeth not shall be damned." Unless the sinner, therefore, can be rendered obedient to

the faith of the Gospel, he must be lost; there is no hope but in the Lord Jesus Christ; and if he reject the Saviour there " remaineth no more sacrifice for sin, but a certain fearful looking-for of judgment and fiery indignation which shall devour the adversaries." It should, therefore, be a prominent object of effort among Christians to bring the Gospel to bear with powerful effect upon the ungodly and disobedient. They should labour and pray and live with special reference to the case of those who are blinded by the god of this world and led captive by the Devil at his will. They should regard themselves as "workers together with God," as humble instruments in His hand of reclaiming a lost and perishing world to its proper allegiance. He that saveth a soul from death hideth a multitude of sins.

In striving, then, for the faith of the Gospel, the prominent objects before the mind of the Christian are the sanctification of believers and the conversion of sinners. These are the great purposes which the Gospel is intended to promote, and let it be remembered that nothing will promote these purposes but the Gospel. We cannot expect that God will bless anything but His own truth, and "philosophy and vain deceit" palmed off upon men under the specious pretence of Divine revelation will prove utterly unavailing in the edification of Christ's mystical body, or in alarming and converting the impenitent and careless. A healthy and vigorous Christian character can be formed only by feeding on the solid and substantial food of uncorrupted truth. Not by any means that the truth has any sanctifying power in itself. All its efficacy depends on the accompanying operations of the Holy Spirit, and the Holy Spirit will accompany nothing but His own Word. Just in proportion as the true faith of the Gospel, the pure doctrines and precepts of Christ are enforced and inculcated by the life and efforts of professors of religion, just in the same proportion will the Church be edified and sinners born into the kingdom of heaven. Hence, the duty of "striving together for the faith of the Gospel" is solemn and imperative; it is no less than striving for the salvation of lost, helpless, immortal souls. It is striving to establish the reign and authority of Christ upon the ruins of sin, iniquity and rebellion. It is no less than striving to open the eyes of the blind, unstop the ears of the deaf, and knock the fetters from the hands of the captive and set the prisoner free.

II. Having now stated the leading objects of Christian effort, the next thing to be noticed is the manner in which that effort should be put forth. And in the first place—
1. Christians should *strive with earnestness*. This characteristic of their efforts is implied in the term which the Apostle uses, and which our translators have rendered *strive*. It is a term descriptive of athletic exercises, and is manifestly borrowed from the Grecian games, in which the wrestlers exerted all their might against each other. We are required, then, by the Apostle to wrestle for the faith of the Gospel—to exert ourselves with as much intensity and earnestness as the wrestlers at the Grecian games. The ardour of pursuit ought to bear some reasonable proportion to the value of success. Great results should be sought with great industry. And what result is so grand and glorious as the salvation of the soul? Heaven or hell, life or death, eternal life or eternal death, depends upon the reception which is given to the Gospel; and if there is anything terrible in hell or desirable in heaven, if the interests of eternity are matters of supreme importance, if the frown of God is above all things to be dreaded, and the smile of God above all things to be won, then the efforts put forth in the salvation of the soul ought to be deep, intense and powerful. There should be no trifling here; our all is at stake, and at stake for eternity. Who can think without emotion of the bare possibility that he or his friends may be damned for ever? and yet who does not know that this must be the case unless a cordial obedience is rendered to the Gospel? The Christian looks around upon sinners, he sees the storm of Divine wrath gathering fearfully above them, there is a burning gulf beneath them,

and they are fast asleep upon its very edge; in a moment they may be lost eternally, and shall he not strive to awake them—strive with an intensity and earnestness proportioned to their danger? Oh if there be an object which from its intrinsic value and tremendous results ought to call forth all the energies of the soul in strong and mighty exercise, it is the faith of the Gospel. If there be anything in the whole universe of God that is worth contending for, it is the salvation of the soul. "Therefore, let us not sleep as do others;" let all who are called Christians awake, let them strive as one man with all possible intensity of effort for the furtherance of the Gospel in the conversion of the world. Here is a commanding object requiring commanding energy. Soldiers of the cross! shall we sleep at our posts, and while we are at ease in Zion shall our fellow-men around us sink into the torments of hell? How terrible is the idea that one soul should be lost, and lost for ever, through a criminal neglect in us!

2. Unanimity is another characteristic of Christian effort which is quite essential to success. When the Holy Ghost was poured out on the memorable day of Pentecost, it is particularly recorded that the disciples were with *one accord* in one place, and the text requires that Christians should with *one mind* strive for the faith of the Gospel. When there are dissensions and animosities in the Church, the moral influence of the saints is distressingly weakened; nay, these unhappy divisions very often exert an influence decidedly against the cause of Christ. And the existence of such a state of things is alleged by the Apostle as a manifest proof of carnality among the Corinthian professors.

Christians have strong and powerful motives to unanimity of effort. They have been redeemed by a common Saviour, regenerated by a common Spirit; they are animated by a common hope and are striving for a common end. Why then should they fall out by the way? Why should they wound the Saviour in the house of His friends by their wranglings and animosities? They may differ in their views on some points, but they should not permit these differences to distract their efforts and mar their success in the grand object of converting the world. They have an important work to do, and it too often happens that when they ought to be working they are only quarrelling. Instead of aiding, abetting and assisting each other in bringing the Gospel to bear upon the hearts of sinners, they are too often found weakening each other's hands and hardening the hearts of the impenitent against the overtures of grace. There should be *one mind*, one spirit among Christians, and that the Spirit of their Master—a spirit of active benevolence and persevering effort for the glory of God and the salvation of men. They ought to feel the solemnity and importance of their business, and then there would be little disposition to wrangle with each other. These remarks are not designed to intimate that Christians should not resist, and resist with firmness, every effort to corrupt the purity of the Church in doctrine and in discipline: such resistance is actually striving for the faith of the Gospel. All that I mean is that private and personal differences should not be indulged by the professors of a common religion and the followers of a common Saviour. Soldiers should act together on the field of battle. Union is strength in religion as well as in everything else.

3. Steadfastness and regularity of effort are also necessary. What I mean by this is, that Christians should not be flighty and unsteady in the exertions which they put forth for the faith of the Gospel, at one time boiling over with zeal, at another frozen up with indifference; now earnest and engaged for the salvation of souls, and now as careless as though there were no souls to save. This irregularity in their exertions for the faith of the Gospel has a decided tendency to throw a shade over their own personal piety; it destroys, by a necessary consequence, their influence in the world, and it defeats the very object at which the Christian professes to be aiming—the success and furtherance of the Gospel. The light of the Christian should be a steady and uniform light. Cases

sometimes happen in which a whole church becomes cold and careless and lifeless, and continues so for a considerable length of time, and then suddenly bursts forth, as if by volcanic action, and puts forth deep, protracted and earnest efforts for the faith of the Gospel, and subsequently relapses to the same state of lukewarm indifference. Such successions of heat and cold make up the whole history of some congregations, and the reason is to be found in the unsteadiness and irregularity of Christian effort. The followers of Christ ought always to be impressed with a deep sense of the transcendent importance of those objects for which they are striving; they should feel their value to the race, and then there would not and could not be those dreary stages of relaxed exertion which too often occur in the history of the Church. Christians become cold and careless only when eternity is out of view and the value of the soul forgotten. The advice of the Apostle requires them to *stand steadfast* in one spirit, striving together for the faith of the Gospel. They were not to be blown about by every wind of doctrine or every gust of feeling, but they were to have correct apprehensions of their Master's business, and then to exert themselves with earnest, intense, united and steady efforts for the success and honour of His name. Their efforts were not to be flighty, but uniform; not irregular, but constant; not heartless, but powerful; and by such efforts they might well expect to advance their Master's cause and glorify their Master's name.

4. The above considerations have suggested the general characteristics of the manner of those efforts which Christians are required to put forth for the faith of the Gospel. But they have determined nothing in regard to the nature of the efforts themselves. Very bad measures may be adopted for advancing the cause of Christ, and yet professing Christians be very earnest, unanimous, steady and decided in pushing them on. These features may be found in the exertions of errorists and fanatics as well as in those of humble and sincere followers of the blessed Saviour. The next reflection,

therefore, that I would present, is that the measures which Christians adopt should be such as become the Gospel of Christ. The spirit of the world should not be suffered to appear in the bosom of the Church. Our weapons are not carnal, but spiritual. The religion of Jesus demands a peculiar temper, and that temper ought to be observable in all the movements of His disciples in striving for the faith of the Gospel. "But the fruit of the Spirit is love, joy, peace, long-suffering, gentleness, goodness, faith, meekness, temperance." "For the fruit of the Spirit is in all goodness and righteousness and truth."

In these days of morbid excitement and reckless enthusiasm there prevails, in some quarters of the Church, a melancholy disposition to receive a counterfeit spirit for the temper of Christ. Measures are adopted and encouraged and defended which manifest more of the cunning and dexterity of worldly-minded policy than the honest simplicity of an unsophisticated Christian. Men are trapped into the Church. A course of committal, or rather of efforts to make them commit themselves, is pursued, which does not indicate the simplicity of the Gospel. "Only let your conversation be as becometh the Gospel of Christ." The censorious spirit which is indulged toward those who are not willing to be duped into a ready acquiescence with these unauthorized measures shows but too plainly the source from which they spring. In all our efforts, then, to promote and strive for the faith of the Gospel, let nothing be done in a spirit which the Gospel must condemn. Let all our measures be characterized by that honest simplicity and unsophisticated charity which are so conspicuously manifest in the character of Jesus. Let there be no breach of that decency, sobriety, dignity and decorum which become us no less as men than as Christians. And in our universal deportment let the world see the natural influence of the Gospel when cordially received and cheerfully obeyed. The Gospel can be *lived* as well as preached—enforced by the life as well as from the desk. Cultivating, then, the Spirit of Christ, let us put forth our efforts earnestly, unanimously, steadily and firmly in striving together for the faith of the Gospel.

5. Everything should be done, however, under a sense of deep and entire dependence upon God for success. Paul may plant and Apollos water, but God alone can give the increase. He alone has power to convert or sanctify the soul. All the help of man, all our earnest, warm and persevering efforts to alarm and awaken the sinner and lead him to the Saviour, will be utterly unavailing unless the Spirit of God should accompany the truth with His gracious and saving operations. The truth of itself can do nothing at all in the way of a saving work, but it is mighty when wielded by the Spirit and driven home upon a heart prepared by the Spirit to receive it. The agency of the Holy Spirit is a fact which, in the fullness of our arrogance and pride, we are shamefully prone to forget. It is an humbling doctrine, but then the Christian must keep it in view, and have his eyes continually directed to that Agent if he would be successful in his efforts for the furtherance of the Gospel. The Holy Spirit must have the glory of His own work; and if we assume to ourselves and ascribe to our own doings what belongs only to Him, we may expect leanness and barrenness and miserable disappointment until we shall have learned the true source of all spiritual strength.

All our Christian efforts, therefore, should be carried on in a spirit of dependence upon God. The blessing of His Holy Spirit must be continually invoked, as that alone which can give efficiency and success to the movements of the Church. "The excellency is of God and not of men." It is God's work and not ours, and we should not dare to assume the glory to ourselves.

We have now seen the *great ends* for which a Christian should strive, the *manner* in which he should strive, and, in conclusion, it might be well to suggest a few considerations showing the *necessity* of striving. The believer in Christ becomes a servant of Christ: "Ye are not your own, ye are bought with a price;" and it is surely the part of an affectionate and faithful servant to feel a strong attachment to the interests of his master. Shall not the Christian, then, labour in the Lord's vineyard with all possible diligence and industry? Shall he not be deeply concerned for his Master's cause, and exert all his powers and energies in carrying it onward? We are not our own. Our great business is to labour for Christ, for heaven, for eternity. We have no right to consult ease and comfort and self-indulgence. We are the Lord's, and His glory is the great end which we should ever have in view.

The consequences which depend upon our efforts are tremendous. Sinners are in the gall of bitterness and the bonds of iniquity, under the wrath of God and the curse of a holy law, and there is no possible way of escape but in the faith of the Gospel.

If Christians, then, value the souls of their fellow-men, if they look upon salvation as a matter of eternal moment, considerations of humanity, independently of any regard to the glory of God, would urge them to labour and toil and pray and strive for the success of the Gospel. It is the only hope of a sinking world; it is in the hands of Christians, and they are required to proclaim its glad tidings of hope and pardon and mercy to every creature. Shall they not strive, then, with earnest, unanimous, steady, persevering efforts for the recovery of their race? Is there a man who professes to have the spirit of the Saviour that would wish to be exempt from a work like this? Is there one who would excuse himself from the delightful task of hastening on the latter-day glory of the Church? This is an age of great enterprises. None are too humble or too poor to labour for the Saviour. All have some influence, all have some work assigned them, and it is the duty of all to be just in that part of the field which the Redeemer has allotted to them. May we all be found of Him in well-doing—faithful, laborious and devoted servants, such as the Lord will delight to honour!

PREFATORY NOTE.

The discourse on THE SACRIFICE OF CHRIST THE TYPE AND MODEL OF MISSIONARY EFFORT, still more fully than the preceding one on CHRISTIAN EFFORT, forms a suitable conclusion and application of the Doctrines of Grace, and is therefore inserted here at the close of their discussion. The former portion of it covers briefly the same ground as the Discourse on the Priesthood of Christ, but the reader will not object to perusing again, in a somewhat different form, that which, we are sure, will be found both edifying and comforting.

This Discourse was a sermon preached by appointment of the Board of Foreign Missions of the General Assembly of the Presbyterian Church in the United States of America (Old School), in the First Presbyterian Church, New York, on Sabbath, May 18, 1856, and was published by order of the General Assembly.

The text of the sermon was, "Therefore doth my Father love me, because I lay down my life that I might take it again. No man taketh it from me, but I lay it down of myself. I have power to lay it down, and I have power to take it again. This commandment have I received of my Father." John x. 17, 18.

It was this sermon respecting which Dr. Addison Alexander, who was a hearer of it, remarked to a friend that it was as fine a specimen of Demosthenian eloquence as he had ever heard from the pulpit, and that it realized his idea of what preaching should be. It is pleasant to record this tribute from one eminent scholar and preacher to another, honourable alike to both.

THE SACRIFICE OF CHRIST

THE

TYPE AND MODEL OF MISSIONARY EFFORT.

THIS passage (John x. 17, 18), so rich, is yet so awful and mysterious that it is not without fear and trembling I have ventured to make it the subject of discussion. It pierces the depths of eternity and lays bare the counsel of peace betwixt the Father and the Son. The "commandment" of which it speaks is nothing more nor less than the commission to the Son to be the Saviour of the world—a commission to which allusion is frequently made in the Scriptures under the emphatic designation of the will of God. "For I came down from heaven, not to do mine own will, but the will of Him that sent me. And this is the Father's will which hath sent me, that of all which He hath given me I should lose nothing, but should raise it up again at the last day. And this is the will of Him that sent me, that every one that seeth the Son, and believeth in Him, may have everlasting life; and I will raise him up at the last day." To the same "commandment" or commission concerning the redemption of men the Psalmist refers when he introduces the Son as exclaiming: "Lo, I come; in the volume of the book it is written of me, I delight to do Thy will, O my God; yea, Thy law is within my heart;" and it is to the infinite satisfaction which Jesus took in the execution of the trust that He Himself refers in the memorable words: "My meat is to do the will of Him that sent me, and to finish His work." This is the will which was supreme with Him in the garden of Gethsemane, and nerved His soul for the horrors of the cross; the will for which He was born, for which He died, for which He rose again, for which He lives and reigns—the rule and measure, in a single word, of the mediatorial economy.

What is particularly remarkable in the text is the light which it throws upon the nature of the trust. Though styled a will, a commandment, a commission, it is not so much an authoritative law as the accepted condition of a voluntary compact. It binds, not by virtue of a right to command, but by virtue of a consent to obey. The Saviour appears not as a subject, but a prince, an equal party to a high and sovereign treaty. He claims complete jurisdiction of Himself: "I have power to lay down my life, and I have power to take it again. No man taketh it from me, but I lay it down of myself." These words bear the burden of the Godhead; no creature could sustain their weight. Jesus here asserts to Himself the essential independence which separates contingent from necessary being, and appropriates that intrinsic immortality which belongs exclusively to Him who lifts His hand to heaven, and says, I live for ever. They are words which none can consistently employ but He who is God over all and blessed for evermore, and may therefore be accepted as an unequivocal testimony that as the Father hath life in Himself, so, by the mysterious communication of His essence, hath He given to the Son to have life in Himself. The absolute sovereignty which Jesus assumes to Himself can be reconciled with no hypothesis short of the acknowledgment that He is the blessed and only potentate, the King of kings and Lord of lords. The natural import of His language is: "I have received a commission from my Father, not as a dependent subject in whom it would be treason to have an independent thought, but as a free and an equal party whose only law is in Himself; and though it is not possible that there can be any discordancy betwixt the Father and myself, yet the harmony is not obedience, but concurrence—the result not of a sense of duty, but of unity of nature. My acceptance of the trust is not the necessary allegiance of a creature, but the voluntary consent of a sovereign. The redemption of the world is not a task imposed upon me as the expression of a superior will which leaves me no liberty to decline, but a work cheerfully assumed, deriving all its obligation from my own cordial assent. It is not a command which, as a servant, I am bound to obey, but a treaty to which, in the depths of eternity, I have plighted my princely faith." This paraphrase which I have ventured to put into the mouth of the Saviour accords precisely with the prevailing tenor of the Scriptures. You cannot fail to recall that exquisite passage in the Psalms already recited, in which, when sacrifices and offerings were pronounced unavailing, and among all the myriads of creatures none could be found to expiate guilt or ransom from the grave—when from the tallest seraph to the humblest beast all were alike unable to take away sin—the Son is introduced as saying from the fullness of His own heart and the exuberance of His own grace, Lo, I come. He did not wait to be commanded. The purpose which heaved in the Father's bosom swelled in His own. It was the common love of a common nature, as free, as cordial, as sovereign in the consent of the Son as in the original conception and proposal of the Father. The whole transaction was a covenant of grace—the only covenant which God ever made in which the parties were equal, the only covenant in which there was no penalty, in which the sovereign faith of the agents was ample security for the fulfilment of the terms. The commission having been accepted, the execution of it necessarily involved relations in which He would have to become a subject and render the obedience of a creature to law. But the act which introduced Him into these relations, the first step in the stupendous enterprise, was sovereign, free, independent. He was the master of Himself.

The text asserts that precisely because He was the master

of Himself, the disposition which He made of Himself rendered Him, in a peculiar sense, the object of the Father's regard. *Therefore* doth my Father love me, because I lay down my life that I might take it again. This passage is very remarkable; it seems to intimate that, in these acts of Jesus—the laying down and the taking of His life again—there was something so glorious as to comprehend all His claims to attention within itself; a brightness which hid the perfections of His nature and being, displayed in other works, as the splendour of the sun conceals the lustre of the stars. The other glories of His name had no glory in this respect by reason of the glory that excelleth. It is a sublime tribute to the death and resurrection of Jesus that they are singled out as the special grounds of Divine complacency and delight. They include within themselves every other motive of love. Here the rays of His excellence are concentrated and a perfect image is reflected. Here the Father beholds Him in a work which expresses the fullness of His being, which gives scope for all the energies and illustrates all the perfections of His nature—which declares Him to be the Son of God with power. Here His Deity appears in full-orbed radiance as Deity in action. Nowhere else can the Son be seen in all the intensity of His glory, and well may He say: Therefore doth My Father love Me, because I lay down My life, that I may take it again. My brethren, if I can in any measure extract the spirit of this passage and present it before you in the light in which it has impressed my own mind, I shall not need to say a word in furtherance of the cause which I have been appointed to plead. It will then speak for itself, and its appeals to the Christian heart will be as resistless and constraining as the love of Christ. The point to which I wish to call your attention is the connection indicated by the illative "therefore," betwixt the laying down and the taking again of the life of Jesus, and the peculiar complacency and approbation of the Father—how it is that these acts of His so illustriously display His glory, and absorb within themselves all the grounds of the Father's love.

In estimating these events we must obviously penetrate beyond the surface. As the transaction is exhibited to the eye of sense, there is nothing in the death of Jesus to justify the claim to a complete jurisdiction of Himself so clearly asserted in the text. He seems to be the passive and helpless victim of violence and hate. He was taken and by wicked hands crucified and slain. And to look merely at the circumstances of His trial as they lie upon the face of the record, one would be inclined to suspect that there was much more pretext for the jeering exultation, "He saved others—Himself He cannot save," than for the lofty prerogative of sovereignty: "My life is my own, I lay it down of myself, no man taketh it from me, I have power to lay it down, and I have power to take it again." It is evident that there must be more here than meets the eye—an interior work, in which Jesus Himself was the actor, in which the Roman soldiers and the cross were but the outward instruments. The phraseology of the text puts it beyond doubt that while Jewish malignity was consummating its scheme of disappointment and revenge, Christ also was engaged in an enterprise of very different character, in which He could be truly said to lay down His life of Himself. The scenes in which man figured were but the outer court of the transaction; an august mystery was enshrined within. Significant intimations of something awful and sublime, in which Jesus was conspicuously the agent, veiled beneath the tragedy which human infatuation was enacting, were afforded in the display of more than mortal power which preceded the arrest, when the band that came to apprehend Him "went backward and fell to the ground," and in His own distinct recognition of the cup, which, in pursuance of the will He had undertaken to execute, the Father had given Him to drink. We here see that His submission was voluntary—that man had no power over Him, except as it was given by Himself. At the very time when He was led as a lamb to the slaughter, and as a sheep before its shearers is dumb so He opened not His mouth, He could have prayed to the Father and received an army of more than twelve legions of angels for His rescue. He had but to speak, and every arm uplifted against Him would have fallen palsied by the side of its possessor. But the Scriptures must be fulfilled, that thus it must be; the commandment He received from the Father must be accomplished—His covenant-engagements must be kept. He gave Himself up to men, and while the scourge, the thorns and the nails, the ostensible instruments of His death, were doing their office, there was passing in the mysteries of His own being a stupendous transaction which filled heaven with wonder and hell with dismay,—that "laying down of His life" as its sovereign proprietor, which, when adequately understood, extorts the confession, Truly this Man was the Son of God, and removes all occasion of surprise that therefore the Father should love Him. It were an idle mockery of language to find nothing more here than patient submission to insult and injury; and no martyrdom for truth, however sublime and noble, could ever sustain the weight and intensity of the inference, Therefore doth My Father love Me. As Jesus has no rival in His Father's heart, we must obviously seek a sense which will leave Him without a rival in the transaction which justifies the Father's love; and as the point of admiration is not so much what He endures, but what He does, we must seek a meaning that shall represent Him rather as an heroic actor than an humble and uncomplaining sufferer.

What, then, is the nature of the act implied in the laying down of His life? I shall not scruple to assert, whatever other interpretations the language may be capable of bearing, that it is here to be taken in a sacrificial sense. It is this which distinguishes the death of Jesus from the death of every other man. He made His soul an offering for sin. A body was expressly prepared for Him that He might, through the eternal Spirit, present an offering which should really achieve what it was not possible that the blood of bulls and goats could accomplish—the taking away of sins. Interpreted in this sense, the apparent contradictions of the text are beautifully harmonized. He lays down His life, He takes it again, and is as truly alive when He lays it down as when He takes it up. All this is readily explained when we remember that as a priest He ever lives, and that the efficacy of His work is dependent upon the circumstance that He is incapable of death. His Divine Person is essentially immortal, and that assumption to Itself of the entire nature of man by virtue of which He becomes a priest involves a union which can never be disturbed. He can never cease to be God and man in two distinct natures and one Person for ever. He is a priest after the power of an endless life. The victim which He offered was His human nature, which was susceptible of death by the separation of its parts, though the union of neither part with the Divine Son could be dissolved. Here, then, the Priest, as living, lays down a life upon which death may seize without affecting the integrity of His own being. He lays it down and He takes it again. Both are His own acts, and the inconsistency of attributing to the dead the properties of the living is fully resolved. The language, indeed, seems to be accommodated to what we are studiously taught in the Epistle to the Hebrews concerning the sacrifice of Christ, and no other exposition—none, at least, which divests Him of either nature—can extricate His words from absurdity or paradox. How He could die and yet be ever alive; how, as dead, He could resume a life which supposes Him not to be dead,—these are contradictions which can only be explained by the mystery of the incarnation, in which the union of the natures is maintained, each in its integrity, without confusion, amalgamation or mixture. The priest lives, the victim dies; the priest is the actor, the victim the sufferer.

The death of Jesus being distinctively a sacrifice, the question arises what there is in this aspect of it which entitles Him to such pre-eminent consideration. It is not a question concerning redemption as an objective work or an outward manifestation of the Divine glory, but concerning the subjective states of the Redeemer, the moral influences under which He accomplished it. The spirit of the Agent, and not the result or tendencies of the work, determines His own worth. The text implies that the motives which animated Jesus were in the highest degree meritorious; that great as His achievement unquestionably was, He Himself was still greater; and whatever moral grandeur it possesses, either in illustrating the perfections of God or ameliorating the prospects of man, is to be attributed to the moral grandeur of Himself. The Agent dignifies the work. Now, in what did the moral greatness of Jesus, as exemplified in His death, consist?

To elucidate this point, all that is necessary is distinctly to apprehend the nature of a sacrifice, which, as to its matter, may be compendiously defined as the satisfaction of the penalty of the law, and, as to its form or specific difference, an act of worship. Guilt expiated by an office of devotion, —this embraces the prominent conceptions. Hence it always implies a Priest, who presents the victim and celebrates the worship. In the death of Christ, therefore, if we would attain to a just conception of the moral excellence reflected by it, we must consider alike the matter and the form—the judicial sentence, and the spirit of religion in which the offering was laid upon the altar. Let us then contemplate, for a moment, the form of His death as an act of worship, evolve the elements of piety which prompted it, and measure their extent and intensity by the trial to which they were subjected.

1. The moral grandeur of the death of Jesus is not a little enhanced when it is apprehended in its distinctive character as an act of worship. If we consider it exclusively in the light of a judicial sentence, and detach from the Saviour those active sentiments of piety and religion which make him a doer rather than a sufferer, we may understand the principles of moral government which underlie the atonement, but we shall fail to appreciate the dignity and glory of Jesus. It is not right to consider Him as the helpless victim of inexorable wrath; and all the imputations upon

the goodness and clemency of God, which the malice of the human heart has made His vicarious punishment the pretext of suggesting, are at once dispelled when we enter into His own mind, and see the spirit of devotion in which He presented His soul as an offering for sin. His satisfaction is not merely the ground upon which others are at liberty to approach and adore the Divine perfections; it is itself a stupendous act of prayer and an amazing tribute of praise. We dare not entertain the thought, even for an instant, that the Father is harsh or vindictive, or that a cloud obscures the benevolence of His nature, when the very circumstances which are most revolting in the tragedy of Calvary are elements of a worship which the Son delighted to render, and felt that the Father was glorious in accepting. Considered as an act of worship, there is a majestic awe, a moral sublimity thrown around the death of Jesus, which fails to be impressed when attention is exclusively confined to the legal principles which made it indispensable to the pardon of the guilty. It is invested with a sacredness which makes us pause and adore. Never was there such a doxology as when Jesus died, and the whole work of redemption is a grand litany which has no parallel in the history of the universe. There can be no wonder that the Father should love the Son. Such worshippers are not to be dismissed from the sanctuary, nor such homage lightly esteemed. Never, never was there displayed before, and never, never will there be displayed again, such piety as that which burned in the bosom of Jesus when He laid down His life of Himself.

2. This will appear from considering the principles involved, or those moral elements without which the form of worship degenerates into an idle mockery. The internal feelings of the priest must correspond to the external significance of the act. His offering must express the spontaneous sentiments of the heart, or the whole service becomes an empty parade of hypocrisy. Now, what are the motives which alone could be adequate to prompt to such an under-

taking as the death of Christ, and to prompt to it specifically in the light of a solemn office of religion? The first, most obviously, is an intense sense and admiration of the holiness and justice of God, and a corresponding sense and detestation of the sinfulness of sin. This is the very language of a sacrifice, considered in its matter as the expiation of guilt and in its form as an act of worship. If there could have been a cheaper redemption for the race, if sin could have been pardoned at a less expense of suffering and of blood, if any other law could have given righteousness consistently with the integrity of the Divine character, we can hardly conceive that Jesus should have consented to experience gratuitous pain; and much less can we comprehend how He could have rendered a tribute of worship to the Father on the ground of an exaction which could not be vindicated from the charge of cruelty. The strongest argument to me for the necessity of the atonement is that Jesus died in the spirit of devotion. When I consider His soul as a pious offering, and then reflect that He celebrates the grace and the condescension of God in accepting the gift; when I consider the extent and severity of His sufferings, and then remember that all were endured to express to the universe His sense of the Divine holiness, I ask no more: I am satisfied that thus it must be—that without the shedding of this precious blood there could be no remission. So intense was His conviction that His death was indispensable to the righteous pardon of the guilty that He seems to have coveted the cross, and to have been straitened for His baptism of blood. He could not brook the thought that man should be saved at the peril of the Divine glory, and whatever His Father's honour demanded He was prepared to render at any cost of self-denial to Himself. Our finite minds are incapable of conceiving the extent to which the principle of holiness, the principle of supreme regard for the character of God, energized within Him when He made His soul an offering for sin; and when I figure to myself the scene, and undertake to penetrate into the workings and emotions of the Saviour's heart, I am irresistibly impressed with the conviction that nothing short of the Divine nature could have been the dwelling-place of such zeal. I see not so much an admiration of the holiness of God as the energies of that holiness itself. I see the Father reflected in the Son. The piety of the Priest flows from a fountain of inexhaustible fullness. I feel that death was to Jesus not so much a penalty inflicted as an offering accepted—rather a favour than a curse. It was His commentary upon the Divine honour, and contemplated in this light all that was revolting and terrible—His groans, amazement, agony and horror, His strong crying and tears—all lose their harshness, except as marking the malignity of sin, and become expressions of love and piety and zeal. I forget the sufferer in the actor, and enter into that awful reverence for God which invests the cross with the sanctities of worship and converts its shame into glory. I feel the moral sublimity of the scene. The beauty of holiness gilds its terrors. I am at no loss to understand that the Father should love the Son because He laid down His life of Himself.

But, secondly, sacrifice expresses, with equal perspicuity, the sentiment of pity for man. Here is the mystery of grace. It is not strange that God should be loved with all the fullness of the Saviour's being, but it *is* strange that our fallen race should be made the object of a condescension which our capacities are incompetent to measure. The philosopher finds mysteries in nature. His inquiries begin with the incomprehensible, and end by attributing an equal wonder to all the phenomena of life. The department of grace is, in this respect, a perfect counterpart to that of nature. All is wonderful, but that which is most amazing, which communicates least with any ordinary measures of probability, is God's love to the sinner. This is the starting-point in the scheme of redemption. The whole necessity of priesthood arises from the miseries of man as viewed by a nature at once supremely holy and good. Sacrifice is the combined expression of righteousness and grace. "God *so* loved the world" is the explanation of one mystery by another equally incomprehensible. The charity for man which sacrifice obviously expresses was conspicuous in the whole career of Jesus. His bosom glowed with love. He had compassion on the ignorant and on them that are out of the way, and such was the ardour of His zeal, such the intense vigour of His philanthropy, that no ingratitude or cruelty could quench its fires. "Father, forgive them, for they know not what they do," is a key which unlocks the secrets of His heart.

3. These two elements—love to God and love to man—which His death, considered as a sacrifice, expresses, constitute the essence of virtue. They are the principles into which every form of moral excellence may be ultimately resolved. The extent to which they pervade the character and regulate the life—the degree, in other words, in which they are possessed—determines the moral worth of the possessor. This degree is ascertained by the severity of the trials to which they are exposed. In the sacrifice of Jesus, therefore, we are to look for the measure of the intensity of His principles; we are to study His character in the light of sufferings. We are to learn how much He loved God and how much He pitied man from the cost of His piety and philanthropy to His own soul. Tried by this standard, He stands without a rival. To appreciate the greatness of His virtue we must bear in mind that the occasion on which it was so triumphantly displayed was one which might have been avoided. He was under no previous obligation to become a priest and a victim. He might have cherished His sentiments of sympathy and love for our race, and enjoyed for ever the communion of the Father, without subjecting Himself to the pains and privations of a mortal state. The glory of His nature might have been content with those exhibitions of its power which nature and providence unfold when they reveal the ever-blessed God. His virtue might have reposed in undisturbed beatitude. There was no claim upon Him to empty Himself of His Divine

glory, and to be found in fashion as a man. He was master of Himself. Nothing but the sublimity of His principles, the godlike greatness of His heart, brought Him to the earth, a man of sorrows and acquainted with grief. Neither, again, was it a momentary enthusiasm or sudden ebullition of heroic ardour. The principles from which He acted were the settled principles of His soul; they were the life of His life. Had they failed or suffered abatement at any stage in the progress of His work, the worship would have been adulterated and the victim blemished. His zeal for God never cooled, His charity for man never lessened. What grandeur do these considerations throw around the character of Jesus! Can there be a loftier height of virtue, an intenser energy of holiness? All creatures here, with their superficial trials, retire into the shade. Jesus stands unrivalled and alone the possessor of a virtue which none can understand, and none can adequately love, but He who can fathom the deep things of God.

"There is reason to believe," says Robert Hall, "that in a moral—that is, in the highest point of view—the Redeemer, in the depth of His humiliation, was a greater object of attention and approbation, in the eye of His Father, than when He sat in His original glory at God's right hand; the one being His natural, the other peculiarly His moral elevation." His virtue was put to the strongest trial which Omnipotence could exact. The work on which He entered, and which, however His humanity sometimes quailed and trembled, the Priest prosecuted with unabated ardour and consistency of purpose, was a work whose difficulties could only be estimated by Him who can take the length and breadth of God's hatred to sin. The tragedy of Calvary was no scenic exhibition of fictitious terror and distress. The victim was roasted with fire. Behold the man! and be astonished at the spectacle. "His visage is so marred more than any man, and His form more than the sons of men." Tell me, ye that pass by, is there any sorrow like unto His sorrow? My brethren, this is holy ground, and we must take the shoes from our feet. We can only admire and adore. There never was witnessed such a scene in the universe before—the infinite holiness and goodness of God sounded to their depths, the whole moral energy of the Godhead in action. Well might the angels stoop from their heights and desire to look into this mystery; well might there be silence, the silence of profound admiration, in heaven; well might the sun be darkened, the earth convulsed and the very dead startled, when moral elements were at work on a scale of infinite grandeur before which the earth, the sea and the sky, and all material things, dwindle into littleness as mirrors of the glory of God. When I contemplate Calvary and comprehend the spirit of the agent who there laid down His life—when I see Jesus putting into action and trying to the utmost the whole essence of virtue—I ask for no other explanation; the text is solved: Therefore doth My Father love me.

The text, it will be noticed, connects the love of the Father not only with the laying down, but with the taking again, of the life of Jesus. From what has been said, the extraordinary merit of the first may be readily perceived, but the influence of the latter consideration is not so obvious. That the resurrection of the Saviour, as the proof of the completeness of His satisfaction, is essential to the justification of the sinner, is manifest from the nature of the case; that it was indispensable to the discharge of the remaining office of His priesthood—intercession before God—and to His entrance into His kingdom, is equally apparent. But these are not the points to which the text alludes. It is represented as having an influence, not upon His work, but upon the feelings of the Father to His Person. The doctrine is, that the love of which He is the object on account of His death demands His resurrection as equally essential. His death could not, in other words, make Him the subject of Divine complacency and delight if that death were regarded as final. Understood in this light, it enhances the tribute to the personal glory of the Saviour. Such were the transcendent merits of His virtue in the laying down of His life that it would be an imputation upon the Divine character to permit such an exhibition to pass without a conspicuous reward. The thought that such a life should hopelessly perish would be intolerable from the very greatness of its worth. The nobleness of the sacrifice demands a proportionate compensation. It was not the heroism of necessity or duty; it was a spontaneous outburst of the most exalted magnanimity, for which there was no call but its own unrivalled greatness. Creatures may do well, but no mere creature can deserve. But here there was merit, and merit of the loftiest character. God's government would have been wanting in essential justice, and the Divine resources been defective, if such virtue could have existed without the opportunity of signalizing its worth by appropriate rewards. It must be honoured or there would have been a blank, a chasm, a dark spot, in the moral administration of Heaven. Jesus, therefore, must rise again, not merely for His people's sake, but for His own name; and when we read the magnificent honours which are heaped upon Him, we feel that they are fairly His due. He deserves to be exalted and to have a name which is above every name—that at the name of Jesus, every knee should bow and every tongue confess that He is Lord to the glory of God the Father. We feel that He is entitled to be made Head over all things, and to have the power not only of presenting His Church without spot or wrinkle before the presence of the Father, but of collecting the angels under His headship, and extending His grace through all the realms of intelligent being, so as finally to destroy the possibility of sin. This is the grand consummation, and it is a beautiful and glorious reward. He is to finish transgression and to make an end of sin, to redeem and sanctify the Church, and to confirm in holiness every order of unfallen being; so that when His work is finished and His glory complete, the intelligent universe by virtue of one grand enterprise of triumphant virtue shall be bound inviolably to the throne of God. There shall be no more sin, no more sorrow, no more darkness. Holiness is to be the eternal distinction of the creatures, because He who is in the midst of the throne is the centre and source of their stability, and their security is the tribute which the Father pays to His transcendent excellence.

I have now briefly and imperfectly developed the force of the illation in the declaration of the text: Therefore doth My Father love Me, because I lay down My life that I might take it again. Jesus appears as a worshipper of God, burning with zeal for the Divine glory and compassion for the souls of men, and performing an act of homage which concentrates in itself every principle of virtue and displays the energies of infinite holiness in intensest action. The cross is the only spot in all the universe of God where the word *merit* should ever be pronounced; and when we contemplate Him who hangs there, and enter into the moral import of the deed; when we rise to the comprehension of all that is included in a sacrifice for sin; when we measure the length and breadth, the height and depth of that moral heroism which dared to undertake it,—we want no other argument; we feel at once that Jesus is Divine. The impulse to worship is irresistible. We cannot help falling down like Thomas and exclaiming, My Lord and my God! There is no glory that we can give to God higher than the glory which our moral nature constrains us to attribute to the High Priest of our profession. These were the sentiments of Jehovah Himself. He loved the Son, because He perceived in the Son the brightness of His own image. None could be capable of such an act as the offering of Jesus but One who was God over all and blessed for evermore. Such merit, which we feel not to be disproportioned to the reward of universal dominion, and for which our moral sentiments demand a compensation that taxes the resources of Omnipotence,—such merit it were blasphemy to ascribe to a creature. It blazes through the universe in Divine characters. It proclaims its own nature. It stands out unrivalled and alone; and if it be not the property of God, we must cease to ascribe to Him absolute supremacy of excellence. For myself, I am bold to say that the moral character of Jesus shuts me up to the belief of His Divinity. There is no brightness in heaven which can transcend the glory of the Cross, and if there be a being greater and mightier than Jesus, there is assuredly none that is purer, holier or better. He fills the love and admiration of my soul.

The application of this subject to the question of *missions* need not detain us long. It has grown into a proverb that the spirit of missions is essentially the spirit of the Gospel; but the grounds of their identity are in many cases so imperfectly apprehended that many who call themselves Christians are not ashamed to slumber over the necessities of the heathen, while others are impelled to exertion by motives which have little analogy to the temper and example of Christ. The proposition, however, is true, and it is of the last importance that the Church should be aroused to a full conviction of its truth. Zeal for the propagation of the Gospel, upon proper principles and for proper ends, is the highest exhibition of Christian integrity. If any man have not the Spirit of Christ, he is none of His. This is true of the spirit which He exemplified as a Priest. We also are made kings and priests unto God. As our union with Him introduces us by adoption into the family of God, so we share an office bearing somewhat the same relation to His priesthood which our adoption bears to His sonship by nature. We are priests in the sense that we must be animated by the same principles which pervaded His offering, and that we must really express them in outward works in the full intensity of which they are susceptible in our hearts. Our priesthood differs from His in the circumstance that our offerings are only expressions of our principles, and have no judicial value in the expiation of guilt; and by the other circumstance that, as we have no jurisdiction of ourselves, they possess no absolute merit. We can neither redeem others nor arrogate praise to our own persons. In other respects there is a full and striking correspondence betwixt the priesthood of the Church and the priesthood of Jesus. As He was, so are His disciples in the world.

1. That supreme reverence for the glory of God which prompted Jesus to regard not His life dear unto Him, provided His Father's honour were maintained, must be the dominant principle of action in every Christian heart. The Divine character must be sacred in our eyes. The jealousy which the prophet Elijah expressed for the Lord God of hosts, which Paul felt when he beheld the Athenians devoted to superstition, is no transient sentiment of extraordinary zeal nor sudden ebullition of romantic impulse: it is the steady, settled, pervading principle of the Christian life. To be a Christian is to love God, and to love God is to reverence His name. In proportion to the intensity of this principle will be our efforts to vindicate the Divine honour from reproach. We hate sin not merely because its consequences are disastrous, or its forms repugnant to our tastes and sensibilities, but because it is a reflection upon God. In all its exhibitions it is essentially enmity against Him, but there are manifestations of it which assume the distinctive character of a libel upon His name. Idolatry, Superstition, Socinianism, all the types of Paganism, do not more conclusively demonstrate that man is by nature a religious being, than they demonstrate that the carnal mind is enmity against God. The abominations of the Gentile world are not the crude rites of mankind, as many philosophers would have us believe, adapted to the infancy of human knowledge, expressing the natural sentiments of piety and reverence in a form as yet imperfectly developed, and promoting the education of the race in larger and juster views. They are not tendencies towards God in the direction of a proper worship. They are not the feeble and obscure utterances of childhood, sincere and honest, but uninstructed. They are not the results of involuntary ignorance. On the contrary, they are stages of degradation which men have successively reached in their apostasy from God; they are the utterances of

alienated hearts, the slanders of malignant and poisoned tongues. The heavens declare God's glory and the firmament showeth His handiwork; the invisible things of Him are clearly seen, even His eternal power and Godhead, being understood by the things that are made. Creation and providence, the structure and laws of our own souls, proclaim His being, His attributes and His will; so that men are without excuse. There are radical principles in the mind which, if cherished and developed according to their proper tendencies, would rebuke the errors of the heathen; so that they may be said to know God as possessing the germs of that knowledge in the constituent elements of reason. The real difficulty is their reluctance to glorify His name. Hence, they become vain in their imaginations, suppress the light of nature, and their foolish heart is darkened. Hence it is that they have changed the glory of the uncorruptible God into an image made like to corruptible man, and to birds and four-footed beasts and creeping things. Hence it is that they have changed the truth of God into a lie, and worshipped and served the creature more than the Creator, who is blessed for ever. Amen. This is the natural history of Paganism. When the Christian man contemplates this spectacle; when he rises to some mount of vision and passes in review before him the heathen and anti-Christian tribes of earth; when he hears one unbroken voice of blasphemy and slander ascending from every tongue against that Name which angels pronounce with awe,—is there no sentiment of indignation, no spirit of zeal for the Lord God of hosts? Can we hear our God traduced and reviled, and yet hold our peace? Can we witness unceasing libels on His character, and yet take no step to vindicate His injured honour? Can we pretend to have the spirit of our Master, who was clad with zeal as a cloak, when we can gaze unmoved upon the abominations of a world lying in wickedness, which have been introduced by the arch-enemy of God in order to insult and reproach Him? Oh tell it not in Gath, publish it not in Askelon! Your national banner is insulted; your blood boils in your veins, and you cannot rest until the wrong has been repaired. Your earthly friend is reviled in your presence; you would scorn yourself if you could submit with patience. But all wrongs are tolerable provided it is only God who is their object! You must not tarnish my country's name, you must not reproach my patron nor my friend, you must taint with infamy no earthly object that I love or prize; but God, the God who made me, the God who redeemed me, the God who keeps me, whose air I breathe, whose earth I walk, and whose heaven I hope to gain,—why upon Him you may trample and pour contempt, with nothing to fear from me! Is this the Christian spirit? Is this the spirit which brought Jesus from the skies and nailed Him to the cross? Is this the *love* which we bear to our Father's name? Oh no, no! Our souls are stirred within us, stirred to their very depths, when we behold a world joined in conspiracy to darken the glory of God. Our hearts are moved, the fire burns within, and we must speak.

But you object that these reproaches cannot injure the Almighty nor disturb the eternal tranquillity of His throne. Why, then, be so concerned about them? Simply because they are lies and frauds. They traduce His character, and withhold from Him His due. Is your indignation against theft measured exclusively by the injury which the party may sustain in the loss of property?—your abhorrence of scandal founded alone upon the probability of its success? Is this the secret of your zeal for the honour of your friend? Is there no sense of right, no sense of justice, no sense of truth? Is there no such thing as an honest desire that the truth should be known because it is the truth? Has a miserable utilitarian philosophy exploded from amongst us the first principles of morals? God is glorious; the Christian man knows it, and he wants all the world to know it, and his anxiety to spread the truth is in proportion to the enormity of the lie which is supplanting it. The Christian man loves God, and loves Him with all his heart, mind, soul and strength; and the spontaneous dictate of love is to maintain the rights and vindicate the worth of the object to which it is directed. The more completely undisturbed the Divine throne is by the calumnies of sin, the more eager is the impulse to set the truth before the nations of the earth, because the more undisturbed it is the more flagrant is the falsehood, the deeper is the shame.

My brethren, this motive is no visionary thing. It has animated the people of God in all ages and under all dispensations of religion; and if we are not sensible of its ascendency in our own hearts, we have reason to question whether we are fit for that communion in which Moses is found, who ground the calf to powder; Elijah, who destroyed the prophets of Baal; and Paul and Barnabas, who were shocked at the proposal to pay them Divine honours. We have reason to distrust our sympathy with Him who made His soul an offering for sin in the spirit of intense adoration of the holiness of God. Our zeal can never be put to any such test as that of our Master. We are not required to expiate guilt. All that is demanded of us is to speak. We are not to energize commensurately with that holiness; we are only to proclaim it, and to proclaim Him in whom it has been conspicuously displayed. Let us look at His work and then at ours, and can we, for very shame, settle down in indifference?

2. The form which our zeal for the Divine glory is to take—that is, the works to which we should be impelled by it—is determined by the influence of the other motive which entered into the sacrifice of Christ. We do not belong to a dispensation which calls down fire from heaven to avenge the impieties of earth. The Son might have maintained His Father's honour by consigning our race to perdition. But pity moved His heart; and while He was indignant at the sins and wickedness of man, He pitied his miseries, His feelings of compassion were moved, and the universe beheld with rapture and astonishment the matchless scheme of grace. This sentiment of pity for the guilty

and the miserable He has imbedded in the hearts of His people. He has cast them in the mould of His own tenderness, and their hearts yearn over a fallen world. They ascend the mount of vision as Jesus from Olivet surveyed Jerusalem, and the spectacle which they behold of misery, degradation and death—the fiends of darkness brooding over guilty and infatuated nations, and the curse of God settling upon their souls—moves them to tears as the approaching ruin of the holy city moved their Master before them.

Wherever they turn their eyes sin and death present their hideous shapes. Every gradation of wretchedness, from the lethargy and insensibility of stolid ignorance to the anxious apprehensions and agonizing fears of awakened consciences seeking a delusive peace in the rites and tortures of will-worship and superstition, is seen on every hand. Darkness covers the earth and gross darkness the people. Without God, they are yet seeking Him; misled by their carnal minds, they can never find Him. They must lie down in sorrow. There is a light which can dispel this darkness, but it has never yet appeared in their hemisphere. There is a name which can heal this sorrow, but it has never yet been pronounced in their dialects. Is there nothing in this spectacle of a world in ruins to stir the compassion of the Christian heart? Can we look upon our fellows, members of the same family, pregnant with the same instincts and destined to the same immortality, and feel no concern for the awful prospect before them? They are perishing, and we have the bread of life; they are famished with thirst, and we have the water of which if a man drink he shall never thirst; they are dead, and we have the spirit of life. We have but to announce our Saviour's name, to spread the story of the Cross, and we open the door of hope to the multitudes that are perishing for lack of knowledge. The secret of their misery is sin, and nothing can do them effectual good but that blood, offered through the eternal Spirit, which purges the conscience and destroys the dominion of this monster. We have but to erect the Cross, and the millions who are dying from the stings of the fiery serpent may look and live. Was there ever such an appeal to the charities of man—a dying world stretching out its arms and imploring by the mute eloquence of its miseries our sympathy and aid?

When the cry of starving Ireland came to our shores the nation rose as one man, and by a noble and generous impulse interposed to arrest, without delay, the progress of the destroyer. The sufferers were bone of our bone and flesh of our flesh—they were our brothers in humanity; that was enough, we gave them the bread which their own soil had denied to them. When the pestilence was spreading its raven wings over the Southern cities of our own land, their brethren at a distance felt it a privilege to relieve their distresses by their sympathy, their assistance and their alms. It was a just tribute to our common nature. But, my brethren, what was the famine in Ireland, what the plague in Charleston and Savannah, Portsmouth and Norfolk, compared with that famine under which nations are starving—that plague under which nations are dying? And if we cannot disregard the call of earthly wretchedness without renouncing that humanity which binds us to our fellow-men, what shall be said of him who refuses to extend a helping hand, or even to entertain a sympathizing wish, for those who are rushing blindly and hopelessly into the thick darkness of the second death? Shall we call him a man? Can we, dare we, call him a Christian man? Can he stand beneath the cross and be warmed by the blood which flows there, can he be joined to the heart which bleeds there, and enter into the prayer which is breathed there, and turn away unmoved from the spiritual miseries of his kind? Is this to imitate Jesus? I shall not insult your understandings by a categorical answer to the question. I shall not doubt the authenticity of the scenes of Gethsemane and Calvary. The truth is, the apathy of the Christian Church to the condition of the heathen can only explained by the supposition of a lurking skepticism in regard to the perils of their state. There is a secret feeling, where there is not a developed conviction, that after all they shall not surely die. This plea may extenuate, but does not justify, the neglect of the Church, for it only denies without destroying the eternal misery of the heathen. The appeal to our principles as Christians, our love for God and our pity for our fellows, is still mighty from the present injuries which idolatry and superstition are endeavouring to heap on the character of God, and from the present sorrows which Paganism entails upon its votaries. These are evils which, with minds and hearts properly tempered, we could not tolerate a moment longer than we were destitute of power to relieve them. We do not turn away from our suffering brother who is helpless with disease because we are persuaded that after all he shall not die. We minister to his present wants. We do not hold our peace when the name of a dear one is reviled because we are convinced that in the course of time his reputation shall come forth like the sun. And so, even if we had scriptural warrant for the impression that the benefits of redemption may, in some way, be mysteriously imparted to the heathen, yet we could not behold their attitude to God and the manifold calamities of their ignorance without feeling our pity and philanthropy equally impelled to dissipate their darkness at once. But the appeal should be irresistible upon the supposition—which is the only one the Scriptures warrant—that they who are destitute of the external means are also destitute of the internal dispensation of grace—that they who are aliens from the commonwealth of Israel and strangers to the covenant of promise are also without Christ, and, because without Christ, without God and without hope in the world.

If there is any force in the figure so often recurring in the Scriptures, it were as idle to expect a crop from a soil in which no seed had been deposited, as to expect the fruits of the Spirit where the Word had not been disseminated. That is the instrument of grace and holiness. To say that the heathen can be saved irrespectively of the work of Christ, is to renounce the whole doctrine of atonement, and to pour contempt upon that very zeal for the holiness of God which lies at the foundation of the Saviour's sacrifice. To suppose that the benefits of redemption can be imparted where the knowledge of redemption is not found, is to violate all the analogies of providence and to contradict the express teachings of Revelation. But granting that by a provision analogous to that which extends redemption to infants, those who are most diligent in improving the light of nature are led by the Spirit and are in a state of salvation, the number, upon the most charitable estimate, is so small that it hardly deserves to be taken into account in considering the prospects of the heathen world. It would create, at best, only a possibility of salvation, while the overwhelming likelihood would remain that hardly one in millions would avail himself of it. The appeal to our sympathies is scarcely affected. The call is almost as loud as it was before. There is no excuse for our apathy and indifference. The spirit of our Master is the spirit of compassion upon the weak and ignorant and them that are out of the way. We must preach good tidings to the meek—we must bind up the broken-hearted, proclaim liberty to the captives, and the opening of the prison to them that are bound.

But such darkness as that which enshrouds the heathen world requires a stronger light than the glimmering of a feeble star. The Dayspring from on high must visit them, the Sun of righteousness must arise with healing in His wings. The good Samaritan cannot pass by on the other side and leave the wounded traveller to the chances of help; he must alight and put him on his own beast, conduct him to the inn and make provision for his wants. We cannot slight the miseries of so many millions of mankind, and quiet our consciences with the vague plea that their case may not be desperate. We know that they are diseased and that we have a remedy, and we do not know that they can be healed without it. We know that there is salvation in the sound of the Gospel; we do not know that there can be salvation where the silver trumpet is not blown. There is certainty on the one side, there is no certainty on the other. Who can hesitate as to what the priestly office of the Church involves in such an aspect of the case? How can we explain the strange infatuation of the people of God? There is a spectacle before us of misery and degradation and ruin, compared with which the decay of states and empires is but the small dust of the balance. A wail comes up from the regions of superstition, idolatry and error deep and terrible as that which brought our Master from the skies. Millions upon millions are plunging into perdition, and we turn unmoved away, because without Scripture, analogy or experience we have fancied to ourselves that here and there a chance individual may be saved. We harden our hearts and steel our sensibilities, and yet dare to lay the flattering unction to our souls that we are the disciples of Him who, though He was rich, yet for our sakes became poor, that we through His poverty might be made rich. Nevertheless, the declaration of God standeth sure: "Whoso hath this world's goods and seeth his brother have need, and shutteth up his bowels of compassion from him, how dwelleth the love of God in him?" If you cannot refuse a cup of cold water without renouncing your title to Christ, how, oh how can you refuse the glorious Gospel of the blessed God?

3. The love to God and the compassion to man which reigned in the Saviour's breast were not permitted to evaporate in sentiment or to expire in transient desires. They were active and operative principles, expressing themselves in a work which exemplified all their intensity, which tried His allegiance to them, and which was really a sacrifice from the cost to Him and the benefit to others. We can make no expiation for guilt. Our piety and philanthropy are not to operate in this way. But we are required to evince the truth and sincerity of our principles by labours which shall really express them, and which, in what shall

be the cost to us, shall be images of the sacrifice of our Master. Those works which put our integrity to the trial are the offerings which as priests we are bound to render unto God. As the dispensation of the Gospel is founded in a real sacrifice, all its duties are stamped with the spirit of sacrifice. The whole Christian life is a sacrifice; the man must present himself to God as a living sacrifice, and with himself he must give all that pertains to him. The law of sacrifice is consequently the law of Christian effort. The first condition of discipleship is to deny ourselves. We must tread in the footsteps of the Master. Our sacrifices must be presented in the same spirit and with the same motives as His; they differ in their nature, their efficacy and their ends.

As Jesus by His sacrifice purchased redemption, we by ours must make it known; and as there were difficulties which He had to remove before He could bring salvation to our race, so there are difficulties which we have to encounter in spreading it abroad. In these respects His priesthood and ours are strikingly analogous, and it is to give us the opportunity of showing that we are imbued with the same mind which was also in Him that so many obstacles have to be surmounted in the work of the world's conversion. It would be contrary to the whole analogy of our religion, contrary to the very genius and constitution of Christianity, to suppose that those whose life has sprung from death, whose holiness is repentance, whose great business is to die, should be remitted to indolence and ease. They are called to sacrifice. Hence, it does not stagger my faith to be told of the magnitude of the enterprise and the comparative inefficiency of the means, to be reminded of the obstinate and bitter prejudices which must be subdued, the fierce opposition which must be allayed, the cruel persecutions which must be endured. It moves me nothing to point me to the long and patient preparation which must fit the missionary for his work, the inclemency of climates, the low and disgusting customs and rites of heathen nations.

All these and a thousand more such obstructions are only proofs that the Church must tread in the footsteps of her Master, and bless the nations by the sacrifice of her own ease and life. These are only proofs that we have ample and glorious opportunities of attesting to angels and to men that we are really consecrated to a royal priesthood and have the materials for princely offerings. I take fresh courage as larger views of the dignity and grandeur of the trust break in upon my soul. The magnitude of the danger illustrates the spirit of the hero. As the whole earthly existence of man is modified by its relations to the cross, that cross has impressed its type upon our whole earthly being, so that nothing great or good, whether in providence or grace, can be achieved without sacrifice. The law of our whole state is life out of death. Learning is the fruit of sacrifice, power is the purchase of sacrifice, character is the result of many and severe sacrifices, liberty comes from sacrifice; and look where you may you will find nothing that deserves to be called a good that has not cost labour, or tears, or blood. The only way to gain life is to lose it. This is pre-eminently true in the sphere of our religion. We are born into the kingdom with pains and throes; we live there in much tribulation. We begin in a conflict, we continue in a conflict, and the conflict never ceases until the crown is put upon our heads. No marvel, then, that our outward labours for Christ should call for the crucifixion of the flesh. We should have reason to doubt their genuineness as Christian works if they involved no test of our principles, if they required no agony, or tears, or blood. In the very difficulties of the world's conversion we see the tokens of our Father's will. These are the signs that we are called to undertake it; we should rejoice that we have the opportunity of showing our love to our Master's name and our charity for our fallen race. These are the crosses which precede the crown, the tribulations through which we pass into glory. If we would reign with Jesus, we must also suffer with Him; if we would sit on His right hand or on

His left, or, what suits us better, at His feet, in His kingdom, we must be baptized with the baptism that He was baptized with, and drink of the cup that He drank of.

I think it of great importance that this peculiarity of our work should be understood. The whole course of reasoning by which many pacify their consciences, while neglecting the only enterprise in which they can acquit themselves as priests before God, is founded upon a radical misconception of the nature of their calling. They expect the mountains to be levelled, the valleys to be elevated, the rough places made smooth, before they herald the advent of their Lord; whereas this is the very labour by which they are required to prepare His way. This is the very work which His Church must do. She must cast up the highway for the progress of the Gospel by her own efforts, self-denial and prayer. She has no questions to ask but what is the will of the Lord; that being known, to be deterred by difficulties is to renounce her faith, and to withhold her sacrifices is to be unworthy of the office to which her Lord has commissioned her. The full and distinct recognition of the truth which I have been endeavouring to present is, it seems to me, all that is necessary to awaken the energies of God's people upon a scale of grandeur which the world has never witnessed before. We have great resources in means and men, in piety, learning, talent and wealth. The world is open before us. Commerce and war have broken down the barriers of centuries, and the rapid and constant intercourse of the nations has brought the heathen to our door. The ships are waiting in port to bear the heralds of salvation to the ends of the earth. The American Eagle and the British Lion are prepared to accompany and protect them wherever they may choose to pitch their tents. The harvest is rich for the sickle, or, to change the figure, the altar is ready for the sacrifice, the materials are all waiting to be offered; nothing, nothing is wanting but the spirit in the priest to avail himself of the golden opportunity. Let the Church comprehend her calling, let her comprehend the times, and there would be presented to God an oblation which would soon change the aspect of the world. We should soon be found rejoicing in sacrifices. The father would bring his son with delight and offer him upon the altar of God. The rich would bring their wealth, the wise their learning, the great their power, the poor their prayers; all would bring something to testify their zeal for God and their sympathy for man. Commerce would consecrate its ships, and war its victories. Soon the name of Jesus would be found in every dialect under heaven. The spirit of sacrifice is all that we want—the offering lies at the door. And, my brethren, can we endure the shame, when God calls us by His providence and commands us in His Word to undertake this work, specifically in the light of a sacrifice, in order that in so doing it we may imitate Him who prepared us for it by a sacrifice which cost Him His life,—can we endure the shame, the deep damnation of our indolence and love of ease, our cowardice and idleness, if we decline to bind the victim with the cords of our love to the horns of the altar? Shall we be deterred by the prospect of self-denial? Who is so base that he would let a nation perish rather than forego some little pleasure or encounter a little pain? Who so mean that for his own personal and private ends he would be content that the earth should be covered with darkness? But your children are dear, and you cannot give them up; you cannot renounce for them the prospects of wealth and influence and fame; you must keep them at home, though continents join with the isles in imploring your aid. What would you think of this plea if your country should call to arms? Could you find capacity in your souls large enough for despising the man who could hold back his sons when patriotism was mustering its hosts for the conflict? At your country's call you would gladly give up all. And is there no magic in the call of Jesus? Under your country's banners you would renounce your homes, your wives and lands; you would endure hardships as good soldiers, and rejoice in them the more the severer they were; the cold ground, the open air, bogs and marshes, disease and hunger and thirst,—all this would be sweet to you if it added to your country's glory. And is there nothing in the glory of Jesus, nothing in attachment to that country of which you hope to be immortal citizens, nothing in the great interests of the human soul, to stir up your energies and to nerve your resolutions? And are you disciples of Jesus? Can you stand beneath the cross, can you behold the Lamb there slain, the blood there poured out like water; can you listen to the cry of agony and feel the shaking earth, and shudder at the darkened heavens, and then talk of *your* sacrifices for that Saviour? Shame, shame, if we draw back in the service of such a Lord! No, no, my brethren, let us gird ourselves for the sacrifices; let us rejoice in making them. They are but shadows after all, mere emblems and images. The *true sacrifice* was made on Calvary. The way has been broken up, the Breaker has gone before us; let us follow in His tracks—we shall know them by the blood. Let us put our hands in His, and bid an eternal farewell to all parleys with flesh and blood.

4. And as there was a joy set before Jesus, for which He endured the cross, despising the shame, so there is a glorious recompense of reward attached to our sacrifices and labours of love. We are not required to spend our strength for naught, nor to waste our energies upon a bootless scheme. The reward of Jesus was won upon the strictest principles of right. He deserved the glory with which for His sacrifice He was crowned. The reward in our case is exclusively of grace. We can never be other than unprofitable servants; but God, in infinite goodness, measures the expressions of His favour by the intensity with which we have manifested the spirit of allegiance to Him. All He asks is that the heart should be in the service; and any effort that really proceeds from love to His name and charity to the race will never be overlooked nor forgotten. A cup of cold water ministered in the spirit and for the sake of Christ is a treasure laid up in heaven. The moral significance of our

actions depends upon the degree and severity of the sacrifice. What costs us little means little. It is not the external splendour of the deed, it is the spirit in which it is performed and the self-denial it involves that determine its value in the sight of God. If vanity, ostentation or secular motives have prompted it, if it have sprung from a mercenary spirit and is presented as a price for the Divine favour, if its asceticism and self-denial are regarded as pleas of merit and occasions of self-gratulation and applause, the water is polluted at the fountain—the victim is blemished, it is the halt and the lame that are presented on the altar. The act must proceed from love, be a cheerful and voluntary expression of love, and vindicate its own sincerity by its cost to the flesh. When these conditions meet, there is a reward, which becomes the more glorious the less we feel it to be deserved—a reward compared with which the poor satisfaction we obtain in the carnal indulgences which we spare in refusing to make sacrifices deserves not to be named. This reward is twofold—it is the reward of success here, and of glory hereafter. The first is not sufficiently understood, nor the latter sufficiently contemplated. I have no hesitation in laying down the proposition that no real sacrifice of the Christian heart is ever lost, even in this world. If it is an exercise of some personal grace, the exercise strengthens the habit and improves the principle of grace in general. If it is an effort for the external kingdom of Christ, it enters as a link in the chain of providence, and contributes its part to the final consummation. Works of grace are as immortal as grace itself—they can never perish. As the sacrifice of Christ, the great High Priest, was infallibly accepted, so the real sacrifice of all whom He has consecrated priests must be as really accepted, and must as really secure, in the way of means, the blessings to which they were directed. Our labours for the conversion of the world, so far as they are spiritual sacrifices, must be crowned with success. What now hinders the result is, that there is so little sacrifice for it. We pray; but what is there of agony in our prayers?

Who wrestles with God? whose soul is burdened with the weight of a perishing world? or who takes an hour from his sleep or foregoes a single meal in order that he may plead the cause of the millions upon millions that know not God? And are such prayers *sacrifices?* Are they more than breath?—and can there be any wonder that mere breath should not move the Lord of hosts?. What was the spirit in which Christ prayed when He made His soul an offering for sin? Again, we give; but who, like the widow, gives all his living? Who denies himself one luxury or refuses one indulgence that he may have the means of contributing more to the cause of the Redeemer? How many give only what they think they will not miss! How many professedly adjust their contributions by the principle that God is entitled only to what they do not want, and accordingly treat His kingdom as they would treat a beggar who supplicates for alms at the door! Are such gifts sacrifices, and is it any wonder that they should stink in the nostrils of the Lord of hosts? He is no pensioner upon our bounty; the cattle upon a thousand hills are His, and what He requires is some proof that we recognize His right—His supreme and absolute right—to us and ours. We are not first, and then the Lord have what we can spare. He is first, and we are to have what He may allow for our sustenance and comfort. If these things are so, it is painfully obvious that the Church collectively is not animated with the spirit of its priesthood; it makes no sacrifices for the heathen world, it detains the victims from the altar, and the darkness continues to cover the earth and gross darkness the people. The few who here and there are awake to their responsibilities, and are struggling to do their duty, will find in the issue that their work has not been in vain. Every prayer has told, every contribution has told, every missionary has told, every martyr-death has told,—all have entered into the complicated web of providence, and all have aided in bringing about the accomplishment of the eternal purposes of God. And when the whole Church shall comprehend the nature of her calling, and summon her energies to make the sacrifice which God exacts at her hands, the period will soon revolve in which sacrifices will give place to praise and trials to glory.

Those who are embarked in the work should not be discouraged because there are not symptoms of immediate success.

As in the discoveries of science, according to the observation of Whewell, so in every great enterprise, there are always three stages—the prelude, the pursuit, the triumph. The prelude is mainly a work of preparation. It is the mustering of forces, the collection and distribution of means, the marshalling of the hosts for the impending conflict. This stage in the missionary work consists in efforts to awaken interest, to arouse the dormant energies of the Church, and to bring it to a full apprehension of its duty and the magnitude and extent of the task to be performed. In the pursuit the battle is joined; and as in the ardour of the contest it is often impossible to determine the chances of victory or to estimate the success of particular evolutions and manœuvres, so in the great work of missions, while the enterprise is still in progress, in the heat and fervour of the struggle, it is hardly possible to comprehend the bearing of particular achievements or to ascertain the measure of what is actually accomplished. Appearances, for the time, may be doubtful, when, after all, there is a real and steady progress.

While Jesus was engaged in His own peculiar work, as He approached its termination the appearance was anything but encouraging to the minds of His disciples, and the victory was gained at the very hour in which all seemed to be lost. The corn of wheat must lie under the ground and seem to perish before it can vegetate and bring forth fruit. In this enterprise, therefore, we are not to be disheartened by unpromising appearances. The day of triumph will come, and our defeats and disasters will be the means of advancing it. What we have to do is to gird ourselves for the fight. The faith of God is pledged for the rest. When we engage in good earnest in the enterprise, offering up the sacrifices of prayers and men and alms, we shall soon see the ensign of the Lord lifted up on high and the nations flocking to His standard. Victory will perch upon our banners, and the shout will thunder through the temple of God, " The kingdoms of this world have become the kingdoms of our Lord and of His Christ!" Is not this a reward worth striving for? And when you add to it that eternal weight of glory which awaits us in the skies, is there not inducement enough to awake the very dead in labours for the honours of Jesus? My brethren, do we believe in our religion? Can we believe in its promises and prospects, and yet be so reluctant to make the sacrifices it requires? What have her labours for the conversion of the world cost the Church collectively? Individuals have suffered, have given themselves and their all as a free-will offering to God. Parents here and there have consecrated their children to the work, and God has accepted the gift. Young men and maidens have taken their lives in their hands and become strangers and pilgrims upon earth; and some here to-night have had the distinguished honour of anointing heathen soil with martyr-blood derived from their veins. These are glorious achievements of grace, and the actors shall flourish in eternal renown. But the Church collectively, what has she suffered for Christ? what has she suffered for the heathen? Where are her sacrifices, where her tears, where the offerings that have cost her dear? What has our Presbyterian Church done worthy of her privileges and resources? How many sacrifices can she count as proofs of her love to God and man? I would not reproach her—with all her faults I love her; and when I cease to love her may my heart cease to beat! It is because I love her that I would have her love her Lord more, and that I would delight to trace upon her the scars and wounds of many a hard-fought battle in His cause. I would have her foremost in sacrifices, as she is foremost in intelligence, purity of doctrine and simplicity of worship.

I have now, brethren—very inadequately, I know—discharged the duty assigned to me. I have taken you to the Cross, and discussed this great subject in the light of the arguments and motives derived from it. My appeal has been to Christian principle, Christian faith and Christian love. I have pointed you to your Saviour, and endeavoured to illustrate the spirit in which He laid down His life that He might take it again. I have explained the nature of your own spiritual priesthood, and insisted on the duty, the privilege, the glory of making sacrifices to communicate that salvation which Jesus made His sacrifice to procure. I have appealed to no selfish, personal or secular considerations. I have drawn no argument from the sympathies, the vanity, the pride of the natural heart. I have resorted to no tricks of rhetoric, no artifices of logic, to seduce your feelings and entrap you into conclusions for a momentary effect. I have simply contemplated you as the anointed priests of the Lord, and have sketched a single department of your work in this high and holy calling. Have I exaggerated aught? Is it so that when our Divine Master had completed His work of sacrifice for the expiation of human guilt, He anointed His followers with His own Spirit, and commissioned them to make the sacrifices which should be needed to propagate the Gospel to the ends of the earth? Is it our business to spread, as it was His business to purchase, salvation by *sacrifice?* Is this so? And does not the call of the heathen world come to us with a solemn, momentous, awful emphasis? They are perishing in their sins. True, it is their own guilt which condemns them. Their idolatry, superstition and will-worship, their impurities, crimes and abominations, are all the result of their own voluntary ignorance, the successive steps and indications of a wicked apostasy from God. They are without excuse; and when they stand before the great white Throne every mouth shall be stopped and all the world shall become guilty before God. Their condemnation is just. But are we free from their blood? Have we manifested the love to them which has been manifested to us? We, too, were perishing in our sins, but the Saviour passed by; and when He extended to us the arms of salvation and of mercy, He commanded us to give to others what we had so freely received ourselves. Can we face the Saviour by whose stripes we were healed—can we encounter the rebuke of that eye which melted Peter into penitence and shame—when we confront the dying millions in reference to whom we must have the agonizing consciousness that we have made no sacrifices for their souls? Who could brook the thought, saved by blood himself and unwilling to endure a little hardship for the salvation of others? Were it not for all-glorious, matchless grace, it seems to me that the faithless Christian, when he meets the wretched tribes of superstition for whom he has done nothing that deserves to be counted a sacrifice, would wish to sink into the earth or be crushed by rocks and mountains, rather than meet that Redeemer who was all sacrifice for him. He could not see the scars and wounds and look upon his own unmangled body. The sense of unfaithfulness, of shame, of baseness, of utter meanness, must be excruciating, would be excruciating beyond degree, were it not that the sacrifice which saves also cancels. This very consideration that God forgives us should make us now more determined not to forgive ourselves. The destinies of the heathen are, in some measure, intrusted to us; we hold the key of life. We are required to make sacrifices for their souls, and we assume a fearful responsibility in declining to do so. It is a vain plea that the work is too great for us—that we have neither the men nor the means. Have we prayed for the men with an earnestness, intensity and fervour that may cause our prayers to be denominated sacrifices? Is not this a part of our office? Have we not the means of supporting all that God shall give? Are not our resources abundant, provided the heart were in the work? Have we done what we could? Nations sitting in darkness and the valley of the shadow of death cry to us for light. These nations we have been commissioned to enlighten; and because the work cannot be done with a sigh or a wish, or a little useless treasure that no one would miss, we, the priests of God, who have been bought with blood and appointed for self-denial, fold our arms and say they must die! We pity them, we are sorry for them, but it would require too much trouble to do all that their case demands, and we must therefore let them perish in their sins! O my God, have mercy upon us! O blessed Saviour, reveal Thy love for ruined man and shed it abroad in our hearts! We are verily guilty concerning our brother, in that we saw the anguish of his soul when he besought us and we would not hear.

When I consider the magnitude and grandeur of the motives which press upon the Church to undertake the evangelization of the world; when I see that the glory of God, the love of the Saviour and pity for the lost all conspire in one great conclusion; when I contemplate our own character and relations as spiritual priests, and comprehend the dignity, the honour, the tenderness and self-denial of the office; and then reflect upon the indifference, apathy and languor which have seized upon the people of God; when I look to the heavens above me and the world around me, and hear the call which the wail of perishing millions sends up to the skies thundered back upon the Church with all the solemnity of a Divine commission; when a world says, Come, and pleads its miseries; when God says, Go, and pleads His glory, and Christ repeats the command, and points to His hands and His feet and His side,—it is enough to make the stone cry out of the wall and the beam out of the timber to answer it.

If Jesus should stand again upon the Mount of Olives and summon before Him this venerable court, as He summoned the disciples of His personal ministry and the apostles of His extraordinary call—if He should collect you and me and all the officers and all the people of His Church on earth—what, think you, would be the language in which He would address us? It would be an august spectacle—a solemn, an awful scene. The words that He would speak would pierce our souls and stir the very depths of our being.

They could never be effaced from the memory. We should think of them by day and dream of them by night; and the most anxious cares of business could never drown them. The voice would ring in our ears wherever we went—at home, in the market, by the wayside, as we lay down and as we rose up. It would be an era in our history never to be forgotten. Is it presumption to imagine what those words would be? Shall we say that He would reproach us? His nature is made of tenderness, His bowels melt with love. His eyes would beam only with pity, but our own hearts would be busy with upbraidings. My brethren, there is no need for any exercise of fancy. He was once present with His collected Church, and He did give her a parting mandate—Go ye into all the world!

Methinks I see Him here to-night, with His hands uplifted to bless us, repeating the same commission to us; and as here present I cannot restrain the prayer that He would breathe upon us as He did upon the Apostles, that we too may receive the Holy Ghost. With a fresh anointing from Him we will look upon the world with new eyes and a new heart, and an impulse be given to our efforts which shall never falter nor fail until the whole earth is filled with the glory of the Lord. Amen, so may it be!

OTHER TITLES BY SOLID GROUND

In addition to *Theology as a Life* by J.H. Thornwell we are honored to have more than 330 volumes that we have reprinted since 2001. Some of those are listed here for your consideration:

Notes on Galatians by Machen is a reprint that is long overdue, especially in light of the present-day battle of the doctrine articulated in Galatians.

The Origin of Paul's Religion by Machen penetrates to the heart of the matter and speaks to many of the contemporary attacks upon the purity of the Gospel of Christ.

The Virgin Birth of Christ: *A Classic Defense of the Deity of our Lord* by Machen remains the most powerful defense ever written on this vital subject.

Biblical and Theological Studies by the professors of Princeton in 1912, at the centenary celebration of the Seminary. Articles are by men like Allis, Vos, Warfield, Machen, Wilson and others.

Theology on Fire: Vols. 1 & 2 by J.A. Alexander is the two volumes of sermons by this brilliant scholar from Princeton Seminary.

A Shepherd's Heart by J.W. Alexander is a volume of outstanding expository sermons from the pastoral ministry of one of the leading preachers of the 19th century.

Evangelical Truth by Archibald Alexander is a volume of practical sermons intended to be used for Family Worship.

The Lord of Glory by B.B. Warfield is one of the best treatments of the doctrine of the Deity of Christ ever written. Warfield is simply masterful.

The Power of God unto Salvation by B.B. Warfield is the first book of sermons ever published of this master-theologian. Several of these are found nowhere else.

The Person & Work of the Holy Spirit by B.B. Warfield is a compilation of all the sermons, articles and book reviews by a master-theologian on a theme that should interest every child of God. Brilliant in every way!

Grace & Glory by Geerhardus Vos is a series of addresses delivered in the chapel to the students at Princeton. John Murray said of him, "Dr. Vos is, in my judgment, the most penetrating exegete it has been my privilege to know, and I believe, the most incisive exegete that has appeared in the English-speaking world in this century."

Princeton Sermons: *Chapel Addresses from 1891-92* by B.B. Warfield, W.H. Green, C.W. Hodge, John D. Davis and More. According to Joel Beeke, this is "a treasure-trove of practical Christianity delivered by some of the greatest preachers and seminary teachers America has ever known."

Call us at **1-205-443-0311**
Send us an e-mail at **mike.sgcb@gmail.com**
Visit us on line at **www.solid-ground-books.com**

www.ingramcontent.com/pod-product-compliance
Lightning Source LLC
Chambersburg PA
CBHW021133230426
43667CB00005B/95